Judicial Review and American Democracy

Judicial Review and American Democracy

Albert P. Melone,
George Mace

BeardBooks

Reprinted 2004 by Beard Books, Washington, D.C.
ISBN 1-58798-239-0

Printed in the United States of America

Authors' Note — Reprint Edition

Since the original publication of this book in 1988, the uses and misuses of judicial power continue to occupy the attention of politicians and judicial scholars alike. This is due in no small part to the present Rehnquist Court — justices who continue to repeat with conviction John Marshall's eloquent phrase in *Marbury v. Madison* (5 U.S. Cranch 137) "That it is emphatically the province and duty of the judicial department to say what the law is." The past Warren and Burger Courts and members of the present high court have seen fit to strike down congressional legislation and to implicate it in issues that a court otherwise interested in exercising judicial restraint might very well steer clear from. In other words, judicial activism remains today a fact of American political life as it did in some turbulent political years during the nineteenth and twentieth centuries when the Supreme Court was assailed by some as a highly suspect institution.

The Rehnquist Court is most commonly criticized for its dual federalism and states' rights perspective and especially the practical naming of a president of the United States in the highly controversial 2000 decision in *Bush v. Gore* (531 U.S. 98). At the same time, some lower federal courts and state appellate courts have actively employed their authority to rule in controversial issue areas such as abortion rights, church/state relations, and same-sex marriages.

Consequently, although most of the readings in this volume are written by constitutional scholars and legal professionals of an earlier era, their arguments remain pertinent today and will most likely remain so in the distant future. Two complex issues remain problematic and each underpin much of the continuing ambivalence about the exercise of judicial review in the United States. Despite its employment, the use of the judicial review remains a matter of honest intellectual debate because its use turns on logical inference and not explicit inclusion in the U.S. Constitution. Additionally, whether judicial review is compatible with democratic theory remains a thorny problem because it runs contrary to majoritarian principles of representative government.

In addition, there is the matter of whether Americans should regard the Supreme Court as the final arbiter of what the Constitution means. Especially in recent years, scholars have challenged the notion of judicial supremacy with the alternative view of provisional judicial review. Congress, the executive, and state authorities sometimes rewrite statutes deemed by the high court as unconstitutional so as to rescue them from the dust bin of constitutional infirmity. These bodies react to controversial court decisions in some instances because politicians understandably want to maintain public policies thought desirable. Contrary to the view of judicial supremacists, in this sense Supreme Court decisions may not represent the final word and the end of the matter. Rather, legislators, executives, and administrative agents together with the courts create a constitutional discourse about what may or may not pass constitutional muster.

It is for this reason that the creation of what is often referred to as "constitutional review" in the latter half of the twentieth century possesses considerable appeal. Serious students of judicial review have much to learn from the experiences in post-World War Two Germany, Italy, France, post-Franco Spain, and in many of the post-communist countries of Eastern Europe. In these venues, judicial review was made explicit from the start. Indeed, there is little argument that review is legitimate and that its exercise is conceived as a way to help these states from backsliding into their authoritarian and totalitarian past. Importantly, judicial review is explicitly provided in the bodies of their constitution as a way to insure the constitutional integrity of those states and of protecting basic human rights. There is also a practical understanding that legislative, executive, and judicial branches of government play an interactive role in determining how specific policy goals may be achieved within the prescriptions and proscriptions of constitutional documents.

Our interactions lead us to believe that knowledgeable colleagues agree with the proposition that the arguments and debates found in this volume have an enduring quality about them when attempting to comprehend the judicial review debate in America. But most of these readings also provide valuable insights when reflecting on the role of judicial power in other political cultures. We are gratified that Beard Books recognizes the lasting value of our effort and are making our volume available to a new generation of readers.

To Publius

CONTENTS

I

JUDICIAL REVIEW AND AMERICAN GOVERNMENT

14

The Antidemocratic Nature of
Judicial Review and a Good Democracy   236

15

Judicial Review and Public Awareness   257

PREFACE

THE BICENTENNIAL CELEBRATION of the framing of the United States Constitution has signaled a renewed interest in our legal heritage and in the Supreme Court. Indeed, in the 1980s, controversial decisions involving civil liberties and criminal justice have rekindled the long-standing debate about the Supreme Court's proper role and function.

Today the political conservatives are attacking judicial activism. They sometimes speak and write of judicial incapacity or, in the case of Attorney General Edwin Meese, the "Jurisprudence of Original Intention." Among other things they subscribe to the notion that the Court should interpret the Constitution as its Framers intended. On the other hand, today's liberals support judicial activism as a way to protect the politically weak from attacks by powerful majorities. History tells us that both right- and left-wing ideologues have been inconsistent on the matter of judicial power. In other periods, conservatives have defended judicial activism while liberals have decried it.

The contemporary debate is ultimately related to more fundamental queries of a timeless character. Whether judicial review is a usurpation of power and whether it is consistent with democratic theory are the underlying problems. This book centers upon these matters, providing a focus for assessing the Court's role in shaping constitutional law, principles, and doctrines. We have combined original expository materials with an anthology of significant and consequential writings to accomplish this goal.

Part I treats basic questions concerning the role and function of the Supreme Court and the nature and character of that role and function. These five chapters relate the political problems raised by the exercise of judicial power, the historic role of the Supreme Court as the interpreter of the Constitution, the scope of judicial review, and a description and explanation of the historical and political setting of the landmark case establishing judicial review, *Marbury* v. *Madison*. The fifth chapter analyzes and reproduces John Marshall's famous opinion.

Parts II and III are collections of important writings. These readings illustrate differing and often clashing views concerning the legitimacy of judicial review within the constitutional order. Scholars widely regard most of these readings as classic statements. Unfortunately, these works are not readily available in most libraries. Because they never before have been placed together in.a single volume, we have reprinted them in their entirety with original footnotes unaltered. A summary and analysis precede each reading. This volume represents a unique contribution to the literature, and we hope that students of political science, jurisprudence, history of law, judicial policy-making, constitutional history, constitutional politics, and the judicial process will find it useful as a source book. We believe that readers will find our attempt at synthesis both stimulating and intellectually rewarding. If we contribute even in a small way to sharpening the historical debate, our effort will be well rewarded. To be sure, putting this book together has proved a fine learning experience for the coauthors.

Part II contains five interrelated chapters focusing on whether the establishment of judicial review represents a usurpation of power. We begin with an analysis of Judge Gibson's famous dissent in *Eakin* v. *Raub*. His excellent criticism of judicial review is followed by Professor Thayer's seminal argument and prescription in support of judicial self-restraint. Though vigorous and well-reasoned, Mr. Justice Lurton's defense of an activist Supreme Court precipitates an outstanding rebuttal. L. B. Boudin decries government by the judiciary, taking Lurton to task on virtually every point. The concluding chapter in Part II centers upon Charles Beard's respected scholarly attempt to prove that the Framers intended judicial review. Yet after careful study, one may nonetheless harbor serious doubts. In short, although we explore fully the various sides of this multifaceted issue, readers are advised to weigh the evidence carefully. The usurpation charge is by no means an open-and-shut case.

Closely related to the issue of usurpation of power is the question of democratic theory. Is judicial review consistent with democratic theory? Part III of this volume contains five chapters that represent contradictory views on what we call the compatibility question. How may one reconcile judicial lawmaking with the doctrine of majority rule? In a society that thinks of itself as democratic, how can one justify nullification of the acts of elected representative bodies by an unelected oligarchy? These and related queries are addressed first and in the negative by the Antifederalist writings of Robert Yates. This chapter is followed by the famous "least dangerous branch" justification offered by Alexander Hamilton in *The Federalist Papers*. Eugene V. Rostow's important twentieth-century contribution to the debate follows. He holds that judicial review is in fact democratic. We think his argument is mistaken. Ironically, though judicial review is antidemocratic, it is nevertheless compatible with democracy. Finally, we address the issue of whether the people may be trusted with the knowledge that judges are fallible and whether an understanding of the issues raised in this book will breed disrespect or, worse yet, rebellion or revolution.

We present and explore the differing and often contradictory positions found in Parts II and III of this volume with a view toward approximating the truth of the matter. We suspect, however, that those seeking certitude may find our book wanting. It is not that we deliberately recoil from reaching hard and firm conclusions. In fact, throughout the book we openly express our views whenever we agree or, as is the case for the usurpation question, when we as coauthors agree to disagree. The nub of the matter is that the questions of both usurpation and compatibility are very difficult to resolve. A fair reading of the book will bear out this observation. It will also lend credence to the tired but true cliché that reasonable persons may disagree.

Lastly, we have included a bibliography of books and articles on judicial review in the United States. Though by no means a complete enumeration, it is among the most thorough subject listings available in print.

Good writing should appear effortless. It is our hope that this volume reflects less pain and strain than actually were involved. We are grateful to Iowa State University Press for expressing an interest in our project. Robert Schultz, Acquisitions Editor, displayed patience and understanding throughout the revision process. Managing Editor Bill Silag followed through with the professionalism befitting his station at a first-rate university press. The assistance of Sponsoring Editor Gretchen Van Houten and Manuscript Editor Kim Vivier is truly appreciated by the authors.

We are also grateful to the anonymous reviewers of this manuscript. Their comments proved very helpful in our revisions.

Liane Kosaki and Robert Clinton, public-law colleagues within the Department of Political Science, Southern Illinois University at Carbondale, reassured us that the project was worth completing and aided us in tracking down source material.

Research assistants Kevin Lyles, Declan Hall, and Micheal Zurek assisted us by proofreading, conducting bibliographical and biographical searches, and providing cogent criticisms. We also thank Cathy Croquer, Sandy Mason, and especially Cass Geis for their expert clerical help, and Dr. Vincent Lacy, Director of the Computer Assisted Instruction and Research Laboratory within the SIU-C College of Liberal Arts, for assistance in word processing.

Finally, we must acknowledge the debt all authors owe to their families and friends. The required isolation and preoccupation with matters other than the temporal needed understanding. We received more than our fair share.

Notes: An Explanation

Because the Readings have numbered notes, we have chosen to signal textual notes with letters.

I

Judicial Review and American Government

It is emphatically the province
and duty of the judicial department,
to say what the law is.

—JOHN MARSHALL
in *Marbury* v. *Madison*

1

Introduction

THE DOCTRINE OF JUDICIAL REVIEW was established by the 1803 opinion in *Marbury* v. *Madison* (1 Cranch 137), viewed by twentieth-century scholars as one of the most significant cases in the history of constitutional law. Judicial review has become a process whereby the Supreme Court rules on the constitutional validity of acts and activities of the several branches of not only the federal government, as in *Marbury*, but state governments as well. By exercising that power, the Supreme Court is involved in far more than a mere review of lower court decisions and procedures.

The ultimate and necessary foundation upon which judicial review rests is the belief that the Constitution is the supreme expression of the people's will. Since it results from the acts of the people in their constituent capacity, it is fundamental law embodying the people's determination of the proper division and extent of governing authority between the various branches of the national government; between the central government and state governments; between the national government and individuals; and, especially under the expanded application of the Fourteenth Amendment, between state governments and individuals.

Viewed in this light, prescriptions of the Constitution can be regarded only as superior to and thereby controlling the subordinate regulations of government officials representing the ordinary course of daily government. At the same time, the Constitution does not speak for itself. Some voice must pronounce when the ordinary, daily acts of government do not comply with the superior dictates of our fundamental law. By the same token, somebody must review those acts to determine when such a pronouncement is necessary.

Chief Justice John Marshall claimed in *Marbury* v. *Madison* that the judiciary was intended, and by its nature was singularly equipped, to say just what the law is—whether subordinate or fundamental. Thus, in the case of *final* pronouncements, the Supreme Court, and only the Court, can, ought, and must speak as the oracle of the Constitution. The Court alone has both the authority and the knowledge to determine which legislative acts and executive and judicial activities do not comply with constitutional prescriptions. Accordingly, presidents, members of Congress, judges, and various state officials have come under the Court's scrutiny.

Given its constitutional role, the judiciary is at the very center of political controversy. Consequently, it is a natural target of those groups, interests, and political opinions that find themselves profoundly affected by judicial decisions. The judiciary is especially vulnerable to the criticisms of those impacted because its members are appointed, not elected, yet are nevertheless entangled in the political thicket. Of course, there would be no cause for concern if the judiciary exercised little or no discretion in arriving at those decisions. No problem would exist, no ambiguity could be possible, if the process were as simple as Justice Roberts implied in *United States* v. *Butler* (297 U.S. 1). He wrote in simple mechanistic terms:

> There should be no misunderstanding as to the function of this court. . . . It is sometimes said that the court assumes a power to overrule or control the action of the people's representatives. This is a misconception. The Constitution is the supreme law of the land ordained and established by the people. All legislation must conform to the principles it lays down. When an act of Congress is appropriately challenged in the courts as not conforming to the constitutional mandate, the judicial branch of the Government has only one duty—to lay the article of the Constitution which is invoked beside the statute which is challenged and to decide whether the latter squares with the former. All the court does, or can do, is to announce its considered judgment upon the question. The only power it has, if such it may be called, is the power of judgment. This court neither approves nor condemns any legislative policy. Its delicate and difficult office is to ascertain and declare whether the legislation is in accordance with, or in contravention of, the provisions of the Constitution; and having done that, its duty ends.[a]

Viewed in this light, judicial review consists merely of comparing two documents and declaring, when necessary, that there is an obvious contradiction between the words of one and the words of the other. It is thus a simple matter of dealing with perspicuous materials that enable the Court to make unequivocal and unerring responses.

If judicial review were actually this cut and dried, the impacted groups – no matter how outraged they might be – would have to bow to the manifest will of the Constitution pronounced by its unambiguous voice, the Supreme Court. But as we will see, much constitutional adjudication is anything but unambiguous. To determine the validity of an act, the Court places an interpretation upon both the act in question and the Constitution. Yet, and here is the crux of the matter, there is no single interpretation that proceeds ineluctably from the wording of the Constitution. The various and even antipathetic interpretations held by different courts, or different members of the same court, demonstrate conclusively the high degree of ambiguity inherent in interpretation.

The best example of such dramatic variation in interpretation is, perhaps, the establishment of judicial review itself. Although it may be inferred, it is not explicitly mentioned in the Constitution. Ironically, had Justice Roberts adhered to his own standard, he would have been unable to justify that power. The only "express wording" that supports that power is the oath of office, the same oath taken by all other members of the federal government.[b] Curiously, then, Roberts would have been found urging that judicial review consists of a simple comparison of words at the same time as he based his justification for its existence on something other than that wording. And as we shall see, the justification in *Marbury* rests not only upon an interpretation of words, but equally upon an interpretation of a much more nebulous *intent* of the entire document.

Given the role judicial review has played in shaping our governmental system, as well as the manner in which judicial review was established, it is difficult to regard Roberts's view as anything other than apocryphal. Judicial review clearly involves something other than a simple meaning. It is a process of judicial interpretation, a kind of interpretation not far removed from law making.

However, it is not our task here to investigate judicial legislation per se. We are more concerned with the implications that the establishment, nature, and role of judicial review hold in light of our democratic polity. In the remaining chapters of Part I we relate how historically the Supreme Court has employed its power to interpret the Constitution, how judicial review has been used to shape the nature of the governmental system, how knowledge of the events surrounding the Court's decision in *Marbury* v. *Madison* aid in understanding that opinion, and finally, we present John Marshall's famous opinion itself. In Parts II and III we concentrate on two central aspects of the many controversies and issues surrounding the American doctrine and practice of judicial review.

The first concerns the establishment of judicial review, which has been questioned from Jefferson's time by many who insist that the Court usurped power when it claimed this function. For them, there is no constitutional justification – whether implicit or explicit. They insist that the Founding Fathers never intended to invest the judiciary with such power. Thus, we will seek to answer the question best phrased by Charles A. Beard: "The Supreme Court – Usurper or Grantee?"

The second aspect concerns the matter of Court rulings that, in the final analysis, seem to be legislative rulings emanating from *legislators* who are not held directly accountable through the electoral process. This has led some to charge that such a power wielded by the judiciary is not consistent with the spirit and form of democratic government.

These two problems are closely linked. Those who believe judicial review is not democratic portray the judiciary not as the unambiguous voice of the Constitution, but as so many individuals who express their own personal or group interests. To them, the judiciary is little more than an outrageous oligarchy masquerading in the black robes of constitutional impartiality.

For the most part, replies to this charge have taken the following form. First, respondents insist that Justice Roberts presented judicial reality, not judicial myth. Second, they further maintain that judicial review is wholly constitutional and was intended by the Founding Fathers. Since it is a purposeful part of the polity created by the Constitution, the question of the compatibility of judicial review with the spirit and form of democracy is undercut. It is argued if the Constitution did create a democratic form of government, and a Court vested with judicial review is a part of that government and is within the Constitution, the Court and the power must be viewed as not only compatible with democracy but, in fact, an inherent part of democracy. On the other hand, if a Court vested with judicial review is a part of the Constitution, and yet the Court and the power are shown to be incompatible with democracy, this would serve to prove that it is the Constitution that is incompatible with democracy. Thus, the Court, even if it actually was an outrageous oligarchy, would simply be reflecting the supreme expression of the people's will, the fundamental law.

Thus, we arrive at the link between the nature and role of judicial review and its establishment. Any charge that judicial review is undemocratic loses much of its force if that power was intended. This, in turn, leads to an intensification of debate on the question of its establishment.

There are indeed other controversies surrounding the role of the judiciary in modern American life. One contemporary debate involves the issue of the extent to which courts should attempt to ascertain and follow the intent of the constitutional Framers. Non-interpretivists hold that the Framers' real intent cannot be known and it is best to make rational policy based upon social reality.[c] Interpretivists believe that the Framers' intent can be known in many important areas of constitutional law, and when judges ignore such evidence they behave undemocratically.[d] A third view holds that it is advisable to ascertain the underlying purposes implicit in the structure of the Constitution and not to insist upon finding the specific intent of the Framers for each constitutional provision.[e]

The controversy is more than an academic fashion. The July 1986 appointments by President Ronald Reagan of William Rehnquist to chief justice and Antonin Scalia to associate justice came at an interesting time. The public debate sparked a year earlier by Attorney General Edwin Meese was fully heated, and it became plain that some political conservatives would like to make commitment to interpretivism a requirement for appointment to the federal bench. Mr. Meese and Judge Robert Bork, for example, have insisted that contemporary jurists should confine themselves to the rules and principles found in the written Constitution as originally intended by its Framers.[f] Indeed, Mr. Bork's 1987 nomination to the Supreme Court went down to defeat due in large measure to his interpretivist view of constitutional interpretation.

Mr. Justice William Brennan has been the torchbearer for political liberals. He has vigorously defended non-interpretivism by first accepting the legitimacy of looking to history in order to understand the principles underlying the basic document. However, he goes on to maintain that

> the ultimate question must be, what do the words of the text mean in our time. For the genius of the Constitution rests not in any static meaning it might have had in a world that is dead and gone, but in the adaptability of its great principles to cope with current problems and current needs. What the constitutional fundamen-

tals meant to the wisdom of other times cannot be their measure to the vision of our time. Similarly, what those fundamentals mean for us, our descendants will learn, cannot be the measure to the vision of their time.[g]

Another controversy of the 1970s and 1980s centers upon the growing willingness on the part of federal judges to involve themselves in matters heretofore regarded as unfit for litigation. The capacity of judges to supervise prisons, mental hospitals, local education policy, and automotive safety are but a few examples of a judicial activism that has precipitated a renewed debate on the proper scope and authority of judicial power and of judges as social engineers.[h]

Though the exercise of judicial power may be viewed as a matter of degree and timing, those interested in the debates concerning judicial capacity and interpretivism necessarily must face the fundamental questions explored in this book. If the federal judiciary may not legitimately exercise review and if that power is incompatible with democracy, no amount of interpretation, selective use of power, or its carefully considered timing may excuse its exercise.

NOTES

a. 297 U.S. at 62–63 (1936).

b. See Judge Gibson's argument in *Eakin* v. *Raub,* Chap. 6, this volume.

c. Thomas C. Grey, "Do We Have an Unwritten Constitution?" *Stanford Law Review* 27(1975): 703–18.

d. Raoul Berger, *Government by Judiciary. The Transformation of the Fourteenth Amendment* (Cambridge: Harvard University Press, 1977).

e. John Hart Ely, *Democracy and Distrust* (Cambridge: Harvard University Press, 1981).

f. Speeches by Attorney General Edwin Meese III and Judge Robert H. Bork in *The Great Debate: Interpreting Our Written Constitution,* ed. The Federalist Society (Washington, D.C.: The Federalist Society, 1986), 1–10, 31–41, 43–52.

g. Speech by Justice William J. Brennan, Jr., ibid., 17.

h. Donald L. Horowitz, *The Courts and Social Policy* (Washington, D.C.: Brookings Institution, 1977).

2

The Historic Role of the Supreme Court
as Interpreter of the Constitution

U NDER the Articles of Confederation the United States government had no third branch. The federal judiciary came into being with the ratification in 1788 of the new Federal Constitution.

In the earliest years of the Republic the Supreme Court was barely perceptible. It met only a few weeks each year, and in its first three years had no disputes to decide. Indeed, several prominent politicians, including such notables as Alexander Hamilton and Patrick Henry, refused appointments to the high bench.[a] The Supreme Court was not even included in the plans for the new Capitol in Washington, D.C.; the Court was forced to take up residence in the basement beneath the Senate chambers.[b] It is not surprising, therefore, that many of the nation's most prominent attorneys preferred seats on the state high courts.

The federal judiciary gained visibility and later influence with the defeat of the Federalist Party and the rise of Thomas Jefferson and his Republican Party. The Federalists, the party of Washington, Hamilton, and Adams, were soundly defeated in the elections of 1800. Responding to the political debacle, they hurriedly created new judgeships, packing the federal courts with nationalist-oriented Federalist Party faithfuls. Not amused, the Republicans, upon taking control of the legislative and executive branches, quickly repealed the Judiciary Act of 1801 and returned the judicial system to its status under the original Judiciary Act of 1789.[c]

Chief Justice John Marshall, a leading Federalist and former secretary of state under John Adams, viewed various Republican attacks upon the federal judiciary with alarm. With the now-famous case of *Marbury* v. *Madison* (1803), John Marshall found a way to assert judicial independence. While giving Jefferson what he wanted – namely, the denial of the commission of justice of the peace to a midnight appointee – Marshall established the power of the Supreme Court to declare an act of Congress unconstitutional. Although the Court refrained from declaring another congressional act unconstitutional until 1857, the stage was set for the high bench to become the final judge of the meaning of the Constitution.

Marshall's imprimatur upon the Constitution is nothing less than impressive, and his nationalistic approach is felt even today. In landmark decisions, his arguments held, for example, that the Constitution derives its authority not from the states but rather from the people; that the Necessary and Proper Clause permits Congress to make laws that carry into effect specifically enumerated powers; that commerce is intercourse, not just traffic, and that the congressional power to regulate commerce is plenary; that states entering into agreements with private parties are subject to the limitations of the Contract Clause; and that the Supremacy Clause dictates that state laws must not be inconsistent with the Constitution.

During Marshall's thirty-four-year tenure (1801–35) as chief justice the internal procedures of the Court changed, reflecting a felt need for a strong united institution; also, to some extent, changes resulted from the personal leadership exerted by this extraordinary man. The seriatim practice by which each justice wrote his own opinion in each case was strongly discouraged and was replaced by the more desirable institutional opinion. Also, the making of the circuit court assignments for each individual justice by the Court's majority was discarded in favor of determination by the chief justice.[d] Whether these internal changes and the increased public visibility and vigor of the Court was due primarily to Marshall's strong personality or to the indolence or incompetence of his associates is a question that need not be resolved here.[e] What is significant is that under Marshall's leadership the Court was transformed into a major political institution with a profound and lasting impact upon the political environment.

Upon the death of John Marshall, President Andrew Jackson appointed Roger B. Taney, an ex-Federalist and loyal cabinet member, as the new Chief Justice. During his tenure on the Court (1836–64) Taney helped to weave some notions of popular democracy into the fabric of

constitutional interpretation. Although not destroying Marshall's archi-
tectonic nationalist design, Taney and his sometimes-divided court
gave advocates of states' rights and popular control of government
some measure of support. The Court upheld state claims to power in
the field of banking and corporate enterprise; it modified Marshall's
reading of the Contract Clause by refusing to accept arguments of
implied contractual provisos and vested rights. The nationalistic position that the regulation of commerce rested solely with Congress was
reinterpreted to permit limited state concurrent power. It must be emphasized, however, that although the Taney Court tended to reflect the
more popular agrarian sentiments of the day, there was no radical
departure from the broad constitutional framework set down by John
Marshall.[f]

The otherwise favorable record of the Taney Court was marred by
its direct involvement in the most passionate and explosive issue of the
age: slavery. Marked by nine separate opinions, including seven majority and two minority, and improperly leaked to President-Elect Bu-
chanan, the 1857 decision in *Dred Scott* v. *Sanford* (19 Howard 393)
invalidated the Missouri Compromise. It held that Dred Scott, a Negro
slave, could not sue because he was not a citizen of the United States.
If it had chosen to apply an 1850 precedent, the Court could have
dismissed the case for want of jurisdiction and thereby avoided the
slavery issue altogether. Instead, the Court's opinion(s), loaded with
what abolitionist critics termed "political obiter dicta," enraged the political opponents of slavery[g] and in some measure contributed to the
dismemberment of the Union.

The issue of slavery was resolved with the bloodshed of the Civil
War. And though the issue of states' rights versus a strong national
government lingers even today, any notion of secession or nullification
was defeated extrajudicially. No doubt the prestige of the Supreme
Court was damaged with the *Dred Scott* decision. Yet in the long run
the fact that judicial review was employed further strengthened the
independence of the Court and prepared it for the tests ahead.

After the Civil War the fundamental issue facing the reunited nation was industrial growth and how to control its impact upon the
human condition. Beginning around 1870 the country was to experience the influence of the new corporate attorney in his attempts to
protect the "vested rights" of business. At first, proponents of the so-
called natural rights of business suffered mild setbacks. For example,
the majority in the 1873 *Slaughterhouse Cases* (16 Wallace 36) rejected
the contention that due process protects vested rights in property and

that the Due Process Clause of the Fourteenth Amendment meant simply traditional procedural and not substantive rights. And in 1877 in *Munn* v. *Illinois* (94 U.S. 113), one of the famous *Granger Cases,* the majority held that a state legislature may regulate business when its activities are clothed with a public interest. Yet in both *Slaughterhouse* and the *Granger Cases* some concessions were made to the forces of newly emerging industrial wealth. By the 1890s the Court came to link the notion of vested rights and due process.[h] The result was a substantive limitation upon the power of both states and the national government to regulate the affairs of private property.[i]

Due process was not the only weapon in the conservative arsenal. Through the application of the doctrine of the separation of powers, the newly formed Interstate Commerce Commission was stripped of most of its authority to fix rates charged by the railroads to its customers.[j] The Sherman Anti-Trust Act was emasculated when the Court held that production or manufacturing is not commerce and is thus not subject to federal regulation under the Constitution's Commerce Clause.[k] The first peacetime income tax was declared unconstitutional as violative of the "direct taxation" provision of Article I, Section 2.[l] Organized labor was punished when the Court upheld the right of the federal government to break up a strike in order to "move the mails."[m] Finally, with the invalidation of child-labor[n] and minimum-wage[o] laws, the Court had clearly earned the dubious reputation of superlegislature.

The liberal impulses of the late nineteenth and early twentieth centuries were sapped by an activist Supreme Court that substituted its public policy judgments for those of the state and national legislatures. In Congress there were cries of outrage, and inside the Court, Justices Holmes, Brandeis, and Stone became vocal critics. The conservative and activist tenor of Supreme Court decisions was maintained from the latter part of the nineteenth century through the first term of President Franklin D. Roosevelt. Finally, in 1937, the Court was forced to yield.

In its attempt to save the country from the grip of the Great Depression, the New Deal invoked legislative experimentation filled with much hope but little consistent ideological content. Yet various legislative enactments were viewed in conservative quarters as socialistic and dangerous to liberty. In a single term of the Court, eleven acts of Congress were declared null and void, and the New Deal was thought to be crippled by nine old men who were characterized as out of touch with the realities of the time. Unlike most presidents, Mr.

Roosevelt did not have the opportunity to appoint a single member to the Court during his first four-year term. As a result he was helpless to change the Court's constitutional interpretation through the normal appointment process. Undaunted, however, President Roosevelt hit upon his famous court-packing scheme.

The patently transparent Court plan, introduced in February 1937, would have provided for voluntary retirement for all Supreme Court justices upon reaching the age of seventy. To assist in the Court's heavy workload, for every justice over seventy, additional justices would be appointed (the total number of justices not to exceed fifteen). In 1789 the number of justices was set at six. It was changed to five in 1801 but went back to six in 1802. In 1837 it was set at nine and in 1863 at ten. It went down to seven in 1866 and since 1869 has remained at nine.[p] Though changing the number of justices on the Supreme Court was nothing new to U.S. history, Roosevelt's bill sparked extended and acrimonious congressional debate. But before Congress could conclude its consideration of the bill, the Supreme Court made its famous "switch in time saves nine." Chief Justice Hughes and Justice Roberts deserted the conservative camp, and the Supreme Court reversed itself within a four-month period. It upheld a state minimum-wage law, the Farm Mortgage Act of 1935, the Railway Labor Act of 1934, the National Labor Relations Act of 1935, and the Social Security Act of 1935. By 1943, through death and resignation, the Supreme Court had experienced almost a complete turnover in personnel and with it a repudiation of conservative economic ideology. Thus the historians' conventional wisdom was demonstrated: although FDR lost the court-packing battle, he eventually won the war.[q]

The Roosevelt Court (1937–45) and its immediate successor the Vinson Court (1946–52) continued to uphold federal and state statutes regulating the economy. At this time attention shifted from economic policy to matters involving civil liberties and rights. Of particular concern to the justices were First Amendment issues arising out of the right to strike and picket and the protection of the nation's minorities from discriminatory state practices. Due process of law, while losing its meaning as a substantive limitation upon economic regulatory power, took on a new meaning as a limitation upon state power in the abrogation of individual rights guaranteed by the Bill of Rights. The issue centered upon the question of the extent to which the Fourteenth Amendment's Due Process Clause makes the Bill of Rights applicable to the states. Closely related to the issue of incorporation was the matter of the proper mode of constitutional interpretation; that is, should provisions of the Bill of Rights be treated in any special way with respect to the burden of proof?

As indicated earlier, the Due Process Clause of the Fourteenth Amendment was employed as early as 1890 in the case of *Chicago, Milwaukee and St. Paul Ry. Co.* v. *Minnesota* (34 U.S. 418). However, it was not until 1925 that the applicability of noneconomic protections involving the Bill of Rights as a limitation upon the states was enunciated. Although the Court concluded in *Gitlow* v. *New York* (268 U.S. 652) that the questioned state criminal anarchy statute was not a violation of the First Amendment, it added by way of obiter dictum that the First Amendment is applicable to the states by virtue of the Due Process Clause of the Fourteenth Amendment.

In several additional decisions in the early 1930s the Court found occasion to strike down state prosecutions as violative of the First and Fourteenth amendments.[r] Incorporation of the Bill of Rights received its first full-scale discussion in the 1937 case of *Palko* v. *Connecticut* (302 U.S. 319).[s] Justice Cardozo created what has been termed an "honor roll" of rights; rather than simply holding that the first eight or nine amendments applied to the states, he argued instead that only those rights "implicit in the concept of ordered liberty" and those notions of justice "so rooted in the traditions and conscience of our people are to be ranked as fundamental" (302 U.S. at 325). Cardozo specifically mentioned the following rights as incorporated by way of the Due Process Clause: speech; press; free exercise of religion; peaceful assembly; and counsel in criminal cases. The other Bill of Rights provisions were presumably not incorporated pending a finding by the Court that they should be.[t] This dichotomy stood for nearly a decade, when in 1947 in *Everson* v. *Board of Education* (330 U.S. 1) the Establishment Clause of the First Amendment was incorporated by virtue of a dicta pronouncement.[u]

With *Palko* the Court was given a tool with which to modernize the Bill of Rights. Interestingly, the same Court that had extinguished substantive due process in the field of economic regulation was to consider applying suspiciously analogous due process principles in the field of civil liberties. The Supreme Court of the late 1930s and 1940s, however, was not united on this issue. In particular, Justices Frankfurter and Jackson insisted that it was important for the maintenance of the federal system as well as for principles of judicial self-restraint to permit the states discretion in civil liberties policy. Justice Black, on the other hand, argued forcefully that due process was shorthand for the Bill of Rights and is thus made obligatory upon the states. Justices

Rutledge and Murphy took an even more extreme view by maintaining that the Bill of Rights should be read broadly to include not only its specific provisions but also additional rights that may be inferred from the Amendments.[v]

Related to the issue of incorporation was the question of the proper mode of constitutional interpretation. Reflecting his position on judicial self-restraint, Frankfurter held that the outcome of civil liberties issues should be determined with a judicial balancing-of-interests test; in each case, the Court should balance the constitutional guarantee against the reasonableness of the questioned social regulation. However, for a short period in the 1930s and 1940s some justices adopted a preferred-freedoms approach, which held, with respect to the First Amendment in particular, that the burden of proof was against the constitutionality of government restriction. It became plain by the end of the Truman administration that the Court's majority had failed to adopt the preferred-freedoms position and tended to accept Frankfurter's conceptualization.[w]

During the 1930s and 1940s the Supreme Court moved toward the vindication of the rights of black Americans.[x] This was made less complicated since constitutional provisions other than the Fourteenth's Due Process Clause could be invoked. Instead, the Court interpreted the Equal Protection Clause of the Fourteenth Amendment and the relatively straightforward right-to-vote requirement of the Fifteenth Amendment. While not eliminating the separate-but-equal doctrine first laid down in 1896 in *Plessy* v. *Ferguson* (163 U.S. 537), the Supreme Court began to consider the less tangible aspects of discrimination and in the process struck down segregation in some educational settings.[y] Also, by carefully construing state action the Court found judicially enforced restrictive covenant agreements constitutionally invalid.[z] Moreover, in the field of political participation the Court moved to eliminate southern restrictions on black voting.[aa]

By the end of the Vinson era the Supreme Court seemed to enjoy broad popular support. The Court's willingness to sustain congressional antisubversion legislation in 1951 in *Dennis* v. *United States* (341 U.S. 494) and its denial of presidential power the following year in *Youngstown Sheet and Tube* v. *Sawyer* (343 U.S. 579) put it in good stead with Congress and with moderate-to-right-wing citizen groups.[bb] However, with the accession in 1953 of Earl Warren as chief justice and a series of dramatic Court decisions spanning the 1950s and most of the 1960s, the Supreme Court experienced one of its most exciting but difficult periods.

In 1954 in his first great opinion, Chief Justice Warren skillfully massed the entire Court behind him in *Brown* v. *Board of Education* (347 U.S. 488).[cc] The Court discarded the separate-but-equal doctrine, holding that separate but equal facilities in public education are "inherently unequal." This decision, combined with a number of opinions restricting federal and state legislation designed to deal with alleged threats to internal security, coalesced southern segregationists and northern conservatives against the Court.[dd] As if this was not opposition enough, the Court went on to strike down prayer in the public schools,[ee] rural domination of state legislatures,[ff] various obscenity regulations,[gg] and common police interrogation practices.[hh]

Perhaps the Warren Court's most enduring contribution to constitutional law was its role in the modernization of the Bill of Rights. From 1961 to 1969 the Court used the Fourteenth Amendment's Due Process Clause to incorporate all but a few of the most minor provisions of the Bill of Rights as limitations upon state power.[ii] Overruling previous precedent, the Supreme Court in *Mapp* v. *Ohio* in 1961 (367 U.S. 643) held that illegally seized materials are inadmissible in a state criminal proceeding. A year later in *Robinson* v. *California* (370 U.S. 660) the Court held that a California criminal statute punishing someone for being addicted to drugs was violative of the Eighth Amendment's prohibition against cruel and unusual punishment. In 1963 in *Gideon* v. *Wainwright* (372 U.S. 335) the right to counsel in criminal cases, whether capital or noncapital, was made obligatory upon the states. The Fifth Amendment provision against self-incrimination was made applicable to the states in 1964 in *Malloy* v. *Hogan* (378 U.S. 1). In the following year the confrontation-of-witnesses provision of the Sixth Amendment was likewise incorporated in *Pointer* v. *Texas* (380 U.S. 400). In 1967 in *Klopfer* v. *North Carolina* (386 U.S. 213) the Sixth Amendment provision of the right to a speedy trial was applied to the states, and in 1968 the right to a jury trial in criminal cases was placed as a restriction upon the states (*Duncan* v. *Louisiana* (391 U.S. 145). Finally, in 1969 in *Benton* v. *Maryland* (395 U.S. 784), the Court overruled the 1937 *Palko* v. *Connecticut* decision (302 U.S. 319), holding that the double-jeopardy provision of the Fifth Amendment applied to the states by virtue of the Fourteenth Amendment's Due Process Clause.

The Warren Court did not proceed in a straight liberal line. The Court did backpedal from time to time, reflecting both adverse reactions to its decisions and conflict within the Court itself.[jj] On balance, however, it is clear that the Court's liberal majority felt compelled to act in the area of civil liberties and rights, although it suffered much counterreaction.

The Court's visibility as a target of conservative agitation was reflected in the presidential campaign of 1968. Seizing upon the Warren Court's unpopularity in many quarters, Richard Nixon promised that if elected he would appoint to the Supreme Court justices who would be "strict constructionists" with strong "law and order" predispositions. Of course, such terms were well-known euphemisms for conservative justices.[kk]

President Nixon encountered senatorial opposition to two of his nominees, but in the end he was able to secure the appointment of four relatively conservative men. These four did not always vote together. Indeed, it is fair to conclude that Chief Justice Burger and Associate Justice Rehnquist were the most conservative of the four, with Justices Powell and Blackmun leaning toward a more centrist position; Justice Blackmun sometimes joined the remnants of the old Warren Court liberal coalition, particularly in matters touching upon the right to privacy. Justice Stewart, an Eisenhower appointee, and Justice White, a Kennedy appointee, often provided the swing votes. And Justice Stevens, appointed by President Ford in 1976 to replace the liberal William O. Douglas, steered a relatively independent course; he was not identified with any particular voting bloc. Appointed in 1981 by President Reagan, Justice Sandra Day O'Connor replaced the moderate Justice Stewart, and despite some contradictory votes she became identified with Justice Rehnquist and the chief justice as one of the most conservative-minded members of the high court. By the end of Chief Justice Burger's tenure on the Court, only two members, Justice Brennan and Justice Marshall, could be counted upon to echo the liberal sentiments of the Warren Court.

It is erroneous to assert that the Burger Court (1969–86) reversed the liberal decisions of the Warren Court. It is true that this Court was not sympathetic to liberal attempts to use the judiciary as an agent of social change. This hostility was sensed by such groups as the National Association for the Advancement of Colored People (NAACP) and the American Civil Liberties Union (ACLU). The latter pursued at times a strategy intended to avoid litigation before the Supreme Court.

Particularly in the areas of obscenity, criminal justice, and minority rights the Burger Court failed to adhere to the implications in many Warren Court opinions. With respect to obscenity cases, the Burger Court discarded some rules created during the Warren era.[ll] For the most part, however, through carefully worded opinions and by limiting holdings to particular rather than broadly applicable fact situations, the Burger Court avoided direct contradiction of many earlier and widely interpreted liberal decisions of the preceding era. In the process the Burger Court limited the scope and modified the legal rules initiated by the Warren Court.

Though the Burger Court seemed to enjoy broad public support, it was not immune from criticism. It upheld the propriety of school busing in order to achieve racial integration,[mm] and it reaffirmed the Warren Court's ban on school prayer.[nn] It also affirmed the constitutionality of affirmative action programs in education and employment.[oo] Its most controversial and debated holdings have been in abortion cases.[pp] There the Supreme Court held that the various blanket limitations upon the ability of pregnant women to obtain abortions is violative of the right to privacy. On the other hand, most Americans applauded the 1974 decision in *U.S. v. Nixon* (418 U.S. 683) in which a unanimous Court, with Justice Rehnquist not participating, rejected President Nixon's claim of executive privilege with respect to the Watergate tapes. It is also noteworthy that, in a departure from the Warren Court tendency, this Court exhibited an antigovernment—including anti-state government—disposition and probusiness attitude in economic cases.[qq]

Although the Burger Court genuflected at the altar of judicial self-restraint, there is evidence that it had little difficulty exercising judicial power when the felt need arose. It did not hesitate to use its power of judicial review, for example, to strike down various provisions of the Federal Election Campaign Act of 1971[rr]; to hold unconstitutional the 1974 Amendment to the Fair Labor Standards Act which provided for minimum-wage protection for municipal workers, only to be overruled nine years later[ss]; to invalidate the one-House legislative veto provision of the Immigration and Nationality Act[tt]; and to veto the automatic triggering device in the Gramm-Rudman-Hollings Balanced Budget Act.[uu]

It is difficult to predict with certitude the policy pronouncements of the Rehnquist Court. The appointment of U.S. Court of Appeals Judge Antonin Scalia to fill the vacancy left by the Rehnquist elevation to chief justice is almost sure to guarantee a significant and articulately led conservative voting bloc within the Court. The resignation of Mr. Justice Powell and the appointment of U.S. Court of Appeals judge Anthony Kennedy may have placed the institution firmly in the control of modern conservative ideologues. One additional conservative appointment will remove all doubt.

No matter what ideology dominates the Court for the remainder of the twentieth century it is clear that the imprint left by John Marshall upon the Supreme Court as a vital political institution of government remains, and it is unlikely to change as long as the Republic endures. The political history of the Supreme Court affirms the proposition that the various uses of judicial review place the Court squarely in the midst of the governmental process as an important allocator of political authority. In the following chapter, we explore more precisely how the power of judicial review has shaped vital political relationships.

NOTES

a. Martin Shapiro and Rocco J. Tresolini, *American Constitutional Law*, 6th ed. (New York: Macmillan, 1983), 14.

b. Elder Witt, ed., *Congressional Quarterly's Guide to the U.S. Supreme Court* (Washington, D.C.: Congressional Quarterly, 1979), 10.

c. Ibid., 70.

d. John R. Schmidhauser, *Judges and Justices: The Federal Appellate Judiciary* (Boston: Little, Brown, 1979), 105–16.

e. Donald O. Morgan, *Justice William Johnson: The First Dissenter* (Columbia, S.C.: University of South Carolina Press, 1954), 181–82.

f. Alfred H. Kelly and Winfred A. Harbison, *The American Constitution: Its Origins and Development* (New York: W. W. Norton, 1955), 342–53.

g. Ibid., 387.

h. Ibid., 515–18. *Chicago, Milwaukee, and St. Paul Ry. Co. v. Minnesota*, 134 U.S. 418 (1890), is the landmark decision marking the turning point.

i. Due process is a limitation upon the state governments by virtue of the Fourteenth Amendment and a limitation upon the federal government through the Fifth Amendment.

j. *Cincinnati, New Orleans, and Texas Pacific Railway Co. v. Interstate Commerce Commission*, 162 U.S. 184 (1896); *Interstate Commerce Commmission v. Alabama Midland Ry. Co.*, 168 U.S. 144 (1897).

k. *United States v. E. C. Knight Co.*, 156 U.S. 1 (1895).

l. *Pollock v. Farmers Loan and Trust Co.*, 157 U.S. 429 (1895); *Pollock v. Farmers Loan and Trust Co.*, 158 U.S. 601 (1895).

m. In *Re Debs*, 158 U.S. 564 (1895).

n. *Hammer v. Dagenhart*, 247 U.S. 251 (1918).

o. *Adkins v. Children's Hospital*, U.S. 525 (1923).

p. Witt, ed., *Guide to the U.S. Supreme Court*, 664–65.

q. Fred Rodell, *Nine Men: A Political History of the Supreme Court of the United States from 1790 to 1955* (New York: Vintage Books, 1955), 213–55.

r. Henry J. Abraham, *Freedom and the Court: Civil Rights and Liberties in the United States*, 4th ed. (New York: Oxford University Press, 1982), 53–56.

s. Ibid., 56.

t. Ibid., 57–59.

u. Ibid., 60.

v. Ibid., 83–91.

w. Kelly and Harbinson, *American Constitution*, 836.

x. Ibid., 821–36.

y. *Missouri Ex rel. Gaines* v. *Canada,* 305 U.S. 337 (1938); *Sipuel* v. *Board of Regents,* 332 U.S. 631 (1948); *Sweatt* v. *Painter,* 339 U.S. 629 (1950); *McLaurin* v. *Oklahoma State Regents,* 339 U.S. 637 (1950).

z. *Shelly* v. *Kraemer,* 334 U.S. 1 (1948).

aa. *United States* v. *Classic,* 313 U.S. 229 (1941); *Smith* v. *Allwright,* 321 U.S. 649 (1944).

bb. Walter F. Murphy, *Congress and the Court* (Chicago: University of Chicago Press, 1962), 74–76.

cc. S. Sidney Ulmer, "Leadership and Group Structure," in *Courts, Law, and Judicial Processes,* ed. S. Sidney Ulmer (New York: Free Press, 1981), 373–79.

dd. John R. Schmidhauser, Larry L. Berg, and Albert P. Melone, "The Impact of Judicial Decisions: New Dimensions in Supreme Court Congressional Relations, 1945–1968," *Washington University Law Quarterly* 209 (1971); Albert P. Melone, "System Support Politics and the Congressional Court of Appeals," *North Dakota Law Rev.* 597 (1975).

ee. *Engel* v. *Vitale,* 370 U.S. 421 (1962).

ff. *Reynolds* v. *Sims,* 377 U.S. 533 (1964).

gg. *Roth* v. *United States, Alberts* v. *California,* 354 U.S. 476 (1957).

hh. *Escobedo* v. *Illinois,* 378 U.S. 478 (1964); *Miranda* v. *Arizona,* 384 U.S. 436 (1966).

ii. For a succinct discussion of the case law, see Abraham, *Freedom and the Court,* 61–83.

jj. G. Gregory Fahlund, "Retroactivity and the Warren Court: The Strategy of a Revolution," *Journal of Politics* 35 (1973): 570–93.

kk. Witt, ed., *Guide to the U.S. Supreme Court,* 245.

ll. *Miller* v. *California,* 413 U.S. 15 (1973); *Paris Adult Theatre* v. *Slaton,* 413 U.S. 49 (1973). Also see Abraham, *Freedom and the Court,* 199–204.

mm. *Swann* v. *Charlotte-Mecklenburg Board of Education,* 402 U.S. 1 (1971).

nn. *Wallace* v. *Jaffree,* 53 L.W. 4665 (1985).

oo. *Regents of the University of California* v. *Bakke,* 438 U.S. 265 (1978); *United Steelworkers of America, AFL-CIO-CLC* v. *Weber,* 443 U.S. 193 (1979).

pp. *Roe* v. *Wade,* 410 U.S. 113 (1973); *Thornburgh* v. *American College of Obstetricians and Gynecologists,* 54 L.W. 4618 (June 11, 1986).

qq. See, for example, *United States Trust Co.* v. *State of New York and New Jersey,* 431 U.S. 1 (1977); *Loretto* v. *Teleprompter Manhattan CATV Corp.,* 458 U.S. 419 (1982); *Penn Central Transportation Co.* v. *City of New York,* 438 U.S. 104 (1975); *National League of Cities* v. *Usery,* 426 U.S. 833 (1976); Richard E. Johnston and John T. Thompson, "The Burger Court and Federalism: A Revolution in 1976?" *Western Political Quarterly* 33 (1980): 197–216; Robert L. Dudley and Craig R. Ducat, "The Burger Court and Economic Liberalism," *Western Political Quarterly* 39 (1986): 236–37.

rr. *Buckley* v. *Valeo,* 424 U.S. 1 (1976).

ss. *National League of Cities* v. *Usery,* 426 U.S. 833 (1976); *Garcia* v. *San Antonio Metro Transit Authority,* 105 S. Ct. 1005 (1985).

tt. *Immigration and Naturalization Service* v. *Chadha,* 462 U.S. 919 (1983).

uu. *Bousker, Comptroller General of the U.S.* v. *Synar, Member of Congress et al.,* No. 85-1377, slip op. (U.S. July 7, 1986).

3

The Scope of Judicial Review

JUDICIAL REVIEW has been applied in three key areas of interaction: (1) between federal and state governments, (2) among the various branches of the national government, and (3) between the federal government and individuals and between state governments and individuals. An appreciation for the role of the Supreme Court in defining these relationships will emphasize the vital relevance of the judicial review debate.

In all its variations judicial review is a singular institution. It is one of the primary political innovations of the American system and has only rudimentary precedents. Nonetheless, the uniqueness of judicial review is overlooked by most Americans. We are so accustomed to the notion that courts can declare acts to be unconstitutional that we consider it to be an ordinary aspect of judicial power. Yet in most other countries the judiciary is not vested with this kind of power. It is fair to conclude that prior to the American experience no judiciary held such power, at least in the open form that we know it today.

Most nation-states operate under a unitary form of government. The central government possesses all authority. Local governmental units are created, altered, and abolished by the central authority. Thus in unitary systems such as England's, local governments lack constitutional autonomy and are but mere conveniences for the central government headquartered in London.

At the polar opposite is the confederation. It is a loose union of sovereign states in which the states create the central government and may abolish it. Only the states act upon the people directly, and the central government has only that authority granted to it by the constituent states. Under the Articles of Confederation (1776–89), the United States had such a government. Other examples include the Netherlands under the Union of Utrecht (1579), Switzerland from its earliest days, Germany (1815–67), the North German Confederation (1867–71), the German Empire (1871–1918), and, of course, the Confederate States of America (1861–65).[a]

If placed on a continuum of government schemes a federation falls somewhere between the unitary and confederate forms. It is a territorial division of powers among governments, each acting directly upon the people. Unlike unitary governments and confederations, both the central and local governments derive authority from the same source — namely, the same written constitution. Besides the United States, the nations of Australia, Canada, West Germany, and to a lesser extent the Soviet Union are contemporary examples of federal systems.

The practice of judicial review seems well suited for the special character of American federalism. In fact, it is widely believed that judicial review is an inescapable result of our *federal* form of democratic government. This is understood most readily by noting the change that took place in the meaning of federalism. At the time of the Philadelphia Convention, 1787, "the then common understanding of federalism involved no distinction between confederation and federalism."[b] Federalism encompassed three characteristics: government over collectivities (the essential characteristic), abstinence from internal administration, and equal suffrage of the members.[c] Such characteristics hardly square with our contemporary understanding of federalism.

Federalism now refers to a system of government wherein political power is divided between a central government and governments of various political subdivisions, both deriving authority from the constitution and, ultimately, "we the people" who ordained and established it. Moreover, the authority of the central government applies not only to "collectivities" (the governments of the political subdivisions), but to *individuals* within those subdivisions as well.

The two remaining characteristics fare little better. The authority of the central government is not proscribed from operating within the sphere of "internal administration." Unlike a confederation, both the central government and the state governments act directly upon the people. If we look to the political system of the United States (which is currently equated with federalism) by way of example, we find the central government enormously involved in internal affairs. Matters affecting the education, health, and even the morals of the people are subjects for central government legislation and regulation as well as the legitimate sphere of authority for state and local governments. With respect to the feature of equal suffrage, the states have equal footing in the Senate with two members each. However, the House of Representatives violates this principle because representation is proportioned according to population. Thus, for example, the state of North Dakota with a population of 652,717 persons is entitled to two senators but only one House member; Illinois with a population of 11,426,518 persons also has two senators but a House delegation of twenty-two members.

The real change in federalism was just this: the shortcomings of a *league* whose primary purpose was to provide protection from foreign danger were exchanged for the advantages of a *national government.* However, there were still disadvantages in this regard. Writing in defense of the proposed federal constitution, James Madison (who is rightly considered the "Father" of the Constitution) noted that "the national countenance of the government . . . seems to be disfigured by a few federal features. But this blemish is perhaps unavoidable."[d] The "disfiguring blemish" concerned some of the federal characteristics of the Constitution which related to the operation of the national government's powers.[e]

In order to attain the ends for which the national government was instituted, some means of providing for the supremacy of that government was necessary. In other words, above all else it needed a means of enforcing the second clause of Article VI of the Constitution, commonly referred to as the Supremacy Clause:

> This Constitution, and the Laws of the United States which shall be made in pursuance thereof; and all treaties made, or which shall be made, under the authority of the United States, shall be the supreme law of the land; and the judges in every State shall be bound thereby, anything in the Constitution or laws of any State to the contrary not withstanding.

In his February 15, 1913, address before the Harvard Law Association on Law and the Court, Associate Justice Oliver Wendell Holmes stated that "the United States would not come to an end if we the Supreme Court lost our power to declare an Act of Congress void." However, such a danger would exist "if we could not make that declaration as to the laws of the several States." Judicial review of state actions promotes national supremacy and places the federal judiciary in the institutional position of umpire and enforcer of the rules within the federal system of government.

This explains at once much of the importance and uniqueness of judicial review. Its greatest significance lies in the fact that it serves to overcome the tension existing between state and national governments. Its uniqueness is similarly explained. Prior to 1787, federalism (or what we call confederation today), did not incur such tension. The central "government" did what various "state" governments permitted. It was only after the central body became a *government* in *fact* that such tension resulted.

W. W. Willoughby appraised the problem thus:

> The reason for giving such unusual power to a judicial tribunal is obvious. It was necessary to give it from the complex character of the Government in the United States, which is in part National, and in part Federal; where two separate governments exercise certain powers of sovereignty over the same territory, each independent of the other within its appropriate sphere of action, and where there was, therefore, an absolute necessity, in order to preserve internal tranquility, that there should be some tribunal to decide between the Government of the United States and the government of a State, whenever any controversy should arise as to their relative and respective powers in the common territory. The Supreme Court was created for that purpose.[1]

Although some questions may be raised as to whether the Supreme Court was created solely for the purpose of resolving controversies between federal and state governments, there can be little doubt about the basis by which they are resolved. The Constitution explicitly states that it and all laws and treaties made for purposes of its implementation are the supreme law of the land. By continuing to require that the respective constitutions and laws of the several states must comply with the supreme law of the land, it becomes the single and controlling standard for Supreme Court judgments.

National supremacy so stated is unequivocal. However, our Constitution grants power to both federal and state governments. Some grants are made exclusively to the national government, some are made concurrently to both national and state governments, and some powers are "reserved" to the states or to the people. The problem of national supremacy arises when a state government, pursuing a rightful or unrightful exercise of power, violates a national law (whether constitutional or statutory). At this point, some means of determining whether the federal or state government must give way is needed.

The best-known example of this confrontation occurred in 1818 as a result of the concurrent power of taxation. Pursuing a course already pioneered by several other states, Maryland laid a heavy stamp tax upon all notes issued by banks it had not chartered. As in the case of the other states, this legislation was directed against the controversial Bank of the United States.

The cashier of the Baltimore branch of the Bank, James McCulloch, refused to comply with the Maryland statute and issued unstamped banknotes. After state courts decided in favor of the state, the case was taken on a writ of error to the United States Supreme Court. The 1819 opinion of the Court in *McCulloch* v. *Maryland* (4 Wheaton 316) stated the question precisely. Chief Justice John Marshall wrote: "The conflicting powers of the general and state governments must be brought into view, and the supremacy of their respective laws, when they are in opposition, must be settled."

In settling this conflict, Marshall first noted that the "government of the Union, though limited in its powers, is supreme within its sphere of action." Admitting that the Constitution did not expressly grant the central government the power to create a Bank, Marshall pointed out at the same time that it did grant "the great powers to lay and collect taxes; to borrow money; to regulate commerce; to declare and conduct war; and to raise and support armies and navies." Moreover, the government was expressly granted the power "of making all laws which shall be necessary and proper, for carrying into execution . . . all other powers vested by this constitution, in the government of the United States." Thus, Marshall found the Bank to be constitutionally valid since the national government derived a legitimate power to create it from the Necessary and Proper Clause.

Although the Constitution also gave Maryland the power to tax, "that authority which is supreme must control." Therefore, the Maryland legislation "imposing a tax on the Bank of the United States, is unconstitutional and void."

By using the power of judicial review, itself something of an "implied power," Marshall declared a legislative act of the State of Maryland to be null and void because it collided with a valid national law. With this decision the supremacy of national laws was firmly established.

The second area in which judicial review may be applied concerns the relationships among the various branches of the central government. There are two salient points of difference. One is the federal balance involving a division of power, and the other is the departmental balance involving a separation of power.

First, division of power involves a quantitative portioning of power; separation of powers involves a distribution of kinds of power. The former is concerned with determining how much of the total amount of power that may be brought to bear upon individuals belongs to the central government on the one hand and state governments on the other. The latter is concerned with a distribution of what are viewed as qualitatively different powers to the various branches of the central government.

Second, the principle of division of power is explicit in the Constitution, whereas the principle of separation of powers is implicit and can be found only through inference from the organization and structure of that document. The Tenth Amendment clearly establishes the principle of a granted amount of power for the central government and a reserved amount for the states and people by providing that the "powers not delegated to the United States by the Constitution or prohibited by it to the States, are reserved to the States respectively, or to the people." (This is not to say that the demands of that principle are evident. Various Court interpretations of what that principle requires as a proper extent of both federal and state powers have tended to expand or diminish the power of either, as in *McCulloch* v. *Maryland.*) Constitutional provision for the principle of separation of powers is not so clear. Such provision as exists is not found in any one statement to that effect. We must look to three different articles: Article I, "All legislative powers herein granted shall be vested in a Congress of the United States . . ."; Article II, "The executive power shall be vested in a President of the United States . . ."; Article III, "The judicial power of the United States shall be vested in one Supreme Court, and in such inferior courts as the Congress may from time to time ordain and estabish. . . ." These statements suggest that only the Congress may exercise legislative power, only the president may exercise executive power, and only the judiciary may exercise judicial power. However, the Constitution also provides for an admixture of those powers.

Article I, which vests "all" legislative power in Congress, is the same article that gives the president his most obvious participation in the legislative process. Section 7 provides that all bills passed by Congress must be presented to the president for his signature before they become law. In the event the president does not approve a bill,

he shall return it, with his objections, to that house in which it
shall have originated, who shall . . . proceed to reconsider it. If
after such reconsideration two-thirds of that house shall agree to
pass the bill, it shall be sent . . . to the other house, by which it
shall likewise be reconsidered, and if approved by two-thirds of
that house, it shall become law.

This provision for presidential veto gives the president immense legislative power. On any vetoed bill the president has the equivalent voting
power of two fewer than two-thirds the membership of both houses
(289 in the House and 66 in the Senate).

Other important provisions for cross-branch participation include
Article I, Section 3, which gives the Senate the judicial power to try
impeachment cases with the chief justice presiding in the event the
president is tried (it also empowers the vice-president to be president
of the Senate and to vote whenever that body is equally divided); Article II, Section 2, which gives the Senate the power to approve treaties
and certain appointments, including those of federal judges; and Article II, Section 3, which not only grants but obliges the president to
propose legislation.

In this light, we readily see that the Constitution by no means
prescribes an absolute separation of powers. Moreover, the Constitution is not clear as to the extent of that nonabsolute separation. In an
attempt to understand the proper extent, we must first look to the
purpose of that principle. It is intended to prevent the "accumulation of
all powers, legislative, executive, and judiciary, in the same hands,
whether of one, a few, or many, and whether hereditary, self-appointed, or elective, may justly be pronounced the very definition of
tyranny."[g] Simply stated, separation of powers is intended to prevent
tyranny by ensuring that the same person, or the same body of persons, does not possess more than one of the three kinds of governmental power.

So convinced were Americans of the necessity that a separation of
powers be sufficient to attain its purpose that one of the major objections directed at the proposed constitution during the ratification debates was that it could not ensure liberty since it did not embody an
absolute separation. James Madison answered the objection by first
noting that not even Montesquieu, who was regarded by both sides as
the greatest proponent of this principle, insisted upon a complete separation.[h] He then turned to an examination of existing state constitu-

tions to show that they also blended and commingled legislative, executive, and judicial powers.¹ He found the true meaning of the principle in the New Hampshire Constitution, a meaning which made clear the necessity of an incomplete separation.

> the legislative, executive, and judiciary powers ought to be kept as separate from, and independent of, each other *as the nature of a free government will admit; or as is consistent with that chain of connection that binds the whole fabric of the constitution in one indissoluble bond of unity and amity.*¹

As the proponents of the Constitution viewed it, two values were involved in ascertaining the proper extent of separation of powers. The first is liberty, which requires that the separation be great enough to prevent tyranny. The second is order. If government is to attain the ends for which it was created, it must be able to bring concerted governmental powers to bear on any issue at hand. For if that power is to be effective, it must consist of a combination of legislative, executive, and judicial powers. Anything less would be futile.

For example, let us suppose Congress passed a law that either the executive or judiciary believed was bad. Were the three branches completely independent of one another, the law would not be binding upon the latter two branches. The executive branch could choose not to enforce that law. Or if the executive did enforce it, and the judiciary were opposed, the latter branch could make the law ineffectual by simply dismissing all charges against defendants brought before them and ordering their release. Of course, in the latter instance, there is no reason to believe the executive branch would adhere to that order.

The inescapable result of an absolute separation is that government would be reduced to institutionalized absurdity. Efficacious government demands that the separation be not absolute.

With this in mind, recall that the Constitution is silent on the nature of the intended separation. Even so vague a standard as the requirement that the various powers must be as independent of one another as free *and* efficacious government will permit must be inferred. Once this is accomplished, someone then must determine that point where the separation is either too great to allow workable government or so insufficient it cannot prevent an unending coalescence of power in one of the branches, resulting in tyranny. Since the Court speaks for the Constitution, the responsibility for that determination is clearly located.

A classic example of the Court's role in this respect is found in the

1952 opinion in *Youngstown Sheet and Tube Company* v. *Sawyer,* (343 U.S. 579), which merits a brief investigation since it not only illustrates the Court's operation concerning a proper separation of powers, but demonstrates the manner in which the Court has limited federal executive power as it relates to individual citizens as well. Approximately two years before this so-called Steel Seizure Case the Court sustained the existence of presidential "inherent" powers in *U.S. ex rel. Knauff* v. *Shaughnessy* (338 U.S. 537). Seeming to accept the Court at its word, President Truman seized the nation's steel mills in 1952 claiming an inherent power to do so stemming from the general powers granted him by the Constitution, and especially from the power he held as commander-in-chief. In an interesting opinion, the Court did not deny that the president might have inherent power in certain instances. However, the facts in this case indicated that this was not one of those instances, and Mr. Justice Black found no "ultimate power as such to take command of private property in order to keep labor disputes from stopping production. This is a job for the Nation's lawmakers, not for its military authorities."[k] Seeing the constitutional question as one of separation of powers, rather than one of inherent powers, the Court continued:

> In the framework of our Constitution, the President's power to see that the laws are faithfully executed refutes the idea that he is to be a lawmaker. The Constitution limits his functions in the lawmaking process to the recommending of laws he thinks wise and the vetoing of laws he thinks bad. And the Constitution is neither silent or equivocal about who shall make laws which the President is to execute. . . .[l]
> The Founders of this Nation entrusted the lawmaking power to Congress alone in both good and bad times. It would do no good to recall the historical events, the fears of power and the hopes for freedom that lay behind their choice. Such a review would but confirm our holding that this seizure order cannot stand."[m]

In this case, a nonunanimous Court overruled what it viewed as arbitrary governmental action aimed at individuals (corporations). However, its arbitrariness lay in the fact that the president had exercised wrongfully a legislative function by usurping the lawmaking power. This was not a question of whether government as a whole rightfully could seize the mills. Nonetheless, it can be seen that the Court's activity is not restricted to the single purpose Willoughby saw as the raison d'etre for judicial review, that is, the resolution of federal-state tension. At issue here is the additional sphere of relations between governmental departments, which, as we have seen, is tied directly to the problem of tyranny. In other words, concern over the sphere of relations between departments exists because of a preceding concern for individual rights and limits upon governmental power.

The third area of application of judicial review concerns the relations between individuals and federal and state governments. Essentially, this is the area of encounter between individual rights and governmental power. Whereas the previous areas concern the proper division of governmental authority, we now consider what has been viewed as the proper extent of that authority.

Ascertainment of the proper extent of governmental power turns upon the same two values involved in arriving at the proper extent of separation of powers: liberty and order. The desired result is also the same, namely, efficacious and free government. We see this in the Declaration of Independence, which states:

> We hold these truths to be self-evident, that all men are created equal. That they are endowed by their Creator with certain unalienable Rights, that among these are Life, Liberty and the pursuit of Happiness. – That to secure these rights, Governments are instituted among Men, deriving their just powers from the consent of the governed, – That whenever any Form of Government becomes destructive of these ends, it is the Right of the People to alter or to abolish it, and to institute new Government, laying its foundation on such principles and organizing its powers in such form, as to them shall seem most likely to effect their Safety and Happiness.

The Declaration brings us to the crux of the matter. Free government is limited government, and limited government is brought about by the existence of individual rights. Whenever rights are considered, the subject of those rights is liberty. The essence of liberty is the belief that there are certain areas in which a government may not rightfully act. This use of *right* has a different meaning than the same word does in the case of "one's rights." We may say we have a right to this or that, which seems to carry with it not only the notion of correctness, but the additional notion of a correct claim to something. In fact, "our rights" are actually conceived as properties for which one is entitled to exclusive control and enjoyment. On the other hand, to say a government may or may not rightfully act in a certain sphere seems only to suggest the notion of correctness, in other words, the notion of right or wrong.

This really is the opposite side of the coin, for rightness or wrongness is usually determined in relation to transgression upon our rights. Government may not rightfully act because our rights prevent that action, and these rights are liberties. Thus we arrive at an aspect of the meaning of liberty and freedom which depends upon spheres of activity.

When individuals have the right to every and all activity they are in a state of license. When they authorize government to restrict certain of those activities, the activities that remain are liberties, or a relative degree of freedom. This freedom also serves as a restriction upon governmental action. It limits that action to specified *authorized* areas. Thus authority is the imputation of permission and thereby *legitimacy* for government action. When government steps outside the area of legitimate action, it commits *unauthorized* (unrightful) acts.

Inalienable rights are rights that cannot be taken away or transferred. They constitute an area in which individuals have freedom of action and at the same time an area that limits government. According to the Declaration this area is comprised of the rights of life, liberty, and the pursuit of happiness. The right to liberty at first glance seems redundant, that is, the right to rights. However, upon further examination we see that it is not redundant but of the utmost necessity.

If there are to be God-given inalienable rights, there must be a right to them. Otherwise, they would not be truly inalienable. The Declaration is really saying here that people have a right to enjoy (inalienable) rights of life and the pursuit of happiness. This is made clear in the following sentence asserting that the foundation of government must be based upon such principles, and governmental power must be organized into such form as will seem most likely to realize "Safety and Happiness" for its people. To this end, the Founding Fathers attempted to rightly organize governmental power by framing a constitution that both granted and limited power. Although some limits upon power are found in the body of the Constitution, the greater portion stem from the first eight amendments. The Ninth and Tenth Amendments are also considered part of the "Bill of Rights," but they were added to lessen the fears of those who believed such an enumeration of rights in the first eight amendments was not only unnecessary but dangerous. Since the Constitution was itself a limit, some feared the addition of such restriction would make the body appear to be a carte blanche grant, save for a few explicit restrictions contained therein.

At the same time, the Constitution provides little by way of defining either powers or limitations. Of course, this is not to say it contains no express grants or limitations of power. The power of Congress to declare war and the prohibition placed upon both state and federal governments preventing ex post facto legislation are obvious examples of specific grants and limitations.

Most limitations or grants are "implicit" in the Constitution and are inferred from either its general provisions or its organization and structure. Moreover, it is these inferred "rules" that take the form of so-called "doctrines" or "principles." Examples of the former, rules inferred from the general provisions of the Constitution, are the doctrines stemming from the Due Process, Equal Protection, Necessary and Proper, and Commerce clauses, and the principle of federalism. Examples of the latter, rules inferred from the organization and structure of the Constitution, are the principles of separation of powers and legislative checks and balances, and the doctrine of judicial review.

The Necessary and Proper Clause of Article I has been invoked so many times as a source of implied power that it has been appropriately labeled "the elastic clause." It may be recalled that Chief Justice John Marshall used it as such when he interpreted it to mean that "the powers given to the government imply the ordinary means of execution." In other words, if the government is granted the power to attain certain ends, it must also have the power to create or attain the means prerequisite to those ends. However, in the case of the Marshall Court, the expansion of federal power was at the expense of state power, not individual rights (whether corporate or personal).

In fact, with the exception of *Marbury* v. *Madison,* the early history of the Court was one of applying judicial review to determine the proper balance between federal and state governments. The Court did not strike down federal legislation again until the infamous decision in *Dred Scott* v. *Sanford* (19 Howard 393) in 1857. In this opinion, we find the establishment of a new constitutional doctrine that later would come to be called Substantive Due Process. Prior to this doctrine, due process concerned only the rights of persons accused of crime in criminal cases and, almost always, little more than proper notice and hearing and compensation in civil cases. However, Chief Justice Taney left little doubt that in the future due process would involve not only these appropriate procedures, but the substance of the matter at hand as well. The employment of judicial review in this manner places the Court in an activist posture and is particularly disturbing to proponents of majority rule.

In a series of cases which followed *Dred Scott* the Court limited the regulatory power of the federal government by restricting the area encompassed by the Commerce Clause through the application of Substantive Due Process and the Tenth Amendment and, in conjunction with the discovery in 1905 in *Lochner* v. *New York* (198 U.S. 45) of the principle of the "Inviolability of Liberty of Contract" inherent in Substantive Due Process, limited the states thereby creating a "no man's land" in the area of commerce." The result was that certain aspects of commerce (for example, mining, manufacturing, agriculture, and certain employer-employee relationships) could not be regulated by either federal or state governments. This doctrine was not overturned until 1937, when the Court, coincident with Franklin D. Roosevelt's "court-packing scheme," discovered in *West Coast Hotel Co.* v. *Parrish* (300 U.S. 379) that Congress did have the power to legislate in the area after all.

Such a sudden and far-reaching reversal of a firmly rooted policy seemed to many as something more than simple coincidence. Nonetheless the series of cases which followed ended the era of a constitutional void. The result was an expansion of governmental power brought about by the very vehicle responsible for the preceding diminution of power. Through judicial interpretation, mining, manufacturing, agriculture, minimum-wage laws, and so on were found to be aspects of interstate commerce and therefore subject to congressional regulation.

The state governments as well as the national government have been subjected to the Supreme Court's exercise of judicial review. Though the bulk of judicial intervention has occurred in recent American history by virtue of the application of the Fourteenth Amendment's Equal Protection and Due Process clauses, earlier cases were important also.

The Supreme Court's 1810 opinion in *Fletcher* v. *Peck* (10 U.S. 6 Cranc.) is the first major decision to strike down a state law as inconsistent with the federal Constitution and thus is the state analogue to *Marbury* v. *Madison*. Georgia's repeal of a corrupt land give-away law was found to be violative of the Constitution's Contract Clause forbidding states to impair the obligation of contract. Interestingly, the Court presumed to intervene in the internal affairs of a state because, in part, as Justice William Johnson put it, of "a general principle, on the reason and nature of things; a principle which will impose laws even on the Deity." Thus the natural law was invoked as a protection of individual rights against state governments, and the notion of vested property rights became firmly embedded in the constitutional consciousness.

As noted in Chapter 2, the courts led by Earl Warren and Warren Burger were very much involved in the protection of individual rights against state intrusions. The use of the Equal Protection and Due Process clauses of the Fourteenth Amendment to litigate matters such as school segregation,[p] apportionment of state legislatures,[q] regulation of abortions,[r] and the sexual preferences of consenting adults in the privacy of their homes,[s] illustrate the Supreme Court's role as the definer of boundaries of individual rights against the power of state governments.

It is thus evident that judicial review affords the judiciary an enormous power in the American political system. Because the Supreme Court is in the position to define the relationships between federal and state governments, among the three branches of the national government, and between governments at all levels and individuals, its visibility and importance in the political system is central to an understanding of government. The exercise of judicial review draws the judiciary deeply into what would be wholly political matters in most other countries. No less an observer of the American system than Alexis de Tocqueville noted that the position of a Supreme Court justice

> is therefore exactly the same as that of the magistrates of other nations; and yet he is invested with immense political power. How does this come about? If the sphere of his authority and his means of action are the same as those of other judges, whence does he derive a power which they do not possess? The cause of this difference lies in the simple fact that the Americans have acknowledged the right of judges to found their decisions on the *Constitution* rather than on the *laws*. In other words, they have permitted them not to apply such laws as may appear to them to be unconstitutional.
>
> I am aware that a similar right has been sometimes claimed, but claimed in vain, by courts of justice in other countries; but in America it is recognized by all the authorities; and not a party, not so much as an individual, is found to contest it. This fact can be explained only by the principles of the American constitutions. In France the constitution is, or at least is supposed to be, immutable; and the received theory is that no power has the right of changing any part of it. In England the constitution may change continually, or rather it does not in reality exist; the Parliament is at once a legislative and a constituent assembly. The political theories of America are more simple and more rational. An American constitution is not supposed to be immutable, as in France; nor is it susceptible of modification by the ordinary powers of society,

as in England. It constitutes a detached whole, which, as it represents the will of the whole people, is no less binding on the legislator than on the private citizen, but which may be altered by the will of the people in predetermined cases, according to established rules. In America the Constitution may therefore vary; but as long as it exists, it is the origin of all authority, and the sole vehicle of the predominating force.[t]

With this understanding of the role judicial review has played in our polity and of the questions it has raised, we next turn to the famous decision itself. A discussion of the historical and political setting of *Marbury* v. *Madison* precedes an edited reproduction of the opinion of the Court. The reader will then be in the position to critically analyze the fundamental questions raised by this book. First, was the power of judicial review usurped by the Supreme Court? Part II of this book contains readings that will help answer this question. Second, is the power of judicial review compatible with the spirit and form of democratic government? The readings in Part III will target this query.

NOTES

a. K. C. Wheare, *Federal Government,* 4th ed. (New York: Oxford Univ. Press, 1964), 32.

b. Martin Diamond, "The Federalists' View of Federalism," in *Essays in Federalism,* ed. George C. S. Benson et al. (Claremont, Calif.: Institute for Studies in Federalism, 1961), 26.

c. Diamond, "Federalists' View," 27.

d. Alexander Hamilton, John Jay, and James Madison, *The Federalist* (New York: Modern Library, 1941), *Federalist* 39, p. 248. Hereafter cited as *Federalist.* See also: Diamond, "Federalists' View," 63 n.9.

e. *Federalist* 39.

f. Quoted by Charles Warren, *The Supreme Court in U.S. History* (Boston: Little, Brown, 1937), 6 n.1.

g. *Federalist* 47, p. 313.

h. Ibid., 314–15.

i. Ibid., 316–20.

j. Ibid., 316.

k. 343 U.S. at 587.

l. Ibid.

m. 343 U.S. at 589. One year after the steel-seizure case, the Court reasserted the existence of inherent presidential powers in *Shaughnessy* v. *U.S. ex. rel. Mezei* (345 U.S. 206).

n. See Edward S. Corwin, "The Passing of a Dual Federalism," *Virginia Law Review* 36(1950): 1.

o. 10 U.S. (Cranc.) at 143.

p. *Brown* v. *Board of Education of Topeka*, 347 U.S. 483 (1954); *Swann* v. *Charlotte-Mecklenburg Board of Education*, 402 U.S. 1 (1971).

q. *Reynolds* v. *Sims*, 377 U.S. 533 (1964); *Davis* v. *Bandemer*, 54 U.S.L.W. 4898 (1986).

r. *Roe* v. *Wade*, 410 U.S. 113 (1973); *Thornburgh* v. *American College of Obstetricians and Gynecologists* 54 U.S.L.W. 4618 (1986).

s. *Bowers* v. *Hardwick and John and Mary Doe*, 54 U.S.L.W. 4919 (1986).

t. Alexis de Tocqueville, *Democracy in America*, trans. Henry Reeve (New York: Knopf, 1948), 1: 100–101.

4

Marbury v. *Madison:*
The Historical and Political Setting

A
S IN MOST INSTANCES in which judicial review has been exercised, its establishment took place in a context highly charged with political controversy. Essentially, there were three factors at work: (1) the personal differences of Marshall and Jefferson; (2) the party differences of Federalists and Antifederalists; and (3) the party history of the judiciary. In order to fully comprehend and appreciate the usurpation charge, let us briefly consider these factors.

First, by 1800 Thomas Jefferson and John Marshall had long been at variance. To Jefferson, his cousin Marshall was little more than a hypocrite and a demagogue,[a] a note of opprobrium picked up by the Antifederalist press. Only seven months before Marshall's appointment as chief justice, the *Aurora* characterized him as "more distinguished as a rhetorician and sophist than as a lawyer and statesman, sufficiently pliant to succeed in a corrupt court, too insincere to command respect or confidence in a republic."[b] Marshall's argumentative powers must have been as great as the degree of reprobation he elicited from Antifederalists. In a conversation with Judge Story, Jefferson said:

> When conversing with Marshall, I never admit anything, so sure as you admit any position to be good, no matter how remote the conclusion he seeks to establish, you are gone. So great is his sophistry you must never give him an affirmative answer or you

will be forced to grant his conclusion. Why, if he were to ask me if
it were daylight or not, I'd reply, "Sir, I don't know, I can't tell."[c]

Marshall's opinion of Jefferson was no better. In a January 1, 1801,
letter to Alexander Hamilton, Marshall explained why he could not
support Jefferson over Aaron Burr for president in the upcoming election in the House of Representatives necessitated by the tied vote in
the Electoral College. Marshall adamantly insisted that Jefferson's
"morals . . . cannot be pure."[d] He also noted two other characteristics
that combined to make Jefferson unfit for the presidency: his admiration for the French—his "foreign prejudices"—and his demagoguery,
the latter being the greater vice. "By weakening the office of President,
he will increase his personal power."[e]

Each antagonist viewed the other as one quite willing to do almost
anything to win political favor. This fact becomes even more significant in light of party differences. For by 1800 and in spite of Washington's warning in his Farewell Address "against the baneful effects of
the spirit of party," the so-called Hamiltonians and Madisonians
coalesced into the Federalist and Antifederalist (Republican) parties,
respectively.

In 1796 each party selected presidential and vice-presidential candidates. Republican Jefferson and Federalist John Adams vied for the
presidency, while Republican Aaron Burr and Federalist Thomas
Pinckney were opposed for the vice-presidency. The results of the
balloting in the Electoral College placed Adams in the presidency and
Jefferson in the vice-presidency. This unforeseen result, unsatisfactory
to all concerned, resulted from the Constitution's requirement that
electors, meeting in their respective states, were to vote for two persons without designating which was their choice for president or vice-
president. The person with the greatest number of votes, if a majority,
became president. The person with the next highest total became vice-
president.

This experience demonstrated the need for each party to pledge
electors to both presidential and vice-presidential candidates. Pursuing
this strategy in the following election, the Republican congressional
caucus in 1800 renominated Jefferson and Burr. The Electoral College
results found Jefferson and Burr tied with the greatest number of
votes. The Constitution again came into play. In accordance with its
procedures, selection between Jefferson and Burr became the responsibility of the House of Representatives.[f]

At this point, circumstances arose which contributed to the ever-widening breach between Jefferson and Marshall. Marshall assumed his duties as chief justice on February 2, 1801, during what had become a long and bitterly contested balloting for president between Jefferson and Burr in the House of Representatives. For several months, a report had been circulating that Marshall had given a legal opinion that Congress under certain contingencies might appoint a president.[g] The possibility that the House could not agree between Jefferson and Burr, was foremost among those contingencies. Indeed, James Monroe wrote Jefferson from Richmond that "Strange reports circulatory here . . . that Federalism means to commit the power by a Legislative to John Marshall . . . or some other person till another election."[h]

Similar reports came from other areas. Whether or not true, they served to increase Jefferson's distrust of Marshall, especially when viewed in the following light. First, it was no secret that Marshall would suffer little discomfort if Burr, not Jefferson, were selected. And second, during January and February 1801 a series of articles unfavorable to Jefferson was published in the *Washington Federalist*. It was popularly believed, and not without cause, that Marshall had at least instigated if not written them.[i]

Moreover, Republican newspapers discovered and reported a direct tie between Marshall and the *Washington Federalist*. The *Aurora* noted that the paper had been "set up by John Marshall and supported by his credit in the banks of the Columbia District."[j] The *Independent Chronicle* also reported that the *Washington Federalist* was published "under the immediate patronage of General Marshall . . . which discharges a great deal of low abuse at Mr. Jefferson." The article continued by noting wistfully, "Who would think that John Marshall, once the fervent worshipper at the altar of Liberty, would become the abuser of Jefferson. 'Tis true, 'tis pity, Pity 'tis, 'tis true."[k]

In the face of so many charges one can see how the already substantial personal differences of Jefferson and Marshall were made even greater by the fact of party differences. Such a condition of opinion seems of itself sufficiently volatile to lead to Jefferson's future charges of usurpation. However, we find further cause in yet another factor, the Supreme Court itself.

The charges directed at Marshall were no different in kind or tone than those directed at the Court. We have already seen that the Republican press viewed the Court as corrupt. Obviously, this had the effect of lowering its prestige. But the most damaging blow to the Court's prestige was the presumed political involvement of the judiciary with the Federalist party.

If the proof is in the pudding, partisan conduct of the Court was self-evident to Republicans. They objected to the lower courts' vigorous enforcement of the detested Alien and Sedition laws, laws aimed for the most part at the Republican press. An irony of American history is that discontent with the Court's power of judicial review first arose, as constitutional historian Charles Warren put it, "not because the Court held an Act of Congress unconstitutional, but rather because it refused to do so." The Antifederalists and the early Republicans assailed the Court because it failed to hold the Sedition Law, among others, unconstitutional.[1]

It is not surpising, therefore, to find Republican silence on the matter of Marshall's declaration of an act of Congress unconstitutional. Jefferson's acquiescence is similarly explained since he too felt that the Supreme Court should have declared the Sedition Law unconstitutional. In Chapter 13 Eugene Rostow interprets this acquiescence as meaning that Jefferson accepted judicial review and that it was not until later in life that he seemed to repudiate its constitutionality. The truth of the matter is that Jefferson did accept judicial review but also rejected its exercise in *Marbury,* and he did both while remaining consistent. The explanation is that Jefferson favored a kind of judicial review that he believed was the same as the kind Marshall established in *Marbury.* It was only when he perceived that Marshall had initiated a different kind that he came to charge Marshall with usurping power.

Let us consider the form of judicial check that Jefferson favored. In 1787, many years before Marshall's decision, Jefferson had demonstrated his approval of the new proposed Constitution by applauding "the negative given to the executive, conjointly with a third of either House; though I should have liked it better had the judiciary been associated for that purpose or invested separately with a similar power."[m] However, this sort of check is not tantamount to judicial review as it is conceived at present, and it was not a *final and ultimate* determination on the membership of Congress. Furthermore, the scope concerned only congressional acts. Jefferson's later statements were wholly consistent with the principle he actually advocated—not judicial review as we understand that power, but judicial review as an extension of separation of powers. Properly understood, the judicial review exercised in *Marbury* was acceptable to Jefferson because the Court was acting on legislation involving judicial power.[n] In fact, earlier Jefferson described the judiciary as the most harmless and helpless of all organs of government. Thus, to hold this view, the truth must be that Jefferson did not foresee the development of the kind of judicial review that permits judges to tell legislators and executives what they may do in their respective spheres of authority.

Further indication of a Jeffersonian kind of judicial review, a much less potent version, is found in a letter to James Madison:

> I learned that Hamilton had expressed the strongest desire that Marshall shall come into Congress from Richmond, declaring that there is no man in Virginia whom he wishes so much to see there; and I am told that Marshall has expressed half a mind to come. Hence, I conclude that Hamilton has plyed him well with flattery and sollicitation, and I think nothing better could be done than to make him a judge.°

Jefferson's willingness to make a judge of a man he both disliked and distrusted, to give Marshall the means by which he later became a thorn in Jefferson's side, indicates that he viewed the judiciary as relatively impotent and that he was unaware the Supreme Court would ever have the power to thwart him.

This explains how Jefferson could remain consistent when saying later in 1825 that although the judiciary was at first considered the most harmless and helpless of all organs it had developed to the point of "sapping and mining . . . the foundation of the Constitution. . . ."ᵖ

However, the most helpless and harmless organ did develop to the point where Jefferson perceived it as a dual threat. First, it was the vehicle of national supremacy, a supremacy that undermined the rights of the states. And second, at least equally objectionable to Jefferson, the freehold estate of the judiciary was enlarged within the national government. Such statements of belief are perfectly compatible with Jefferson's earlier remarks about the desirability of a judicial veto. This was made clear in a letter to Abigail Adams in 1804. Jefferson argued:

> You seem to think it devolved on the judges to decide on the validity of the Sedition law. But nothing in the Constitution has given them a right to decide for the executive, more than to the executive to decide for them. Both magistrates are equally independent in the sphere of action assigned to them. The judges, believing the law constitutional, had a right to pass a sentence of fine and imprisonment; because the power was placed in their

hands by the Constitution. But the executive, believing the law to be unconstitutional, were bound to remit the execution of it; because that power has been confided to them by the Constitution. That instrument meant that its coordinate branches should be checks on each other. But the opinion which gives to the judges the right to decide what laws are constitutional, and what not, not only for themselves in their own sphere of action, but for the legislature and executive also, in their spheres, would make the judiciary a despotic branch. Nor does the opinion of the unconstitutionality, and consequent nullity of that law, remove all restraint from the overwhelming torrent of slander, which is confounding all vice and virtue, all truth and falsehood, in the United States. The power to do that is fully possessed by the several State Legislatures. It was reserved to them, and was denied to the General Government, by the Constitution, according to our construction of it. While we deny that Congress have a right to control the freedom of the press, we have asserted the right of the States, and their exclusive right to do so.[q]

Jefferson believed, in sum, that each department ought to determine for itself whether acts were unconstitutional. This explains his belief expressed prior to the *Marbury* decision that, regardless of the Court's view of the Sedition Law, he considered it be no law. Because it was in opposition to the Constitution, he would whenever it might come in the way of his functions treat it as nullity. We only can conclude that the judicial check envisioned by Jefferson was certainly not the kind of check judicial review now involves—one that is binding and controlling upon the federal executive and legislative branches and upon state governments.[r]

For Jefferson, this was more than a simple matter of theoretical concern over possible future events. The election of 1800, which resulted in the destruction of the Federalist party, left a Federalist-controlled Congress to finish its term. We have seen that Jefferson believed the Federalists were trying to temporarily capture the presidency. Jefferson further suspected, and had insisted for some time, that Federalists unable to *win* office were retiring into the judiciary to continue their assault against the Antifederalists. For Jefferson and the Antifederalists, the Circuit Court Act of 1801 gave ample proof of this. By that act, the Federalists "multiplied useless judges merely to strengthen their phalanx."[s]

The act provided for a suspension of the circuit court duties of Supreme Court justices, reduced their number to five, and established six new circuit courts with sixteen new judges. The bill became law on

February 13, 1801. On February 26 the Senate received Adams's list of
nominations, and it completed confirmation of the nominees by March
2, only two days before political control passed into the hands of the
Antifederalists.ᵗ

Changes in positions included John Marshall's switch from secretary of state under Adams to chief justice of the Supreme Court. Of the
lesser judgeships, so little time was left Adams to sign the commissions (some sixty-seven) that his administration worked into the night
of the final day in office.ᵘ The recipients of these eleventh-hour commissions were called accurately, although uncharitably, the "midnight
judges" by the Antifederalists.ᵛ

The ascendancy of the Antifederalists to office the following day
led to two significant developments. First, the new secretary of state,
James Madison, found four commissions that, though signed and affixed with the seal of the United States, had not been delivered. Jefferson ordered Madison to withhold them.

On December 21, ten days after the Supreme Court convened for
its December term, William Marbury, Dennis Ramsay, Robert Hooe,
and William Harper presented a petition in an original suit to require
Madison to show cause why a writ of mandamus should not be granted
requiring him to deliver their commissions.

The Court's power to issue writs of mandamus stemmed from the
following. The Constitution of 1787 provided that the Supreme Court
had two sorts of jurisdiction: original and appellate. In matters of original jurisdiction, cases could be initiated in the Court without previous
trial in lower federal or state courts. Article III defined original jurisdiction as extending to "all cases affecting Ambassadors, other public
ministers and counsuls . . . and those in which a State shall be party."
The same article gave Congress the power to establish lower federal
courts as well as regulations and exceptions to the Court's appellate
jurisdiction. Therefore, Congress proceeded to pass the Judiciary Act
of 1789 as "necessary and proper for carrying into execution . . .
powers vested by the Constitution in the Government of the United
States, or any department or officer thereof."ʷ

The more pertinent provisions of the 1789 act provided for the
appointment of a chief justice and five associate justices, the establishment of lower courts consisting of three circuit courts and thirteen
district courts, an extension of responsibilities of Supreme Court justices to include circuit court duty, and Supreme Court authority "to
issue writs of mandamus in cases warranted by the principles and
usages of law, to any courts appointed, or persons holding office, under

the authority of the United States."[x] In accordance with this provision of the Judiciary Act, the Court granted the petitioners a preliminary motion for a rule to show cause and scheduled the fourth day of the June term for the determination of whether the writ of mandamus would be issued.

The second development occurred in Congress. On January 6, 1802, one month after the Court's show-cause ruling, a motion was introduced in the Senate to repeal the Circuit Court Act of 1801. The motion was passed less than one month later and became law with the approval of the House on March 31. Fearing that the Court might rule the Repeal Law unconstitutional, the Congress then proceeded to pass another bill that abolished the June and December terms of the Court in favor of a February term—some eleven months in the future.[y]

When the Court convened again in 1803 the air was alive with partisan charges. The two greatest fears of the Antifederalists were (1) that the Court would issue a writ of mandamus against Madison, and (2) that it would also declare the Circuit Court Act of 1802 unconstitutional.

Marshall had several surprises. In *Stuart* v. *Laird,* 1 Cranch 299 (1803), the Court upheld the validity of the Circuit Court Act of 1802. Only six days earlier his opinion in *Marbury* v. *Madison* held the greater surprise. Marshall did not issue the writ of mandamus. Instead, he declared unconstitutional that section of the Judiciary Act which gave the Court power to issue it. Nevertheless, he was unwilling to let an opportunity to chastise Jefferson slip by. To this end, Marshall first noted "the peculiar delicacy of this case," which demanded a complete exposition of the principles on which the Court's opinion was founded.[z] This in turn structured the order of the consideration of the issues in the case:

> 1st. Has the applicant a right to the commission he demands?
> 2dly. If he has a right, and that right has been violated, do the laws of his country afford a remedy?
> 3dly. If they do afford a remedy, is it a mandamus issuing from this Court?[aa]

In answering the first two queries, Marshall found that Jefferson had improperly withheld the commission and that there were legal remedies available. However, his answer to the third question was that no mandamus could be issued by the Supreme Court since that power was unconstitutionally granted. This meant that the Court had no jurisdiction in the matter.

Decision making in this case followed an extraordinary route. Even the strongest admirers of Marshall admitted that his manner of dealing with this case was unusual. When a judgment was to turn on a question of jurisdiction, the Court commonly considered that point as first and final. In the *Marbury* case the Court had no original jurisdiction, and so decided; but instead of beginning at that point and dismissing the motion, the Court began by discussing the merits of the case.[bb]

Jefferson, being something less than a strong admirer of Marshall, attacked the *in extensio* opinion in *Marbury*. In later years he retained the same objections:

> This practice of Judge Marshall, of travelling out of his case to prescribe what the law would be in a moot case not before the court, is very irregular and very censurable. I recollect another instance, and the more particularly, perhaps, because it in some measure bore on myself. Among the midnight appointments of Mr. Adams, were commissions to some federal justices of the peace for Alexandria. These were signed and sealed by him, but not delivered. I found them on the table of the Department of State, on my entrance into office, and I forbade their delivery. Marbury, named in one of them, applied to the Supreme Court for a mandamus to the Secretary of State (Mr. Madison) to deliver the commission intended for him. The Court determined at once, that being an original process, they had no cognizance of it; and therefore the question before them was ended. But the Chief Justice went on to lay down what the law would be, had they jurisdiction of the case, to wit: that they should command the delivery. The object was clearly to instruct any other court having the jurisdiction, what they should do if Marbury should apply to them. Besides the impropriety of this gratuitous interference, could anything exceed the perversion of law? For if there is any principle of law never yet contradicted, it is that delivery is one of the essentials to the validity of a deed. Although signed and sealed, yet as long as it remains in the hands of the party himself, it is *in fieri* only, it is not a deed and can be made so only by its delivery. In the hands of a third person it may be made as escrow. But whatever is in the executive offices is certainly deemed to be in the hands of the President; and in this case, was actually in my hands, because, when I countermanded them, there was as yet no Secretary of State. Yet this case of Marbury and Madison is continually cited by bench and bar, as if it were settled law, without any animadversion on its being merely an *obiter* dissertation of the Chief Justice.[cc]

Jefferson's mild-tempered reaction to *Stuart* v. *Laird* and *Marbury* may be attributed to Marshall's shrewd political acumen. In effect, Marshall so contrived as to have his cake and eat it too, accompanied by the smallest possible dose of castor oil given the circumstance. On the one hand, he all but placated keyed-up Republicans by not realizing their greatest fears: namely, invalidation of the Circuit Court Act of 1802 and a mandamus issued against Madison. On the other hand, Marshall still accomplished his desired ends by employing other means, which carried only one unwanted circumstance – the continuation of circuit court duty for Supreme Court justices.

Most commentators agree that Marshall had two purposes. He wished to firmly establish judicial review and to embarrass Jefferson.[dd] By declaring Section 13 of the Judiciary Act unconstitutional, and not the Circuit Court Act of 1802, he thereby created a sympathetic and accepting audience. The Republicans got what they wanted most, even as Marshall established what he wanted most. And the establishment took place in an atmosphere of willing acceptance, rather than one of vitriolic rejection.

At the same time, the opinion was also the most prudent means of embarrassing the Jefferson administration. Had Marshall chosen the mandamus instead, he would have run the risk of putting a tool into Jefferson's hands which could be employed to further lower the prestige of the Court. The fact is that once the mandamus was issued there was no means of enforcing it. After all, the Court could not enforce a writ directed to its only means of enforcement – the executive branch. Jefferson simply could have sat back and ignored and even laughed at the Court while the rest of the country took note of its impotency. Perhaps an even more detrimental consequence for the future of judicial power was that it would have given Jefferson the opportunity to establish his own view of constitutional review, the view noted above wherein each branch determines the constitutionality of an issue for itself. Jefferson could have refused to honor the mandamus on the basis that it violated separation of power, the very principle he claimed justified constitutional review by all three branches.

If the latter possibility had occurred, we can be sure that Jefferson's reaction to Marshall's notion of judicial review would have been quite different. Marshall would have been forced to enter debate as to whether only the judiciary could exercise constitutional review. Jefferson then would have been wholly aware of the significance of Marshall's argument in *Marbury,* and his charge of usurpation would have sounded loud and clear at a much earlier time.

Let us turn now to Marshall's argument in *Marbury* as told in his own words.

NOTES

a. Charles Warren, *The Supreme Court in U.S. History* (Boston: Little, Brown, 1937), 182. Also see Donald O. Dewey, *Marshall versus Jefferson: The Political Background of Marbury v. Madison* (New York: Alfred A. Knopf, 1970), 36–38.

b. Warren, *Supreme Court in U.S. History,* 181.

c. Ibid., 182 n. 1.

d. Dewey, *Marshall versus Jefferson,* 41; Warren, *Supreme Court in U.S. History,* 184.

e. Dewey, *Marshall versus Jefferson,* 41–42,; Warren, *Supreme Court in U.S. History,* 184.

f. To prevent any similar recurrence Jefferson later advocated an amendment to separate presidential and vice-presidential balloting. The Twelfth Amendment, ratified on September 25, 1804, allowed electors to "name in their ballots the person voted for as President, and in distinct ballots the person voted for as Vice-President."

g. Warren, *Supreme Court in U.S History,* 182.

h. Ibid., 182 n. 2. See also Dewey, *Marshall versus Jefferson,* 42–44.

i. Warren, *Supreme Court in U.S. History,* 183; Dewey, *Marshall versus Jefferson,* 43.

j. Warren, *Supreme Court in U.S. History,* 184, n. 2.

k. Ibid.

l. Ibid., 5. Warren also notes that the Federalists were displeased because the Court did not hold the Embargo Act unconstitutional. Thus both Federalists and Antifederalists criticized the Court for not employing the power of judicial review.

m. Andrew A. Lipscomb, ed., *The Writings of Thomas Jefferson* (Washington, D.C.: Thomas Jefferson Memorial Association, 1904), 6:387.

n. Dewey, *Marshall versus Jefferson,* 142.

o. Paul L. Ford, ed., *The Writings of Thomas Jefferson* (New York: G. P. Putnam's Sons, 1892–99), 6:95.

p. H. A. Washington, ed., *The Writings of Thomas Jefferson* (Washington, D.C.: Taylor and Maury, 1854), 7:404.

q. Washington, ed., *Writings,* 4:561.

r. See letter to W. H. Torrence, 1801, Washington, ed., *Writings,* 6:461–62; and Ford, ed., *Writings,* 9:517–18.

s. Letter to John Dickinson, 1801, Washington, ed., *Writings,* 4:425.

t. Warren, *Supreme Court in U.S. History,* 188–89.

u. The total of sixty-seven appointments stemmed from two facts. First, the Circuit Court Act of 1801 provided sixteen new positions, some of which were filled by district court judges. Thus there were also replacement appointments. Second, the Act of the District of Columbia, passed on February 27, provided for the appointment of forty-two justices of the peace for the District. All, save four, of the sixty-seven commissions were delivered (among the four was that of William Marbury).

v. Warren, *Supreme Court in U.S. History,* 188.

w. *U.S. Constitution,* Article I, sec. 8, para. 18.

x. Judiciary Act of 1789, First Congress, Sess. 1. Ch. 20, sec. 13.

y. Dewey, *Marshall versus Jefferson,* 68–69.

z. 1 Cranch at 154.

aa. Ibid.

bb. Henry Adams, *History of the United States of America* (New York: Scribner's Sons, 1903), 2:146.

cc. Albert Ellery Bergh, ed., *The Writings of Thomas Jefferson* (Washington, D.C.: Thomas Jefferson Memorial Association, 1907), 15:447–48. Letter to Judge William Johnson, June 12, 1823.

dd. For a contrary viewpoint see Robert Lowry Clinton, "The Populist-Progressive Reinterpretation of Constitutional History: The Scapegoating of John Marshall, His Court, and the Founding Fathers" (Ph.D. diss., University of Texas, Austin, 1984), 167–213.

5

The Opinion

I N THIS CHAPTER we present an edited *Opinion of the court* in *Marbury* v. *Madison*. It should not be read without an appreciation for the rich political circumstances surrounding the case. We attempted in Chapter 4 to acquaint readers with those facts. Yet even without a knowledge of the political scene one may nonetheless appreciate the reasoning employed by the chief justice. Marshall presents the claim to the power of judicial review as though it were a matter of simple logic.

One is struck by the clarity with which Marshall states the issues in the case; indeed, he goes so far as to number them. He then proceeds to answer each numbered query. However, as we noted in the previous chapter, the order in which Marshall raises and disposes of the issues is questionable. In fact, the last issue, namely the jurisdiction question, might logically have been the first. If the Supreme Court was without the power to issue a writ of mandamus directed against Secretary of State James Madison, it was unnecessary to involve the Court in the issues of whether Mr. Marbury had a right to the commission he demanded and whether the laws of this country afforded him a remedy. The point is that without jurisdiction no court may provide any legal remedy. Thus we conclude that although at first blush the ordering of the legal issues appears to exhibit the workings of a logical mind, it may also reveal the sophistry of a goal-oriented political actor.

Of course, the goal sought and achieved was nullification of a portion of Section 13 of the Judiciary Act of 1789. However, it has been widely surmised that this goal was but a proximate one. The final end sought was the establishment in practice of judicial review. In fairness, it should be pointed out that such a conclusion cannot be discerned from the plain words written by Marshall in *Marbury* v. *Madison*. In fact, the author of a 1984 doctoral dissertation argues that Marshall's opinion has been used by certain historians in a straw-man argument in order to discredit the practice of judicial review.[a] Whether or not that interpretation is correct, the fact remains that the ordering of the legal issues was, to say the least, odd.

The reason the Court lacked jurisdiction, according to Chief Justice Marshall, is that the case before it was a matter arising out of the original jurisdiction of the Court, and that in its original jurisdiction the Supreme Court lacked the power to issue writs of mandamus. Article III contains the whole of the Court's jurisdiction. Though Congress may grant appellate jurisdiction to the Court, the legislative branch is not afforded a similar authority over the Court's original jurisdiction. Section 13 of the Judiciary Act of 1789 was unconstitutional because, according to Marshall, it added to the Court's original jurisdiction.

Notice the apparent modesty of Marshall's claim. The Supreme Court must reject an authority that the Constitution does not grant it; Congress may not add to its jurisdiction. Yet simultaneously Marshall claims for the Court a power that is not stated explicitly in the Constitution. Thus on one hand he insists upon a strict reading of the words in the Constitution, but on the other he is quite willing to make an argument without benefit of a specific written provision.

The offending legislation is said by Marshall to add to the Court's original jurisdiction. But does it? The exact words of Section 13 are as follows:

> *And be it further enacted,* That the Supreme Court shall have exclusive jurisdiction of all controversies of a civil nature, where a state is a party, except between a state and its citizens; and except also between a state and citizens of other states, or aliens, in which latter case it shall have original but not exclusive jurisdiction.(*b.*) And shall have exclusively all such jurisdiction of suits or proceedings against ambassadors, or other public ministers, or their domestics, or domestic servants, as a court of law can have or exercise consistently with the law of nations; and original, but not exclusive jurisdiction of all suits brought by ambassadors, or other public ministers, or in which a consul, or vice consul, shall be a party.(*a*) And the trial of issues in fact in the Supreme Court, in all actions at law against citizens of the United States, shall be by jury. *The Supreme Court shall also have appellate jurisdiction from*

*the circuit courts and courts of the several states, in the cases herein
after specially provided for; (b) and shall have power to issue writs of
prohibition (c) to the district courts, when proceeding as courts of
admiralty and maritime jurisdiction, and writs of mandamus, (d) in
cases warranted by the principles and usages of law, to any courts
appointed, or persons holding office, under the authority of the United
States.*[b] [italics added]

Constitutional scholar Craig Ducat has pointed out that Section 13
may be read to mean the Court may issue writs of mandamus in its
appellate jurisdiction. It need not have been interpreted to mean Congress intended for the Court to issue the writ in its original jurisdiction.
Indeed, given the way the language is employed it may be fair to
conclude that Congress was referring to the Court's appellate jurisdiction and not to its original jurisdiction. The opening lines of Section 13
address exclusive and original jurisdiction whereas the later part treats
appellate jurisdiction, including the issuing of writs of mandamus.[c]

Professor Ducat further suggests that Marshall could have dismissed the case for want of jurisdiction; he may have held that the
Supreme Court could not issue a mandamus sitting as a court of original jurisdiction. Marshall might have suggested to fellow Federalist
Marbury that he pursue his case in the circuit court for the District of
Columbia. In time the legal cause of action could find its way to the
Supreme Court, whereupon the Court could properly issue a writ of
mandamus as an exercise of its appellate jurisdiction. But Marshall
rejected this option by finding that "the essential criterion of appellate
jurisdiction . . . is that it revises and corrects the proceedings in a
cause already instituted, and does not create that cause." In other
words, if Marshall directed Marbury to begin his case again in another
court and the Supreme Court were subsequently asked to issue a mandamus against Secretary of State James Madison, the Court would
have created the cause of action. Therefore, any writ so issued would
be in the Supreme Court's original jurisdiction. Professor Ducat's comment about this reasoning is perceptive: "To those who have just sat
through several paragraphs of Marshall's making the point that original jurisdiction is original jurisdiction and appellate jurisdiction is appellate jurisdiction, this seems downright contradictory."[d] Readers are
well advised to consider Ducat's point when evaluating Marshall's opinion as a simple matter of straightforward logical analysis. Persuasive-
ness should not be mistaken for logical argument.

Moving beyond the apparent difficulties in Marshall's jurisdictional discussion may for some be too much to overcome. Nonetheless, the remainder of Marshall's opinion contains the reasoned argument or justification for judicial review. Though not without problems, as the reading in the next chapter indicates, Marshall's argument is clear and to the point. It may be summarized in the following fashion:

(1) The Constitution established by the people organized a government of limited powers. These powers may not be transgressed.

(2) The Constitution controls any legislative act repugnant to it; that is, the Constitution is superior to ordinary legislation. Consequently, a legislative act contrary to the Constitution is not law and is void. To hold otherwise would render a written constitution useless.

(3) The courts are not under an obligation to give effect to an unconstitutional law. Because the function of courts entails saying what the law is, they have no choice but to ascertain whether a law is in opposition to the written Constitution. Because it is superior to a law, the Constitution must govern the disposition of a given case. In such a situation, to uphold the law over the Constitution would require courts to "close their eyes on the constitution, and see only the law." This could not have been intended by those who brought the Constitution into existence.

(4) The oath of judicial office requires judges to uphold the Constitution. It would be immoral to ask judges to take the oath without expecting that it should guide them in their official conduct. Thus the Supreme Court in the matter of Marbury against Madison was under a moral obligation to hold the particular section of the Judiciary Act of 1789 unconstitutional.

(5) Given the phraseology of the Constitution wherein the Supremacy Clause (Article VI, paragraph 2) mentions the Constitution before it mentions laws and not the other way around, it must have been intended by the Framers that the Constitution be treated as superior to laws.

John Marshall cites no precedents in support of judicial review. Yet there is a longstanding commitment among Anglo-American jurists to the wisdom of basing judicial opinions upon previous experience. Does this suggest that Marshall created judicial review out of whole cloth? The answer depends upon the interpretation and upon the reception of the so-called precedents.

Because it declared a Parliamentary enactment null and void, Sir Edward Coke's 1610 decision in *Dr. Bonham's Case* is often cited as an early English precedent favoring judicial review. During the colonial period, many laws and judicial opinions of the colonists underwent mandatory review by the Privy Council. State supreme court decisions rendered before and after Marshall's era may also be interpreted as instances of judicial review. In addition, prior to the *Marbury* decision the Supreme Court alluded to the judicial veto in a number of its decisions.[e] However, investigation of the so-called precedents reveals two points worth considering. First, some of them may be only loosely construed as precedents. Second, evidence suggests that elite and public reactions were decidedly negative in those few instances when judicial review was exercised.

Rhetorical skills are routinely employed to convince legal professionals that a given set of facts in a previous case or set of cases is similar enough to serve as precedent for the present case. Karl Llewellyn teaches that both welcomed and unwelcomed precedents may be treated in a strict or loose fashion by skillful minds to bring about desired policy outcomes, depending, of course, upon one's perspective.[f] Employing a loose view to welcomed precedent, it is surely possible to find precedent in support of Marshall's opinion. In Chapter 8 of this volume Mr. Justice Lurton's claim of precedent for the *Marbury* decision is, in part, based upon this unstated view. Until the rebuttal by L. B. Boudin in Chapter 9, Lurton's argument seems reasonable enough.

First, Louis Boudin employs legal reasoning to cut away "unwelcomed precedent." He confines previous cases to the particular facts of each case. The assumption is that unless the facts of the previous case or cases are the same as what is actually before the court in the present case, the legal rule in the two or more cases need not be the same. Llewellyn's often cited metaphorical image vividly illustrates the point. Confining the case to its particular facts results in a rule applying only to "redheaded Walpoles in pale magenta Buick cars." Strictly construing *Marbury* v. *Madison,* Boudin summarily finds that several cases cited as precedent are easily distinguished. Further, though Boudin does not make the point himself, there are no pre-*Marbury* cases involving a legislature granting to the judiciary more jurisdictional authority than it is constitutionally entitled. Similarly, it may also be argued that *Marbury* v. *Madison* should serve as a precedent only for a court to strike down a legislative enactment expanding judicial power in an unconstitutional manner. In fact, however, *Marbury* has been cited in the latter part of the twentieth century to mean much more. Legislative and executive enactments and orders have been struck down which in no way affect court jurisdiction. Clearly, the courts have adopted a loose view of precedent when citing Marshall's decision.

Even if one is willing to adopt a loose rather than a strict view, it is uncertain that the so-called precedents have much value after all. Unless judges can make their opinions stick, there can be little if any claim to the status of a legal rule. As Boudin points out, in the few instances in which state courts dared to strike down legislative enactments, general public indignation was aroused and the judges were rebuked for their conduct.

Thus, it is clear that in part the answer to the question of whether Marshall created judicial review out of whole cloth depends upon whether one takes a loose or a strict view of precedent. Loosely speaking, there are precedents. Strictly speaking, few – if any – exist. Of the possible few, there is evidence the opinions were poorly received.

One last point deserves reflection. If an opinion writer does not cite so-called precedents, how can others claim years later that the original decision maker acted in a manner consistent with established legal principle? It may be that John Marshall was ignorant of existing precedent; consequently, he was unable to cite the cases. This seems unlikely because a 1782 decision of his own Virginia Court of Appeals is one of those instances in which judicial review is said to have occurred.[g] Perhaps he regarded the matter as so well settled that reference to precedent was thought unnecessary. Or, alternatively, Marshall knew that previous experience could not support the claim. Instead he resolved to assert judicial review employing other arguments. Rather than to expose himself to greater criticism, it seems reasonable that this well-seasoned politician would choose the prudent course of action.

We suggest readers study the *Marbury* opinion with an open mind. This is no doubt difficult given the fact that most Americans have been taught from a very early age the virtues of judicial review and of John Marshall's famous opinion. Ironically, the matter may have been made more difficult by our own comments. Nevertheless, it is hoped that our foregoing discussion may serve to hone critical powers. We reserve the most cogent and noteworthy reviews of Marshall's opinion, and of the theory and practices of judicial review, to the readings found in the remainder of this volume.

William Marbury v. James Madison,
Secretary of State of the United States

(1 Cranch 137)

February, 1803

Opinion of the court

At the last term on the affidavits then read and filed with the clerk, a rule was granted in this case, requiring the secretary of state to show cause why a mandamus should not issue, directing him to deliver to William Marbury his commission as a justice of the peace for the county of Washington, in the District of Columbia.

No cause has been shown, and the present motion is for a mandamus. The peculiar delicacy of this case, the novelty of some of its circumstances, and the real difficulty attending the points which occur in it, require a complete exposition of the principles, on which the opinion to be given by the court, is founded.

These principles have been, on the side of the applicant, very ably argued at the bar. In rendering the opinion of the court, there will be some departure in form, though not in substance, from the points stated in that argument.

In the order in which the court has viewed this subject, the following questions have been considered and decided.

1st. Has the applicant a right to the commission he demands?

2dly. If he has a right, and that right has been violated, do the laws of his country afford him a remedy?

3dly. If they do afford him a remedy, is it a *mandamus* issuing from this court?

The first object of enquiry is,

1st. Has the applicant a right to the commission he demands?

His right originates in an act of congress passed in February 1801, concerning the District of Columbia.

After dividing the district into two counties, the 11th section of this law enacts, "that there shall be appointed in and for each of the said counties, such number of discreet persons to be justices of the peace as the president of the United States shall, from time to time, think expedient, to continue in office for five years."

It appears, from the affidavits, that in compliance with this law, a commission for William Marbury as a justice of the peace for the county of Washington, was signed by John Adams, then president of the United States; after which the seal of the United States was affixed to it, but the commission has never reached the person for whom it was made out.

In order to determine whether he is entitled to this commission, it becomes necessary to enquire whether he has been appointed to the office. For if he has been appointed, the law continues him in office for five years, and he is entitled to the possession of those evidences of office, which, being completed, became his property. . . .

. . . The clauses of the constitution and laws of the United States, which affect this part of the case . . . seem to contemplate three distinct operations:

1st. The nomination. This is the sole act of the President, and is completely voluntary.

2d. The appointment. This is also the act of the President, and is also a voluntary act, though it can only be performed by and with the advice and consent of the senate.

3rd. The commission. To grant a commission to a person appointed, might perhaps be deemed a duty enjoined by the constitution. "He shall," says that instrument, "commission all the officers of the United States."

The acts of appointing to office, and commissioning the person appointed, can scarcely be considered as one and the same; since the power to perform them is given in two separate and two distinct sections of the constitution. The distinction between the appointment and the commission will be rendered more apparent, by adverting to that provision in the second section of the second article of the constitution, which authorizes congress "to vest, by law, the appointment of such inferior officers, as they think proper, in the President alone, in the courts of law, or in the heads of departments;" thus contemplating cases where the law may direct the President to commission an officer appointed by the courts, or by the heads of departments. In such a case, to issue a commission would be apparently a duty distinct from the appointment, the performance of which, perhaps, could not legally be refused.

The last act to be done by the President, is the signature of the commission. He has then acted on the advice and consent of the senate to his own nomination. The time for deliberation has then passed. He has decided. His judgment, on the advice and consent of the senate concurring with his nomination, has been made, and the officer is appointed. This appointment is evidenced by an open, unequivocal act; and being the last act required from the person making it, necessarily excludes the idea of its being, so far as respects the appointment, an inchoate and incomplete transaction. . . .

The commission being signed, the subsequent duty of the Secretary of State is prescribed by law, and not to be guided by the will of the President. He is to affix the seal of the United States to the commission, and is to record it.

This is not a proceeding which may be varied, if the judgment of the executive shall suggest one more eligible; but is a precise course accurately marked out by law, and is to be strictly pursued. It is the duty of the secretary of state to conform to the law, and in this he is an officer of the United States, bound to obey the laws. He acts in this respect, as has been very properly stated at the bar, under the authority of law, and not by the instructions of the President. It is a ministerial act which the law enjoins on a particular officer for a particular purpose. . . .

It is therefore decidedly the opinion of the court, that when a commission has been signed by the President, the appointment is made; and that the commission is complete when the seal of the United States has been affixed to it by the Secretary of State. . . .

Mr. Marbury, then, since his commission was signed by the President, and sealed by the secretary of state, was appointed; and as the law creating the office, gave the officer a right to hold for five years, independent of the executive, the appointment was not revocable, but vested in the officer legal rights, which are protected by the laws of his country.

To withhold his commission, therefore, is an act deemed by the court not warranted by law, but violative of a vested legal right. This brings us to the second inquiry; which is,

2dly. If he [Marbury] has a right, and that right has been violated, do the laws of his country afford him a remedy?

The very essence of civil liberty certainly consists in the right of every individual to claim the protection of the laws, whenever he receives an injury. One of the first duties of government is to afford that protection. . . .

By the constitution of the United States, the President is invested with certain important political powers, in the exercise of which he is to use his discretion, and is accountable only to his country in his political character and to his own conscience. To aid him in the performance of these duties, he is authorized to appoint certain officers, who act by his authority and in conformity with his orders.

In such cases, their acts are his acts; and whatever opinion may be entertained of the manner in which executive discretion may be used, still there exists, and can exist, no power to control that discretion. The subjects are political. They respect the nation, not individual rights, and being entrusted to the executive, the decision of the executive is conclusive. The application of this remark will be perceived by adverting to the act of congress for establishing the department of foreign affairs. This officer, as his duties were prescribed by that act, is to conform precisely to the will of the President. He is the mere organ by whom that will is communicated. The acts of such an officer, as an officer, can never be examinable by the courts.

But when the legislature proceeds to impose on that officer other duties; when he is directed peremptorily to perform certain acts; he is so far the officer of the law; is amenable to the laws for his conduct; and cannot at his discretion sport away the vested rights of others.

The conclusion from this reasoning is, that where the heads of departments are the political or confidential agents of the executive, merely to execute the will of the President, or rather to act in cases in which the executive possesses a constitutional or legal discretion, nothing can be more perfectly clear than that their acts are only politically examinable. But where a specific duty is assigned by law, and individual rights depend upon the performance of that duty, it seems equally clear that the individual who considers himself injured, has a right to resort to the laws of his country for a remedy.

If this be the rule, let us enquire how it applies to the case under the consideration of the court.

The power of nominating to the senate, and the power of appointing the person nominated, are political powers, to be exercised by the President according to his own discretion. When he has made an appointment, he has exercised his whole power, and his discretion has been completely applied to the case. If, by law, the officer be removable at the will of the President, then a new appointment may be immediately made, and the rights of the officer are terminated. But as a fact which has existed cannot be made never to have existed, the appointment cannot be annihilated; and consequently if the officer is by law not removable at the will of the President; the rights he has acquired are protected by the law, and are not resumable by the President. They cannot be extinguished by executive authority, and he has the privilege of asserting them in like manner as if they had been derived from any other source.

The question whether a right has vested or not, is, in its nature, judicial, and must be tried by the judicial authority. If, for example, Mr. Marbury had taken the oaths of a magistrate, and proceeded to act as one; in consequence of which a suit had been instituted against him, in which his defence had depended on his being a magistrate, the validity of his appointment must have been determined by judicial authority.

So, if he conceives that, by virtue of his appointment, he has a legal right, either to the commission which has been made out for him, or to a copy of that commission, it is equally a question examinable in a court, and the decision of the court upon it must depend on the opinion entertained of his appointment.

That question has been discussed, and the opinion is, that the latest point of time which can be taken as that at which the appointment was complete, and evidenced, was when, after the signature of the president, the seal of the United States was affixed to the commission.

It is then the opinion of the Court,

1st. That by signing the commission of Mr. Marbury, the president of the United States appointed him a justice of peace for the county of Washington in the District of Columbia; and that the seal of the United States, affixed thereto by the secretary of state, is conclusive testimony of the verity of the signature, and of the completion of the appointment; and that the appointment conferred on him in a legal right to the office for the space of five years.

2dly. That, having this legal title to the office, he had a consequent right to the commission; a refusal to deliver which, is a plain violation of that right, for which the laws of his country afford him a remedy.

It remains to be enquired whether,

3dly. He is entitled to the remedy for which he applies. This depends on,

1st. The nature of the writ applied for and,

2dly. The power of this court.

1st. The nature of the writ. . . .

It was at first doubted whether the action of *detinue* was not a specific legal remedy for the commission which has been withheld from Mr. Marbury; in which case a mandamus would be improper. But this doubt has yielded to the consideration that the judgment in *detinue* is for the thing itself, *or* its value. The value of a public office not to be sold, is incapable of being ascertained; and the applicant has a right to the office itself, or to nothing. He will obtain the office by obtaining the commission, or a copy of it from the record.

This, then, is a plain case for a mandamus, either to deliver the commission, or a copy of it from the record; and it only remains to be enquired,

Whether it can issue from this court.

The act to establish the judicial courts of the United States authorized the supreme court "to issue writs of mandamus in cases warranted by the principles and usages of law, to any courts appointed, or persons holding office, under the authority of the United States."

The secretary of state, being a person holding an office under the authority of the United States, is precisely within the letter of the description, and if this court is not authorized to issue a writ of mandamus to such an officer, it must be because the law is unconstitutional, and therefore absolutely incapable of conferring the authority, and assigning the duties which its words purport to confer and assign.

The constitution vests the whole judicial power of the United States in one Supreme Court, and such inferior courts as congress shall, from time to time, ordain and establish. This power is expressly extended to all cases arising under the laws of the United States; and, consequently, in some form, may be exercised over the present case; because the right claimed is given by a law of the United States.

In the distribution of this power it is declared that "the supreme court shall have original jurisdiction in all cases affecting ambassadors, other public ministers and consuls, and those in which a state shall be a party. In all other cases, the Supreme Court shall have appellate jurisdiction."

It has been insisted, at the bar, that as the original grant of jurisdiction, to the supreme and inferior courts, is general, and the clause, assigning original jurisdiction to the supreme court, contains no negative or restrictive words; the power remains to the legislature, to assign original jurisdiction to that court in other cases than those specified in the article which has been recited; provided those cases belong to the judicial power of the United States.

If it had been intended to leave it in the discretion of the legislature to apportion the judicial power between the supreme and inferior courts according to the will of that body, it would certainly have been useless to have proceeded further than to have defined the judicial power, and the tribunals in which it should be vested. The subsequent part of the section is mere surplusage, is entirely without meaning, if such is to be the construction. If congress remains at liberty to give this court appellate jurisdiction, where the constitution has declared their jurisdiction shall be original; and original jurisdiction where the constitution has declared it shall be appellate; the distribution of jurisdiction, made in the constitution, is form without substance.

Affirmative words are often, in their operation, negative of other objects than those affirmed; and in this case, a negative or exclusive sense must be given to them, or they have no operation at all.

It cannot be presumed that any clause in the constitution is intended to be without effect; and therefore, such a construction is inadmissable, unless the words require it.

If the solicitude of the convention, respecting our peace with foreign powers, induced a provision that the Supreme Court should take original jurisdiction in cases which might be supposed to affect them; yet the clause would have proceeded no further than to provide for such cases, if no further restriction on the powers of congress had been intended. That they should have appellate jurisdiction in all other cases, with such exceptions as congress might make, is no restriction; unless the words be deemed exclusive of original jurisdiction.

When an instrument organizing fundamentally a judicial system, divides it into one supreme, and so many inferior courts as the legislature may ordain and establish; then enumerates its powers, and proceeds so far to distribute them, as to define the jursidiction of the supreme court by declaring the cases in which it shall take original jurisdiction, and that in others it shall take appellate jurisdiction; the plain import of the words seems to be, that in one class of cases its jursidiction is original, and not appellate; in the other it is appellate, and not original. If any other construction would render the clause inoperative, that is an additional reason for rejecting such other construction, and for adhering to their obvious meaning.

To enable this court, then to issue a mandamus, it must be shown to be an exercise of appellate jurisdiction, or to be necessary to enable them to exercise appellate jurisdiction.

It has been stated at the bar that the appellate jurisdiction may be exercised in a variety of forms, and that if it be the will of the legislature that a mandamus should be used for that purpose that will must be obeyed. This is true, yet the jurisdiction must be appellate, not original.

It is the essential criterion of appellate jurisdiction, that it revises and corrects the proceedings in a cause already instituted, and does not create that cause. Although, therefore, a mandamus may be directed to courts, yet to issue such a writ to an officer for the delivery of a paper, is in effect the same as to substain an original action for that paper, and therefore seems not to belong to appellate, but to original jurisdiction. Neither is it necessary in such a case as this, to enable the court to exercise its appellate jurisdiction.

The authority, therefore, given to the Supreme Court, by the act establishing the judicial courts of the United States, to issue writs of mandamus to public officers, appears not to be warranted by the constitution; and it becomes necessary to enquire whether a jurisdiction, so conferred, can be exercised.

The question, whether an act, repugnant to the constitution, can become the law of the land, is a question deeply interesting to the United States; but, happily, not of an intricacy proportioned to its interest. It seems only necessary to recognize certain principles, supposed to have been long and well established, to decide it.

That the people have an original right to establish, for their future government, such principles, as, in their opinion, shall most conduce to their own happiness, is the basis, on which the whole American fabric has been erected. The exercise of this original right is a very great exertion; nor can it, nor ought it to be frequently repeated. The principles, therefore, so established, are deemed fundamental. And as the authority from which they proceed, is supreme, and can seldom act, they are designed to be permanent.

This original and supreme will organizes the government, and assigns, to different departments, their respective powers. It may either stop here; or establish certain limits not to be transcended by those departments.

The government of the United States is of the latter description. The powers of the legislature are defined, and limited; and that those limits may not be mistaken, or forgotten, the constitution is written. To what purpose are powers limited, and to what purpose is that limitation committed to writing, if these limits may, at any time, be passed by those intended to be restrained? The distinction, between a government with limited and unlimited powers, is abolished, if those limits do not confine the persons on whom they are imposed, and if acts prohibited and acts allowed, are of equal obligation. It is a proposition too plain to be contested, that the constitution controls any legislative act repugnant to it; or, that the legislature may alter the constitution by an ordinary act.

Between these alternatives there is no middle ground. The constitution is either a superior, paramount law, unchangeable by ordinary means, or it is on a level with ordinary legislative acts, and, like other acts, is alterable when the legislature shall please to alter it.

If the former part of the alternative be true, then a legislative act contrary to the constitution is not law: if the latter part be true, then written constitutions are absurd attempts, on the part of the people, to limit a power, in its own nature illimitable.

Certainly all those who have framed written constitutions contemplate them as forming the fundamental and paramount law of the nation, and consequently the theory of every such government must be, that an act of the legislature, repugnant of the constitution is void.

This theory is essentially attached to a written constitution, and is consequently, to be considered, by this court, as one of the fundamental principles of our society. It is not therefore to be lost sight of in the further consideration of this subject.

If an act of the legislature, repugnant to the constitution, is void, does it, not withstanding its invalidity, bind the courts, and oblige them to give it effect? Or, in other words, though it be not law, does it constitute a rule as operative as if it was a law? This would be to overthrow in fact what was established in theory; and would seem, at first view, an absurdity too gross to be insisted on. It shall, however, receive a more attentive consideration.

It is emphatically the province and duty of the judicial department to say what the law is. Those who apply the rule to particular cases, must of necessity expound and interpret the rule. If two laws conflict with each other, the courts must decide on the operation of each.

So if a law be in opposition to the constitution; if both the law and the constitution apply to a particular case, so that the court must either decide the case conformably to the law, disregarding the constitution; or conformably to the constitution, disregarding the law; the court must determine which of these conflicting rules governs the case. This is of the very essence of judicial duty.

If then the courts are to regard the constitution; and the constitution is superior to any ordinary act of the legislature; the constitution, and not such ordinary act, must govern the case to which they both apply.

Those then who controvert the principle that the constitution is to be considered, in court, as a paramount law, are reduced to the necessity of maintaining that courts must close their eyes on the constitution, and see only the law.

This doctrine would subvert the very foundation of all written constitutions. It would declare that an act, which, according to the principles and theory of our government, is entirely void; is yet, in practice, completely obligatory. It would declare, that if the legislature shall do what is expressly forbidden, such act, notwithstanding the express prohibition, is in reality effectual. It would be giving to the legislature a practical and real omnipotence, with the same breath which professes to restrict their powers within narrow limits. It is prescribing limits, and declaring that those limits may be passed at pleasure.

That it thus reduces to nothing what we have deemed the greatest improvement on political institutions a written constitution would of itself be sufficient, in America, where written constitutions have been viewed with so much reverence, for rejecting the construction. But the peculiar expressions of the constitution of the United States furnish additional arguments in favour of its rejection.

The judicial power of the United States is extended to all cases arising under the constitution.

Could it be the intention of those who gave this power, to say that, in using it, the constitution should not be looked into? That a case arising under the constitution should be decided without examining the instrument under which it arises?

This is too extravagant to be maintained.

In some cases then, the constitution must be looked into by the judges. And if they can open it at all, what part of it are they forbidden to read, or to obey?

There are many other parts of the constitution which serve to illustrate this subject.

It is declared that "no tax or duty shall be laid on articles exported from any state." Suppose a duty on the export of cotton, of tobacco, or of flour, and a suit instituted to recover it. Ought judgment to be rendered in such a case? Ought the judges to close their eyes on the constitution, and only see the law?

The constitution declares "that no bill of attainder or ex post facto law shall be passed."

If, however, such a bill should be passed and a person should be prosecuted under it; must the court condemn to death those victims whom the constitution endeavours to preserve?

"No person," says the constitution, "shall be convicted of treason unless on the testimony of two witnesses to the same overt act, or on confession in open court."

Here the language of the constitution is addressed especially to the courts. It prescribes, directly for them, a rule of evidence not to be departed from. If the legislature should change the rule, and declare *one* witness, or a confession *out* of court, sufficient for conviction, must the constitutional principle yield to the legislative act?

From these, and many other selections which might be made, it is apparent, that the framers of the constitution contemplated that instrument, as rule for the government of *courts,* as well as of the legislature.

Why otherwise does it direct the judges to take an oath to support it? This oath certainly applies, in an especial manner, to their conduct in their official character. How immoral to impose it on them, if they were to be used as the instruments, and the knowing instruments, for violating what they swear to support!

The oath of office, too, imposed by the legislature, is completely demonstrative of the legislative opinion of this subject. It is in these words, "I do solemnly swear that I will administer justice without respect to persons, and do equal right to the poor and to the rich; and that I will faithfully and impartially discharge all the duties incumbent on me as ___, according to the best of my abilities and understanding, agreeably to the *constitution,* and laws of the United States."

Why does a judge swear to discharge his duties agreeably to the constitution of the United States, if that constitution forms no rule for his government? if it is closed upon him, and cannot be inspected by him?

If such be the real state of things, this is worse than solemn mockery. To prescribe, or to take this oath, becomes equally a crime.

It is also not entirely unworthy of observation, that in declaring what shall be the *supreme* law of the land, the *constitution* itself is first mentioned; and not the laws of the United States generally, but those only which shall be made in *pursuance* of the constitution, have that rank.

Thus, the particular phraseology of the constitution of the United States confirms and strengthens the principle, supposed to be essential to all written constitutions, that a law repugnant to the constitution is void; and that *courts,* as well as other departments, are bound by that instrument.

The rule must be discharged.

NOTES

a. Robert Lowry Clinton, "The Populist-Progressive Reinterpretation of American Constitutional History: The Scapegoating of John Marshall, His Court, and the Founding Fathers" (Ph.D. diss., University of Texas, Austin, 1984).

b. Judiciary Act of 1789, First Congress, Sess. 1. Ch. 20, sec.13.

c. Craig R. Ducat, *Modes of Constitutional Interpretation* (St. Paul: West Publishing, 1978), 23.

d. Ibid., 24.

e. Henry J. Abraham, *The Judicial Process. An Introductory Analysis of the Courts of the United States, England, and France,* 5th ed. (New York: Oxford Univ. Press, 1986), 323–24; Clinton, "Populist-Progressive Reinterpretation," 37–100. Also see Chaps. 8, 9, and 10 of this volume.

f. Karl N. Llewellyn, *The Bramble Bush* (New York: Oceana Publications, 1960), 66–69.

g. See Chap. 9, this volume, 124.

II

The Usurpation Question

Shall we permit this revolution to take place
without even calling the attention of the people of
the United States to its momentous character?

—L. B. BOUDIN in
"Government by Judiciary"

6

The Classic Rebuttal

O UR FIRST READING to address the question of usurpation
of power is from Judge John B. Gibson's 1825 dissenting
opinion in a Pennsylvania Supreme Court case. This opinion is considered by many to be the most effective answer
given to John Marshall's famous arguments in support of judicial review.[a] The facts and the court's seriatim opinions in *Eakin* v. *Raub* are
of no particular importance to our discussion. Therefore, we have
edited only those portions of Judge Gibson's opinion relevant to the
issue of judicial review per se.

When reading Gibson, note at least six related points. First,
he states that the ordinary and essential powers of the judiciary do not
extend to the annulling of an act of the legislature. In other words, the
everyday duty of courts is to interpret the meaning of laws. Today we
would call this the duty of statutory interpretation; and indeed, courts
spend considerable time and effort in deciding what the legislature
meant when it enacted a given piece of legislation, and how the legislation should be interpreted given the fact situation of the particular case
or controversy before it. This task, argues Gibson, is the ordinary and
essential aspect of judicial power.

Second, Judge Gibson argues that what is good for one
coequal branch of the government ought to be good for the others. He
exclaims that it would be viewed as a usurpation of judicial power if
the legislature should attempt to reverse a Supreme Court decision.
Yet it is not regarded as a usurpation of legislative power when the
judiciary holds a statute unconstitutional. This argument is all the

more cogent in light of twentieth-century experience. Interest groups have attempted and sometimes have succeeded in reversing controversial Supreme Court decisions by proposing the rewriting of statutes so as to avoid previously held unconstitutional provisions, removing appellate jurisdiction, or even campaigning for constitutional amendments. Defenders of Court decisions often appeal to a sense of deep commitment to the Court as the guardian of what the Constitution means. Though reason may require equal regard for the authority of the legislative branch, as Gibson points out, the judiciary occupies a special status within the governmental system unaffected by the rules of logic.

Third, Gibson argues that the concept of checks and balances does not include the idea of a judicial veto. Within the legislative branch itself a proposal must pass through two legislative chambers. If the Framers intended to impose the judiciary as an additional barrier, they would have explicitly granted the power to the judges instead of leaving the matter in doubt.

Fourth, Gibson takes up the matter of the oath, which John Marshall regarded as a high moral duty. For Gibson the oath of office taken by judicial officers, or for that matter any government official, extends only to supporting the Constitution as far as it extends to official conduct. If one's duty does not entail excursions into the legislative realm, neither does one's oath. This conclusion gives rise to a rhetorical question that we may treat as Gibson's fifth point.

Does a judge violate the Constitution when he permits an unconstitutional legislative act to stand? Gibson answers, No! The enactment and the interpretation of a legislative act are not concurrent. In other words, the judge does not adopt unconstitutional legislation as his own simply because he interprets it. Members of the legislative branch enacted the legislation, not the judiciary.

The sixth and last major point clearly follows. If the legislature enacts an unconstitutional law, the people may petition their elected representatives to repeal it. If the judiciary makes a mistake, a constitutional amendment is needed. The former remedy is clearly preferable to the latter, given the relatively drastic and cumbersome process of amending a constitution.

The remainder of Gibson's dissent is an exposition of the authority of state courts under the Constitution. However, what is of lasting value is his contribution to the debate over judicial review. Interestingly, Gibson later recanted his bold view because the Pennsylvania legislature had "sanctioned the pretensions of the courts to deal freely with the acts of the legislature, and from experience of the necessity of the case."ᵇ

Though Gibson's appointment to the United States Supreme Court was mentioned, it never materialized. However, he went on to win great prestige as a state jurist. His most famous opinion was delivered in *De Chastellue* v. *Fairchild* (3 Harris 18). Completely ignoring his previous position and overturning all accepted precedent, he established the proper limits of legislative power in that state through an exercise of judicial review based upon the Pennsylvania constitution.

Few state jurists enjoyed a more distinguished career. Gibson was appointed chief justice in 1827 and held that position until 1851, when a constitutional amendment retired the entire bench. "The Old Chief," as he was affectionately known, was nominated and elected an associate justice on the new court, a position he held until his death in 1853.

Eakin v. *Raub*

12 Sergeant and Rawle 330

(Philadelphia, April 16, 1825)

I WILL . . . express an opinion which I have deliberately formed on the abstract right of the judiciary to declare an unconstitutional act of the legislature void.

. . . I am aware, that a right to declare all unconstitutional acts void, without distinction as to either constitution, is generally held as professional dogma; but I apprehend, rather as a matter of faith than of reason. I admit, that I once embraced the same doctrine, but without examination, and I shall, therefore, state the arguments that impelled me to abandon it, with great respect for those whom it is still maintained. But I may premise, that it is not a little remarkable, that although the right in question has all along been claimed by the judiciary, no judge has ventured to discuss it, except Chief Justice Marshall (in *Marbury* v. *Madison,* 1 Cranch, 176); and if the argument of a jurist so distinguished for the strength of his ratiocinative powers be found inconclusive, it may fairly be set down to the weakness of the position which he attempts to defend. . . .

I begin, then, by observing, that in this country, the powers of the judiciary are divisable into those that are POLITICAL, and those that are purely CIVIL. Every power by which one organ of the government is enabled to control another, or to exert an influence over its acts, is a political power. The political powers of the judiciary are *extraordinary* and *adventitious;* such, for instance, as are derived from certain peculiar provisions in the constitution of the *United States,* of which hereafter: and they are derived by direct grant, from the common fountain of all political power. On the other hand, its civil, are its *ordinary* and *appropriate* powers; being part of its essence, and existing independently of any supposed grant in the constitution. But where the government exists by virtue of a *written* constitution the judiciary does not necessarily derive from that circumstance, any other than its ordinary and appropriate powers. Our judiciary is constructed on the principles of the common law, which enters so essentially into the composition of our social institution as to be inseparable from them, and to be, in fact, the basis of the whole scheme of our civil and political liberty. In adopting any organ or instrument of the common law, we take it with just such powers and capacities as were incident to it, at the common law, except where these are expressly, or by necessary implication, abridged or enlarged in the act of adoption; and, that such act is a written instrument, cannot vary its consequences or construction. . . . Now, what are the powers of the judiciary at the common law? They are those that necessarily arise out of its immediate business; and they are, therefore, commensurate only with the judicial execution of the municipal law, or in other words, with the administration of distributive justice, without extending to anything of a political cast whatever. . . .

With us, although the legislature be the depository of only so much of the sovereignty as the people have thought fit to impart, it is, nevertheless, sovereign within the limit of its powers, and may relatively claim the same pre-eminence here, that it may claim elsewhere. It will be conceded, then, that the ordinary and essential powers of the judiciary do not extend to the annulling of an act of the legislature. . . .

The constitution of *Pennsylvania* contains no express grant of political powers of the judiciary. But to establish a grant by implication, the constitution is said to be a law of superior obligation; and consequently, that if it were to come into collision with an act of the legislature, the latter would have to give way; this is conceded. But it is a fallacy, to suppose, that they can come into collision *before the judiciary.* What is a constitution? It is an act of extraordinary legislation, by which the people establish the structure and mechanism of their government; and in which they prescribe fundamental rules to regulate the motion of the several parts. What is a statute? It is an act of ordinary legislation, by the appropriate organ of the government; the provisions of which are to be executed by the executive or judiciary, or by officers subordinate to them. The constitution, then, contains no practical rules for the administration of *distributive justice,* with which alone the judiciary has to do; these being furnished in acts of ordinary legislation, by that organ of the government, which, in this respect, is exclusively the representative of the people; and it is generally true, that the provisions of a constitution are to be carried into effect immediately by the legislature, and only mediately, if at all, by the judiciary. . . .

The Constitution and the *right* of the legislature to pass the act, may be in collision but is that a legitimate subject for judicial determination? If it be, the judiciary must be a peculiar organ, to revise the proceedings of the legislature, and to correct its mistakes; and in what part of the constitution are we to look for the proud preeminence? Viewing the matter in the opposite direction, what would be thought of an act of assembly in which it should be declared that the Supreme Court had, in a particular case put a wrong construction on the Constitution of the *United States,* and that the judgment should therefore be reversed? It would, doubtless, be thought a usurpation of judicial power. But it is by no means clear, that to declare a law void, which has been enacted according to the forms prescribed in the constitution, is not a usurpation of legislative power. It is an act of sovereignty; and sovereignty and legislative power are said by Sir William *Blackstone* to be convertible terms. It is the business of the judiciary to interpret the laws, not scan the authority of the lawgiver; and without the latter, it cannot take cognisance of a collision between a law and the constitution. So that, to affirm that the judiciary has a right to judge of the existence of such collision, is to take for granted the very thing to be proved; and that a very cogent argument may be made in this way, I am not disposed to deny; for no conclusions are so strong as those that are drawn from the *petitio principii.*

But it has been said to be emphatically the business of the judiciary, to ascertain and pronounce what the law is; and that this necessarily involves a consideration of the constitution. It does so: but how far? If the judiciary will inquire into anything besides the form of enactment, where shall it stop? . . .

. . . In theory, all the organs of the government are of equal capacity, or, if not equal, each must be supposed to have superior capacity only for those things which peculiarly belong to it; and, as legislation peculiarly involves the consideration of those limitations which are put on the law-making power, and the interpretation of the laws when made, involves only the construction of the laws themselves, it follows, that the construction of the constitution, in this particular, belongs to the legislature, which ought, therefore, to be taken to have superior capacity to judge of the constitutionality of its own acts. But suppose all to be of equal capacity in every respect, why should one exercise a controlling power over the rest? That the judiciary is of superior rank, has never been pretended, although it has been said to be co-ordinate. It is not easy, however, to comprehend how the power which gives law to all the rest, can be of no more than equal rank with one which receives it, and is answerable to the former for the observance of its statutes. Legislation is essentially an act of sovereign power; but the execution of the laws by instruments that are governed by prescribed rules, and exercise no power of volition, is essentially otherwise. . . . It may be said, the power of the legislature, also, is limited by prescribed rules: it is so. But it is, nevertheless, the power of the people, and sovereign as far as it extends. It cannot be said, that the judiciary is co-ordinate, merely because it is established by the constitution; if that were sufficient, sheriffs, registers of wills, and recorders of deeds, would be so too. Within the pale of their authority, the acts of these officers will have the power of the people for their support; but no one will pretend, they are of equal dignity with the acts of the legislature. Inequality of rank arises not from the manner in which the organ has been constituted, but from its essence and the nature of its functions; and the legislative organ is superior to every other, inasmuch as the power to will and to command, is essentially superior to the power to act and to obey. . . .

Every one knows how seldom men think exactly alike on ordinary subjects; and a government constructed on the principle of assent by all its parts, would be inadequate to the most simple operations. The notion of a complication of counter-checks has been carried to an extent in theory, of which the framers of the constitution never dreamt. When the entire sovereignty was separated into its elementary parts, and distributed to the appropriate branches, all things incident to the exercise of its powers were committed to each branch exclusively. The negative which each part of the legislature may exercise, in regard to the acts of the other, was thought sufficient to prevent material infractions of the restraints which were put on the power of the whole; for, had it been intended to interpose the judiciary as an additional barrier, the matter would surely not have been left in doubt. The judges would not have been left to stand on the insecure and ever shifting ground of public opinion as constructive power; they would have been placed on the impregnable ground of an express grant; they would not have been compelled to resort to the debates in the convention, or the opinion that was generally entertained at the time. A constitution, or a statute, is supposed to contain the whole will of the body from which it emanated; and I would just as soon resort to the debates in the legislature, for the construction of an act of assembly, as to the debates in the convention, for the construction of the constitution. . . .

But the judges are sworn to support the constitution, and are they not bound by it as the law of the land? In some respects they are. In the very few cases in which the judiciary, and not the legislature, is the immediate organ to execute its provisions, they are bound by it, in preference to any act of assembly to the contrary; in such cases, the constitution is a rule to the courts. But what I have in view in this inquiry, is, the supposed right of the judiciary, to interfere, in cases where the constitution is to be carried into effect through the instrumentality of the legislature, and where that organ must necessarily first decide on the constitutionality of its own act. The oath to support the constitution is not peculiar to the judges, but is taken indiscriminately by every officer of the government, and is designed rather as a test of the political principles of the man, than to bind the officer in the discharge of his duty: otherwise, it were difficult to determine what operation it is to have in the case of a recorder of deeds, for instance, who, in the execution of his office, has nothing to do with the constitution. But granting it to relate to the official conduct of the judge, as well as every other officer, and not to his political principles, still, it must be understood in reference to supporting the constitution, *only as far as that may be involved in his official duty;* and, consequently, if his official duty does not comprehend an inquiry into the authority of the legislature, neither does his oath.

It is worthy of remark here, that the foundation of every argument in favor of the right of the judiciary, is found, at last, to be an assumption of the whole ground in dispute. Granting that the object of the oath is to secure a support of the constitution in the discharge of official duty, its terms may be satisfied by restraining it to official duty in the exercise of the *ordinary* judicial powers. Thus, the constitution may furnish a rule of construction, where a particular interpretation of a law would conflict with some constitutional principle; and such interpretation, where it may, is always to be avoided. But the oath was more probably designed to secure the powers of each of the different branches from being usurped by any of the rest; for instance, to prevent the House of Representatives from erecting itself into a court of judicature, or the Supreme Court from attempting to control the legislature: and in this view, the oath furnishes an argument equally plausible *against* the right of the judiciary. But if it require a support of the constitution in anything besides official duty, it is, in fact, an oath of allegiance to a particular form of government; and considered as such, it is not easy to see, why it should not be taken by the citizens at large, as well as by the officers of the government. It has never been thought, that an officer is under greater restraint as to measures which have for their avowed end a total change of the constitution, than a citizen who has taken no oath at all. The official oath, then, relates only to the official conduct of the officer, and does not prove that he ought to stray from the path of his ordinary business, to search for violations of duty in the business of others; nor does it, as supposed, define the powers of the officer.

But do not the judges do a *positive* act in violation of the constitution, when they give effect to an unconstitutional law? Not if the law has been passed according to the forms established in the constitution. The fallacy of the question is, in supposing that the judiciary adopts the acts of the legislature as its own; whereas, the enactment of a law and the interpretation of it are not concurrent acts, and as the judiciary is not required to concur in enactment, neither is it in the breach of the constitution which may be the consequence of the enactment; the fault is imputable to the legislature, and on it the responsibility exclusively rests. In this respect, the judges are in the predicament of jurors who are bound to serve in capital cases, although unable, under any circumstances, to reconcile it to their duty to deprive a human being of life. To one of these, who applied to be discharged from the panel, I once heard it remarked, by an eminent and humane judge: "You do not deprive a prisoner of life, by finding him guilty of a capital crime; you but pronounce his case to be within the law, and it is therefore, those who declare the law, and not you, who deprive him of life." . . .

But it has been said, that his construction would deprive the citizen of the advantages which are peculiar to a written constitution, by at once declaring the power of the legislature, in practice, to be illimitable. . . . But there is no magic or inherent power in parchment and ink, to command respect, and protect principles from violation. In the business of government, a recurrence to first principles answers the end of an observation at sea, with a view to correct the dead-reckoning; and for this purpose, a written constitution is an instrument of inestimable value. It is of inestimable value also, in rendering its first principles familiar to the mass of people; for, after all, there is no effectual guard against legislative usurpation, but public opinion, the force of which, in this country, is inconceivably great. . . . Once let public opinion be so corrupt as to sanction every misconstruction of the constitution, and abuse of power, which the temptation of the moment may dictate, and the party which may happen to be predominant, will laugh at the puny efforts of a dependent power to arrest it in its course.

For these reasons, I am of opinion, that it rests with the people, in whom full and absolute sovereign power resides, to correct abuses in legislation, by instructing their representatives to repeal the obnoxious act. What is wanting to plenary power in the government, is reserved by the people, for their own immediate use; and to redress an infringement of their rights in this respect, would seem to be an accessory of the power thus reserved. It might, perhaps, have been better to vest the power in the judiciary; as it might be expected, that its habits of deliberation, and the aid derived from the arguments of counsel, would more frequently lead to accurate conclusions. On the other hand, the judiciary is not infallible; and an error by it would admit of no remedy but a more distinct expression of the public will, through the extraordinary medium of a convention; whereas, an error by the legislature admits of a remedy by an exertion of the same will, in the ordinary exercise of the right of suffrage – a mode better calculated to attain the end, without popular excitement. It may be said, the people would probably not notice an error of their representatives. But they would as probably do so, as notice an error of the judiciary; and besides, it is a *postulate* in the theory of our government, and the very basis of the superstructure, that the people are wise, virtuous, and competent to manage their own affairs: and if they are not so, in fact, still, every question of this sort must be determined according to the principles of the constitution, as it came from the hands of the framers, and the existence of a defect which was not foreseen, would not justify those who administer the government, in applying a corrective in practice, which can be provided only by convention. . . .

But in regard to an act of assembly, which is found to be in collision with the constitution, laws, or treaties of the *United States,* I take the duty of the judiciary to be exactly the reverse. By becoming parties to the federal constitution, the states have agreed to several limitations of their individual sovereignty, to enforce which, it was thought to be absolutely necessary, to prevent them from giving effect to laws in violation of those limitations, through the instrumentality of their own judges. Accordingly, it is declared in the sixth article and second section of the federal constitution, that "This constitution, and the laws of the *United States* which shall be made in pursuance thereof, and all treaties made, or which shall be made under the authority of the *United States,* shall be the *supreme* law of the land; and the *judges* in every *state* shall be BOUND thereby; anything in the *laws* or *constitution* or any *state* to the contrary not withstanding."

This is an express grant of a political power, and it is conclusive, to show that no law of inferior obligation, as every state law must necessarily be, can be executed at the expense of the constitution, laws, or treaties of the *United States.* It may be said, these are to furnish a rule only when there is no state provision on the subject. But in that view, they could, with no propriety, be called supreme; for supremacy is a relative term, and cannot be predicted of a thing which exists separately and alone: and this law, which is called supreme, would change its character and become subordinate, as soon as it should be found in conflict with a state law. But the judges are to be bound by the federal constitution and laws, notwithstanding anything in the constitution or laws of the particular state *to the contrary.* If, then, a state were to declare the laws of the *United States* not to be obligatory on her judges, such an act would unquestionably be void; for it will not be pretended, that any member of the union can dispense with the obligation of the federal constitution; and if it cannot be done directly, and by a general declaratory law, neither can it indirectly, and by by-laws dispensing with it in particular cases. . . .

NOTES

a. Alpheus Thomas Mason, William M. Beaney, and Donald Grier Stephenson, Jr., *American Constitutional Law: Introductory Essays and Selected Cases,* 7th ed. (Englewood Cliffs, N.J.: Prentice-Hall, 1983), 50.

b. Ibid.

7

Thayer on Restraint

F ORTY YEARS after Gibson's death, James B. Thayer stood
before the Congress on Jurisprudence and Law Reform on
August 9, 1893, to deliver the paper you are about to read.
After noting with favor Judge Gibson's argument in *Eakin*
v. *Raub,* he went on to argue for the view of the judiciary he had
adopted early in life. Namely, if the Supreme Court exercised judicial
review at all, it must be with great restraint, declaring acts void only
when their constitutionality was beyond all reasonable doubt.

The Harvard law professor reviews carefully the historical ante-
cedents to the establishment of judicial review. He comes to the skeptical conclusion that the "judiciary may well reflect that if they had been
regarded by the people as the chief protection against legislative violation of the constitution, they would not have been allowed . . . incidental and postponed control." Yet Thayer accepts judicial review as a
legitimate judicial function and not a usurpation per se of legislative
power. What is unacceptable is the employment of judicial review in
those instances in which reasonable persons may disagree. Judicial
review should be reserved for those cases for which there is no "reasonable doubt" that the legislature enacted an unconstitutional law.

Thayer counsels for judicial self-restraint because the very independence of the judiciary may be jeopardized without it. He argues
that repeated and unnecessary use of the judicial veto could excite
institutional jealousy and diminish public reverence for the laws.

Note the acknowledgment that judges are part of the political
process and therefore should "apply methods and principles that befit

their task." It is this view of the court's relationship with the other branches of government that clearly distinguishes advocates of judicial self-restraint from the others: for example, jurists such as Justice Roberts, who described the judicial function in *Butler* v. *United States* in simple, mechanistic terms, on the one hand, or, on the other hand, judges who are committed to using courts to right the many wrongs abroad in the land in the manner of a superlegislature.

James Bradley Thayer was born in Haverhill, Massachusetts, on January 15, 1831, and graduated from the Harvard Law School in 1856. He began his legal career only after first exploring his interests in divinity and the Greek and Latin classics. Upon graduation from law school he became a leading legal practitioner in Boston and turned down an offer to become a Harvard English professor only to accept a professorship at the law school in 1874.[a]

He joined the Harvard faculty at the same time the case method was inaugurated under the leaderhip of Dean Christopher Columbus Landgell. There he was associated with the legal titans of the age, including John Chipman Gray and James Barr Ames. Thayer wrote an important treatise on the law of evidence which his student, John H. Wigmore, built upon to produce some years later the classic statement on the law of evidence. In the tradition of Langdell, who was responsible for the case method as a paradigm of legal teaching, Professor Thayer compiled the first constitutional law casebook, *Cases on Constitutional Law*. His most lasting contribution to scholarship is the article contained in this chapter.[b]

This famous essay is the foundation on which Justices Holmes, Brandeis, and Frankfurter constructed their judicial philosophies. All three were associated with Harvard and connected with Thayer as faculty member or student. All three acknowledged the intellectual impact of Thayerism upon their own thinking. The three justices represent the most articulate spokespersons for judicial self-restraint for sixty years, from 1902 to 1962. Their judicial opinions provide scholar and practitioner alike with the finest primer available in any form on the doctrine of judicial self-restraint.[c]

The timelessness of the Thayer article is evident when we consider contemporary criticisms of the Supreme Court.The charge that the Supreme Court has become a policy-making institution, one with little regard for popular opinion and proper deference toward the legislature, is one that modern conservative ideologues, including those in the Reagan administration, have trumpeted with great resonance. But the political noise directed against the Court is not limited to our time.

The same arguments were directed against the Court by liberals in an earlier age who opposed the Court's tendency to strike down social and economic legislation designed to protect the masses from those with economic wealth and power.

Without intending to promote undue cynicism, we must point out that, from a historical perspective, positions on judicial activism versus restraint often turn on whose ox is being gored. Yesterday's liberals often criticized the Court for its activism; today it is the conservatives who condemn the Court for the same sin. Though this fact does not alter the validity, if any, of Professor Thayer's views, it nonetheless reinforces his basic underlying assumption of the Supreme Court as a political institution.

The Origin and Scope of the American Doctrine of Constitutional Law[d1]

James B. Thayer

I. How did our American doctrine, which allows to the judiciary the power to declare legislative Acts unconstitutional, and to treat them as null, come about, and what is the true scope of it?

It is a singular fact that the State constitutions did not give this power to the judges in express terms; it was inferential. In the earliest of these instruments no language was used from which it was clearly to be made out. Only after the date of the Federal constitution was any such language to be found; as in Article XII of the Kentucky constitution of 1792. The existence of the power was at first denied or doubted in some quarters; and so late as the year 1825, in a strong dissenting opinion, Mr. Justice Gibson, of Pennsylvania, one of the ablest of American judges, and afterwards the chief justice of that State, wholly denied it under any constitution which did not expressly give it. He denied it, therefore, under the State constitutions generally, while admitting that in that of the United States the power was given; namely, in the second clause of Article VI, when providing that the constitution, and the laws and treaties made in pursuance thereof, "shall be the supreme law of the land; and the judges in every State shall be bound thereby, anything in the constitution or laws of any State to the contrary notwithstanding."[2]

So far as the grounds for this remarkable power are found in the mere fact of a constitution being in writing, or in judges being sworn to support it, they are quite inadequate. Neither the written form nor the oath of the judges necessarily involves the right of reversing, displacing, or disregarding any action of the legislature or the executive which these departments are constitutionally authorized to take, or the determination of those departments that they are so authorized. It is enough, in confirmation of this, to refer to the fact that other countries, as France, Germany, and Switzerland, have written constitutions, and that such a power is not recognized there. "The restrictions," says Dicey, in his admirable Law of the Constitution, "placed on the action of the legislature under the French constitution are not in reality laws, since they are not rules which in the last resort will be enforced by the courts. Their true character is that of maxims of political morality, which derive whatever strength they possess from being formally inscribed in the constitution, and from the resulting support of public opinion."[3]

How came we then to adopt this remarkable practice? Mainly as a natural result of our political experience before the War of Independence, – as being colonists, governed under written charters of government proceeding from the English Crown. The terms and limitations of these charters, so many written constitutions, were enforced by various means, – by forfeiture of the charters, by Act of Parliament, by the direct annulling of legislation by the Crown, by judicial proceedings and an ultimate appeal to the Privy Council. Our practice was a natural result of this; but it was by no means a necessary one. All this colonial restraint was only the usual and normal exercise of power. An external authority had imposed the terms of the charters, the authority of a paramount government, fully organized and equipped for every exigency of disobedience, with a king and legislature and courts of its own. The superior right and authority of this government were fundamental here, and fully recognized; and it was only a usual orderly, necessary procedure when our own courts enforced the same rights that were enforced here by the appellate courts in England. These charters were in the strict sense written *law*: as their restraints upon the colonial legislatures were enforced by the English courts of last resort, so might they be enforced through the colonial courts, by disregarding as null what went counter to them.[4]

The Revolution came, and what happened then? Simply this: we cut the cord that tied us to Great Britain, and there was no longer an external sovereign. Our conception now was that "the people" took his place; that is to say, our own home population in the several States were now their own sovereign. So far as existing institutions were left untouched, they were construed by translating the name and style of the English sovereign into that of our new ruler, – ourselves, the People. After this the charters, and still more obviously the new constitutions, were not so many orders from without, backed by an organized outside government, which simply performed an ordinary function in enforcing them; they were precepts from the people themselves who were to be governed, addressed to each of their own number, and especially to those who were charged with the duty of conducting the government. No higher power existed to support these orders by compulsion of the ordinary sort. The sovereign himself, having written these expressions of his will, had retired into the clouds; in any regular course of events he had no organ to enforce his will, except those to whom his orders were addressed in these documents. How then should his written constitution be enforced if these agencies did not obey him, if they failed, or worked amiss?

Here was really a different problem from that which had been presented under the old state of things. And yet it happened that no new provisions were made to meet it. The old methods and the old conceptions were followed. In Connecticut, in 1776, by a mere legislative Act, the charter of 1662 was declared to continue "the civil Constitution of the State, under the sole authority of the People thereof, independent of any King or Prince whatsoever;" and then two or three familiar fundamental rules of liberty and good government were added as a part of it. Under this the people of Connecticut lived til 1818. In Rhode Island the charter, unaltered, served their turn until 1842; and, as is well known, it was upon this that one of the early cases of judicial action arose for enforcing constitutional provisions under the new order of things, as against a legislative Act; namely, the case of Trevett v. Weeden, in the Rhode Island Supreme Court in 1786.[5]

But it is instructive to see that this new application of judicial power was not universally assented to. It was denied by several members of the Federal convention, and was referred to as unsettled by various judges in the last two decades of the last century. The surprise of the Rhode Island legislature at the action of the court in Trevett v. Weeden seems to indicate an impression in their minds that the change from colonial dependence to independence had made the legislature the substitute for Parliament, with a like omnipotence.[6] In Vermont it seems to have been the established doctrine of the period that the judiciary could not disregard a legislative Act; and the same view was held in Connecticut, as expressed in 1795 by Swift, afterwards chief justice of that State. In the preface to I. D. Chipman's (Vermont) Reports, *22 et seq.*, the learned reporter, writing (in 1824) of the period of the Vermont Constitution of 1777, says that "No idea was entertained that the judiciary had any power to inquire into the constitutionality of Acts of the legislature, or to pronounce them void for any cause, or even to question their validity." And at page 25, speaking of the year 1785, he adds: "Long after the period to which we have alluded, the doctrine that the constitution is the supreme law of the land, and that the judiciary have authority to set aside . . . Acts repugnant thereto, was considered anti-republican." In 1814,[7] for the first time, I believe, we find this court announcing an Act of the State legislature to be "void as against the constitution of the State and the United States, and even the laws of nature." It may be remarked here that the doctrine of declaring legislative Acts void as being contrary to the constitution, was probably helped into existence by a theory which found some favor among our ancestors at the time of the Revolution, that courts might disregard such acts if they were contrary to the fundamental maxims of morality, or, as it was phrased, to the laws of nature. Such a doctrine was thought to have been asserted by English writers, and even by judges at times, but was never acted on. It has been repeated here, as matter of speculation, by our earlier judges, and occasionally by later ones; but in no case within my knowledge has it even been enforced where it was the single and necessary ground of the decision, nor can it be, unless as a revolutionary measure.[8]

In Swift's "System of the Laws of Connecticut," published in 1795,[9] the author argues strongly and elaborately against the power of the judiciary to disregard a legislative enactment, while mentioning that the contrary opinion "is very popular and prevalent." "It will be agreed," he says, "it is as probable that the judiciary will declare laws unconstitutional which are not so, as it is that the legislature will exceed their constitutional authority." But he makes the very noticeable admission that there may be cases so monstrous, − *e.g.*, an Act authorizing conviction for crime without evidence, or securing to the legislature their own seats for life, − "so manifestly unconstitutional that it would seem wrong to require the judges to regard it in their decisions." As late as 1807 and 1808, judges were impeached by the legislature of Ohio for holding Acts of that body to be void.[10]

II. When at last this power of the judiciary was everywhere established, and added to the other bulwarks of our written constitutions, how was the power to be conceived of? Strictly as a judicial one. The State constitutions had been scrupulous to part off the powers of government into three; and in giving one of them to each department, had sometimes, with curious explicitness, forbidden it to exercise either of the others. The legislative department, said the Massachusetts constitution in 1780,[11] −

> "Shall never exercise the executive and judicial powers, or either of them; the executive shall never exercise the legislative and judicial powers or either of them; to the end, it may be a government of laws, and not of men."

With like emphasis, in 1792, the constitution of Kentucky[12] said: −

> "Each of them to be confided to a separate body of magistracy; to wit, those which are legislative to one, those which are executive to another, and those which are judiciary to another. No person or collection of persons, being of one of these departments, shall exercise any power properly belonging to either of the others, except in the instances hereinafter expressly permitted."

Therefore, since the power now in question was merely a purely judicial one, in the first place, there were many cases where it had no operation. In the case of purely political acts and of the exercise of mere discretion, it mattered not that other departments were violating the constitution, the judiciary could not interfere; on the contrary, they must accept and enforce their acts. Judge Cooley has lately said:[13] −

"The Common impression undoubtedly is that in the case of any
legislation where the bounds of constitutional authority are disregarded,
. . . the judiciary is perfectly competent to afford the adequate remedy; that
the Act indeed must be void, and that any citizen, as well as the judiciary
itself, may treat it as void, and refuse obedience. This, however, is far from
being the fact."

Again, where the power of the judiciary did have place, its whole scope
was this; namely, to determine, for the mere purpose of deciding a litigated
question properly submitted to the court, whether a particular disputed exercise of power was forbidden by the constitution. In doing this the court was so
to discharge its office as not to deprive another department of any of its proper
power, or to limit it in the proper range of its discretion. Not merely, then, do
these questions, when presenting themselves in the courts for judicial action,
call for a peculiarly large method in the treatment of them, but especially they
require an allowance to be made by the judges for the vast and not definable
range of legislative power and choice, for that wide margin of considerations
which address themselves only to the practical judgment of a legislative body.
Within that margin, as among all these legislative considerations, the constitutional law-makers must be allowed a free foot. In so far as legislative choice,
ranging here unfettered, may select one form of action or another, the judges
must not interfere, since *their* question is a naked judicial one.

Moreover, such is the nature of this particular judicial question that the
preliminary determination by the legislature is a fact of very great importance,
since the constitutions expressly intrust to the legislature this determination;
they cannot act without making it. Furthermore, the constitution not merely
intrust to the legislatures a preliminary determination of the question, but they
contemplate that this determination may be the final one; for they secure no
revision of it. It is only as litigation may spring up, and as the course of it may
happen to raise the point of constitutionality, that any question for the courts
can regularly emerge. It may be, then, that the mere legislative decision will
accomplish results throughout the country of the profoundest importance before any judicial question can arise or be decided, — as in the case of the first
and second charters of the United States Bank, and of the legal tender laws of
thirty years ago and later. The constitutionality of a bank charter divided the
cabinet of Washington, as it divided political parties for more than a generation. Yet when the first charter was given, in 1791, to last for twenty years, it
ran through its whole life unchallenged in the courts, and was renewed in
1816. Only after three years from that did the question of its constitutionality
come to decision in the Supreme Court of the United States. It is peculiarly
important to observe that such a result is not an exceptional or unforeseen one;
it is a result anticipated and clearly foreseen. Now, it is the legislature to
whom this power is given, — this power, not merely of enacting laws, but of
putting an interpretation on the constitution which shall deeply affect the
whole country, enter into, vitally change, even revolutionize the most serious

affairs, except as some individual may find it for his private interest to carry the matter into court. So of the legal tender legislation of 1863 and later. More important action, more intimately and more seriously touching the interests of every member of our population, it would be hard to think of. The constitutionality of it, although now upheld, was at first denied by the Supreme Court of the United States. The local courts were divided on it, and professional opinion has always been divided. Yet it was the legislature that determined this question, not merely primarily, but once for all, except as some individual, among the innumerable chances of his private affairs, found it for his interest to raise a judicial question about it.

It is plain that where a power so momentous as this primary authority to interpret is given, the actual determinations of the body to whom it is intrusted are entitled to a corresponding respect; and this not on mere grounds of courtesy or conventional respect, but on very solid and significant grounds of policy and law. The judiciary may well reflect that if they had been regarded by the people as the chief protection against legislative violation of the constitution, they would not have been allowed merely this incidental and postponed control. They would have been let in, as it was sometimes endeavored in the conventions to let them in, to a revision of the laws before they began to operate.[14] As the opportunity of the judges to check and correct unconstitutional Acts is so limited, it may help us to understand why the extent of their control, when they do have the opportunity, should also be narrow.

It was, then, all along true, and it was foreseen, that much which is harmful and unconstitutional may take effect without any capacity in the courts to prevent it, since their whole power is a judicial one. Their interference was but one of many safeguards, and its scope was narrow.

The rigor of this limitation upon judicial action is sometimes freely recognized, yet in a perverted way which really operates to extend the judicial function beyond its just bounds. The court's duty, we are told, is the mere and simple office of construing two writings and comparing one with another, as two contracts or two statutes are construed and compared when they are said to conflict; of declaring the true meaning of each, and, if they are opposed to each other, of carrying into effect the constitution as being of superior obligation, – an ordinary and humble judicial duty, as the courts sometimes describe it. This way of putting it easily results in the wrong kind of disregard of legislative considerations; not merely in refusing to consider them at all. Instead of taking them into account and allowing for them as furnishing possible grounds of legislative action, there takes place a pedantic and academic treatment of the texts of the constitution and the laws. And so we miss that combination of a lawyer's rigor with a statesman's breadth of view which should be found in dealing with this class of questions in constitutional law. Of this petty method we have many specimens; they are found only too easily to-day in the volumes of our current reports.

In order, however, to avoid falling into these narrow and literal methods, in order to prevent the courts from forgetting, as Marshall said, that "it is a constitution we are expounding," these literal precepts about the nature of the judicial task have been accompanied by a rule of administration which has tended, in competent hands, to give matters a very different complexion.

III. Let us observe the course which the courts, in point of fact, have taken, in administering this interesting jurisdiction.

They began by resting it upon the very simple ground that the legislature had only a delegated and limited authority under the constitutions; that these restraints, in order to be operative, must be regarded as so much law; and, as being law, that they must be interpreted and applied by the court. This was put as a mere matter of course. The reasoning was simple and narrow. Such was Hamilton's method in the Federalist, in 1788,[15] while discussing the Federal constitution, but on grounds applicable, as he conceived, to all others. So, in 1787, the Supreme Court of North Carolina had argued that no Act of the legislature could alter the constitution;[16] that the judges were as much bound by the constitution as by any other law, and any Act inconsistent with it must be regarded by them as abrogated. Wilson, in his lectures at Philadelphia in 1790–1791,[17] said that the constitution was a supreme law, and it was for the judges to declare and apply it; what was subordinate must give way; because one branch of the government infringed the constitution, it was no reason why another should abet it. In Virginia, in 1793, the judges put it that courts were simply to look at all the law, including the constitution: they were only to expound the law, and to give effect to that part of it which is fundamental.[18] Patterson, one of the justices of the Supreme Court of the United States, in 1795, on the Pennyslvania circuit,[19] said that the constitution is the commission of the legislature; if their Acts are not conformable to it, they are without authority. In 1796, in South Carolina,[20] the matter was argued by the court as a bald and mere question of conformity to paramount law. And such, in 1802, was the reasoning of the General Court of Maryland.[21] Finally, in 1803 came Marbury *v.* Madison,[22] with the same severe line of argument. The people, it was said, have established written limitations upon the legislature; these control all repugnant legislative Acts; such Acts are not law; this theory is essentially attached to a written constitution; it is for the judiciary to say what the law is, and if two rules conflict, to say which governs; the judiciary are to declare a legislative Act void which conflicts with the constitution, or else that instrument is reduced to nothing. And then, it was added, in the Federal instrument this power is expressly given.

Nothing could be more rigorous than all this. As the matter was put, the conclusions were necessary. Much of this reasoning, however, took no notice of the remarkable peculiarities of the situation; it went forward as smoothly as if the constitution were a private letter of attorney, and the court's duty under it were precisely like any of its most ordinary operations.

But these simple precepts were supplemented by a very significant rule of administration, – one which corrected their operation, and brought into play large considerations not adverted to in the reasoning so far mentioned. In 1811,[23] Chief Justice Tilghman, of Pennsylvania, while asserting the power of the court to hold laws unconstitutional, but declining to exercise it in a particular case, stated this rule as follows: –

> "For weighty reasons, it has been assumed as a principle in constitutional construction by the Supreme Court of the United States, by this court, and every other court of reputation in the United States, that an Act of the legislature is not to be declared void unless the violation of the constitution is so manifest as to leave no room for reasonable doubt."

When did this rule of administration begin? Very early. We observe that it is referred to as thoroughly established in 1811. In the earliest judicial consideration of the power of the judiciary over this subject, of which any report is preserved, – an *obiter* discussion in Virginia in 1782,[24] – while the general power of the court is declared by other judges with histrionic emphasis, Pendleton, the president of the court, in declining to pass upon it, foreshadowed the reasons of this rule, in remarking, –

> "How far this court, in whom the judiciary powers may in some sort be said to be concentrated, shall have power to declare the nullity of a law passed in its forms by the legislative power, without exercising the power of that branch, contrary to the plain terms of that constitution, is indeed a deep, important, and, I will add, a tremendous question, the decision of which would involve consequences to which gentlemen may not . . . have extended their ideas."

There is no occasion, he added, to consider it here. In 1793, when the General Court of Virginia held a law unconstitutional, Tyler, Justice, remarked,[25] –

> "But the violation must be plain and clear, or there might be danger of the judiciary preventing the operation of laws which might produce much public good."

In the Federal convention of 1787, while the power of declaring laws unconstitutional was recognized, the limits of the power were also admitted. In trying to make the judges revise all legislative acts before they took effect, Wilson pointed out that laws might be dangerous and destructive, and yet not so "unconstitutional as to justify the judges in refusing to give them effect."[26] In 1796 Mr. Justice Chase, in the Supreme Court of the United States,[27] said, that without then determining whether the court could declare an Act of Congress void, "I am free to declare that I will never exercise it but in a very clear case." And in 1800, in the same court,[28] as regards a statute of Georgia, Mr. Justice Patterson, who had already, in 1795, on the circuit, held a legislative Act of Pennsylvania invalid, said that in order to justify the court in declaring any law void, there must be "a clear and unequivocal breach of the Constitution, not a doubtful and argumentative implication."

In 1808 in Georgia[29] it was strongly put, in a passage which has been cited by other courts with approval. In holding an Act constitutional, Mr. Justice Charlton, for the court, asserted this power, as being inseparable from the organization of the judicial department. But, he continued, in what manner should it be exercised?

> "No nice doubts, no critical exposition of words, no abstract rules of interpretation, suitable in a contest between individuals, ought to be resorted to in deciding on the constitutional operation of a statute. This violation of a constitutional right ought to be as obvious to the comprehension of every one as an axiomatic truth, as that the parts are equal to the whole. I shall endeavor to illustrate this: that the first section of the second article of the constitution declares that the executive function shall be vested in the governor. Now, if the legislature were to vest the executive power in a standing committee of the House of Representatives, every mind would at once perceive the unconstitutionality of the statute. The judiciary would be authorized without hesitation to declare the Act unconstitutional. But when it remains doubtful whether the legislature have or have not trespassed on the constitution, a conflict ought to be avoided, because there is a possibility in such a case of the constitution being with the legislature."

In South Carolina, in 1812,[30] Chancellor Waties, always distinguished for his clear assertion of the power in the judiciary to disregard unconstitutional enactments, repeats and strongly reaffirms it: –

> "I feel so strong a sense of this duty that if a violation of the constitution were manifest, I should not only declare the Act void, but I should think I rendered a more important service to my country than in discharging the ordinary duties of my office for many years. . . . But while I assert this power and insist on its great value to the country, I am not insensible of the high deference due to legislative authority. It is supreme in all cases where it is not restrained by the constitution; and as it is the duty of legislators as well as judges to consult this and conform their acts to it, so it should be presumed that all their acts do conform to it unless the contrary is manifest. This confidence is necessary to insure due obedience to its authority. If this be frequently questioned, it must tend to diminish the reverence for the laws which is essential to the public safety and happiness. I am not, therefore, disposed to examine with scrupulous exactness the validity of a law. It would be unwise on another account. The interference of the judiciary with legislative Acts, if frequent or on dubious grounds, might occasion so great a jealousy of this power and so general a prejudice against it as to lead to measures ending in the total overthrow of the independence of the judges, and so of the best preservative of the constitution. The validity of the law ought not then to be questioned unless it is so obviously repugnant to the constitution that when pointed out by the judges, all men of sense and reflection in the community may perceive the repugnancy. By such a cautious exercise of this judicial check, no jealousy of it will be excited, the public confidence in it will be promoted, and its salutary effects be justly and fully appreciated."[31]

IV. I have accumulated these citations and run them back to the beginning, in order that it may be clear that the rule in question is something more than a mere form of language, a mere expression of courtesy and deference. It means far more than that. The courts have perceived with more or less distinctness that this exercise of the judicial function does in truth go far beyond the simple business which judges sometimes describe. If their duty were in truth merely and nakedly to ascertain the meaning of the text of the constitution and of the impeached Act of the legislature, and to determine, as an academic question, whether in the court's judgment the two were in conflict, it would, to be sure, be an elevated and important office, one dealing with great matters, involving large public considerations, but yet a function far simpler than it really is. Having ascertained all this, yet there remains a question – the really momentous question – whether, after all, the court can disregard the Act. It cannot do this as a mere matter of course, – merely because it is concluded that upon a just and true construction the law is unconstitutional. That is precisely the significance of the rule of administration that the courts lay down. It can only disregard the Act when those who have the right to make laws have not merely made a mistake, but have made a very clear one, – so clear that it is not open to rational question. That is the standard of duty to which the courts bring legislative Acts; that is the test which they apply, – not merely their own judgment as to constitutionality, but their conclusion as to what judgment is permissible to another department which the constitution has charged with the duty of making it. This rule recognizes that, having regard to the great, complex, ever-unfolding exigencies of government, much which will seem unconstitutional to one man, or body of men, may reasonably not seem so to another; that the constitution often admits of different interpretations; that there is often a range of choice and judgment; that in such cases the constitution does not impose upon the legislature any one specific opinion, but leaves open this range of choice; and that whatever choice is rational is constitutional. This is the principle which the rule that I have been illustrating affirms and supports. The meaning and effect of it are shortly and very strikingly intimated by a remark of Judge Cooley,[32] to the effect that one who is a member of a legislature may vote against a measure as being, in his judgment, unconstitutional; and, being subsequently placed on the bench, when this measure, having been passed by the legislature in spite of his opposition, comes before him judicially, may there find it his duty, although he has in no degree changed his opinion, to declare it constitutional.

Will any one say, You are over-emphasizing this matter, and making too much turn upon the form of a phrase? No, I think not. I am aware of the danger of doing that. But whatever may be said of particular instances of unguarded or indecisive judicial language, it does not appear to me possible to explain the early, constant, and emphatic statements upon this subject on any slight ground. The form of it is in language too familiar to courts, having too definite a meaning, adopted with too general an agreement, and insisted upon quite too emphatically, to allow us to think it a mere courteous and smoothly transmitted platitude. It has had to maintain itself against denial and dispute. Incidentally, Mr. Justice Gibson disputed it in 1825, while denying the whole power to declare laws unconstitutional.[33] If there be any such power, he insisted (page 352), the party's rights "would depend, not on the greatness of the supposed discrepancy with the constitution, but on the existence of any discrepancy at all." But the majority of the court reaffirmed their power, and the qualifications of it, with equal emphasis. This rule was also denied in 1817 by Jeremiah Mason, one of the leaders of the New England bar, in his argument of the Dartmouth College case, at its earlier stage, in New Hampshire.[34] He said substantially this: "An erroneous opinion still prevails to a considerable extent, that the courts . . . ought to act . . . with more than ordinary deliberation, . . . that they ought not to declare Acts of the legislature unconstitutional unless they come to their conclusion with absolute certainty, . . . and where the reasons are so manifest that none can doubt." He conceded that the courts should treat the legislature "with great decorum, . . . but . . . the final decision, as in other cases, must be according to the unbiassed dictate of the understanding." Legislative Acts, he said, require for their passage at least a majority of the legislature, and the reasons against the validity of the Act cannot ordinarily be so plain as to leave no manner of doubt. The rule, then, really requires the court to surrender its jurisdiction. "Experience shows that legislatures are in the constant habit of exerting their power to its utmost extent." If the courts retire, whenever a plausible ground of doubt can be suggested, the legislature will absorb all power. Such was his argument. But notwithstanding this, the Supreme Court of New Hampshire declared that they could not act without "a clear and strong conviction;" and on error, in 1819, Marshall, in his celebrated opinion at Washington, declared, for the court, "that in no doubtful case would it pronounce a legislative Act to be contrary to the Constitution."

Again, when the great Charles River Bridge Case[35] was before the Massachusetts courts, in 1829, Daniel Webster, arguing, together with Lemuel Shaw, for the plaintiff, denied the existence or propriety of this rule. All such cases, he said (p. 442) involve some doubt; it is not to be supposed that the legislature will pass an Act palpably unconstitutional. The correct ground is that the court will interfere when a case appearing to be doubtful is made out to be clear. Besides, he added, "members of the legislature sometimes vote for a law, of the constitutionality of which they doubt, on the consideration that the question may be determined by the judges." This Act passed in the House of Representatives by a majority of five or six.

> "We could show, if it were proper, that more than six members voted for it because the unconstitutionality of it *was* doubtful; leaving it to this court to determine the question. If the legislature is to pass a law because its unconstitutionality is doubtful, and the judge is to hold it valid because its unconstitutionality is doubtful, in what a predicament is the citizen placed! The legislature pass it *de bene esse;* if the question is not met and decided here on principle, responsibility rests nowhere. . . . It is the privi-

lege of an American judge to decide on constitutional questions . . . Judicial tribunals are the only ones suitable for the investigation of difficult
questions of private right."

But the court did not yield to this ingenious attempt to turn them into a
board for answering legislative conundrums. Instead of deviating from the line
of their duty for the purpose of correcting errors of the legislature, they held
that body to its own duty and its own responsibility. "Such a declaration," said
Mr. Justice Wilde in giving his opinion, "should never be made but when the
case is clear and manifest to all intelligent minds. We must assume that the
legislature have done their duty, and we must respect their constitutional
rights and powers." Five years later, Lemuel Shaw, who was Webster's associate counsel in the case last mentioned, being now Chief Justice of Massachusetts, in a case[36] where Jeremiah Mason was one of the counsel, repeated with
much emphasis "what has been so often suggested by courts of justice, that
. . . courts will . . . never declare a statute void unless the nullity and invalidity
are placed beyond reasonable doubt."

A rule thus powerfully attacked and thus explicitly maintained, must be
treated as having been deliberately meant, both as regards its substance and
its form. As to the form of it, it is the more calculcated to strike the attention
because it marks a familiar and important discrimination, of daily application
in our courts, in situations where the rights, the actions, and the authority of
different departments, different officials, and different individuals have to be
harmonized. It is a distinction and a test, it may be added, that come into more
and more prominence as our jurisprudence grows more intricate and refined.
In one application of it, as we all know, it is constantly resorted to in the
criminal law in questions of self-defense, and in the civil law of tort in questions of negligence, – in answering the question what might an individual who
has a right and perhaps a duty of acting under given circumstances, reasonably have supposed at that time to be true? It is the discrimination laid down for
settling that difficult question of a soldier's responsibility to the ordinary law of
the land when he has acted under the orders of his military superior. "He may,"
says Dicey, in his "Law of the Constitution,"[37] "as it has been well said, be liable
to be shot by a court-martial if he disobeys an order, and to be hanged by a
judge and jury if he obeys it. . . . Probably," he goes, quoting with approval one
of the books of Mr. Justice Stephen, ". . . it would be found that the order of a
military superior would justify his inferiors in executing any orders for giving
which they might fairly suppose their superior officer to have good reasons.
. . . The only line that presents itself to my mind is that a soldier should be
protected by orders for which he might reasonably believe his officer to have
good grounds."[38] This is the distinction adverted to by Lord Blackburn in a
leading modern case in the law of libel.[39] "When the court," he said, "come to
decide whether a particular set of words . . . are or are not libellous, they have
to decide a very different question from that which they have to decide when
determining whether another tribunal . . . might not unreasonably hold such

words to be libellous." It is the same discrimination upon which the verdicts of juries are revised every day in the courts, as in a famous case where Lord Esther applied it a few years ago, when refusing to set aside a verdict.[40] It must appear, he said, "that reasonable men could not fairly find as the jury have done. . . . It has been said, indeed, that the difference between [this] rule and the question whether the judges would have decided the same way as the jury, is evanescent, and the solution of both depends on the opinion of the judges. The last part of the observation is true, but the mode in which the subject is approached makes the greatest difference. To ask "Should we have found the same verdict," is surely not the same thing as to ask whether there is room for a reasonable difference of opinion." In like manner, as regards legislative action, there is often that ultimate question, which was vindicated for the judges in a recent highly important case in the Supreme Court of the United States,[41] viz., that of the reasonableness of a legislature's exercise of its most undoubted powers; of the permissible limit of those powers. If a legislature undertakes to exert the taxing power, that of eminent domain or any part of that vast, unclassified residue of legislative authority which is called, not always intelligently, the police power, this action must not degenerate into an irrational excess, so as to become, in reality, something – different and forbidden, – e.g., the depriving people of their property without due process of law; and whether it does so or not, must be determined by the judges.[42] But in such cases it is always to be remembered that the judicial question is a secondary one. The legislature in determining what shall be done, what it is reasonable to do, does not divide its duty with the judges, nor must it conform to their conception of what is prudent or reasonable legislation. The judicial function is merely that of fixing the outside border of reasonable legislative action, the boundary beyond which the taxing power, the power of eminent domain, police power, and legislative power in general, cannot go without violating the prohibitions of the constitution or crossing the line of its grants.[43]

It must indeed be studiously remembered, in judicially applying such a test as this of what a legislature may reasonably think, that virtue, sense, and competent knowledge are always to be attributed to that body. The conduct of public affairs must always go forward upon conventions and assumptions of that sort. "It is a *postulate*," said Mr. Justice Gibson, "in the theory of our government . . . that the people are wise, virtuous, and competent to manage their own affairs."[44] "It would be indecent in the extreme," said Marshall, C. J.,[45] "upon a private contract between two individuals to enter into an inquiry respecting the corruption of the sovereign power of a State." And so in a court's revision of legislative acts, as in its revision of a jury's acts, it will always assume a duly instructed body; and the question is not merely what persons may rationally do who are such as we often see, in point of fact, in our legislative bodies, persons untaught it may be, indocile, thoughtless, reckless, incompetent, – but what those other persons, competent, well-instructed, sagacious, attentive, intent only on public ends, fit to represent a self-governing people, such as our theory of government assumes to be carrying on our public affairs, – what such persons may reasonably think or do, what is the permissible view for them. If, for example, what is presented to the court be a question as to the constitutionality of an Act alleged to be *ex post facto,* there can be no assumption of ignorance, however probable, as to anything involved in a learned or competent discussion of that subject. And so of the provisions about double jeopardy, or giving evidence against one's self, or attainder, or jury trial. The reasonable doubt, then, of which our judges speak is that reasonable doubt which lingers in the mind of a competent and duly instructed person who has carefully applied his faculties to the question. The rationally permissible opinion of which we have been talking is the opinion reasonably allowable to such a person as this.

The ground on which courts lay down this test of a reasonable doubt for juries in criminal cases, is the great gravity of affecting a man with crime. The reason that they lay it down for themselves in reviewing the civil verdict of a jury is a different one, namely, because they are revising the work of another department charged with a duty of its own, – having themselves no right to undertake *that* duty, no right at all in the matter except to hold the other department within the limit of a reasonable interpretation and exercise of its powers. The court must not, even negatively, undertake to pass upon the facts in jury cases. The reason that the same rule is laid down in regard to revising legislative acts is neither the one of these nor the other alone, but it is both. The courts are revising the work of a co-ordinate department, and must not, even negatively, undertake to legislate. And, again, they must not act unless the case is so very clear, because the consequences of setting aside legislation may be so serious.

If it be said that the case of declaring legislation invalid is different from the others because the ultimate question here is one of the construction of a writing; that this sort of question is always a court's question, and that it cannot well be admitted that there should be two legal constructions of the same instrument; that there is a right way and a wrong way of construing it, and only one right way; and that is ultimately for the court to say what the right way is, – this suggestion appears, at first sight, to have much force. But really it begs the question. Lord Blackburn's opinion in the libel case[46] related to the construction of a writing. The doctrine which we are now considering is this, that in dealing with the legislative action of a co-ordinate department, a court cannot always, and for the purpose of all sorts of questions, say that there is but one right and permissible way of construing the constitution. When a court is interpreting a writing merely to ascertain or apply its true meaning, then, indeed, there is but one meaning allowable; namely, what the court adjudges to be its true meaning. But when the ultimate question is not that, but whether certain acts of another department, officer, or individual are legal or permissible, then this is not true. In the class of cases which we have been considering, *the ultimate question is not what is the true meaning of the constitution, but whether legislation is sustainable or not.*

It may be suggested that this is not the way in which the judges in fact

put the matter; *e.g.,* that Marshall, in McCulloch *v.* Maryland,[47] seeks to establish the court's own opinion of the constitutionality of the legislation establishing the United States Bank. But in recognizing that this is very often true, we
must remember that where the court is sustaining an Act and finds it to be
constitutional in its own opinion, it is fit that this should be said, and that such
a declaration is all that the case calls for; it disposes of the matter. But it is not
always true; there are many cases where the judges sustain an Act because
they are in doubt about it; where they are not giving their own opinion that it is
constitutional, but are merely leaving untouched a determination of the legislature; as in the case where a Massachusetts judge concurred in the opinion of
his brethren that a legislative Act was "competent for the legislature to pass,
and was not unconstitutional," "upon the single ground that the Act is not so
clearly unconstitutional, its invalidity so free from reasonable doubt, as to
make it the duty of the judicial department, in view of the vast interests
involved in the result to declare it void."[48] The constant declaration of the
judges that the question for them is not one of the mere and simple prepon-
derance of reasons for or against, but of what is very plain and clear, clear
beyond a reasonable doubt, – this declaration is really a steady announcement
that their decisions in support of the constitutionality of legislation do not, as
of course, import their own opinion of the true construction of the constitution,
and that the strict meaning of their words, when they hold an Act constitutional is merely this, – not unconstitutional beyond a reasonable doubt. It may
be added that a sufficient explanation is found here of some of the decisions
which have alarmed many people in recent years, – as if the courts were turning out but a broken reed.[49] Many more such opinions are to be expected, for,
while legislatures are often faithless to their trust, judges sometimes have to
confess the limits of their own power.

It all comes back, I think, to this. The rule under discussion has in it an
implied recognition that the judicial duty now in question touches the region of
political administration, and is qualified by the necessities and proprieties of
administration. If our doctrine of constitutional law – which finds itself, as we
have seen, in the shape of a narrowly stated substantive principle, with a rule
of administration enlarging the otherwise too restricted substantive rule – admits now of a juster and simpler conception, that is a very familiar situation in
the development of law. What really took place in adopting our theory of
constitutional law was this: we introduced for the first time into the conduct of
government through its great departments a judicial sanction, as among these
departments, – not full and complete, but partial. The judges were allowed,
indirectly and in a degree, the power to revise the action of other departments
and to pronounce it null. In simple truth, while this is a mere judicial function,
it involves, owing to the subject-matter with which it deals, taking a part, a
secondary part, in the political conduct of government. If that be so, then the
judges must apply methods and principles that befit their task. In such a work
there can be no permanent or fitting *modus vivendi* between the different de-

partments unless each is sure of the full co-operation of the others, so long as its own action conforms to any reasonable and fairly permissible view of its constitutional power. The ultimate arbiter of what is rational and permissible is indeed always the courts, so far as litigated cases bring the question before them. This leaves to our courts a great and stately jurisdiction. It will only imperil the whole of it if it is sought to give them more. They must not step into the shoes of the law-maker, or be unmindful of the hint that is found in the sagacious remark of an English bishop nearly two centuries ago, quoted lately from Mr. Justice Holmes[50]:

> "Whoever hath an absolute authority to interpret any written or spoken laws, it is he who is truly the lawmaker, to all intents and purposes, and not the person who first wrote or spoke them."[51]

V. Finally, let me briefly mention one or two discriminations which are often overlooked, and which are important in order to a clear understanding of the matter. Judges sometimes have occasion to express an opinion upon the constitutionality of a statute, when the rule which we have been considering has no application, or a different application from the common one. There are at least three situations which should be distinguished: (1) where judges pass upon the validity of the acts of a co-ordinate department; (2) where they act as advisers of the other departments; (3) where as representing a government of paramount authority, they deal with acts of a department which is not co-ordinate.

(1) The case of a court passing upon the validity of the act of a co-ordinate department is the normal situation, to which the previous observations mainly apply. I need say no more about that.

(2) As regards the second case, the giving of advisory opinions, this, in reality, is not the exercise of the judicial function at all, and the opinions thus given have not the quality of judicial authority.[52] A single exceptional and unsupported opinion upon this subject, in the State of Maine, made at a time of great political excitement,[53] and a doctrine in the State of Colorado, founded upon considerations peculiar to the constitution of that State,[54] do not call for any qualification of the general remark, that such opinions, given by our judges, – like that well-known class of opinions given by the judges in England when advising the House of Lords, which suggested our own practice, – are merely advisory, and in no sense authoritative judgments.[55] Under our constitutions such opinions are not generally given. In the six or seven States where the constitutions provide for them, it is the practice to report these opinions among the regular decisions, much as the responses of the judges in Queen Caroline's Case, and in MacNaghten's Case, in England, are reported, and sometimes cited, as if they held equal rank with true adjudications. As regards such opinions, the scruples, cautions, and warnings of which I have been speaking, and the rule about a reasonable doubt, which we have seen emphasized by the courts as regards judicial decisions upon the constitutionality of

laws, have no application. What is asked for is the judge's own opinion.

(3) Under the third head come the questions arising out of the existence of our double system, with two written constitutions, and two governments, one of which, within its sphere, is of higher authority than the other. The relation to the States of the paramount government as a whole, and its duty in all questions involving the powers of the general government to maintain that power as against the States in its fullness, seem to fix also the duty of each of its departments; namely, that of maintaining this paramount authority in its true and just proportions, to be determined by itself. If a State legislature passes a law which is impeached in the due course of litigation before the national courts, as being in conflict with the supreme law of the land, those courts may have to ask themselves a question different from that which would be applicable if the enactments were those of a co-ordinate department. When the question relates to what is admitted not to belong to the national power, then whoever construes a State constitution, whether the State or national judiciary, must allow to that legislature the full range of rational construction. But when the question is whether State action be or be not conformable to the paramount constitution, the supreme law of the land, we have a different matter in hand. Fundamentally, it involves the allotment of power between the two governments, – where the line is to be drawn. True, the judiciary is still debating whether a legislature has transgressed its limit; but the departments are not co-ordinate, and the limit is at a different point. The judiciary now speaks as representing a paramount constitution and government, whose duty it is, in all its departments, to allow to that constitution nothing less than its just and true interpretation; and having fixed this, to guard it against any inroads from without.

I have been speaking of the national judiciary. As to how the State judiciary should treat a question of the conformity of an Act of their own legislature to the paramount constitution, it has been plausibly said that they should be governed by the same rule that the Federal courts would apply. Since an appeal lies to the Federal courts, these two tribunals, it has been said, should proceed on the same rule, as being parts of one system. But under the Judiciary Act an appeal does not lie from every decision; it only lies when the State law is *sustained* below. It would perhaps be sound on general principles, even if an appeal were allowed in all cases, here also to adhere to the general rule that judges should follow any permissible view which the co-ordinate legislature has adopted. At any rate, under existing legislation it seems proper in the State court to do this, for the practical reason that this is necessary in order to preserve the right of appeal.[56]

The view which has thus been presented seems to me highly important. I am not stating a new doctrine, but attempting to restate more exactly and truly an admitted one. If what I have said be sound, it is greatly to be desired that it should be more emphasized by our courts, in its full significance. It has been often remarked that private rights are more respected by the legislatures of some countries which have no written constitution, than by ours. No doubt our doctrine of constitutional law has had a tendency to drive out questions of justice and right, and to fill the mind of legislators with thoughts of mere legality, of what the constitution allows. And moreover, even in the matter of legality, they have felt little responsibility; if we are wrong, they say, the courts will correct it.[57] If what I have been saying is true, the safe and permanent road towards reform is that of impressing upon our people a far stronger sense than they have of the great range of possible harm and evil that our system leaves open, and must leave open, to the legislatures, and of the clear limits of judicial power; so that responsibility may be brought sharply home where it belongs. The checking and cutting down of legislative power, by numerous detailed prohibitions in the constitution, cannot be accomplished without making the government petty and incompetent. This process has already been carried much too far in some of our States. Under no system can the power of courts go far to save a people from ruin; our chief protection lies elsewhere. If this be true, it is of the greatest public importance to put the matter in its true light.[58]

JAMES B. THAYER

Cambridge

NOTES

a. Wallace Mendelson, "The Influence of James B. Thayer upon the Work of Holmes, Brandeis and Frankfurter," in *Supreme Court Statecraft: The Rule of Law and Men,* ed. Wallace Mendelson (Ames, Iowa: Iowa State Univ. Press, 1985), 3.

b. Ibid.

c. Ibid., 5–17.

d. *Harvard Law Review* 7(October 1893): 129–56. Copyright © 1893 by the Harvard Law Review Association. Used by permission.

1. Read at Chicago, August 9, 1893, before the Congress on Jurisprudence and Law Reform.

2. This opinion has fallen strangely out of sight. It has much the ablest discussion of the question which I have ever seen, not excepting the judgment of Marshall in Marbury *v.* Madison, which, as I venture to think, has been overpraised. Gibson afterwards accepted the generally received doctrine. "I have changed that opinion," said the Chief Justice to counsel, in Norris *v.* Clymer, 2 Pa. St., p. 281 (1845), "for two reasons. The late convention [apparently the one preceding the Pennsylvania constitution of 1838] by their silence sanctioned the pretensions of the courts to deal freely with the Acts of the legislature; and from experience of the necessity of the case."

3. Ch. ii.p. 127, 3d ed. President Rogers, in the preface to a valuable collection of papers on the "Constitutional History of the United States, as seen in the Development of American Law," p. II, remarks that "there is not in Europe to this day a court with authority to pass on the constitutionality of national laws. But in Germany and Switzerland, while the Federal courts cannot annul a Federal law, they may, in either country,

declare a cantonal or State law invalid when it conflicts with the Federal law." Compare Dicey, *ubi supra*, and Bryce, Am. Com., i. 430, note (1st ed.), as to possible qualifications of this statement.

4. For the famous cases of Lechmere *v.* Winthrop (1727–28), Phillips *v.* Savage (1734), and Clark *v.* Tousey (1745), see the Talcott Papers, Conn. Hist. Soc. Coll., iv. 94, note. For the reference to this volume I am indebted to the Hon. Mellen Chamberlain, of Boston. The decree of the Privy Council, in Lechmere *v.* Winthrop, declaring "null and void" a provincial Act of nearly thirty years' standing, is found in Mass. Hist. Soc. Coll., sixth series, v. 496.

5. Varnum's Report of the case (Providence, 1787); s.c.2 Chandler's Crim. Trials, 269.

6. And so of the excitement aroused by the alleged setting aside of a legislative Act in New York in 1784, in the case of Rutgers *v.* Waddington. Dawson's edition of this case, "With an Historical Introduction" (Morrisania, 1866), pp. xxiv *et seq.* In an "Address to the People of the State," issued by the committee of a public meeting of "the violent Whigs," it was declared (pp. xxxiii) "That there should be a power vested in Courts of Judicature, whereby they might control the Supreme Legislative power, we think is absurd in itself. Such powers in courts would be destructive of liberty, and remove all security of property." For the reference to this case, and a number of others, I am indebted to a learned article on "The Relation of the Judiciary to the Constitution" (19 Am. Law Rev. 175) by William M. Meigs, Esq., of the Philadelphia bar. It gives all the earliest cases. As Mr. Meigs remarks, the New York case does not appear to be really one of holding a law *unconstitutional.*

7. Dupuy *v.* Wickwire, I. D. Chipman, 237.

8. This subject is well considered in a learned note to Paxton's Case (1761), Quincy's Rep. 51, relating to Writs of Assistance, understood to have been prepared by Horace Gray, Esq., now Mr. Justice Gray, of the Supreme Court of the United States. See the note at pp. 520–530. James Otis had urged in his argument that "an Act of Parliament against the Constitution is void" (Quincy, 56, n., 474). The American cases sometimes referred to as deciding that a legislative Act was void, as being contrary to the first principles of morals or of government, – *e.g.*, in Quincy, 529, citing Bowman *v.* Middleton, I Bay, 252, and in I Bryce, Am. Com., 431, n., 1st ed., citing Gardner *v.* Newburgh, Johns. Ch. Rep. 162, – will be found, on a careful examination, to require no such explanation.

9. Vol. i., pp. 50 *et seq.*

10. Cooley, Const. Lim., 6th ed., 193, n.; I Chase's Statutes of Ohio, preface, 38–40. For the last reference I am indebted to my colleague, Professor Wambaugh.

11. Part I. Art. 30.

12. Art. I.

13. Journal of the Michigan Pol. Sc. Association, vol. i, p. 47.

14. The constitution of Columbia, of 1886, art. 84, provides that the judges of the Supreme Court may take part in the legislative debates over "bills relating to civil matters and judicial procedure." And in the case of legislative bills which are objected to by "the government" as unconstitutional, if the legislature insist on the bill, as against a veto by the government, it shall be submitted to the Supreme Court, which is to decide upon this question finally. Arts. 90 and 150. See a translation of this constitution by Professor Moses, of the University of California, in the supplement to the Annals of the American Academy of Political and Social Science, for January, 1893.

We are much too apt to think of the judicial power of revising the acts of the other departments as our only protection against oppression and ruin. But it is remarkable how small a part this played in any of the debates. The chief protections were a wide suffrage, short terms of office, a double legislative chamber, and the so-called executive veto. There was, in general, the greatest unwillingness to give the judiciary any share in the law-making power. In New York, however, the constitution of 1777 provided a Council of Revision, of which several of the judges were members, to whom all legislative Acts should be submitted before they took effect, and by whom they must be approved. That existed for more than forty years, giving way in the constitution of 1821 to the common expedient of merely requiring the approval of the executive, or in the alternative, if he refused it, the repassing of the Act, perhaps by an increased vote, by both branches of the legislature. In Pennsylvania (Const. of 1776, –47) and Vermont (Const. of 1777, –44) a Council of Censors was provided for, to be chosen every seven years, who were to investigate the conduct of affairs, and point out, among other things, all violations of the constitution by any of the departments. In Pennsylvania this arrangement lasted only from 1776 to 1790; in Vermont from 1777 to 1870. In framing the constitution of the United States, several of these expedients, and others, were urged, and at times adopted; *e.g.*, that of New York. It was proposed at various times that the general government should have a negative on all the legislation of the States; that the governors of the States should be appointed by the United States, and should have a negative on State legislation; that a Privy Council to the President should be appointed, composed in part of the judges; and that the President and the two houses of Congress might obtain opinions from the Supreme Court. But at last the convention, rejecting all these, settled down upon the common expedients of two legislative houses, to be a check upon each other, and of an executive revision and veto, qualified by the legislative power of reconsideration and enactment by a majority of two-thirds; – upon these expedients, and upon the declaration that the constitution, and constitutional laws and treaties, shall be the supreme law of the land, and shall bind the judges of the several States. This provision, as the phrasing of it indicates, was inserted with an eye to secure the authority of the general government as against the States, *i.e.* as an essential feature of any efficient Federal system, and not with direct reference to the other departments of the government of the United States itself. The first form of it was that "legislative Acts of the United States, and treaties, are the supreme law of the respective States, and bind the judges there as against their own laws."

15. No. 78, first published on May 28, 1788. See Lodge's edition, pp. xxxvi and xliv.

16. Den d. Bayard *v.* Singleton, I Martin, 42.

17. Vol I, p. 460.

18. Kemper *v.* Hawkins, Va. Cas. 20.

19. Vanhorne's Lessee *v.* Dorrance, 2 Dall. 304.

20. Lindsay *v.* Com'rs, 2 Bay, 38.

21. Whittington *v.* Polk, I H. & J. 236.

22. I Cranch, 137.

23. Com. *v.* Smith, 4 Bin. 117.

24. Com. *v* Call, 4 Call, 5.

25. Kemper *v.* Hawkins, Va. Cases, p. 60.

26. 5 Ell. Deb. 344.

27. Ware *v.* Hylton, 3 Dall. 171.

28. Cooper *v.* Telfair, 4 Dall. 14.

29. Grimball *v.* Ross, Charlton, 175.

30. Adm'rs of Byrne *v.* Adm'rs of Stewart, 3 Des. 466.

31. This well-known rule is laid down by Cooley (Const. Lim., 6th ed., 216), and supported by emphatic judicial declarations and by a long list of citations from all parts of the country. In Ogden *v.* Saunders, 12 Wheat. 213 (1827), Mr. Justice Washington, after remarking that the question was a doubtful one, said: "If I could rest my opinion in favor of the constitutionality of the law . . . on no other ground than this doubt, so felt and acknowledged, that alone would, in my estimation, be a satisfactory vindication of it. It is but a decent respect due to the . . . legislative body by which any law is passed, to presume in favor of its validity, until its violation of the constitution is proved beyond all reasonable doubt. This has always been the language of this court when that subject has called for its decision; and I know it expresses the honest sentiments of each and every member of this bench." In the Sinking Fund Cases, 99 U.S. 700 (1878), Chief Justice Waite, for the court, said: "This declaration [that an Act of Congress is unconstitutional] should never be made except in a clear case. Every possible presumption is in favor of the validity of a statute, and this continues until the contrary is shown beyond a rational doubt. One branch of the government cannot encroach on the domain of another without danger. The safety of our institutions depends in no small degree on a strict observance of this salutary rule." In Wellington *et al.,* Petitioners, 16 Pick. 87 (1834), Chief Justice Shaw, for the court, remarked that it was proper "to repeat what has been so often suggested by courts of justice, that when called upon to pronounce the invalidity of an Act of legislation [they will] never declare a statute void unless the nullity and invalidity of the Act are placed, in their judgment, beyond reasonable doubt." In Com. *v.* Five Cents Sav. Bk., 5 Allen, 428 (1862), Chief Justice Bigelow, for the court, said: "It may be well to repeat the rule of exposition which has been often enunciated by this court, that where a statute has been passed with all the forms and solemnities required to give it the force of law, the presumption is in favor of its validity, and that the court will not declare it to be . . . void unless its invalidity is established beyond reasonable doubt." And he goes on to state a corollary of this "well-established rule." In *Ex-parte* M'Collum, I Cow. p. 564 (1823), Cowen, J. (for the court), said: "Before the court will deem it their duty to declare an Act of the legislature unconstitutional, a case must be presented in which there can be no rational doubt." In the People *v.* The Supervisors of Orange, 17 N.Y. 235 (1858), Harris, J. (for the court), said: "A legislative Act is not to be declared void upon a mere conflict of interpretation between the legislative and the judicial power. Before proceeding to annul, by judicial sentence, what has been enacted by the law-making power, it should clearly appear that the Act cannot be supported by any reasonable intendment or allowable presumption." In Perry *v.* Keene, 56 N.H. 514, 534 (1876), Ladd, J. (with the concurrence of the rest of the court), said: "Certainly it is not for the court to shrink from the discharge of a constitutional duty; but, at the same time, it is not for this branch of the government to set an example of encroachment upon the province of the others. It is only the enunciation of a rule that is now elementary in the American States, to say that before we can declare this law unconstitutional, we must be fully satisfied – satisfied beyond a reasonable doubt – that the purpose for which the tax is authorized is private, and not public." In The Cincinnati, etc., Railroad Company, I Oh. St. 77 (1852), Ranney, J. (for the court), said: "While the right and duty of interference in a proper case are thus undeniably clear, the principles by which a court should be guided in such an inquiry are equally clear, both upon principle and authority. . . . It is only when manifest assumption of authority and clear incompatibility between the constitution and the law appear, that the judicial power can refuse to execute it. Such interference can never be permitted in a doubtful case. And this results from the very nature of the question involved in the

inquiry. . . . The adjudged cases speak a uniform language on this subject. . . . An unbroken chain of decisions to the same effect is to be found in the State courts." In Syndics of Brooks *v.* Weyman, 3 Martin (La.), 9, 12 (1813), it was said by the court: "We reserve to ourselves the authority to declare null any legislative Act which shall be repugnant to the constitution; but it must be manifestly so, not susceptible of doubt." (Cited with approval in Johnson *v* Duncan, Ib. 539.) In Cotton *v.* The County Commissioners, 6 Fla. 610 (1856), Dupont, J. (for the court), said: "It is a most grave and important power, not to be exercised lightly or rashly, nor in any case where it cannot be made plainly to appear that the legislature has exceeded its powers. If there exist upon the mind of the court a reasonable doubt, that doubt must be given in favor of the law. . . . In further support of this position may be cited any number of decisions by the State courts. . . . If there be one to be found which constitutes an exception to the general doctrine, it has escaped our search."

32. Const. Lim., 6th ed., 68; cited with approval by Bryce, Am. Com., 1st ed., i. 431.

33. Eakin *v.* Raub, 12 S. & R. 330.

34. Farrar's Rep. Dart. Coll. Case, 36.

35. 7 Pick. 344.

36. Wellington, Petr., 16 Pick. 87.

37. 3d ed., 279–281.

38. It was so held in Riggs *v.* State, 3 Cold. 85 (Tenn., 1866), and United States *v.* Clark, 31 Fed. Rep. 710 (U.S. Circ. Ct., E. Dist. Michigan, 1887, Brown, J.). I am indebted for these cases to Professor Beale's valuable collection of Cases on Criminal Law (Cambridge, 1893). The same doctrine is laid down by Judge Hare in 2 Hare, Am. Const. Law, 920.

39. Cap. & Counties Bank *v.* Henty, 7 App. Cas., p. 776.

40. Belt *v.* Lawes, Thayer's Cas. Ev. 177, n.

41. Chic. &c. Ry. Co. *v.* Minnesota, 134 U.S. 418. The question was whether a statute providing for a commission to regulate railroad charges, which excluded the parties from access to the courts for an ultimate judicial revision of the action of the commission, was constitutional.

42. Compare Law and Fact in Jury Trials, 4 Harv. Law Rev. 167, 168.

43. There is often a lack of discrimination in judicial utterances on this subject, – as if it were supposed that the legislature had to conform to the judge's opinion of reasonableness in some other sense than that indicated above. The true view is indicated by Judge Cooley in his Principles of Const. Law, 2d ed., 57, when he says of a particular question: "Primarily the determination of what is a public purpose belongs to the legislature, and its action is subject to no review or restraint as long as it is not manifestly colorable. All cases of doubt must be solved in favor of the validity of legislative action, for the obvious reason that the question is legislative, and only becomes judicial when there is a plain excess of legislative authority. A court can only arrest the proceedings and declare a levy void when the absence of public interest in the purpose for which the funds are to be raised is so clear and palpable as to be perceptible to any mind at first blush." And again, on another question, by the Supreme Court of the United States, Waite, C. J., in Terry *v.* Anderson, 95 U.S. p. 633: "In all such cases the question is one of reasonableness, and we have therefore only to consider whether the time allowed in this Statute [of Limitations] is, under all the circumstances, reasonable. Of that the legislature is primarily the judge; and we cannot overrule the decision of that department of the government, unless a palpable error has been committed." See Pickering Phipps *v.* Ry.

Co., 66 Law Times Rep. 721 (1892), and a valuable opinion by Ladd, J., in Perry v. Keene, 56 N.H. 514 (1876).

44. Eakin v. Raub, 12 S. & R., p. 355.

45. Fletcher v. Peck, 6 Cr., p. 131.

46. Cap. & Count, Bank v. Henty, 7 App. Cas. 741.

47. 4 Wheat. 316.

48. Per Thomas, J., the Opinion of Justices, 8 Gray, p. 21.

49. "It matters little," says a depressed, but interesting and incisive writer, in commenting, in 1885, upon the Legal Tender decisions of the Supreme Court of the United States, "for the court has fallen, and it is not probable it can ever again act as an effective check upon the popular will, or should it attempt to do so, that it can prevail." The "Consolidation of the Colonies," by Brooks Adams, 55 Atlantic Monthly, 307.

50. By Professor Gray in 6 Harv. Law Rev. 33, n., where he justly refers to the remark as showing "that gentlemen of the short robe have sometimes grasped fundamental legal principles better than many lawyers."

51. Bishop Hoadly's Sermon preached before the King, March 31, 1717, on "The Nature of the Kingdom or Church of Christ." London: James Knapton, 1717. It should be remarked that Bishop Hoadly is speaking of a situation where the supposed legislator, after once issuing his enactment, never interposes. That is not strictly the case in hand; yet we may recall what Dicey says of amending the constitution of the United States: "The sovereign of the United States has been roused to serious action but once during the course of ninety years. It needed the thunder of the Civil War to break his repose, and it may be doubted whether anything short of impending revolution will ever again arouse him to activity. But a monarch who slumbers for years is like a monarch who does not exist. A federal constitution is capable of change, but, for all that, a federal constitution is apt to be unchangeable."

52. Com. v. Green, 12 Allen, p. 163; Taylor v. Place, 4 R.I., p. 362. See Thayer's Memorandum on Advisory Opinions (Boston, 1885), Jameson, Const. Conv., 4th ed., Appendix, note e, p. 667, and a valuable article by H. A. Dubuque, in 24 Am. Law Rev. 369 on "The Duty of Judges as Constitutional Advisers."

53. Opinion of Justices, 70 Me., p. 583 (1880). Contra, Kent, J., in 58 Me., p. 573 (1870): "It is true, unquestionably, that the opinions given under a requisition like this have no judicial force, and cannot bind or control the action of any officer of any department. They have never been regarded as binding on the body asking for them." And so Tapley, J., ibid, p. 615: "Never regarding the opinions thus formed as conclusive, but open to review upon every proper occasion;" and Libby, J., in 72 Me., p. 562-3 (1881): "Inasmuch as any opinion now given can have no effect if the matter should be judicially brought before the court by the proper process, and lest, in declining to answer, I may omit the performance of a constitutional duty, I will very briefly express my opinion upon the question submitted." Walton, J., concurred; the other judges said nothing on this point.

54. In re Senate Bill, 12 Colo. 466,—an opinion which seems to me, in some respects ill considered.

55. Macqueen's Pract. Ho. of Lords, pp. 49, 50.

56. Gibson, J., in Eakin v. Raub, 12 S. & R., p. 357. Compare Ib., p. 352. The same result is reached by the court, on general principles, in the Tonnage Tax Cases, 62 Pa. St. 286: "A case of simple doubt should be resolved favorably to the State law, leaving the correction of the error, if it be one, to the Federal judiciary. The presumption in favor of a co-ordinate branch of the State government, the relation of her courts to the State, and,

above all, the necessity of preserving a financial system so vital to her welfare, demand this at our hands" (Agnew, J., for the court).

57. "A singular result of the importance of constitutional interpretation in the American government . . . is this, that the United States legislature has been very largely occupied in purely legal discussions. . . . Legal issues are apt to dwarf and obscure the more substantially important issue of principle and policy, distracting from these latter the attention of the nation as well as the skill of congressional debaters." – I Bryce, Am. Com., 1st ed., 377. On page 378 he cites one of the best-known writers on constitutional law, Judge Hare, as saying that "In the refined and subtle discussion which ensues, right is too often lost sight of, or treated as if it were synonymous with might. It is taken for granted that what the constitution permits it also approves, and that measures which are legal cannot be contrary to morals." See also Ib., 410.

58. La volonté populaire: tel est, dans les pays libres de l'ancien et du Nouveau Monde, la source et la fin de tout pouvoir. Tant qu'elle est saine, les nations prospèrent malgré les imperfections et les lacunes de leurs institutions; si le bon sens fait defaut, si les passions l'emportent, les constitutions les plus parfaites, les lois les plus sages, sont impuissantes. La maxime d'un ancien: *quid leges sine moribus?* est, en somme, le dernier mot de la science politique. – *Le Système Judiciaire de la Grande Bretagne,* by le Comte de Franqueville, i. 25 (Paris: J. Rothschild, 1893).

8

In Defense of Judicial Review

P ROFESSOR THAYER'S seminal argument in favor of judicial self-restraint seemed to have little initial impact upon the behavior of the Supreme Court. In *Lochner* v. *New York* (198 U.S. 45) in 1905 the Court moved to strike down a New York statute regulating the working conditions of bakery workers. In his famous dissent Oliver Wendell Holmes applied the Thayer standard, finding the law in question reasonable and therefore constitutional.

In the face of rising controversy surrounding the Court's activism in apparent opposition to government regulation of the economy, Supreme Court Associate Justice Horace H. Lurton rose to defend the institution against its critics. Few men were more suitable for the task, whether on the basis of conviction or of deed.

One-time law professor and dean at the Vanderbilt University Law School, Lurton was an elected member of the Tennessee Supreme Court, where he served for a few months as its chief justice. He was then appointed by President Cleveland to the Circuit Court of Appeals for the sixth circuit, of which William Howard Taft was the presiding judge. When Lurton, a Democrat, was appointed in 1910 at the age of sixty-six to the U.S. Supreme Court by Republican President Taft, some were surprised. Political party affiliation is an important factor in presidential nominations to the high court. However, in this instance ideology and personal friendship played a dominant role. The conservative Taft was pleased to appoint a man who had little sympathy for the

notion that the Constitution should be interpreted to reflect changing
social conditions—that the Supreme Court is a continuous constitutional convention.

Mr. Justice Lurton argues that public opinion and the oath of office are not sufficient guarantees that legislators will stay within constitutional boundaries when promulgating laws. Lurton proceeds from
the premises first enunciated by Montesquieu in *The Spirit of the Laws*
(1748). The great French scholar of the eighteenth century maintained
that liberty could not be maintained without a separation of powers
among the legislative, executive, and judicial functions. Lurton argues
that American history supports the contention that the exercise of
judicial review is an obligation of the judiciary as a guarantor of liberty.

Not only does Lurton present early case law in support of judicial
review, but he also asserts that its practice was accepted by the people
in the early years of the Republic. Unfortunately, however, the enormous mass of new immigrants, "unaccustomed to democratic government," consider the judicial veto to be a usurpation of legislative
authority. Justice Lurton then proceeds to instruct that in a government of laws there is no such thing as unlimited power. Rather, all
power is delegated.

Thus when courts exercise judicial review they are not legislating
or employing uncontrolled political power. They are applying the elementary principle that "the acts of an agent in excess of his authority
do not bind his principal." Judges in such instances have no choice but
to "enforce the constitution as the law of highest obligation."

When reading Lurton's article, consider the unstated premise that
law and politics are somehow separate and distinct; that the judge's
role is simply to find the law, not to make it. Indeed, the widespread
belief that legal rules are superior to individual choice is the genesis of
the phrase "a nation of laws, not of men." The ideology of legalism
which is summarized in this phrase has as much attraction today as it
did when Lurton wrote his article more than three quarters of a century ago. The search for neutral principles of law and objectivity in
decision making is a recurring theme in American law. As long as
humans believe that their decisions should be based upon principles
transcending self-interest and subjectivity, essays such as the one that
follows will be written. Nonetheless, how we believe we *ought* to behave is not always how we in *fact* behave. The confusion of a value
prescription with a factual description is as common to judges as it is to
ordinary mortals.

A Government of Law or a
Government of Men?[a]

Horace H. Lurton

WHICH SHALL IT BE, a government of law or a government of men? As the alternative to a government of law is a despotism, whether the despots be many or one, benevolent or malignant, the question admits of but one answer. But are we not more or less conscious of a restless tugging against the bonds of the law and the yoke of the Constitution? Is there not a growing disposition to disregard the limitations which we have placed upon those in authority and a tendency to applaud the doing of things which we wish done, regardless of whether lawful or unlawful? If one in power does things which displease us, we are swift to inquire into his authority; but is that so if the thing done meets with our approval?

The tendency to throw off the obligation of a rigid Constitution has attracted the attention of so wise and intelligent an observer as Mr. James Bryce, now British Ambassador to the United States, who, in a forceful essay on Flexible and Rigid Constitutions, when referring to the protection afforded by rigid constitutions to the minority as a leading argument for their continuance, says:

> "A change of view has, however, become noticeable within the last few years. In the new democracies of the United States . . . the multitude no longer fear abuse of power by its rulers. It is itself the ruler, accustomed to be coaxed and flattered. It feels no need for the protection which rigid constitutions give. And in the United States it chafes under these restrictions of legislative power embodied in the Federal Constitution or State Constitutions (as the case may be) which have surrounded the rights of property and the obligation of subsisting contracts with safeguards obnoxious not only to the party called 'Socialists,' but to reformers of other type. As these safeguards are sometimes thought to prevent the application of needed remedies and to secure impunity for abuses which have become intrenched behind them, the aforesaid constitutional provisions have incurred criticism and censure from various sections, and many attempts have been made by State Legislature . . . to disregard or evade these restrictions. These attempts are usually defeated by the action of Courts, when it happens that both the Federal Constitution and the functions of the Judiciary are often attacked in the country which was so extravagantly proud of both institutions a half-century ago. This strife between the bench as the defenders of old-fashioned doctrines, embodied in the provisions of a rigid constitution (Federal or State) and of State Legislatures acting at the bidding of a large section of voters, is a remarkable feature of contemporary America."

Has this disinterested and most wise observer overdrawn the dangers which threaten our institutions? Has he mistaken the direction in which we are drifting, or the magnitude of the factors which are undermining our fundamental law, National and State?

Is the obligation to support and uphold the Constitution and the laws made in pursuance thereof dependent upon whether the legislative body, the executive or the judge shall think the public welfare will be best promoted by its enforcement or its disregard? May a legislative body disregard a plain constitutional limitation merely because it may think the public welfare thereby promoted? May a Court disregard a plain law constitutionally passed merely because it may think it unjust or unwise? May one charged with the enforcement or execution of the law decline to execute it as written and modify it if it deems the public good thereby advanced?

One may read and hear upon every hand such sentiments as this: "The law is a means, not an end; a means to be used for the public good, to be modified for the public good and to be interpreted for the public good." Neither do the outcries against constitutional restraints come only from those who find in them barriers against assaults upon property and contract rights, but from the very class who are supposed to be sheltered from popular legislation by the safeguards which a large section of voters wish to sweep away. There is a widely circulated address by one of the ablest of our business men, the head of one of the most important of our great business corporations, complaining of the restraints and inconveniences due to the authority exercised by the States and by limitations upon Federal power, wherein he says:

> "Cries for Federal control are the growing-pains of a great people. Let Senator Root and all others who are leaders make no mistake. The people of the country are not afraid of themselves, and they are no more doubtful of their power as citizens of the United States than they are of their power as citizens of the States. They see their opportunity and they will not try to run away from it. On the contrary, they will crowd every opportunity. Having a given thing to do in common, no one can persuade them that they cannot do it better by doing it once for all than by doing it forty-six times."

Despairing of relief by amending the Federal Constitution from the fate of effort in that direction in the past, he points out that the needful enlargement of Federal power will arise from the action of the Supreme Court, saying:

> "But the Constitution has been changed, nevertheless, and it will be changed again. Whatever the demands of the nation's growth and of the nation's welfare may be, whatever new and strange governmental problems may arise, the unwritten Constitution and the Supreme Court will be equal to them."

In the same line, a great journal, representing a large conservative class, lately referred to the Supreme Court as a "Continuous Constitutional Convention."

These views, taken from opposite poles of opinion, concur in establishing the existence of a great and impressive body of criticism of the very fundamentals upon which our American constitutional system rests. The seriousness of the matter lies not so much in that relaxation is desired with reference to restraint upon legislative power, Federal and State, as in the fact that such change is largely anticipated through an exercise of legislative powers by the Courts in expanding or modifying the Federal Constitution, under guise of constitutional construction, and in obedience to the bidding of an apparent majority public sentiment, as to obviate the necessity of amendment in the manner required by the instrument itself.

I do not propose to touch upon the merits of the ends which either class of opinion seek to advance by a letting down of the constitutional bars which stand in the way of assaults upon contract or property rights nor upon the advantages which are supposed to result to the "business interests" of the country by the unification of legislation affecting them. The thought to which I address myself is the effect upon our institutions if the time shall come when the judiciary shall cease to regard the line which separates judicial and legislative functions by either abdicating their authority as the expounders and defenders of constitutional restraint or by arrogating to themselves the right to destroy or modify a plain expression of legislative will when constitutionally expounded. The appeal to and criticism of the Courts is one which concerns the State Courts no less than the Courts of the Union, for the tendency is to obliterate the line which divides the legislative and judicial powers as well as the obligation which rests upon every Court to apply and enforce the law of the Constitution whenever it conflicts with the inferior law of ordinary legislation. The contention that the obligation of a Constitution is to be disregarded if it stands in the way of that which is deemed of public advantage, or that a valid law, under the Constitution, is to be interpreted or modified so as to accomplish that which the executive administering it, or a Court called upon to enforce it, shall deem to the public advantage, is destructive of the whole theory upon which our American Commonwealths have been founded, to say nothing of the constitutional relation of the Union and the States to each other. It is a substitution of a government of men for a government of law. It is against this that I warn.

Two political dogmas were of universal acceptance among the generation which converted thirteen dependent colonies into thirteen independent sovereign States, and which later converted these States into an indissoluble union of indissoluble States. These dogmas were: first, that all power resides in the people and that they might institute such government as they saw fit, and that authority conferred by the organic instrument creating such governments was a delegated authority limited by the creative act of the people; and, second, that the best security against usurpation of power would be found in a distribution of the functions of government between independent departments.

In passing, it may be observed that the idea of an absolute democracy found no favor whatever. However valuable or desirable direct popular legislation may be in a small community of intelligent and conservative citizens, the

notion was universally regarded as absolutely unworkable upon any large
scale. Hence, the model upon which the State and Federal Governments were
constituted was that of a representative constitutional democracy, and the
guarantee to each State of a republican form of government found in the
Federal Constitution refers obviously to the character of republican governments which then existed, a form inconsistent with a pure or absolute democracy.

The thought to which I particularly wish to direct attention concerns the
distribution of the powers of government.

Nearly a half-century before our Federal Constitution emerged, Montesquieu formulated and defended upon unanswerable philosophical and historical considerations the dogma that neither public nor private liberty could be
maintained without a division of the legislative, executive and judicial functions of government. His great treatise upon the Spirit of Laws had then been
long translated into the language of every civilized country; was well known to
the thoughtful and educated of every nation and had acquired a prodigious
influence throughout Europe and America. Concerning the influence of Montesquieu upon the men who made or brought about the adoption of our Federal
Constitution, Mr. Bryce, the most discerning and capable of those foreigners
who have written of our institutions, in his "American Commonwealth," says:

> "No general principle of politics laid such hold on the Constitution-makers
> and statesmen of America as the dogma that the separation of these three
> functions is essential to freedom. It had already been made the groundwork
> of several State Constitutions. It is always reappearing in their writings; it
> was never absent from their thoughts."

After a comparison of the condition of the people of Continental Europe
with that of the English and a consideration of the governments which then
existed, Montesquieu thus states his conclusion in respect to the wisdom of
such a division of power:

> "There is no liberty, if the judiciary power be not separated from the legis-
> lative and executive. Were it joined with the legislative, the life and liberty
> of the subject would be exposed to arbitrary control; for the judge would
> then be the legislator. Were it joined to the executive power, the judge
> might behave with violence and oppression. Then would be an end of
> everything, were the same men or the same body to exercise these three
> powers, that of enacting laws, that of executing them and of trying the
> cases of individuals."

Fundamental as such a separation has come to be regarded by all who
love liberty regulated by law, it was almost a novel conception when developed
by Montesquieu. The government of England afforded the nearest approach to
such a system, and from a comparison of the operation of the English plan and
of the English people and their institutions with the governments and condition of the people of Continental States, he deduced the dogma as one of

necessary application in every free State. The colonies as they converted themselves into States took care to embody this separation dogma in their Bill of Rights, a method of putting the matter upon an even higher authority than the Constitution itself, if that were possible. Thus Virginia wrote into her Bill of Rights of June 12th, 1776, that the legislative and executive powers of the State should be separate and distinct from the judiciary. Maryland inserted in her Bill of Rights of November 11th, 1776, the statement:

> "That the legislative, executive and judicial powers of government ought to be forever separate and distinct from each other."

The declaration in the Massachusetts Bill of Rights is particularly emphatic. It reads:

> "In the government of this commonwealth, the legislative department shall never exercise the executive and judicial powers, or either of them; the executive shall never exercise the legislative and judicial powers, or either of them; the judiciary shall never exercise the legislative and excutive powers, or either of them; to the end it may be a government of laws and not men."

It followed from the settled practice of the States in the organization of their respective State governments that when, many years later, the formation of the present Federal Constitution was begun the same separation of powers to be exercised by the Union was made the corner-stone of the structure. Thus by Section 1, Article 1, it is provided that:

> "All legislative powers herein granted shall be vested in a Congress of the United States, which shall consist of a Senate and a House of Representatives."

By Section 1, of Article 2, it is declared that the executive power shall be vested in a President of the United States of America, and by Section 1, of Article 3, it is said that:

> "The judicial power of the United States shall be vested in one Supreme Court, and in such inferior Courts as the Congress may from time to time ordain and establish."

In the organization of the States the same plan is adopted, and the judicial power is vested in the Courts created by the State in much the same definite terms.

That the exercise of power vested in one branch by another would be a usurpation, and as such null and void, is too plain to need argument.

Thus, to take the case of Congress, it is vested with the entire legislative power delegated by the Constitution. By necessary implication no other department can constitutionally exercise any power which is legislative. Neither can the Congress exercise any power which is either executive or judicial, for the very obvious reason that no such power has been granted to it, and also for the reason that whatever the executive power of the United States is, it has been exclusively vested in the President. So with the judicial power of the United States—that power, whatever it is, is, by the Constitution, vested only in the Courts of the United States, and may, therefore, be exerted only by the Courts.

What is the security against a usurpation of power by one department which belongs to another?

There is, of course, the force of public opinion. So long as there is entertained by any decided majority of the people a serious and earnest conviction that the encroachment of one branch of the government upon the domain of another must be resisted at every cost, the boundary line is not likely to be wilfully overstepped. Then there is the solemn obligation of the oath which presumptively binds the conscience of every legislator, executive and judge, that he will respect and obey the organic law, which includes this distribution of powers. These are the only sanctions possessed by the people of any other land for the maintenance of any limitation upon the legislative power. But if these prove unavailing, as they have proven many times, and the executive undertakes to exercise legislative or judicial power, or the legislative body shall assume to combine the functions which pertain to either of the other departments, how shall such usurpation of power be resisted, or the executive trespass be restrained, or the legislative enactment be nullified? Other nations have endeavored, by organic popular legislation called constitutions, to restrain the power of the executive and legislative authority, but the only security provided against the violation of the boundaries thus set consisted in public opinion and the sanctity of an oath. Neither has proven effective. Having an unlimited power to interpret and apply such restrictions, the legislative power has in France, where there has been a succession of constitutions, been found unrestrainable by any such barriers.

> "The limitations imposed by French constitutions are not [says Dicey in his Law of the Constitution] in reality laws, since they are not rules which in the last resort will be enforced by the Courts. Their true character is that of maxims of political morality, which derive whatever strength they have from being formally placed in the Constitution and from the resulting force of public opinion."

But under our American system of constitutional government, the power which the Courts have to determine the invalidity of a legislative or executive act as in excess of delegated constitutional power extends also to acts which are in violation of the distribution of governmental functions made by the organic law. While the executive power may not be restrained from the exercise of any executive duty, imperative or discretionary, yet if an official undertakes to do an act clearly unauthorized he is but a trespasser and may not resist the restraints of the Courts by holding up as a shield either the office which he holds, if he has exceeded his lawful power, or a statute which is no law because in excess of legislative power. It follows, of course, that rights cannot be enforced which wholly depend upon either a void executive or legislative foundation. The principle that the acts of an executive in excess of his lawful authority are void and restrainable is a well-settled principle of English law. "The principle," says Mr. Bryce in his "American Commonwealth," "is a corner-stone of English liberty."

In the one case as in the other the question can only arise for judicial determination in a justiciable matter involving rights of persons or property affected by the act of usurpation. Unless, therefore, the encroachment by one department upon the domain of the other becomes involved in a case justiciable in character, there is no way by which the separation of the functions of government may be made effective through the Courts.

Much of the popular opinion concerning the scope of the power of the Courts grows out of a misconception of the authority under which Courts assume to declare a legislative enactment void if found repugnant to the organic law of a constitution. From the beginning it has been claimed by American Courts as a proper function of the Courts under our American constitutional system. It is a doctrine which originated in the Courts of the States long before the adoption of the Federal Constitution. Professor Thayer, in his Constitutional Cases, refers to no less than five decisions by State Courts prior to the adoption of the Constitution of the United States, in which it was held that the power of State legislation was limited by constitutional restrictions, and that it was the duty of the judicial power to declare legislation repugnant to such superior law void and unenforceable whenever necessary to determine the rights of parties in pending cases. The earliest of reported cases is that of Commonwealth *v.* Caton, decided by the Virginia Court of Appeals in 1782. Neither that case, nor either of the decisions I refer to, are cited by Chief-Justice Marshall in Marbury *v.* Madison, although they afforded a body of opinion of commanding influence which one cannot suppose the great Chief Justice to have been ignorant of, especially as one of them was from his own State.

This doctrine was challenged by many extreme Republicans, and the principle was asserted by no less a statesman than Mr. Jefferson that a Legislature was itself the judge of the meaning and scope of a State Constitution, and that the Courts had no authority superior to the Legislature in applying the Constitution. The doctrine, however, was generally accepted, and at this time is regarded as a proper judicial function by an overwhelming majority of public opinion. But of late, with the great influx of an enormous mass of immigrants unaccustomed to democratic government and wholly unfamiliar with the American constitutional idea, there has been a great increase in the number of those voters who object to any restraint upon the will of the majority as voiced in either Congress or the State legislative assemblies, and therefore consider this power to annul a law as the usurpation of legislative authority.

That the power thus exercised in doing these things is not legislative, but judicial, will be plainly evident if we do but stop to consider the nature of an

American Constitution. If those instruments are merely accepted declarations of moral and political principles to which the people have given their assent and which officials are pledged to uphold, as is the case with a political party platform, then it is a flagrant act of usurpation and a defiance of the legislative will when the Courts refuse to give effect to legislation, even though it may violate so-called constitutional principles. The very corner-stone of American constitutional law is, that the instruments under which the State governments were organized, and the same is true of the Federal Constitution, were acts of organic sovereign legislation, defining and limiting the scope of the governments organized thereunder. It is, therefore, a profound fact that both State and Federal governments are governments exercising delegated, and therefore limited, powers. *There is no deposit of unlimited power in any government organized under the American system of constitutional governments.* It follows, therefore, that neither State nor Congressional legislation which is in excess of delegated power may be enacted or enforced without a disregard of the supreme will of the people as expressed in the underlying legislation contained in the constating instruments enacted by them.

From these conceptions result two kinds of law differing in authority:

(*a*) The organic underlying law, which we call a constitution, being law enacted by the people in their collective capacity as the source of authority and whereby they defined the powers delegated to each of the great governmental departments created by such primary enactments.

(*b*) Secondary law—that is, enactments by the legislative bodies organized under the primary and superior law contained in the Constitution.

But when the union of States was organized under the present Constitution, whereby there was delegated to the central government the powers therein enumerated, there arose another body of law superior to the primary law found in the State Constitutions. Thenceforward the legislation of a State Legislature was subject to comparison with three higher and superior kinds of law, and it was valid only: first, if it did not conflict with the Constitution of the State; second, if it did not conflict with a valid law of Congress; and, third, if it did not conflict with the Constitution of the United States.

The enactments of Congress were also subject to comparison with the Constitution of the United States, for if they conflicted therewith they were invalid as in excess of the granted powers of Congress.

As a result of these limitations upon the lawmaking power, Federal and State, the judicial power, when a case arose which required for its determination an application of the existing law, if there appeared to be a conflict between two applicable laws, is required to decide which was the law of higher obligation. There was nothing novel in the exercise of this authority. It was a function similar in character to that which the Courts had from all time been exercising when a conflict between two laws appeared. In such case, whether the conflict was between two sections of the same statute, or two statutes passed by the same legislative authority, the judge was compelled to say which was the law which it was his duty to enforce. If a conflict arose between a legislative enactment and a constitutional provision, it must follow that the law of higher obligation must be enforced and the conflicting law declared of no force because its enactment was in excess of the power of the enacting body. The authority exercised is no assumption of political or legislative power, but an application of the elementary rule that the acts of an agent in excess of his authority do not bind his principal. The clear obligation of the judge is to enforce the Constitution as the law of highest obligation. If the exercise of that duty requires him to declare that an enactment in the form of law is no law, because repugnant to the law of primary obligation, he is obviously obeying the supreme expression of the popular will as found in a law directly enacted by the sovereign authority of the people. That this function should not be understood by the millions who have come among us from lands where constitutional limitations are either unknown or are unenforceable for lack of any definite means of compelling obedience, and therefore regarded as an exercise of legislative power, is not strange. The American dogma that all power resides in the people, and that public officials of every class are but agents executing the power delegated to them through the direct legislation, which constitutes what we call a constitution, is the very root principle upon which we have organized our Federal as well as our State Governments. When this is understood there is no mystery to be explained, no usurpation to be defended when the judge declares that he must follow the superior rather than the inferior law.

That no English judge would venture to declare a statute void which had been in due course passed by the English Parliament is due to conditions fundamentally different from those which confront an American judge.

The so-called Constitution of that country consists only in a body of ancient usages, practices, understandings and statutes declaratory of the principles upon which the government is supposed to be administered. But none of the precedents or statutes have any authority higher than the Parliament itself, and hence do not stand in the way of any legislation whatever, although the effect be to repeal or alter the most fundamental of the principles upon which the government is supposed to be administered. Of these practices, usages or understandings constituting the English Constitution, the one least challenged or questioned is that the Parliament stands for and speaks with the voice of the whole British people. Its enactments stand, therefore, upon the same plane and are entitled to the same authority as the extraordinary legislation embodied in an American Constitution. So long as the English people are content to regard the voice of the English Parliament as the voice of the English people, and its enactments uncontrollable except by and through a subsequent Parliament, the English judge has no function to exercise which corresponds with that of an American judge when he declares a legislative act void as in conflict with a superior law of obligation. The constitutional duty of the English judge is to apply the enactments of Parliament as the law of highest obligation, there being under English institutions no superior law with which he may compare it, and hence no repugnancy to render it void and no excess of authority in its enactment.

The primary purpose of every such organic instrument of government is to limit the power and control the conduct of the legislative authority by an overruling Constitution, an instrument amendable or repealable only by the people in the manner of its enactment, or as provided by the instrument itself. In the course of events exigencies have arisen and may again arise where constitutional impediments prevent the attainment of ends through ordinary legislation which a temporary majority, or an impatient executive officer, may deem necessary in the public interest. Every such occasion operates as a strain upon the fundamental structure of our government. Whether the general interests will be best subserved by a disregard of constitutional barriers or by obedience to the slow processes for constitutional amendments is a question which goes to the very fundamentals of our institutions. To override constitutional methods spells revolution and tends to the destruction of a government of law. To yield to the clamor of a temporary majority upon the pretence that otherwise popular government is prevented is but to overthrow the barriers which the people themselves, under great deliberation, have erected against their own impulsive majorities. These impediments to hasty action are intended not only as bulwarks for the defence of minorities, but as defences against hotfooted action by temporary majorities in supposed exigencies.

The American scheme of limiting and controlling not only executive but legislative power by express constitutional limitations enforceable through the Courts was the single unique improvement in the art and science of government made by the generation which first embodied the idea in their several State Constitutions and then in that of the Union.

Speculative jurists have suggested that if legislation should be found absolutely unreasonable or opposed to a universal idea of natural justice that a Court might refuse to enforce or apply it, and here and there may be found a dictum to that effect. But Sir William Blackstone regarded the legislative power as so uncontrollable that no Court might justify a refusal to enforce it as law for any reason. Thus he says:

> "If the Parliament will positively enact a thing to be done which is unreasonable, I know of no power which can control it . . . for that were to set the judicial power above that of the legislative, which would be subversive of all government."

But he adds:

> "if some collateral matter arises out of the general words and happens to be unreasonable, then the judges are in decency to conclude that this consequence was not foreseen by the Parliament, and therefore they are at liberty to expound the statute by equity and only *quoad hoc* disregard it. Thus if an act of Parliament give a man power to try all causes that may

arise in his manor; yet if a cause should arise in which he himself is a party, the act is construed not to mean that, because it is unreasonable that any man should determine his own quarrel."

But this would not be to disregard or reject the act at all, but to enforce it according to the intent and purpose of the lawmakers, which, if the words be doubtful, is not to be regarded as intending that which would be unreasonable or contrary to natural justice. But Sir William Blackstone lays down in a very positive way that if the legislative power be unqualified, "no Court has the power to defeat the intent of the Legislature, when couched in such evident and express words as leave no doubt whether it was the intent of the Legislature or no."

In Calder *v.* Bull, 3 Dallas, 388, this question of whether it is within the scope of judicial power to refuse to give effect to a plain legislative enactment, which is not repugnant to the Constitution merely because the statute seems to be absurd and unreasonable, was discussed, and Mr. Justice Chase lays down one limitation which is of far-reaching importance—namely, that "the nature and ends of legislative power will limit the exercise of it." Mr. Justice Iredell in the same case seems to concur with Sir William Blackstone in the view that it is not for the Courts to set up their judgment against that of the lawmaking power as to the reasonableness or justice of a statute if its meaning be plain and the intent of the law unobscure.

The Constitution of the United States includes a specific enumeration of the subjects in respect to which the Congress may legislate. This is not true of most, if true of any, of our State Constitutions. There is usually a grant of legislative power limited by specific reservations. Referring to this, Judge Raney, in Cincinnati, etc., R. Co. *v.* Commission, 1, Ohio State, 77, 86, said, in reference to the extent of the legislative power under such grant, that "this must therefore always be determined from the nature of the power exercised. If it is found to fall within the general terms of the grant, we can only look to other parts of the Constitution for limitations upon it; if none are found none exist." He adds:

"But as the General Assembly, like the other departments of government, exercises only a delegated authority, it cannot be doubted that any act passed by it not falling fairly within the scope of legislative power is as clearly void as though expressly prohibited."

In Loan Association *v.* Topeka, 20 Wall, 655, Mr. Justice Miller, referring to the implied limitations upon the legislative power, said:

"There are limitations on such power which grow out of the essential nature of all free governments,"

and that legislation under the guise of taxation might, if the purpose was not public,

"none the less be robbery because it is done under the form of law and is called taxation. This is not legislation. It is a decree under legislative form."

When a legislative enactment goes so far as to infringe upon the fundamental maxims of a free government and disregard rights of person or property which it is the declared object of our governments, State and National, to secure, it will be generally found that every such act conflicts with some positive provision of both State and National organic law, and that it will not be necessary to resort to general maxims and unexpressed restraints dependent upon implied limitations.

Montesquieu has been cited as entertaining the notion that the judges have no power of construing or interpreting any constitutional or statute law. He says:

> "In republics the very nature of the constitution requires the judges to follow the letter of the law; otherwise the law might be explained to the prejudice of citizens in cases where their honor, property or life is concerned."

This is a narrow view of his meaning. What he obviously meant was that the function of a judge does not include any alteration, modification or amendment of any authoritative enactment of the legislative body, and that a judge may not explain it away if he happens to think it a bad or unwise law. Thus construed, the statement is sound and is the accepted rule laid down with little or no variation by our Courts, National and State.

The duty of interpretation can only arise in a judicial proceeding when words of doubtful meaning are used, or the structure of the law is ungrammatical or the meaning confused. Neither constitutions nor statutes can escape scrutiny for the purpose of ascertaining their meaning and the intent of the lawmaker. No function can be less subject to the accusation of usurpation than that of endeavoring to carry out a law according to the intent and purpose of the lawmaking department of government.

In this indisputable function of interpreting and construing applicable constitutional or statutory law to the case in hand there lurks, however, an immeasurable power, which is all the more dangerous to the public welfare because under its cover it is possible for a bad or ignorant judge to defeat the legislative purpose. There are doubtless instances where, through ignorance and mistake, a legislative purpose has been misconstrued, and doubtless there are rare instances where judges have conceived it within the scope of the interpreting function to so shape and mould a statute, or even a constitutional provision, as to minimize the effect of a law deemed unwise, as to render it harmless or capable of subserving some genuine public good. That there is a large and intelligent body of public opinion which regards this trimming down or modifying function as quite within the scope of the judicial power and which looks to the Courts with confidence for relief against what they regard as bad and dangerous legislation must be confessed by all who have observed the public press. This is another manifestation of the decay of respect for the limitations imposed by our fundamental law and of the yearning for a government of men rather than a government of laws. If we have outgrown the institutions which have made us the greatest people of the earth, let us change them by direct rather than by indirect means. If our Constitution is too rigid and the restraints upon the legislative power too great, let us amend the Constitution. The theory that the law is only a means to an end is truth. But who is to alter, modify or annul a constitutionally valid law? The executive, who has no function but to execute the law as he finds it; the judge, who has no lawmaking power and whose single duty is to apply the law as he finds it to an existing case? The best means of securing the alteration or repeal of a vicious law is to enforce it.

Any such contention is totally subversive of our institutions and involves a willingness to accept a government of men rather than a government of laws. Neither a Constitution nor a statute is to be treated by either the executive or the judiciary as if it were a "nose of wax," to be twisted and moulded according to the fancy of the occasion. It is against this most dangerous notion of judicial power that I most earnestly protest. There is nothing in the past history of either the National or State judiciary which gives sanction to any such abuse of power or supports an expectation that the function of interpreting will be tortured into an exercise of legislative power. The rules of construction are plain and simple of application. They are in substance identical, whether the instrument for interpretation be a statute or a contract. The Courts possess neither the power of taxation nor that of the sword. They are dependent upon the legislative power for their existence and upon the executive for the force needful to enforce their judgments. Set in the place of an arbiter between the branches among which the functions of government have been parcelled, they constitute the balance-wheel in our unique and splendid governmental system. They are the guardians of the fundamental law which conducts and controls the otherwise uncontrollable legislative power. Their dominating authority is moral. They will continue to retain the authority necessary to their free action so long only as they shall respect their own limitations, scrupulously avoiding the exercise of powers which they have not and fearlessly exercising those which they have. But this duty of keeping within the limits of the organic law is one which does not rest upon the judicial branch with any greater force than it rests upon the co-ordinate departments of government. The lawmaker no less than the judge exercises his office under the same solemn obligation to support and uphold the limitations of the organic law. Why shall that oath rest more lightly upon one than the other? In the forum of conscience may the legislator say, as he too often does, "I will not consider that side of the matter— that I will turn over to the Courts." Yet, as we all know, this is not an unusual attitude for a legislator who finds questionable legislation desirable if valid. This is not honest, nor is it expedient.

An important rule of constitutional construction is that legislation shall not be annulled for antagonism to the organic law unless its invalidity is clear. This has its genesis, first, in a proper respect for the Legislature, and, second, upon an assumption that the legislator has himself acted under the obligation of the same oath which forbids his assent to any law which contravenes the Constitution.

The forces which from opposite poles are endeavoring to break down the restraints which safeguard us against the despotic power of an uncontrollable legislative or executive power are not the progressive, but the retrogressive element of our people. The mightiest advance against despotism was made when our fathers devised and put into operation a government of law for a government of men. We read in Holy Writ of one of the prophets who in his despair went a day's journey into the wilderness and laid himself down under a juniper-tree and prayed, "Now, O Lord, take away my life, for I am not better than my fathers." Let us rather rejoice that in standing by the institutions which have for more than a century made us the most law-abiding people of the earth, that we are walking in the footsteps of our fathers when we maintain in letter and spirit that division of the great functions of government which the men of Massachusetts, and the men of Virginia and the men of Maryland declared with Montesquieu to be the best security for a government of laws and the only safeguard against a return to a government of men.

NOTES

a. *North American Review* 193 (January 1911):9–25. Used by permission.

9

Justice Lurton Rebutted

MR. JUSTICE LURTON'S vigorous defense of judicial review is answered with an equally spirited essay. Louis Boudin, New York jurist, labor lawyer, and one of the more prominent members of the American Labor Party during the early part of this century, challenges, point by point, Lurton's arguments. The debate joined here reached well beyond cloistered academic halls. The fact is that the Supreme Court had deployed constitutional concepts such as substantive due process and liberty of contract to strike down legislation designed to protect working persons. Organized labor and progressives viewed the Supreme Court during the period of the turn of the century as an important force of reaction and opposition.

Boudin sets out to convince his readers of two major points. First, he presents evidence to discredit Justice Lurton's claim that judicial review was intended by the Framers of the Constitution. Second, he argues that as a matter of fact the power of judicial review as exercised by the turn-of-the-century Supreme Court is nothing less than revolutionary.

The author maintains that judicial review was not a recognized power at the time of the American Revolution. He argues that the authority was not recognized in England and that Lurton's reliance on the writings of Montesquieu is misplaced. The failure of John Marshall to cite so-called existing precedents from state courts was wise because, according to Boudin, the "precedents" demonstrate opinion in favor not of judicial review, but of its very opposite.

Boudin examines evidence concerning the Framers' intent. He concludes that some who gathered at Philadelphia favored judicial review, but given their explicit silence on the subject "the great majority of the framers never suspected a general power of the judiciary to control legislation could be interpreted into the new constitution."

Citing Judge Gibson's dissent approvingly, Boudin characterizes Marshall's decision in *Marbury* v. *Madison* in the first instance as "amazing." Then, *a fortiori,* Boudin makes two additional points worthy of consideration. First, the *Marbury* decision related particularly to judicial power and not to general legislation. It is one thing for the Supreme Court to defend the judicial branch against legislative encroachment; it is quite another to claim that the Court is the sole and binding interpreter of the Constitution. Second, Jefferson won the immediate battle because Marbury was denied the commission he sought. Thus, the unpopular Federalist attempt to stack the judiciary with the party faithful was spoiled. The decision in *Marbury* provoked no extended public debate because it had no practical importance. The lack of a huge public outcry should therefore not be interpreted as acceptance of judicial review.

If by chance one line of reasoning fails to convince judge and jury, try another. This maxim is true even if the two arguments proceed from different premises. This typical lawyer tactic is employed by Boudin in his "brief" against the Supreme Court of his day. After making the case that there is nothing in preconvention history, court precedents, intent of the Framers, and Supreme Court decisions to justify judicial review, Boudin then argues, in essence, that if all the arguments just presented are rejected, and one accepts the exercise of judicial review as a legitimate authority, the contemporary Court has nonetheless employed the power improperly. In short, a posture of self-restraint is prescribed. Let the policy judgments of the legislatures stand. If the legislative branch violates the Constitution, the best protection against such abuse is the people, not the courts. At this point in the essay, Boudin reads like Thayer (see Chapter 7).

The essay ends with a consideration of how the Supreme Court has abused its power in a number of important recent cases. Boudin argues that the Court's conservative majority substituted their personal policy views for that of legislatures. The Court's famous decisions in *Lochner, Adair,* and others are pointed to as proof that there are no plain and simple rules of constitutional interpretation as claimed by Justice Lurton: "on the contrary, there are now practically no rules at all." Once again, we are reminded of contemporary criticism. The principal difference is that since the mid-1950s the critical voices have come from the political right instead of the political left.

Government by Judiciary[a]

L. B. Boudin

THE MOST MOMENTOUS QUESTION before the people of this country today is undoubtedly the question of the limits of the power of the judiciary to annul legislation for alleged unconstitutionality. When Mr. Roosevelt opened his campaign for the so-called "new nationalism," he was forced to make what was called by his opponents "an attack upon the judiciary." The general election that followed was largely fought, at least in the eastern part of the country, on the issue thus made; and the fight against the new nationalism has since been largely a fight for the preservation of the powers of the judiciary as they exist today.

The fact that Mr. Roosevelt denied the allegation, claiming to have made no "attack" upon the judiciary does not change the situation. It is of course true that Mr. Roosevelt did not attack the judiciary as an institution: he merely criticised some of the decisions of one of our courts. But that court is the highest court in the land. And criticism of courts must be admitted to stand on an entirely different footing from criticism of other public functionaries, notably from that directed against legislative assemblies. Legislators—and within certain circumscribed limits, executives—are vested with discretion to act as the public interest may, in their opinion, from time to time require. Criticism of their public acts does not necessarily involve anything more than the expression of a different opinion as to what is best calculated to promote the public good under certain circumstances. It is different with judges. They are not supposed to be vested with any discretion to act as they see fit in the interest of the public welfare. They are supposed to find the law written down in former decisions or in statutes, in the making of which they have no share, and to apply the law which they find to the facts of the cases presented to them, irrespective of their opinion of its wisdom or unwisdom. Ordinarily, therefore, criticism of the judgments of a court implies a reflection upon either the legal knowledge or the integrity of its members.

Our courts are, however, in a different position—or, at least, it is claimed that they are in a different position—with respect to their power to declare legislation void for alleged unconstitutionality. It is claimed by those who criticise certain of the decisions of our courts on that subject that in dealing with constitutional questions our courts exercise legislative powers under form of judicial decrees, and that the canons of criticism which usually apply to acts of legislatures are therefore applicable to our courts with respect to such decisions. It is this that Mr. Roosevelt implied, when he said, in his Denver speech:

> The courts occupy a position of importance in our government such as they occupy in no other government, because, instead of dealing only with the rights of one man face to face with his fellow-men, as is the case in other governments, they here pass upon the fundamental governmental rights of the people as exercised through their legislative and executive officers.

And it is the same position that is expressed in a very forcible and striking manner in an editorial article on "The Flexibility of the Law," which appeared recently in *The Outlook*. The editor of *The Outlook* said:

> In our judgment the real Constitution of the United States, the Constitution under which we are living, the Constitution to which the decision of all our subordinate courts must conform, the Constitution to which all legislative acts, whether State or National, are subject, is not the written Constitution which was formed in 1787. It is that written Constitution *plus* the decisions of the Supreme Court of the United States interpreting and applying it, and the habit of the Nation which has grown up under it. *The Outlook* has been criticised for talking about the written Constitution as though there were any other. There is another; and in its binding force upon the American people this other Constitution is quite as important as the written document.
>
> The Supreme Court of the United States decided by majority of one that an income tax was constitutional. Then one judge changed his mind and the Supreme court decided that an income tax was unconstitutional. It is now unquestioned, or at least unquestionable, that an income tax cannot constitutionally be levied by Congress upon the people of the United States. What makes such a tax unconstitutional is the Supreme Court's decision interpreting the written Constitution. What made the Supreme Court's decision, interpreting the written Constitution, is the decision of the one judge who changed his mind.[1]

But this is by no means admitted by the other side. Indeed, it is emphatically denied, at least as far as the conclusions are concerned.

Some time after Mr. Roosevelt delivered his famous speech at Denver, Mr. Justice Lurton, of the United States Supreme Court, delivered an address on the subject to the joint bar associations of Virginia and Maryland. That address was subsequently published as the leading article in the January issue of the *North American Review,* under the title: "A Government of Law or a Government of Men?" In that article the distinguished jurist states what may be termed the "conservative" position on the subject, which is diametrically opposed to that just stated. Judge Lurton categorically denies that the courts now exercise any legislative powers, that is to say, powers involving the exercise of discretion or the following out of political policies. He asserts heroically that, in declaring legislation unconstitutional, our courts merely apply the law as they find it plainly written in the Constitution, precisely as any court applies the law in any ordinary judgment. He then proceeds to defend this power generally, and he closes with an appeal to his reader to

> rejoice that in standing by the institutions which have for more than a century made us the most law-abiding people of the earth, that we are walking in the footsteps of our fathers when we maintain in letter and spirit that division of the great functions of government which the men of Massachusetts and the men of Virginia and the men of Maryland declared with Montesquieu to be the best security for a government of laws and the only safeguard against a return to a government of men.[2]

Judge Lurton's appeal to American traditions put his opponents in the awkward position of unpatriotic men, trying to undo the work of the greater men who established this government, and of reactionaries, attempting to abolish one of the most effective safeguards of our free institutions against the tyranny of a mere "government of men." It is, therefore, but fair that we should inquire into the facts of the case, historical and contemporary, and compare them with the assertions on which Judge Lurton bases his conclusions, in an endeavor to arrive at an independent judgment as to whether or not his conclusions are warranted by the facts of the case.

The salient points of Judge Lurton's argument, asserted by him as matters of fact, are as follows:

(1) That the framers of the Constitution, owing to their philosophical training in the school of Montesquieu and the governmental usage of the states prior to the adoption of the United States Constitution, considered it necessary, or at least expedient, as part of the scheme of division of all governmental powers into three independent departments, to invest the judiciary with the power to annul legislation whenever the judges should find it to be unconstitutional.

(2) That by the Constitution framed by them, they intended to invest, and did in fact invest, the judiciary with such power.

(3) That the judiciary of this country has exercised that power ever since, in the manner in which the framers of the Constitution intended it to be exercised, without any change; and that the exercise of this power for "more than a century" has made us "the most law-abiding people of the earth."

(4) That the rules of "constitutional construction" applied by our courts in the exercise of this power are so plain and simple that their application does not, in fact, involve any element of discretion; and that the courts, therefore, never have exercised, nor do they now exercise, any legislative powers in annulling legislative acts on the ground of alleged unconstitutionality.

On this last point, which is perhaps the most important, Judge Lurton says:

> There is nothing in the past history of either the National or State judiciary which gives sanction to any such abuse of power or supports an expecta-

tion that the function of interpreting will be tortured into an exercise of legislative power. The rules of construction are plain and simple of application. They are in substance identical, whether the instrument for interpretation be a statute or a contract.[3]

A careful examination of "the facts of the case," it seems to me, will show conclusively that each and every one of these propositions is erroneous. Indeed, the evidence against some of them is so overwhelming that its complete presentation would require several volumes. It is my purpose in the following pages to take up Judge Lurton's position point by point, and to present as much of what I consider to be the evidence against it as may be compressed into the narrow limits of a magazine essay. An examination of these points, in the order stated by me, will also serve to present to the reader a historical picture of the growth of the power under consideration, showing its gradual development and the vast, indeed revolutionary, changes which have taken place in its application. And this examination will, it seems to me, establish conclusively at least two points: first, that the power under consideration did not emerge in its present form from the brains of the framers, as Minerva sprang, fully panoplied, from the head of Jupiter; and, second, that the epithet "revolutionary," applied by Judge Lurton to the demands of the progressives, could be more fitly applied to the latest actions of our courts.

I

In this inquiry we may take as a starting point the proposition, which is not disputed by Judge Lurton, that at the time of the American Revolution the power of the judiciary to annul legislation regularly enacted by the legislative department did not exist anywhere in the civilized world. It did not exist in England, which we took as a model in framing our government. Blackstone, who enjoyed in the United States great influence as a writer on all legal subjects during the years following the Revolution, in discussing the question whether "acts of parliament contrary to reason are void," said:

> If the parliament will positively enact a thing to be done which is unreasonable, I know of no power in the ordinary forms of the constitution that is vested with authority to control it; and the examples usually alleged in support of this sense of the rule do none of them prove that, where the main object of a statute is unreasonable, the judges are at liberty to reject it; for that were to set the judicial power above that of the legislature, which would be subversive of all government . . . There is no court that has power to defeat the intent of the legislature, when couched in such evident and express words as to leave no doubt whether it was the intent of the legislature or no.[4] . . . So long therefore as the English constitution lasts, we may venture to affirm that the power of parliament is absolute and without control.[5]

And Montesquieu, whose authority Judge Lurton invokes, gives no support to the judge's argument. It is indeed one of the ironies of fate that Montesquieu should be cited as authority for the supremacy of the judiciary over the legislature, in view of that Philosopher's well-known admiration for the English government system of that day, upon which he based his theory of the division of the governmental powers. A reading of his works will prove conclusively that nothing could have been further from his mind than the ideas imputed to him by Judge Lurton. Judge Lurton himself quotes from Montesquieu the following passage, which to the ordinary mind would seem to dispose of the matter very effectually: "In republics," says the great French philosopher, "the very nature of the constitution requires the judges to follow the letter of the law; otherwise the law might be explained to the prejudice of citizens in cases where their honor, property or life is concerned." But Judge Lurton, true to our judicial tradition, established in recent years, "interprets" this passage by a method which is neither plain nor simple, but which does violence to ordinary common sense; and he certainly "explains it to the prejudice" of its author. Significantly enough, Judge Lurton is not able to quote a single line from Montesquieu which would in any way countenance his fanciful interpretation.

In his appeal to American usage Judge Lurton fares no better than in his appeal to foreign authority. He says on this point:

> From the beginning it [the power to declare legislation void for unconstitutionality] has been claimed by American Courts as a proper function of the Courts under our American constitutional system. It is a doctrine which originated in the Courts of the States long before the adoption of the Federal Constitution. Professor Thayer, in his Constitutional Cases, refers to no less than five decisions by State Courts prior to the adoption of the Constitution of the United States, in which it was held that the power of State legislation was limited by constitutional restrictions, and that it was the duty of the judicial power to declare legislation repugnant to such superior law void and unenforceable whenever necessary to determine the rights of parties in pending cases. The earliest of reported cases is that of Commonwealth v. Caton, decided by the Virginia Court of Appeals in 1782.

And then he adds, wonderingly:

> Neither that case, nor either of the decisions I refer to, are cited by Chief Justice Marshall in Marbury v. Madison, although they afford a body of opinion of commanding influence which one cannot suppose the great Chief Justice to have been ignorant of, especially as one of them was from his own State.[6]

The fact that Chief Justice Marshall did not quote these cases should have warned Judge Lurton that they do not "afford a body of opinion of commanding influence." In fact, they afford nothing of the sort. They simply prove that, shortly before the time of the adoption of the Constitution, a few judges made isolated and timid attempts to exercise such powers. These attempts aroused general indignation, and the judges were called to account for their conduct. A brief statement of three of these cases will suffice to reproduce the historical atmosphere. The first two cases which Judge Lurton finds in Professor Thayer's collection may be ignored, because they do not deal with legislative enactments which were in conflict with written constitutions.[7] The three cases which require notice are: Rutgers v. Waddington (New York, 1784); Trevett v. Weeden (Rhode Island, 1786); and Den v. Singleton, also known as Bayard v. Singleton (North Carolina, 1787).

Rutgers v. Waddington[8] was decided by an inferior New York court, the mayor's court of New York City. The law under consideration was a New York statute which was claimed to be in conflict with the law of nations and the' treaty of peace with Great Britain. The court specifically declared the power of the legislature to be supreme in all matters of legislation and not subject to any revisory power of the court; but it disregarded the portion of the statute which was called into question on the theory that the legislature could not have intended to violate the law of nations and bring the United States into conflict with treaty obligations.

This decision brought forth a storm of protests. Mass meetings were called to protest against the usurpation of power by the judiciary, and ringing resolutions denouncing it were adopted. The New York Assembly took a hand in the matter, and passed the following resolution:

> Resolved, that the judgment aforesaid is, in its tendency, subversive of all law and good order and leads directly to anarchy and confusion; because if a court instituted for the benefit and government of a corporation may take upon them to dispense with and act in direct violation of a plain and known law of the State, all other courts, either superior or inferior, may do the like; and therewith well end all our dear-bought rights and privileges, and legislatures become useless.[9]

The case was compromised and never went to the supreme court.

Trevett v. Weeden[10] was the first of these cases in which it may fairly be said that a law was declared unconstitutional. The legislature of Rhode Island tried to force a paper currency upon an unwilling people. It made the refusal to take paper money instead of specie a criminal offence and abolished trial by jury in this class of cases. It was the abolition of trial by jury that was declared unconstitutional.

The legislature immediately passed a resolution condemning the decision and cited the judges to appear before its bar and answer for their conduct. The judges obeyed the summons but justified their conduct by claiming independence. A motion was made to remove them from office; but, as their term of office was soon to expire, the legislature, which had the appointment of their successors, let them serve out their term, and then dropped them all except one, and appointed others who did not claim any such powers for the judiciary.[11]

Bayard v. Singleton,[12] which was decided in North Carolina while the Philadelphia Constitutional Convention was in session, was also a case where the legislature attempted to force upon an unwilling people an unjust law depriving those whom it affected of a jury trial. In this case, also, the law abolishing trial by jury was declared unconstitutional. And in this case also the decision called forth a storm of excitement and protest. One of its severest critics was Richard D. Spaight, one of the framers of the Constitution, and afterwards governor of his state. In his denunciation of this decision he said:

> I do not pretend to vindicate the law which has been the subject of con-
> troversy; it is immaterial what law they have declared void; it is their
> usurpation of the authority to do it, that I complain of as I do positively
> deny that they have any such power. . . . It would have been absurd, and
> contrary to the practice of all the world, had the constitution vested such
> power in them, as would have operated as an absolute negative on the
> proceedings of the legislature, which no judiciary ought ever to possess,
> and the state, instead of being governed by the representatives in general
> assembly would be subject to the will of three individuals, who united in
> their own persons the legislative and judiciary powers, which no monarch
> in Europe enjoys, and which would be more despotic than the Roman
> decemvirate, and equally insufferable.[13]

Such were the state "precedents,"[14] and such was the temper of the people at the time the Philadelphia Convention met to frame the United States Constitution. Small wonder that Chief Justice Marshall did not refer in his decision in Marbury v. Madison to these "precedents." He was too near in point of time to this "body of opinion" to hazard citing it in support of his contention without considerable damage to his reputation.

II

Turning now from pre-convention history to the Constitutional Convention itself, and to the document which that convention framed, the candid student must admit that there is absolutely no evidence whatever of any intention on the part of that body to invest the judiciary with any sort of control over federal legislation, or over state legislation in matters admittedly within the legislative competence of the states. And even if it be assumed, as it is commonly assumed to-day, that in those matters in which state legislation was made subordinate to the federal Constitution and laws it was the judiciary, rather than any other federal governmental department, that was to act as the guardian of federal power against state aggression, there is not the slightest evidence that the framers intended to confer upon the judiciary anything approaching the degree of control over state legislation which in later times and by slow expansion of "implied" authority the judges came to exercise. There undoubtedly were some men in the Convention who favored the investing of the federal judiciary with general revisory powers over the legislation; but all attempts to make the judiciary part of the legislative power of the federal government failed signally and had to be abandoned by their sponsors. The provisions of the Constitution as they now stand contain no reference whatever to any such powers, either expressly or by obvious implication. And there is ample historical proof that—whatever the hopes of some, from the complete

silence of the document, as to possible future development—the great majority
of the framers never suspected that a general power of the judiciary to control
legislation could be interpreted into the new Constitution. They evidently assumed that such an extraordinary power could not be exercised unless expressly granted.

The judiciary article as finally formulated was adopted without a dissenting vote and almost without discussion. It is absurd to assume that the many
avowed opponents of judicial control of legislation who sat in the Convention
would have agreed to the article without a murmur had they suspected that it
contained even a part of the enormous power which our judiciary now exercises. Richard Spaight for one, whose fiery denunciation of this power I have
quoted above, would have made the halls in which the Convention met ring to
the echo with his emphatic protest, had he suspected any such implications.
And it is equally certain that had the Convention given to the courts that
power, either expressly or by necessary implication, apparent to the ordinary
mind, the Constitution would have been overwhelmingly rejected by the people.

A careful examination of all the evidence on the subject now extant leads
to the conclusion that the Constitution was adopted by the Philadelphia Convention, and ratified by the people of the states, without any belief, without
even a suspicion on the part of the great majority of those voting for it,
whether in or out of the Constitutional Convention, that it contained any such
implications. Even Hamilton, who saw more clearly than did the others the
possibilities arising from the silence of the document on this vital point, probably never dreamed of any such development of the judicial power as has taken
place since his day. Mr. Joseph P. Cotton, Jr., puts the case rather mildly when
he says, in his introductory essay to the latest edition of John Marshall's constitutional decisions, in speaking of Marbury v. Madison:

> Common as this conception of the power of our courts now is, it is hard to
> comprehend the amazing quality of it then. No court in England had such a
> power; there was no express warrant for it in the words of the Constitution;
> the existence of it was denied by every other branch of the government and
> by the dominant majority of the country. Moreover, no such power had
> been clearly anticipated by the framers of the Constitution, nor was it a
> necessary implication from the scheme of government they had es-
> tablished.

Mr. Cotton may well call the decision in Marbury v. Madison "amazing,"
for prior to that decision the federal judiciary itself did not claim to have
obtained the powers in question by the adoption of the Constitution. Hayburn's
case, so-called, gives a fair picture of the way in which the judges themselves
regarded the relative positions of legislature and judiciary, under the government established by the Constitution, during the first years after its adoption.
The consideration of that case should be prefaced by the remark that, upon the
adoption of the Constitution, and because the powers now under consideration

were not then believed to have been granted by the Constitution, the federal judiciary was considered of little importance, and so inferior and subordinate to the legislative and executive departments that our first presidents had great difficulty in getting men of high standing to accept positions on the United States Supreme Court. The judges themselves were evidently in fear of encroachments by the legislative department upon their dignity and prerogatives. That was the atmosphere in which arose the following facts, which are usually referred to as "Hayburn's case."[15]

The first United States Congress passed an act to "provide for the settlement of the claims of widows and orphans barred by the limitations heretofore established, and to regulate the claims to invalid pensions." Under the provisions of this act the claims were to be passed upon the federal circuit courts, whose decisions were to be subject to the consideration of the secretary of war, and, if the secretary saw fit, to suspension, and to the revision of Congress itself. The question of unconstitutionality, in the modern sense of the word, was not involved. But the judges saw in this act of Congress an encroachment upon the dignity and independence of the judicial department. For this view there was good reason; for if the duties assigned to the judges were regarded as non-judicial and ministerial, it was not fit that such a burden should be imposed upon them; and if, on the other hand, these new duties were regarded as judicial, the independence of the courts was endangered by assigning to the executive and legislative departments power to revise judicial decisions.

What were the courts to do? We can readily imagine what they would do now, in any similar emergency. What they actually did then shows how far we have traveled from the points of view held by the men of Massachusetts and of Virginia and of Maryland, who formed this government of ours.

The members of the circuit court for the district of New York (Mr. Jay, chief justice of the United States, Mr. Cushing, associate justice of the United States Supreme Court, and Mr. Duane, district judge) stated, in writing, their objection to the law. They held that the duties which Congress had assigned to the court were "not judicial, nor directed to be performed judicially," and that the court as such could not perform them, but, they said, "as the judges desire to manifest, on all proper occasions, and in every proper manner, their high respect for the national legislature," they would execute this act in the capacity of commissioners. And they proceeded to perform the duties imposed upon them.

The members of the circuit court for the district of Pennsylvania (Messrs. Wilson and Blair, associate justices of the United States Supreme Court, and Mr. Peters, district judge) and the members of the circuit for the district of North Carolina (Mr. Iredell, associate justice of the United States Supreme Court, and Mr. Sitgreaves, district judge) declined to act; and they sent "representations" to the president, explaining their apparently insubordinate conduct.[16] These "representations" are strange reading to the lawyers of to-day.

We are used to different language from members of the "most august judicial tribunal in the world."

The matter was afterwards brought up by the attorney-general before the United States Supreme Court, on the question whether the judges had a right to decline to act. And the official report says, that, although the judges were all agreed as to the unconstitutionality of the law, "the Court observed, that they would hold the motion under advisement until the next term; but no decision was ever pronounced, as the legislature, at an intermediate session, provided, in another way, for the relief of the pensioners."[17]

No decision pronouncing an act of legislation void because repugnant to the federal constitution was rendered prior to Marbury v. Madison. The case of Calder v. Bull,[18] decided in 1789, in which an act of the Connecticut legislature was upheld, is interesting, just as Otis's argument in the Paxton case is interesting, because in delivering the opinion of the Supreme Court Mr. Justice Chase went out of his way to give his views on the abstract proposition of the right of the courts to annul legislation, irrespective of consitutional limitations, on the ground that it is "contrary to the great first principles of the social compact." The case is interesting, further, because, in asserting *obiter* the authority of the court to declare unconstitutional laws void, Mr. Justice Iredell described the authority as "of a delicate and awful nature" and said that "the court will never resort to that authority but in all clear and urgent cases." To the view propounded by Chief Justice Chase, Justice Iredell took exception, saying:

> If, on the other hand, the legislature of the union or the legislature of any member of the union shall pass a law within the general scope of their constitutional power, the court cannot pronounce it to be void, merely because it is in their judgment contrary to the principles of natural justice. The ideas of natural justice are regulated by no fixed standard; the ablest and the purest men have differed upon the subject; and all that the court could properly say in such an event would be, that the legislature (possessed of an equal right of opinion) had passed an act, which, in the opinion of the judges, was inconsistent with the abstract principles of natural justice.

III

In 1803 came Chief Justice Marshall's decision in Marbury v. Madison. Since this is not an inquiry into the broad question whether or not the courts should have the power to declare legislation unconstitutional under any circumstances, but rather a historical sketch of the development of that power, I shall not enter upon a discussion of the merits of that decision. Suffice it to say that historically it was, as Mr. Cotton calls it, "amazing"; and that as a matter of legal reasoning it has been pronounced by many eminent thinkers unsatisfactory. Nearly twenty-five years later Chief Justice Gibson of the Pennsylvania supreme court, one of the ablest judges that ever sat on that great bench, called Marshall's argument "inconclusive."

Its "amazing" quality does not, however, exhaust its historical interest. It was undoubtedly a turning point in the history of our political institutions. But it lacked much of being what it has since been often represented to be, and what it is generally understood to be by students of and writers on the subject. It is therefore worth our while to examine a little more closely into its immediate significance, at the time when it was rendered.[19] Its positive historical importance lies in the fact that here, for the first time in our federal history, a court undertook to base a decision on its alleged power to declare a law null and void for alleged repugnance to the written constitution. The right previously asserted by some judges as an abstract proposition was thereby turned into a concrete power, to be reckoned with as a part and parcel of our political system. It created the politico-legal foundation upon which the imposing edifice of that power as it now exists was gradually erected.

But the power which was actually exercised in this case was a very limited power. Two points should be carefully noted. In the first place, the law which the decision annulled was one peculiarly relating to the judicial department and its powers, much like the law which was questioned in Hayburn's case. In this instance, however, the law conferred upon one of the federal courts, namely, the Supreme Court, a distinctly judicial power. In fact it increased the power of the Supreme Court. What was really decided, in Marbury v. Madison, was that the Supreme Court had received certain powers from the Constitution itself, which Congress would not be permitted by that Court either to increase or to diminish. One might very well agree with that contention, without attributing to the Supreme Court a general right of reviewing the acts of Congress in matters of general legislation. From the claim that the judicial department is a co-equal branch of the government, and that its purely judicial powers and jurisdiction, in so far as they are expressly given by the Constitution, cannot be encroached upon by Congress, which is all that the case actually decided, it is a far cry to the claim that the Supreme Court is the sole interpreter of the Constitution and that its interpretation is binding on the legislative department in all matters of legislation. In the second place, there is a wide difference, particularly in political matters, between the refusal to exercise a power which one's opponent believes to exist – which is all that those who did not agree with Marshall could say – and the actual exercise of a power which that opponent believes not to exist. To the opponent the first may be unnecessary modesty or weakness or, at the very worst, neglect of duty; but the second is usurpation.

A further point deserves notice. The practical result of the decision, and the only result that the ordinary man could see, was a victory for Marshall's political opponents, the Jeffersonians. Marbury, a Federalist appointee of Adams, applied to a court controlled by Federalists for a writ of *mandamus* compelling Jefferson's secretary of state to give him the commission signed by the outgoing Federalist secretary of state. He claimed the writ under a law passed by the Federalists. The Supreme Court annulled the Federalist law and non-suited the Federalist claimant. Jefferson won a practical and substantial victory. What did it matter what reasoning Marshall employed in giving Jefferson the victory? The "man in the street" knew nothing of Marshall's reasons. And if he did, he did not care. He seldom does care for such niceties. He is so intensely "practical." He may have thought that Marshall used a great deal of technical language and acute reasoning in order to save the face of the court. In short, there was nothing in the decision to bring its importance, whatever that was, home to the "practical man"–a fact which is often of controlling importance in historical events.

Of course there were not wanting at that time those who could read the future. One of them was Jefferson. They saw the legal significance of this decision and its possible implications, and they denounced it in unmeasured terms. Jefferson bade it defiance; and it is safe to say that, had there been any attempt to do anything under this decision while Jefferson was president, it would have provoked a conflict in which the judiciary might easily have come out second-best.

But in fact nothing was done under the power asserted by the court in Marbury v. Madison during the following thirty-odd years of Marshall's chief-justiceship. Why this was so, it is not necessary here to inquire. I will say however, in passing, that Marshall's position as a constitutional lawyer and statesman has been much misapprehended, owing to later attempts to base the judicial power on his decision in Marbury v. Madison. In my opinion Marshall's great place in the history of our country is due, not to any doctrine of the limitations of the legislative power, which others deduced from that decision more than half a century after and with but doubtful warrant, but to the liberal spirit in which he interpreted, and thus helped to develop, the legislative powers of Congress.

Nor was the power to annul federal legislation used by the federal judiciary for many years after Marshall's death, not indeed until the troublous times which immediately preceded the Civil War. During Marshall's chief-justiceship and under his successors, a number of state enactments were declared void because in conflict with the federal Constitution, and particularly because of attempted encroachment upon powers attributed to Congress; but the first case in which an ordinary law of Congress was declared unconstitutional was that of Dred Scott. And the only case besides Marbury v. Madison in which any law of Congress can be said to have been declared unconstitutional before the fateful Dred Scott decision was the negligible case of Fereira v. the United States, decided but a few years earlier. It will thus be seen that for at least half a century no attempt was made by the federal judiciary to exercise the power asserted in Marbury v. Madison. And when it did act in this sense, it acted under extraordinary circumstances, in an attempt to solve by judicial decree an extraordinary political problem; and the attempt had extraordinary and disastrous results.

In the meantime the conflict over this power was raging in other fields. The state courts in several instances attempted to follow up the logic of Marbury v. Madison. The state courts were in this respect in a much better situation than the federal courts. The acts of the state legislatures were admittedly subject to review by the judiciary, both federal and state, on the score of repugnancy to the federal Constitution, treaties and statutes, in matters of a federal character. From this it was but one step – and a step which a layman could not always see – to the power of review on the score of repugnancy to the respective state constitutions. And yet this step was not taken unopposed, even after Marbury v. Madison. The ensuing conflicts form one of the most interesting chapters in our history – a chapter unfortunately now entirely neglected, the common lot of all struggles which end in defeat.[20] It may be said in general, that the actual exercise of this power by the judiciary of the several states during the first fifty years after the adoption of the Constitution was very rare; that it was used only under extraordinary circumstances; and that its use almost always provoked great public excitement and sometimes entailed results of a more serious sort. In Kentucky it at one time led to the creation of two rival courts, each defying the other and it almost led to the creation of two state governments.[21] In view of these conflicts, and of the disastrous results attending the first important use of the federal judicial power to annul an act of Congress in the Dred Scott case, it sounds like bitter irony when Judge Lurton says that this power has made us "for more than a century the most law-abiding people of the earth."

In most of the states, however, the power in question, although generally asserted, was not used at all during the first half of Judge Lurton's "more than a century." This was the case, for example, in Pennsylvania, then the leading state of the Union. During the half-century following the adoption of the United States Constitution the Pennsylvania courts did not declare a single law unconstitutional, although the judges, with one notable exception, usually asserted that right. There may have been other exceptions, for it is probable that the doctrine was not quite so universally accepted even by the judiciary, either in Pennsylvania or elsewhere, as is now imagined; but the one exception known to us is that of Judge John B. Gibson, for many years judge of the Pennsylvania supreme court, part of the time its chief justice, and one of the ablest men who ever sat on that renowned bench. His opinion, officially stated in 1825, is a convincing (and in my judgement quite unanswerable) argument against the existence as well as against the expediency of the power of the judiciary to review legislation under any circumstances.[22] Its historical importance, however, lies in the fact that, nearly a quarter of a century after Marbury v. Madison, one of the three judges who then composed the highest court of the great state of Pennsylvania, in an official judicial opinion, denied the existence of the power asserted by Marshall. And it is not without historical interest, as an evidence of the spirit of his time and a commentary upon the changed spirit of ours, that Judge Gibson's views did not impede his promotion to the chief-justiceship of his state.

IV

A change no less striking has taken place, since the power of the courts to annul legislation has been more freely exercised and has come to be generally recognized, in the attitude of our judges and in the opinions of our public men as regards the question: How far shall this power extend? Even after the decision in the Dred Scott case the existence of this power was not admitted by our leading statesmen except in a very limited sense. Lincoln denied its binding force in our modern sense, that is, as a rule of political conduct. And even those who admitted it as a rule of political conduct did not by any means, until very recent times, give it the broad scope which it now possesses. The older and more conservative point of view is clearly stated in the opinions of the very judges who asserted and used this power in its earlier stages of development.

Judge Iredell was one of the first members of the United States Supreme Court to claim this power. He advocated it even before the adoption of the federal Constitution; for he was leading counsel in the case of Bayard v. Singleton, noticed above, on the side which urged the right of the North Carolina state court to declare unconstitutional the state law at that time under review. As an associate justice of the United States Supreme Court he asserted this power before the decision in Marbury v. Madison, as we have seen in our examination of the case of Calder v. Bull.[23] We have also seen that he regarded this power as of an "awful nature," never to be resorted to except in a clear and urgent case. A further examination of his opinion will show that he considered the power to be limited to those cases in which the legislative enactment violated the very letter of an express prohibition of the Constitution. He emphatically repudiated, as we have seen, the theory that an act passed by Congress or by a state legislature, within the general scope of its constitutional power, could be pronounced to be void merely because it was deemed by the court to be contrary to the principles of natural justice. He based this conclusion on the assumption that each and every legislature was "possessed of an equal right of opinion" with any court as to what the principles of natural justice were. The hundred-odd years which have passed since Justice Iredell wrote this opinion have certainly wrought havoc with his antiquated ideas regarding the competence of legislatures and the functions of courts.

More than half a century later, at a time when the judicial power had firmly established itself and on the eve of its great *coup* in the Dred Scott case, the utterances of the courts regarding the limitations upon their authority remained the same. In 1853 the judges of the Pennsylvania supreme court wrote a series of notable opinions on this subject, in the case of Sharples v.

The Mayor.[24] The leading opinion was written by Chief Justice Jeremiah S. Black, one of the greatest constitutional lawyers of his generation, and soon afterwards successively attorney-general and secretary of state of the United States. The decision rendered in this case and the opinions upon which it is based are very interesting reading. They give much food for thought to the constitutional lawyer of to-day and to the student of our existing political institutions. Among the points decided in that case are the following:

> In determining whether an act of the legislature is constitutional or not, we must look to the body of the constitution itself for reasons. The general principles of justice, liberty and right, not contained or expressed in that instrument, are no proper elements of a judicial decision upon it.
>
> If such act be within the general grant of legislative power, that is, if it be in its character and essence a law, and if it be not forbidden, expressly or impliedly, either by the state or federal constitution, it is valid.
>
> To make it void, it must be clearly not an exercise of legislative authority, or else be forbidden so plainly, as to leave the case free from all doubt.

In their opinions the judges specifically state that by "forbidden expressly or impliedly" they mean just what they say: that there must be something in the Constitution, state or federal, which shows plainly, so as to leave no room for any doubt, that the Constitution intends to forbid just such a law as that under consideration, and that such general prohibitions as that "no person shall be deprived of life, liberty or property without due process of law" do not furnish a sufficient basis for declaring a legislative act unconstitutional, unless, indeed, the act be such as cannot be properly called a law or an act of legislation at all. Chief Justice Black said, in his opinion:

> We are urged to hold that a law, though not prohibited, is void if it violates the spirit of our institutions, or impairs any of those rights which it is the object of a free government to protect, and to declare it unconstitutional if it be wrong and unjust. But we cannot do this. . . . I am thoroughly convinced that the words of the constitution furnish the only test to determine the validity of a statute, and that all arguments based on general principles outside of the constitution must be addressed to the people, and not to us. A proposition which results so plainly as this does, from the reason of the thing, can scarcely need the aid of authority. . . . But, if the doctrine I am denying could be allowed to prevail, it would decide this case in favor of the plaintiffs without looking into the constitution at all; for it must be admitted that such measures cannot be sustained on principles of moral justice or propriety. . . . There is another rule which must govern us in cases like this; namely, that we can declare an act of Assembly void only when it violates the constitution clearly, palpably, plainly, and in such manner as to leave no doubt or hesitation in our minds.

And Mr. Justice Knox, in a concurring opinion said:

> The presumption is that the legislature has judged correctly of its own constitutional power, and the contrary must be clearly demonstrated

before a coordinate branch of the government can be called upon to interfere between the people and their immediate representatives.

In ascertaining whether there has been this clear usurpation by the law-making power, I agree with the Chief Justice and Mr. Justice Woodward, that the tests to be applied are: 1. Is the act in the nature of a legislative power? 2. Does the constitution expressly, or by necessary implication, forbid the exercise of such a power? . . .

I am aware that under this rule acts may be passed which will, in the minds of many persons, be contrary to natural justice, and subversive of the just rights of the people. The remedy is to be found in further constitutional restrictions upon legislation, not in restraints imposed by the judiciary. The limit of the power of the people's representatives should be written upon the pages of the constitution, rather than remain in the breasts of our judges.

There is great danger in recognizing the existence of a power in the judiciary to annul legislative action, without some fixed rule by which such power is to be measured. Our opinions are so diversified and varied, that what to one mind may seem clearly right and proper, to another will appear to be fraught with imminent danger. If we have not a certain standard by which to test the constitutionality of legislative enactments, if each judge is to be governed by his own convictions of what is right or otherwise, I fear that restraints upon judicial, rather than upon legislative action, will be demanded by the people, ever jealous of the accumulation of power in the hands of a few.

And only a generation ago Justice Clifford of the United States Supreme Court said:

Courts cannot nullify an act of the state legislature on the vague ground that they think it opposed to a general latent spirit supposed to pervade or underlie the Constitution, where neither the terms nor the implications of the instrument disclose any such restriction. *Such a power is denied to the courts, because to concede it would be to make the courts sovereign over both the constitution and the people, and convert the government into a judicial despotism.*[25]

As a corollary to the principle mentioned by Judge Knox, that there must be some fixed rule by which the power of the courts to annul legislative action may be measured and by which the constitutionality of legislative enactments may be tested, and in order to prevent our government from becoming what Mr. Justice Clifford warned us it might become – a "judicial despotism" – the courts have, until very recently, adhered to the well defined and clearly expressed rule of interpretation, that every inquiry into the constitutionality of a legislative enactment must be strictly limited to the question whether the legislature enacting it had power to legislate at all in the premises. Once such power was found to exist, the manner of its exercise could not be inquired into. No law could be declared unconstitutional on the ground that it was an unwise, inexpedient or improper use of a recognized power. The courts distinctly disclaimed any power or right to protect the people against an abuse of power by the legislature in matters on which it admittedly had power to legislate. Each legislature, accordingly, was left absolutely free to use, according to its own best judgment, those powers at least which by the court's own admission were granted or left to it by the Constitution. The power of taxation, for instance, being admittedly reposed in the legislature, no court could interfere with its exercise, no matter how unwise, improvident or even dishonest its use might be deemed. The same was held to be true of the power delegated to congress to regulated commerce with foreign nations. This power was held to be unlimited; it could be used even to the extent of completely forbidding commerce, as was actually done by the Embargo Act.

This rule was laid down by Chief Justice Marshall, who declared that "the interest, wisdom and justice of the representative body furnished the only security in a large class of cases not regulated by any constitutional provision." It has been reiterated by the Supreme Court of the United States on innumerable occasions. In the famous case of Munn *v.* Illinois[26] decided in 1876, the Supreme Court said:

> We know that this is a power which may be abused; but that is no argument against its existence. For protection against abuses by legislation the people must resort to the polls, not to the courts. . . . For us the question is one of power, not of expediency. . . . Of the propriety of legislative interference within the scope of legislative power, the legislature is the exclusive judge.

This rule was absolutely necessary in order to prevent the judiciary from exercising legislative functions, thereby converting our government into a "judicial despotism."

V

Turning now from a study of the past to a consideration of the present, we must be appalled by the enormous change which has taken place in the distribution of powers in our government, not only from the time when the men of Massachusetts, Virginia and Maryland, guided by Montesquieu and English precedent, first formed our government, but also from those later days when our judges, under the able leadership of John Marshall, succeeded in establishing their position as guardians of the Constitution.

Instead of "walking in the footsteps" of either the founders of our government or the earlier judicial interpreters of our Constitution, we have now abandoned all restraints upon the judicial power. We have thrown to the winds all those great limitations, embodied in principles and rules of interpretation, which the earlier judges imposed upon their own power—a power which they deemed necessary for our orderly development, but the danger of which, when not properly limited, they clearly foresaw. One cannot read the latest decision of our courts, either state or federal, without being forced to admit that they have usurped supreme legislative power, and that we have reached the condition of "judicial despotism" which Justice Clifford feared. Benevolent this despotism may be, or otherwise: that depends on the individuals who wield the power. Its benevolence is so largely a matter of opinion, depending on a variety of considerations, some moral and some material. As is well known, it makes a great difference whose ox is gored. But whatever difference of opinion there may be as to the spirit in which this power is exercised, it must be admitted by all candid students that the power itself spells despotism. The essence of despotism is the right of a few to make the laws or to control their making, without being responsible to the people. This condition is admitted by many able and learned jurists. They seldom employ the harsh term which I have borrowed from Justice Clifford; but despotism retains its sting no matter what it be called.

The first restraint to go by the board was the principle that this power was of an "awful nature," as Justice Iredell expressed it, an extraordinary power to be used only on extraordinary occasions for extraordinary purposes. It has become an ordinary power, used by our courts without hesitation as one of their regular functions. It is well within the truth to say that our federal and state courts now annul in one year more laws than they annulled during the entire first half of our national existence. The power is now used by every petty magistrate, and we are so accustomed to its every-day use that to speak of its "awful nature" seems like a bad joke.

The next restraint to be thrown off was the principle that a law cannot be declared unconstitutional unless it contravenes some special provision of the Constitution applicable to the subject, expressly stated in the Constitution or contained in it "by necessary implication," and that neither the general protection accorded to life, liberty and property nor the so-called "spirit of our institutions" gives sufficient cause for such annulment. Most of the important decisions declaring legislation unconstitutional are now rendered in violation of this principle. The chief grounds for annulment of legislation in recent years have been the modern doctrines of "due process of law" and of "liberty of contract." According to the earlier views, neither of these doctrines would have justified the courts in assuming the control over legislation which they now exercise.

When the phrase "due process of law" was first used in this country, as part of the usual bill of rights in our state constitutions, from which it was subsequently taken over into our federal Constitution, this phrase had a well known and clearly defined legal meaning, which was the same as its literal meaning, namely, that of a procedure under general law, with proper trial or hearing. And it was in this sense that the phrase was used until comparatively recent times. But now it has acquired an entirely different meaning. As it is now used by our courts, when they declare legislation unconstitutional for contravening it, it means substantially the same thing that was meant by "natural justice," "principles of liberty and justice" and similar expressions in the earlier days of our constitutional history. Denial of "due process of law" is now discoverable in any law that requires or permits something to be done which the judges deem unjust or not in accord with the "free spirit of our institutions."

The doctrine of "liberty of contract," when used as a test of the constitutionality of legislation, is a still more glaring violation of the older rule. The federal Constitution nowhere mentions any such "liberty." It is claimed however, by our judges (in modern decisions, of course), that this is part of the liberty guaranteed in the phrase contained, in one form or another, in all our constitutions that "no person shall be deprived of his life, liberty or property without due process of law." Aside from the question of the meaning of "due process of law," which has just been considered, there is an additional difficulty with this particular "liberty," namely, that it was entirely unknown and undreamed of at the time we borrowed our "life, liberty and property" phrases from English constitutional law. It is therefore evident that this particular "liberty" was not originally contained in our constitutions. And in fact no such "liberty" was asserted until recent years. When did this "liberty" get into the Constitution? Evidently when we infused into the old words the new "spirit" of extreme individualism. And now we declare legislation unconstitutional on the ground that it is repugnant to this "spirit," and we call this "walking in the footsteps" of our forefathers!

The rule that the violation of the Constitution must be "clear, palpable, and free from all doubt" had to disappear with the other restraining rules when the express provisions of the Constitution were disregarded as a test of constitutionality of legislation and the vague "spirit of our institutions" was substituted therefor. The "spirit of the Constitution," the "spirit of our institutions" and the "principles of our government," which are now used as criteria of constitutionality, are in themselves empty phrases, into which not only each generation but each individual puts a different content, according to his own philosophical, political and social principles. What Justice Iredell said of "the principles of natural justice" is equally true of these newer principles: "The ablest and the purest men have differed on the subject." In this realm nothing can be said to be "free from doubt." Uniformity of opinion, except among close political associates and kindred philosophical spirits, is here extremely unlikely. And so we have lived to see the power which was originally supposed to be used only in cases "clear, palpable, and free from all doubt," used almost regularly by divided courts, often by bare majorities. And the uninitiated wonder: how is it that a provision, of which one judge emphatically asserts that he is able to find no trace whatever in the Constitution, is asserted by another, and with equal emphasis to be clearly and plainly written therein?

The reading of a few important recent decisions, such as Lochner v. New York,[27] Adair v. United States,[28] People v. Williams[29] and Ives v. South Buffalo Railway Company,[30] will sufficiently illustrate the points just made.

These same cases will also show that we have very effectually disposed of the last safeguard against the establishment of a judicial veto upon any and all acts of our legislative assemblies by discarding the rule that the courts must limit their inquiry to the question of the existence of the power which the legislature has undertaken to exercise, and that where the power exists its exercise is beyond the judicial sphere of influence. The courts now openly review the use made by the legislature of its conceded powers, thus arrogating to themselves a distinctly legislative function.

The result of all these changes may be summed up in a sentence. There are now no such "plain and simple" rules of interpretation as Judge Lurton claims; on the contrary, there are now practically no rules at all. Each case is supposed to stand "on its own merits," which, translated into ordinary English, simply means that each law is declared "constitutional" or "unconstitutional" according to the opinion the judges entertain as to its wisdom. This is another reason for the fact that almost all important constitutional cases are now decided by divided courts. Since there are no longer any set rules by which the judges can be guided, since they are left to determine the propriety and wisdom of laws according to the canons of politics and statemanship, they naturally exhibit those differences of opinion which we expect to find in legislative bodies.

This leads our Supreme Court as well as our other courts, into the position – anomalous and absurd for a court, though perfectly proper for a legislature – of deciding in different ways cases similar in principle. Thus in the case of Holden v. Hardy[31] the Supreme Court decided, by a vote of six to three, that a law limiting the hours of labor in mines was constitutional; but in Lochner v. New York[32] it decided, by a vote of five to four, that a law limiting the hours of labor in bakeries was unconstitutional. In principle the two cases are of course identical. Under the old rules of interpretation, which limited judicial inquiry to the matter of legislative competence, these two cases must have been decided in the same way. Either both laws were constitutional or they were both unconstitutional. In the earlier case, Holden v. Hardy, the Supreme Court decided that the state legislature had the power to pass a law limiting the hours of work in any industry when it – the legislature – came to the conclusion that longer hours would endanger the health of those employed in that industry. It followed as an irresistible conclusion that the baker law was constitutional, the legislature enacting it having come to the conclusion that it was necessary for the protection of the health of those working in bakeries. The decision in Lochner v. New York, declaring that law unconstitutional, startled the legal profession and evoked vigorous protest from many constitutional lawyers. They could not understand it. They accused the Supreme Court of inconsistency. But the truth is that the court had discarded the old rules of constitutional interpretation and had adopted an entirely different theory. An examination of the dissenting opinion in that case, when it was before the New York Court of Appeals, and of the prevailing opinion in the United States Supreme Court, clearly shows this shifting of ground. Under the new rule of interpretation, it is no longer a question whether the legislature has the power to limit the hours of labor, when it determines that such a limitation is necessary for the health of those engaged in a particular industry; the question is whether that power has been wisely used. The power of the legislature is conceded, but

its discretion is reviewed and is determined to have been improperly exercised. The legislature has found that work in a bakery beyond a certain number of hours is dangerous to health. But, says the court, we don't consider it so.
And it was their judgment on the matter of the healthfulness of work in a
bakery, not their judgment on the constitutional power of the legislature, that
led five out of the nine judges to declare the law unconstitutional.

We are not now concerned with the question whether their conclusion
was correct or erroneous. What concerns us is the fact that the court assumed
the distinctively legislative function of deciding whether circumstances existed which required remedial legislation. This position is opposed to that
which the court took in Munn v. Illinois.[33] Even in that comparatively late case
the Supreme Court still held that such an inquiry was part of the functions of
the legislature, and none of the court's business. It said: "For our purposes we
must assume that if a state of facts could exist that would justify such legislation, it actually did exist when the statute under consideration was passed." In
other words: if the legislature has the power to limit the hours of labor when
the health of the employees demands it, the court must presume that the
health of the employees in the particular industry which the legislature has
undertaken so to regulate does in fact demand such a limitation of hours.
Neither Judge Lurton, nor anybody else, will contend that if this rule had been
followed in Lochner v. New York the bakery law would have been declared
unconstitutional. It was declared unconstitutional because the rule still recognized in Munn v. Illinois was repudiated.

Another glaring instance of the open assumption of legislative discretion
by the judiciary is furnished by the recent decision of the United States Supreme Court in the Case of Muller v. Oregon.[34] In that case the Oregon statute
under consideration limited the hours of work for women in "mechanical establishments, factories and laundries," to ten hours a day. This law was declared
constitutional "as to laundries." The Supreme Court conceded the power of the
state legislature to limit the hours of work for women, on the ground that "as
healthy mothers are necessary for healthy offspring" the health of women is a
matter of special concern to the state. And yet the court limited its approval of
the exercise of that power to the case of laundries, reserving the right to
declare the law unconstitutional as to "mechanical establishments" and "factories" if it should conclude on future investigation that the state legislature had
made an unwise use of its conceded powers as regards such establishments.

Approval of the decision in Muller v. Oregon as a matter of legislative
policy, because of its effect upon the condition of the working class of this
country, should not blind us to its significance as regards the distribution of
political power in our governmental system. In the latter respect it openly, I
may say almost defiantly, maintains the position that to the judiciary belongs
the supreme control of all legislation and that it means to use it.

To say, in the face of these decisions and the many more that could be
cited but for lack of space, that our courts do not exercise any legislative

power, seems like adding insult to injury. And it is certainly a strange commentary on Judge Lurton's declaration, that the judicial power insures to us "a
government of laws and not a government of men," that within three months
after the publication of these words the New York court of appeals rendered a
decision[35] which led the editors of two important magazines to the doleful
conclusion that nothing can help us—not even an amendment to the Constitution—except the election to the judiciary of *proper men,* not men learned in the
law and in the Constitution, but men with a knowledge of life and plenty of
common sense.[36] These editors meekly accept the political situation created by
the latest phase of the development of the judicial power and merely suggest a
remedy for our social and economic ills on the basis of that political situation.
But the great question before the people of the United States is: Shall we
permit this political situation to become firmly and irrevocably established?
Shall we permit this great revolution in our political institutions to take place
undisputed? And the question before our leaders of thought is: Shall we permit
this revolution to take place without even calling the attention of the people of
the United States to its momentous character?

NOTES

a. *Political Science Quarterly* 26 (June 1911):238–70.

1. *The Outlook,* December 17, 1910, vol. xcvi, p. 848.
2. *North American Review,* vol. 193, p. 25.
3. *North American Review,* vol. 193, p. 24.
4. Commentaries (Lewis's edition), Introduction. p. 91.
5. *Ibid.* book, i, p. 162.
6. *Loc. cit.* pp. 16, 17.
7. Paxton's case (Massachusetts Superior Court, 1761), is not in point, because
the writ of assistance issued to Paxton, of which the validity was questioned, was not
issued by the legislature of the colony but by the judges; and its validity was questioned,
not because its issue was alleged to be in conflict with any written constitution, for there
was no such constitution in existence, but because its issue was alleged to be contrary to
English law. The justices were unanimously of the opinion that the writ might be
granted. Professor Thayer does not reproduce the case (which is briefly reported in
Quincy, pp. 51–57); but from the appendix to Quincy's Reports p. 520, he reprints (Cases
on Constitutional Law, vol. i. p. 48) an abstract of the argument of counsel (Otis), to the
effect that the act of Parliament under which the writ was issued was of no effect
because contrary to the laws of nature. Some English judges had expressed the same
notion—that laws contrary to natural law were void—but no such doctrine was ever
established in Great Britain, nor does the decision in Paxton's case indicate that the
Massachusetts judges accepted it.
   Commonwealth *v.* Caton (Virginia Court of Appeals, 1782; 4 Call, 5; Thayer, Cases,
vol. i, p. 55)—the only case which Judge Lurton names—is not in point, because the court
had before it nothing resembling a legislative enactment. What was before the court was

an attempt on the part of one house of the legislature to grant to certain persons, convicted of treason, a pardon, which could be granted only by the concurrent action of the two houses. On its face the alleged pardon was nothing but a bill which had failed to become the law, and no court in the world would have treated it as possessing any force. Professor Thayer reprints the case because the judges declared *obiter* that they were competent to determine the validity of legislative enactments alleged to be in conflict with the constitution of the state.

8. Thayer, Cases on Constitutional Law, vol. i, p. 63.

9. Thayer, Cases, vol. i, note on pp. 72, 73, citing Dawson's introduction to the pamphlet in which the case was printed, and Coxe, Judicial Power, pp. 223 *et seq.*

10. *Ibid.* p. 73.

11. Coxe, *op. cit.,* pp. 234 *et seq. Cf.* Baldwin, The American Judiciary, p. 110.

12. Martin (N.C.) p. 42. Thayer, Cases, vol. i, p. 78.

13. Coxe, Judicial Power, p. 252.

14. There is another case, earlier than Commonwealth *v* Caton, which is not mentioned by Professor Thayer or Judge Lurton, but which seems in point. The text of the decision is not preserved, but its character seems well attested. In Holmes *v.* Walton (New Jersey Supreme Court, 1780; *American Historical Review,* vol. iv, pp. 456 *et seq.*), a state law making certain cases triable by a jury of six was set aside, apparently because in conflict with the state constitution. This decision aroused popular protests similar to those noted above in the other cases: complaints "poured in upon the Assembly." The lower house attempted to confirm the law; but the Council opposed this action, and the matter was compromised.

For the sake of making our review complete, it may be said that in a letter from John B. Cutting to Thomas Jefferson, dated London, July 11, 1788, it is stated that a law of Massachusetts has been pronounced unconstitutional by the supreme court of that state, and that it had been repealed at the next session of the legislature (Massachusetts Historical Society, Proceedings, 1903, second series, vol. xvii, p. 507). Of this case there is no record nor is there any other mention.

15. 2 Dallas, 409.

16. The "representation" which the Pennsylvania circuit court sent to the president reads as follows:

"To you it officially belongs to 'take care that the laws of the United States 'be faithfully executed.' Before you, therefore, we think it our duty to lay the sentiments, which, on a late painful occasion, governed us with regard to an act passed by the legislature of the union.

"The people of the United States have vested in Congress all *legislative* powers 'granted in the constitution.' They have vested in one Supreme court, and in such inferior courts as the Congress shall establish, 'the *judicial* power of the United States.' It is worthy of remark, that in Congress the *whole* legislative power of the United States is not vested. An important part of that power was exercised by the people themselves, when they 'ordained and established the Constitution.' This constitution is 'the Supreme Law of the Land.' This supreme law 'all judicial officers of the United States are bound, by oath or affirmation, to support.'

"It is a principle important to freedom, that in government, the *judicial* should be distinct from, and independent of, the legislative department. To this important principle, the people of the United States, in forming their Constitution, have manifested the highest regard. They have placed their *judicial* power, not in Congress, but in '*courts.*' They have ordained that the 'Judges of those courts shall hold their offices during good behaviour, ' and that 'during their continuance in office, their salaries shall not be diminished.'

"Congress have lately passed an act, to regulate, among other things, 'the claims to invalid pensions.' Upon due consideration, we have been unanimously of opinion, that, under this act, the Circuit court held for the Pennsylvania district could not proceed.

"1st. Because the business directed by this act is not of a judicial nature. It forms no part of the power vested by the Constitution in the courts of the United States; the Circuit court must, consequently, have proceeded *without* constitutional authority. 2nd. Because, if, upon that business, the court had proceeded, its *judgments* (for its *opinions* are its judgments) might, under the same act, have been revised and controuled by the legislature, and by an officer in the executive department. Such revision and controul we deemed radically inconsistent with the independence of that judicial power which is vested in the courts; and, consequently, with that important principle which is so strictly observed by the Constitution of the United States.

"These, Sir, are the reasons for our conduct. Be assured that, though it became necessary, it was far from being pleasant. To be obliged to act contrary, either to the obvious directions of Congress, or to a constitutional principle, in our judgment equally obvious, excited feelings in us, which we hope never to experience again."

17. Hayburn's Case, 2 Dallas, 409.

18. 3 Dallas, 386.

19. The facts of this celebrated case, in so far as they are material to understanding of the decision, were as follows. After the great victory of the Republicans in the election of 1800 – "the Revolution of 1800" as Jefferson called it – the Federalists utilized the brief term of power which was left them to remodel the federal judicial system and to fill the federal courts with their partisans. As part of that work they created, by an act passed February 27, 1801, certain justiceships for the District of Columbia; and one William Marbury, the plaintiff in the case, was appointed to one of these justiceships. His nomination was confirmed by the Senate March 3, the last day of the Adams administration, and his commission was signed that night by the president and sealed by Marshall, then secretary of state. On that night Marshall himself was commissioned as chief justice of the United States. Marbury's commission, however, was left undelivered for lack of time; and when Jefferson took office he forbade its issuance, on the ground that the appointment did not take effect until the delivery of the commission, and he was therefore free to revoke it. Marbury then applied to the Supreme Court, now headed by Marshall, for a *mandamus* compelling Madison, Jefferson's secretary of state, to issue to him his commission. To the order made by the court, commanding the new secretary of state to show cause why the *mandamus* should not issue, Madison paid no attention. After long deliberation, the court gave its decision in 1803, refusing to issue the *mandamus*. In the opinion delivered by Marshall, the court based its decision, not on the contention put forward on behalf of the administration, that Marbury was not legally appointed and therefore not entitled to the commission, which contention it expressly overruled, but on the alleged lack of power in the Supreme Court to issue a *mandamus*. In order to arrive at this latter conclusion, the court had to declare unconstitutional a statute passed by Congress giving the Supreme Court such power. And it is this part of the opinion that has made it famous.

20. In reference to these struggles, *cf* American State Papers, Misc., vol. ii, pp. 2, 6; Sketch of Hon. Calvin Pease, *Western Law Monthly*, June, 1863, quoted in Cooley, Constitutional Limitations (7th ed.), pp. 229, 230; Niles Register, vol. xxiii supplement, p. 155; Collins, History of Kentucky, vol. i, pp. 218 *et seq*

21. Baldwin, The American Judiciary, pp. 113–115.

22. *Cf.* Eakin *v.* Raub, 12 Sergeant and Rawle, 330, 343.

23. *Cf. supra*, pp. 252, 253.

24. 21 Pennsylvania State Reports, 147.

25. Loan Association *v.* Topeka (1874), 20 Wallace, 655, 669.

26. 94 U.S. 113.

27. 198 U.S. 45 and 177 N.Y. 145.

28. 208 U.S. 161.

29. 189 N.Y. 131.

30. New York *Law Journal*, April 3, 4, 1911.

31. 169 U.S. 366.

32. 198 U.S. 45.

33. *Cf. supra*, p. 263.

34. 208 U.S. 412.

35. Ives *v.* South Buffalo Railway Company (New York *Law Journal*, April 3, 4, 1911), declaring unconstitutional the Workmen's Compensation Act.

36. "Economics, Philosophy and Morals *v.* the Court of Appeals"; *The Survey*, April 8, 1911, vol. xxvi, pp. 77–80. "The Judge and the People"; *The Outlook*, April 15, 1911, vol. xcvii, pp. 809, 810.

10

The Answer: Judicial Review and the Framers' Intent

MR. BOUDIN'S ACCUSATIONS and those of his fellow doubters did not pass unnoticed. This is due in great part to the fact that his charges were something more than the makeweight arguments of a disgruntled politician. Accordingly, Charles A. Beard wrote of him as one of the "legal writers of respectable authority," but nevertheless one whose "sweeping generalizations" had to be examined in "the interest of historical accuracy." Later to become president of both the American Historical Association and the American Political Science Association, Beard was regarded as one of the great authorities in American history and politics. When he wrote the article reproduced below, Beard was a popular professor at the institution that was the pioneering leader in the study of American political science, Columbia University.

Through an examination of the direct and indirect declarations of certain members of the Philadelphia Convention, of various judicial opinions, and of the "purpose and spirit of the federal Constitution," Beard concludes that judicial review was not usurped; it was intended by the Constitutional framers. The evidence adduced in support of his conclusion and the assumptions underlying his research methodology not only shed light upon the usurpation question, but also point to the many difficulties inherent in constitutional interpretation.

Beard begins his argument by conceding that the delegates to the Constitutional Convention did not consider a proposition to grant to the judicial branch a veto over legislative acts. In fact, none was submitted. A council of revision was proposed which would have joined a number of judges with the executive to revise laws passed by Congress. But that is, according to Beard, a different proposition from judicial review. Readers may want to contemplate whether this difference is sufficiently dissimilar to sustain Beard's point. Also note that later in the article Beard cites apparent support of a number of delegates for the revisionary council proposition as persuasive evidence of their belief in judicial review. It seems that Professor Beard wants it both ways. In any event, he claims that the "question of judicial control . . . did not come squarely before the Convention, in such form that a vote could be taken." With that statement, friend or foe of judicial supremacy will agree.

The bulk of Beard's article is devoted to the difficult question of what the Framers intended. He prefaces this research approach with the caution that any such inquiry must be incomplete because new research could uncover additional information. But the search for intent is fraught with even greater difficulties, not the least of which are its underlying assumptions. These are succintly outlined by Professors Walter Murphy and C. Herman Pritchett.[a]

The first assumption is that future generations should be bound by the specific intentions of the Framers, not the general principles that guided their actions. If this assumption is accepted, Americans will be constitutionally mired in the eighteenth century. In this view the Constitution must be interpreted as a set of rules that can be clearly understood as articulated by the Framers. In fairness, we must note that both Beard and his intellectual antagonist Boudin silently accept this questionable assumption. Yet given the nature of the argument it is reasonable for Beard to search for specific intent. It is Boudin and others who claim that because the Framers were silent on the matter of judicial review they could not have intended to make it a part of the Constitution. Beard uses evidence of the specific intent of the individual Framers to counter this point.

In our estimation, the second assumption underlying the search for the Framers' intent is more difficult to defend than the first. It is that the Framers had a single intention. It is conceivable, nay, probable, that the Framers had many different, sometimes contradictory and even irreconcilable "intentions." Reflecting on one's own group experiences, is enough to show that the "group mind" is often elusive. Indeed, the Philadelphia Convention was not an exercise in ascertaining the "general will" or Confucian harmony. Rather it was a matter of compromise, logrolling, and negotiation about matters that do not lend themselves to simple solutions. The politics of such a setting renders the ascertainment of a solid and unified group intention difficult at best.

Beard mitigates the problem of intent by breaking the group down into its constituent parts, namely, the individual delegates. He does this by examining the Convention debates and the letters and private documents of a good number of delegates.

Note that Beard does not examine the views of all fifty-five delegates to the Philadelphia Convention. Rather he first investigates the views of what he calls the leading, or the most influential, members of the convention. He concludes that of these no fewer than thirteen believed that judicial power extended to the nullification of an act of Congress. He adds four more delegates to his total by virtue of their subsequent votes in Congress in support of the Judiciary Act of 1789.

Of the less influential delegates, seven either expressed themselves in favor of judicial review or approved of it by virtue of their votes on the 1789 act. Incidentally, Beard's reference to the Judiciary Act is to that part of the bill dealing with federal-state relations under the Constitution's Supremacy Clause. The argument supposes that favoring judicial review of state actions is the equivalent to supporting judicial control over congressional acts. Though the two are related, readers should consider whether one might reasonably support the federalism principle without favoring the third-branch veto over congressional enactments. Finally, with respect to the Judiciary Act, note that the methodological problems inherent in ascertaining legislative intent are, in principle, similar to those encountered in studying constitutional intent.

Readers should ask themselves whether the evidence presented for each delegate's position of judicial review is clear and convincing. In any event, Beard's best-case argument does not show that a majority of the delegates favored judicial review. He finds that twenty-three were for judicial review, five were against it, and the views of the remaining twenty-seven are unknown. Edward S. Corwin, whose authority ranks with Beard's, found only seventeen in favor of judicial review.[b] Nevertheless, both scholars insist that the Framers intended judicial review. It is troublesome nonetheless, that as influential as the twenty-three or seventeen delegates may have been, it requires considerable faith in their leadership abilities to conclude that all, most, or even a majority of the delegates would have voted for judicial review if the proposition had been presented squarely to them.

However, as one progresses through the argument it is discovered that numbers are not everything. Beard's fall-back position is clear enough: "the constitution is not designed to be perfectly explicit on all points and to embody definitely the opinions of a majority of the Convention." One might wonder that, if this is true, why did Beard make the case for the specific intent of as many convention delegates as he could?

Beard does not rest his case with the submission of evidence on the Framers' intentions. He continues the "brief" against Boudin and other named and unnamed opposing counsels by addressing the remaining usurpation charges and evidence.

Constitutions are not only framed. They are also ratified. Note the presentation of admittedly fragmentary evidence. Beard presents information from the debates in four of thirteen state ratifying conventions in support of his argument that the people who ratified the Constitution favored judicial review. Also note that Beard is unimpressed by arguments of his intellectual opponents that state judicial opinions do not serve as adequate precedents for judicial review. Finally, Beard defends John Marshall against the charge that he created judicial review out of whole cloth. Beard points out that the concept was known within legal circles at the time of the founding, and indeed, prior to the decision in *Marbury* the Supreme Court had alluded to judicial review in a number of decisions.

After reading the chapters in this part of the book, readers may honestly differ on the usurpation question. It is clear to us that reasonable persons may disagree about the answer. Perhaps, as former Chief Justice Warren Burger has stated, "it is now accepted that the original assertion of the power was not judicial usurpation as Jefferson considered it."[c] However, whether that acceptance is based upon reasoned analysis or the facts of political life may be another matter altogether.

The Supreme Court—Usurper or Grantee?[d] [1]

Charles A. Beard

DID THE FRAMERS of the federal Constitution intend that the Supreme Court should pass upon the constitutionality of acts of Congress? The emphatic negative recently given to this question by legal writers of respectable authority[2] has put the sanction of the guild on the popular notion that the nullification of statutes by the federal judiciary is warranted neither by the letter nor by the spirit of the supreme law of the land and is, therefore, rank usurpation. Thus the color of legality, so highly prized by revolutionaries as well as by apostles of law and order, is given to a movement designed to strip the courts of their great political function. While the desirability of judicial control over legislation may be considered by practical men entirely apart from its historical origins, the attitude of those who drafted the Constitution surely cannot be regarded as a matter solely of antiquarian interest. Indeed, the eagerness with which the "views of the Fathers" have been marshalled in support of the attack upon judicial control proves that they continue to exercise some moral weight, even if they are not binding upon the public conscience.

The arguments advanced to show that the framers of the Constitution did not intend to grant to the federal judiciary any control over federal legislation may be summarized as follows. Not only is the power in question not expressly granted, but it could not have seemed to the framers to be granted by implication. The power to refuse application to an unconstitutional law was not generally regarded as proper to the judiciary. In a few cases only had state courts attempted to exercise such a power, and these few attempts had been sharply rebuked by the people. Of the members of the Convention of 1787 not more than five or six are known to have regarded this power as a part of the general judicial power; and Spaight and three or four others are known to have held the contrary opinion. It cannot be assumed that the other forty-odd members of the Convention were divided on the question in the same proportion. If any conclusion is to be drawn from their silence, it is rather that they did not believe that any such unprecedented judicial power could be read into the Constitution. This conclusion is fortified by the fact that a proposition to confer upon the federal judges revisory power over federal legislation was four times made in the Convention and defeated.

A careful examination of the articles cited fails to reveal that the writers have made any detailed analysis of the sources from which we derive our knowledge of the proceedings of the Convention and of the views held by its members. They certainly do not produce sufficient evidence to support their sweeping generalizations. In the interest of historical accuracy, therefore, it is well to inquire whether the evidence available on the point is sufficient to convict the Supreme Court of usurping an authority which the framers of the Constitution did not conceive to be within the judicial province. If the opinions of the majority of the Convention cannot be definitely ascertained, any categorical answer to the question proposed must rest upon the "argument of silence," which, as Fustel de Coulanges warned the Germans long ago, is a dangerous argument.

Now at the outset of this inquiry one important fact should be noted. No proposition to confer directly upon the judiciary the power of passing upon the constitutionality of acts of Congress was submitted to the Convention. On this point a statement made in Chief Justice Clark's address, cited above, is misleading. The proposition to which he refers, and which formed a part of the Randolph plan, was to associate a certain number of the judges with the executive in the exercise of revisionary power over the laws passed by Congress. This was obviously a different proposition. Indeed, some members of the Convention who favored judicial control opposed the creation of such a council of revision.[3] The question of judicial control, accordingly, did not come squarely before the Convention, in such form that a vote could be taken.

How are we to know what was the intention of the framers of the Constitution in this matter? The only method is to make an exhaustive search in the documents of the Convention and in the writings, speeches, papers and recorded activities of its members. It is obviously impossible to assert that any such inquiry is complete, for new material, printed or in manuscript, may be produced at any moment. This paper therefore makes no claim to completeness or to finality. It is designed to throw light on the subject and to suggest ways in which more light may be obtained.

In view of the fact that no vote was taken on this issue, we are compelled to examine the notes of the debates on every part of the Constitution and to search the letters, papers and documents of the members of the Convention to find out how many of them put themselves on record, in one way or another.

I

There were in all fifty-five members of the Convention who were present at some of its meetings. Of these at least one-third took little or no part in the proceedings or were of little weight or were extensively absent. Among these may be included: Blount, Brearley, Broom, Clymer, Fitzsimons, Gilman, W. C. Houston, William Houston, Ingersoll, Lansing, Livingston, McClurg, Alexander Martin, Mifflin, Pierce and Yates. It is of course difficult to estimate the influence of the several members of the Convention, and between the extremes there are a few regarding whom there may reasonably be a difference of opinion. The preceding list is doubtless open to criticism, but it may be safely asserted that a large majority of the men included in it were without any considerable influence in the framing of the Constitution.

Of the remaining members there were (say) twenty-five whose character, ability, diligence and regularity of attendance, separately or in combination, made them the dominant element in the Convention. These men were:

Blair	Franklin	*King*	*Morris, R.*	Rutledge
Butler	*Gerry*	*Madison*	*Patterson*	Sherman
Dayton	Gorham	*Martin, L.*	Pinckney, Charles	*Washington*
Dickinson	*Hamilton*	Mason	Pinckney, C. C.	*Williamson*
Ellsworth	*Johnson*	*Morris, G.*	*Randolph*	Wilson

This list, like the one given above, is tentative; and it is fair to say that, among those whose judgment is entitled to respect, there is no little difference of opinion about the weight of some of the men here enumerated. It cannot be doubted, however, that the list includes the decided majority of the men who were most influential in giving the Constitution its form and its spirit. Among these men were leaders, of whose words and activities we have the fullest records.

Of these men, the seventeen whose names are italicized declared, directly or indirectly, for judicial control. Without intending to imply that the less influential members were divided on the question in the same ratio as these twenty-five, or that due respect should not be paid to the principle of simple majority rule, it is illuminating to discover how many of this dominant group are found on record in favor of the proposition that the judiciary would in the natural course of things pass upon the constitutionality of acts of Congress. The evidence of each man's attitude is here submitted, the names being arranged, as above, in their alphabetical order.

John Blair, of Virginia, was a member of the Virginia court of appeals which decided the case of Commonwealth *v.* Caton,[4] in 1782, and he agreed with the rest of the judges "that the court had power to declare any resolution or act of the legislature, or of either branch of it, to be unconstitutional and void."[5] Ten years later he was one of the three judges of the federal circuit court for the district of Pennsylvania who claimed that they could not perform certain duties imposed upon them by a law of Congress, because the duties were not judicial in nature and because under the law their acts would be subject to legislative or executive control. These judges — Blair, Wilson[6] and Peters — joined in a respectful letter of protest to President Washington, April 18, 1792, in which they declared that they held it to be their duty to disregard the directions of Congress rather than to act contrary to a constitutional principle.[7] It may also be noted that, as a member of the federal Senate, Blair supported the Judiciary Act of 1789, which accorded to the Supreme Court the power to review and reverse or affirm the decisions of state courts denying the validity of federal statutes.[8]

John Dickinson, of Delaware, is usually placed among the members of the Convention who did not recognize the power of the courts to pass upon the constitutionality of statutes; for in the debate on August 15, just after Mercer[9] declared against judicial control, Dickinson said that "he was strongly impressed with the remark of Mr. Mercer as to the power of the Judges to set aside the law. He thought no such power ought to exist. He was at the same time at a loss what expedient to substitute."[10] Later, however, he accepted the principle of judicial control, either because he thought it sound or because he could find no satisfactory substitute. In one of his "Fabius" letters, written in advocacy of the Constitution in 1788, he says:

> In the senate the sovereignties of the several states will be equally represented; in the house of representatives the people of the whole union will be equally represented; and in the president and the federal independent judges, so much concerned in the execution of the laws and in the determination of their constitutionality, the sovereignties of the several states and the people of the whole union may be considered as conjointly represented.[11]

Whatever his personal preference may have been, he evidently understood that the new instrument implicitly empowered the federal judiciary to determine the constitutionality of laws; and he presents this implication to the public as a commendable feature of the Constitution.

Oliver Ellsworth, of Connecticut, held that the federal judiciary, in the discharge of its normal function, would declare acts of Congress contrary to the federal Constitution null and void. In the Connecticut convention, called to ratify the federal Constitution, he was careful to explain this clearly to the assembled delegates.[12] Later, he was chairman of the Senate committee which prepared the Judiciary Act of 1789 and took a leading part in the drafting of that measure.[13]

Elbridge Gerry, of Massachusetts. When, on June 4, the proposition relative to a council of revision was taken into consideration by the Convention, Gerry expressed doubts

> whether the Judiciary ought to form a part of it, as they will have a suffi-
> cient check against encroachments on their own department by their expo-
> sition of the law, which involved a power of deciding on their constitu-
> tionality. In some States the Judges had actually set aside laws as being
> against the Constitution. This was done, too, with general approbation. It
> was quite foreign from the nature of the office to make them judges of the
> policy of public measures.[14]

During the debate in the first Congress on the question whether the president had the constitutional right to remove federal officers without the consent of the Senate, Gerry more than once urged that the judiciary was the proper body to decide the issue finally. On June 16, 1789, he said:

> Are we afraid that the President and Senate are not sufficiently informed to
> know their respective duties? . . . If the fact is, as we seem to suspect, that
> they do not understand the Constitution, let it go before the proper tri-
> bunal; the judges are the constitutional umpires on such question.[15]

Speaking on the same subject again, he said:

> If the power of making declaratory acts really vests in Congress and the
> judges are bound by our decisions, we may alter that part of the Constitu-
> tion which is secured from being amended by the fifth article; we may say
> that the ninth section of the Constitution, respecting the migration or im-
> portation of persons, does not extend to negroes; that the word persons
> means only white men and women. We then proceed to lay a duty of twenty
> or thirty dollars per head on the importation of negroes. The merchant
> does not construe the Constitution in the manner that we have done. He
> therefore institutes a suit and brings it before the supreme judicature of the
> United States for trial. The judges, who are bound by oath to support the
> constitution, declare against this law; they would therefore give judgment
> in favor of the merchant.[16]

Alexander Hamilton, of New York. In *The Federalist* written in defence of the Constitution, and designed to make that instrument acceptable to the electorate, Hamilton said:

> The interpretation of the laws is the proper and peculiar province of the courts. A constitution is, in fact, and must be, regarded by the judges as fundamental law. It must, therefore, belong to them to ascertain its meaning, as well as the meaning of an particular act proceeding from the legislative body. If there should happen to be an irreconcilable variance between the two, that which has the superior obligation and validity ought, of course, to be preferred, or in other words, the Constitution ought to be preferred to the statute, the intention of the people to the intention of their agents.[17]

Rufus King, of Massachusetts. In the discussion of the proposed council of revision which took place in the Convention on June 4, King took the same position as Gerry, observing "that the judges ought to be able to expound the law as it should come before them free from the bias of having participated in its formation."[18] According to Pierce's notes he said that he

> was of opinion that the judicial ought not to join in the negative of a law because the judges will have the expounding of those laws when they come before them; and they will no doubt stop the operation of such as shall appear repugnant to the constitution.[19]

James Madison, of Virginia. That Madison believed in judicial control over legislation is unquestionable, but as to the exact nature and extent of that control he was in no little confusion. His fear of the legislature is expressed repeatedly in his writings, and he was foremost among the men who sought to establish a revisionary council of which the judges should form a part. In the Convention he said:

> Experience in all the states had evinced a powerful tendency in the legislature to absorb all power into its vortex. This was the real source of danger to the American Constitutions; and suggested the necessity of giving every defensive authority to the other departments that was consistent with republican principles.[20]

The association of the judges with the executive, he contended, "would be useful to the judiciary department by giving it an additional opportunity of defending itself against legislative encroachments."[21] He was evidently greatly disappointed by the refusal of the Convention to establish a revisionary council; for, in after years, he said that "such a control, restricted to constitutional points, besides giving greater stability and system to the rules of expounding the instrument would have precluded the question of a judiciary annulment of legislative acts."[22]

From the first, however, he accepted judicial control only with limitation; and complete judicial paramountcy over the other branches of the federal government he certainly deprecated. When it was proposed to extend the jurisdiction of the Supreme Court to cases arising under the Constitution as well as under the laws of the United States, he

> doubted whether it was not going too far to extend the jurisdiction of the court generally to cases arising under the Constitution and whether it ought not to be limited to case of a judiciary nature. The right of expounding the constitution in cases not of this nature ought not to be given to that department.[23]

The refusal of the Convention to establish a council of revision, in his opinion left the judiciary paramount, which was in itself undesirable and not intended by the framers of the Constitution. In a comment on the proposed Virginia Constitution of 1788, he wrote in that year:

> In the state constitutions and indeed in the federal one also, no provision is made for the case of a disagreement in expounding them [the laws], and as the courts are generally the last in making the decision, it results to them, by refusing or not refusing to execute a law, to stamp it with its final character. This makes the Judiciary Department paramount in fact to the Legislature, which was never intended and can never be proper.[24]

The right of the courts to pass upon constitutional questions in cases of a judicial nature we fully acknowlege; but this did not, in his mind, preclude the other departments from declaring their sentiments on points of constitutionality and from marking out the limits of their own powers. This view he expressed in the House of Representatives (first Congress) when the question of the president's removing power was under debate:

> The great objection . . . is that the legislature itself has no right to expound the Constitution; that wherever its meaning is doubtful, you must leave it to take its course, until the judiciary is called upon to declare its meaning. I acknowledge, in the ordinary course of government, that the exposition of the laws and Constitution devolves upon the judicial; but I beg to know upon what principle it can be contended that any one department draws from the Constitution greater powers of the several departments. The Constitution is the charter of the people in the government; it specifies certain great powers as absolutely granted, and marks out the departments to exercise them. If the constitutional boundary of either be brought into question I do not see that any one of these independent departments has more right than another to declare their sentiments on that point.
>
> Perhaps this is an admitted case. There is not one government on the face of the earth, so far as I recollect—there is not one in the United States—in which provision is made for a particular authority to determine the limits of the constitutional division of power between the branches of the government. In all systems, there are points which must be adjusted by the departments themselves, to which no one of them is competent. If it cannot be determined in this way, there is no resource left but the will of the community, to be collected in some mode to be provided by the Constitution, or one dictated by the necessity of the case. It is, therefore, a fair

question, whether this great point may not as well be decided, at least by
the whole legislature, as by part – by us, as well as by the executive or the
judicial. As I think it will be equally constitutional, I cannot imagine it will
be less safe, that the exposition should issue from the legislative authority,
than any other; and the more so, because it involves in the decision the
opinions of both of those departments whose powers are supposed to be
affected by it. Besides, I do not see in what way this question could come
before the judges to obtain a fair and solemn decision; but even if it were
the case that it could, I should suppose, at least while the government is not
lead by passion, disturbed by faction, or deceived by any discolored medium of sight, but while there is a desire in all to see and be guided by the
benignant ray of truth, that the decision may be made with the most advantage by the legislature itself.[25]

Madison's views on the point may be summed up as follows: In cases of a
political nature involving controversies between departments, each department enjoys a power of interpretation for itself (a doctrine which Marshall
would not have denied); in controversies of a judicial nature arising under the
Constitution, the Supreme Court is the tribunal of last resort; in cases of
federal statutes which are held to be invalid by nullifying states, the Supreme
Court possesses the power to pass finally upon constitutionality.[26]

Luther Martin, of Maryland, although he opposed the proposition to form
a revisionary council by associating judges with the executive, was nevertheless strongly convinced that unconstitutional laws would be set aside by the
judiciary. During the debate on July 21, he said:

> A knowledge of mankind, and of Legislative affairs cannot be presumed to
> belong in a higher degree to the Judges than to the Legislature. And as to
> the Constitutionality of laws, that point will come before the Judges in their
> proper official character. In this character they have a negative on the laws.
> Join them with the Executive in the Revision and they will have a double
> negative. It is necessary that the Supreme Judiciary should have the confi-
> dence of the people. This will soon be lost, if they are employed in the task
> of remonstrating against popular measures of the Legislature.[27]

George Mason, of Virginia, favored associating the judges with the executive in revision laws. He recognized that the judges would have the power to
declare unconstitutional statutes void, but he regarded this control as insufficient. He said:

> Notwithstanding the precautions taken in the constitution of the Legisla-
> ture, it would so much resemble that of the individual states, that it must
> be expected frequently to pass unjust and pernicious laws. This restraining
> power was therefore essentially necessary. It would have the effect not only
> of hindering the final passage of such laws, but would discourage dema-
> gogues from attempting to get them passed. It had been said (by Mr. L.
> Martin) that if the Judges were joined in this check on the laws, they would
> have a double negative, since in their expository capacity of Judges they

would have one negative. He would reply that in this capacity they could impede in one case only, the operation of laws. They could declare an unconstitutional law void. But with regard to every law, however unjust, oppressive or pernicious, which did not come plainly under this description, they would be under the necessity as Judges to give it a free course. He wished the further use to be made of the Judges, of giving aid in preventing every improper law. Their aid will be the more valuable as they are in the habit and practice of considering laws in their true principles, and in all their consequences.[28]

Gouverneur Morris, of Pennsylvania, declared in the debate on July 21, that some check on the legislature was necessary; and he concurred in thinking the public liberty in greater danger from the legislative usurpations than from any other source."[29] He was apprehensive lest the addition of the judiciary to the executive in the council of revision would not be enough to hold the legislature in check. Later, when Dickinson questioned the right of the judiciary to set aside laws, Morris said:

He could not agree that the judiciary, which was a part of the executive, should be bound to say that a direct violation of the Constitution was law. A control over the legislature might have its inconveniences. But view the danger on the other side. . . . Encroachments of the popular branch of the government ought to be guarded against.[30]

This view he later confirmed in the debate on the repeal of the Judiciary Act of 1801, when he said:

It has been said, and truly too, that governments are made to provide against the follies and vices of men. . . . Hence checks are required in the distribution of power among those who are to exercise it for the benefit of the people. Did the people of America vest all power in the Legislature? No; they had vested in the judges a check intended to be efficient – a check of the first necessity, to prevent an invasion of the Constitution by unconstitutional laws – a check which might prevent any faction from intimidating or annihilating the tribunals themselves.[31]

Edmund Randolph, of Virginia, does not seem to have expressed himself in the Convention on the subject of judicial control over congressional legislation. In the plan which he presented, however, provision was made for establishing a council of revision, composed of the executive and a convenient number of the judiciary, "with authority to examine every act of the National Legislature before it shall operate." He must, therefore, have been convinced of the desirability of some efficient control over the legislative department. Subsequently, as attorney-general, when it came his duty to represent the government in Hayburn's case[32] and he was moving for a *mandamus* to compel the circuit court for the district of Pennsylvania to execute a law under which the judges had declined to act on the ground of its unconstitutionality, Randolph accepted the view of the judges that they were not constitutionally bound to enforce a law which they deemed beyond the powers of Congress. The meager abstract of his argument before the Supreme Court in Dallas's *Reports* gives no hint of its precise character; but in a letter to Madison, dated August 12, 1792, Randolph said: "The sum of my argument was an admission of the power to refuse to execute, but the unfitness of the occasion."[33] That he approved the provision of the Judiciary Act of 1789, giving the Supreme Court appellate jurisdiction to review and reverse or affirm a decision of a state court denying the constitutionality of a federal statute, is apparent from his report to Congress on the judicial system in 1790. After enumerating the instances in which cases might be carried up to the Supreme Court from the state courts, he says: "That the avenue to the federal court from the state ought, in these instances, to be unobstructed, is manifest." The only question with which he was concerned was: "In what stage and by what form shall their interposition be prayed?"[34]

Hugh Williamson, of North Carolina, certainly believed in judicial control over federal legislation; for in the debate on the proposition to insert a clause forbidding Congress to pass *ex post facto* laws, he said: "Such a prohibitory clause is in the constitution of North Carolina, and though it has been violated, it has done good there and may do good here, because the judges can take hold of it."[35] It is obvious that the only way in which the judges can "take hold of" *ex post facto* laws is by declaring them void.

James Wilson of Pennsylvania, expressed himself in favor of judicial control in the course of the debate on July 21, when the proposition to associate the national judiciary with the executive in the revisionary power was again being considered. He declared:

> The Judiciary ought to have an opportunity of remonstrating against projected encroachments on the people as well as on themselves. It had been said that the Judges as expositors of the Laws would have an opportunity of defending their constitutional rights. There was weight in this observation; but this power of the Judges did not go far enough. Laws may be unjust, may be unwise, may be dangerous, may be destructive; and yet not be so unconstitutional as to justify the Judges in refusing to give them effect. Let them have a share in the Revisionary power, and they will have an opportunity of taking notice of these characters of a law, and of counteracting, by the weight of their opinions, the improper views of the Legislature.[36]

Speaking again, on August 23, in favor of giving the national legislature a negative over the state legislation, he said that he

> considered this as the key-stone wanted to complete the wide arch of Government we are raising. The power of self-defence had been urged as necessary for the State Governments. It was equally necessary for the General Government. The firmness of Judges is not of itself sufficient. Something further is requisite. It will be better to prevent the passage of an improper law than to declare it void when passed.[37]

The rejection of the plan to establish a revisionary council did not lead Wilson to infer that thereby the right of the court to pass upon the constitutionality of statutes was denied. On the contrary, in the debates in the Pennsylvania ratifying convention, he declared that the proposed Constitution empowered the judges to declare unconstitutional enactments of Congress null and void.[38]

Examination of the speeches, papers and documents of the influential members of the Convention enumerated above fails to disclose any further direct declarations in favor of the principle of judicial review of legislation. However, there is reasonably satisfactory evidence that four other members of this group understood and indorsed the doctrine.

William Johnson, of Connecticut, *Robert Morris,* of Pennsylvania, *William Paterson,* of New Jersey and *George Washington.* The evidence of their opinions is their approval of the Judiciary Act of 1789. Section 25 of that act provided:

> A final judgment or decree in any suit, in the highest court of law or equity of a state in which a decision in the suit could be had, where is drawn in question the validity of a treaty or statute of, or an authority exercised under, the United States, and the decision is against their validity; . . . or where is drawn in question the construction of any clause of the Constitution, or of a treaty or state of, or commision held under, the United States, and the decision is against the title, right, privilege or exemption specially set up or claimed by either party, under such clause of the said Constitution, treaty, statute or commision, — may be reexamined and reversed or affirmed in the Supreme Court of the United States upon a writ of error.

In other words: the Supreme Court may review and affirm a decision of a state court holding unconstitutional a statute of the United States. It surely is not unreasonable to assume that the men who established this rule believed that the Supreme Court could declare acts of Congress unconstitutional independently of decisions in lower state courts. Indeed, it would seem absurd to assume that an act of Congress might be annulled by a state court with the approval of the Supreme Court, but not by the Supreme Court directly.

William Johnson, Robert Morris and William Paterson[39] were members of the first Senate and voted in favor of the Judiciary Act[40]; and Washington, as president, approved the measure.

In addition to these eminent members of the Convention who directly or indirectly supported the doctrine of judicial control over legislation there were several members of minor influence who seem to have understood and approved it. There is direct or indirect evidence in the following cases.

Abraham Baldwin, of Georgia, had no extensive faith in the probity of a legislature based on a widely extended suffrage. In speaking on the composition of the Senate, on June 29, he said: "He thought the second branch ought to be the representation of property, and that in forming it, therefore, some reference ought to be had to the relative wealth of their constituents and to the principles on which the Senate of Massachusetts was constituted."[41] Baldwin does not seem to have spoken on the subject of the judicial control in the Convention; but two years later, on June 19, 1789, he participated in the discussion of the bill constituting the Department of Foreign Affairs. The point at issue was whether the president could remove alone or only with the consent of the Senate; and some members of the House of Representatives held that this was a judicial question. To this Baldwin replied:

> Gentlemen say it properly belongs to the Judiciary to decide this question. Be it so. It is their province to decide upon our laws and if they find this clause to be unconstitutional, they will not hesitate to declare it so; and it seems to be a very difficult point to bring before them in any other way. Let gentlemen consider themselves in the tribunal of justice called upon to decide this question on a *mandamus*. What a situation! almost too great for human nature to bear, they would feel great relief in having had the question decided by the representatives of the people. Hence, I conclude, they also will receive our opinion kindly.[42]

Here is a direct statement that it is the duty of the judges to pass upon the constitutionality of statutes; and the statute in question was not one involving an encroachment upon the sphere of the judiciary but one touching the respective powers of the president and Senate. Baldwin here seems to think however, that the court would, and ought to, receive with gratitude the expressed opinion of the House of Representatives. Such an opinion, he apparently thought, would aid the judges in reaching a decision but would not be binding upon them. In his later years, however, after the struggle between the Federalists and the Jeffersonians for the control of the national government had begun, Baldwin seems to have retracted his earlier view; for in a debate in the Senate concerning the powers of the presidential electors, in January, 1800, he said:

> Suppose either of the other branches of the government, the Executive or the Judiciary or even Congress, should be guilty of taking steps which are unconstitutional, to whom is it submitted or who has control over it, except by impeachment? The Constitution seems to have equal confidence in all branches on their own proper ground, and for either to arrogate superiority, or a claim to greater confidence, shows them in particular to be unworthy of it, as it is in itself directly unconstitutional.[43]

It is small wonder that Baldwin thought the powers of the judiciary one of the questions that the Convention had left unsettled;[44] but his clear statement on June 19, 1789, may reasonably be taken to represent his understanding of the power conferred on the judiciary by the Constitution. At that time, at least, he believed it a function of the judiciary to pass upon the constitutionality of the statutes.

Richard Bassett, of Delaware, was a member of the Senate committee which introduced the Judiciary Act of 1789, and he voted for the measure.[45] Bassett was also one of Adams's Federalist judges, appointed under the act of

February 13, 1801; and when the Jeffersonians repealed the law he joined
several of his colleagues in a protest against the repeal, on the ground that it
was an impairment of the rights secured to them as judicial officers under the
Constitution. In a memorial to Congress the deposed judges declared that they
were

> compelled to represent it as their opinion that the rights secured to them by
> the Constitution, as members of the judicial department, have been im-
> paired. . . . The right of the undersigned to their compensation . . . involv-
> ing a personal interest, will cheerfully be submitted to judicial examina-
> tions and decision, in such manner as the wisdom and impartiality of
> Congress may prescribe.[46]

The memorialists proposed that their rights should be decided by the judicial
department; and such a decision would have involved an inquiry regarding the
constitutionality of the repeal of the Judiciary Act of 1801.[47] That Bassett
believed the repeal unconstitutional, as to his deprivation of judicial functions
and salary, and held the judiciary to be the proper authority for deciding the
point, is quite evident.

George Wythe, of Virginia, was a member of the Virginia Court of appeals
which decided the case of Commonwealth *v.* Caton[48] in 1782. Justice Wythe, in
his opinion, referred to the practice of certain English chancellors, who had
defended the rights of subjects against the rapacity of the crown, and ex-
claimed:

> If the whole legislature, an event to be deprecated, should attempt to
> overleap the bounds prescribed to them by the people, I in administering
> the public justice of the country, will meet the united powers at my seat in
> this tribunal; and, pointing to the constitution, will say to them, here is the
> limit of your authority and hither you shall go but no further.

The duty of a court to declare unconstitutional laws void could hardly be more
energetically asserted. Of course this is not direct evidence that Wythe held
that the federal Constitution embodied the principle, but it is clear that he
favored the doctrine.

William Few, of Georgia, *George Read,* of Delaware, and *Caleb Strong,* of
Massachusetts, who were members of the first Senate under the new government, voted for the Judiciary Act[49] and may therefore, for the reasons indicated above, be regarded as having accepted the principle of the judicial review of federal statutes.

Summing up the evidence: we may say that of the leading members of the
Convention no less than thirteen believed that judicial power included the right
and duty of passing upon the constitutionality of acts of Congress. Satisfactory
evidence is afforded by the vote on the Judiciary Act that four other leading
members held to the same belief. Of the less prominent members we find that
three expressed themselves in favor of judicial control and three others approved it by their vote on the Judiciary Act. We are accordingly justified in

asserting that twenty-three members of the Convention favored or at least accepted some form of judicial control. That they all had equal understanding of the implications of the doctrine, that they clearly foresaw the possible development of the judicial power, cannot, of course, be claimed. But it seems to be unquestionable that they all understood that refusal to recognize unconstitutional enactments was a part of the judicial function.

II

We may now turn to the evidence that judicial control was not regarded by the framers of the Constitution as a normal judicial function under the new Constitution. The researches of those who contend that the doctrine propounded in Marbury v. Madison is sheer usurpation have placed only four members of the Convention on record against judicial control; and one of these, John Dickinson, of Delaware, must be stricken from the list.[50] The evidence in the case of the remaining three members is as follows:

Gunning Bedford, of Delaware, speaking in the Convention on June 4 on the subject of the executive veto, expressed himself as

> opposed to every check on the legislative, even the council of revision first proposed. He thought it would be sufficient to mark out in the Constitution the boundaries to the legislative authority, which would give all the requisite security to the rights of the other departments. The representatives of the people were the best judges of what was for their interest and ought to be under no external controul whatever. The two branches would produce a sufficient controul within the legislature itself.[51]

John F. Mercer, of Maryland. On August 15 Madison moved that all acts, before they became laws, should be submitted to both the executive and supreme judiciary departments and, upon being vetoed by either or both of these departments, be repassed only by extraordinary majorities. Mercer

> heartily approved the motion. It is an axiom that the judiciary ought to be separate from the legislative; but equally so that it ought to be independent of that department. The true policy of the axiom is that legislative usurpation and oppression may be obviated. He disapproved of the doctrine that the judges as expositers of the Constitution should have authority to declare a law void. He thought laws ought to be well and cautiously made and then to be uncontroulable.[52]

Mercer evidently feared "legislative oppression," and when the motion to have acts submitted to the judiciary before they should become laws was rejected, he may have changed his mind on the subject of judicial control. However that may be, he stands on record as distinctly disapproving the doctrine.

Richard Spaight, of North Carolina, was undoubtedly opposed to judicial control over legislation, although he does not appear to have said anything on the subject in the constitutional convention. In the spring of 1787 the superior court of North Carolina, in the case of Bayard v. Singleton, declared an act of legislature of that state null and void on the ground that it was not warranted by the constitution of the commonwealth. The decision aroused much popular opposition and Spaight joined in the protest against the action of the court. In a letter dated Philadelphia, August 12, 1787, and directed to Mr. Iredell, Spaight wrote:

> I do not pretend to vindicate the law which has been the subject of con-
> troversy; it is immaterial what law they have declared void; it is their
> usurpation of the authority to do it that I complain of, as I do most posi-
> tively deny that they have any such power; nor can they find anything in
> the constitution, either directly or impliedly, that will support them, or give
> them any color of right to exercise that authority. Besides it would have
> been absurd, and contrary to the practice of all the world, had the constitu-
> tion vested such power in them, as would have operated as an absolute
> negative on the proceedings of the legislature, which no judiciary ought
> ever to possess. . . .

He further declared that "many instances might be brought to show the absurdity and impropriety of such power being lodged in the judges." He was aware, he explained, of the desirability of a check on the legislature, but he thought an annual election the best that could be devised.[53]

Pierce Butler, of South Carolina, and *John Langdon,* of New Hampshire, were members of the first Senate of the new Union, and both voted against the Judiciary Act of 1789.[54] Their reasons for so voting are not apparent; and it may be questioned whether a vote cast against the act as a whole is evidence of opposition to the principle of judicial control of federal legislation recognized in the twenty-fifth section of the act. If, however, these two names be added, the list of opponents of judicial control contain five members of the Convention, and but one of the five, Butler, belong to the influential group.

III

Mr. Boudin lays much stress on the silence of those who disliked judicial control of legislation. He says:

> It is absurd to assume that the many avowed opponents of judicial control
> of legislation who sat in the convention would have agreed to the [judiciary]
> article without a murmur had they suspected that it contained even a part
> of the enormous power which our judiciary now exercises. Richard Spaight
> for one, whose fiery denunciation of this power I have quoted above, would
> have made the halls in which the Convention met ring to the echo with his
> emphatic protest, had he suspected any such implications.[55]

The "avowed opponents" do not seem to have been "many"; but whether they and the unavowed opponents were many or few, they must have been fully aware that most of the leading members regarded the nullification of unconstitutional laws as a normal judicial function. The view was more than once clearly voiced in the Convention, and any delegate who was not aware of "such implication" must have been very remiss in the discharge of his duties. On

June 4 King definitely stated that the judges in the exposition of the laws would no doubt stop the operation of such as appeared repugnant to the Constitution.[56] On that day there were present representatives from Massachusetts, Connecticut, New York, Pennsylvania, Delaware, Maryland, Virginia, North Carolina, South Carolina and Georgia. In addition to members in the group of twenty-five enumerated above there were recorded as present on the occasion Bedford, McClurg, Pierce and Yates.[57] Several other members including Spaight, were in Philadelphia at that time and were probably in attendance at that particular session, but as there was no preliminary roll call the list of those actually present must be made up from those who addressed the Convention or appeared in the roll on a divided vote. There was also a large attendance on July 21, when the doctrine of judicial control was again enunciated in even more emphatic tones. In view of these facts it cannot be assumed that the Convention was unaware that the judicial power might be held to embrace a very considerable control over legislation and that there was a high degree of probability (to say the least) that such control would be exercised in the ordinary course of events.

The accepted canons of historical criticism warrant the assumption that, when a legal proposition is before a law-making body and a considerable number of the supporters of that proposition definitely assert that it involves certain important and fundamental implications, and it is nevertheless approved by that body without any protests worthy of mention, these implications must be deemed part of that legal proposition when it becomes law; provided, of course, that they are consistent with the letter and spirit of the instrument. To go further than this — to say that the Convention must have passed definitely upon every inference that could logically be drawn from the language of the instrument that it adopted — would of course be an absurdity.

In balancing conflicting presumptions in order to reach a judgment in the case, it must be remembered that no little part of the work of drafting the Constitution was done by the Committee of Detail and the Committee of Style.

The former committee, appointed on July 24, consisted of Rutledge, Wilson, Ellsworth, Randolph and Gorham. Of these five men two, Ellsworth and Wilson, had expressly declared themselves in favor of judicial control, and Wilson seems to have been the "dominating mind of the committee." This committee had before it the resolutions referred to it by the Convention on July 23. It had also before it the Pinckney plan, or an outline of it, and the New Jersey plan. The members of the committee had been assiduous in their attendance upon the debates during the two months previous, and they prepared a draft of a constitution which they presented to the Convention on August 6. The article dealing with federal judicial power, as reported by the committee,[58] contained most of the provisions later embodied in the federal Constitution.

After lengthy debates on the draft submitted by the Committee of Detail, a committee of five was created to revise and arrange the style of the articles agreed to by the Convention; and Johnson, Hamilton, Gouverneur Morris, Madison and King were selected as members of this committee. Of these five

men four, Hamilton, Morris, Madison and King, are on record as expressly
favoring judicial control over legislation. There is some little dispute as to the
share of the glory to be assigned to single members of the committee, but
undoubtedly Gouverneur Morris played a considerable part in giving to the
Constitution its final form. Speaking of his work on the Constitution, Mr.
Morris later wrote:

> Having rejected redundant and equivocal terms, I believed it as clear as
> our language would permit; excepting, nevertheless, a part of what relates
> to the judiciary. On that subject conflicting opinions had been maintained
> with so much professional astuteness that it became necessary to select
> phrases which expressing my own notions would not alarm others nor
> shock their self-love.[59]

That the Constitution was not designed to be perfectly explicit on all
points and to embody definitely the opinions of a majority of the Convention is
further evidenced by a speech made by Abraham Baldwin, a member of the
Convention from Georgia, in the House of Representatives on March 14, 1796.
In speaking of the clause of the Constitution which provides that treaties are to
be the supreme law of the land, he said:

> He would begin it by the assertion, that those few words in the Constitution
> on this subject were not those apt, precise, definite expressions, which
> irresistibly brought upon them the meaning which he had been above con-
> sidering. He said it was not to disparage the instrument, to say that it had
> not definitely, and with precision, absolutely settled everything on which it
> had spoken. He had sufficient evidence to satisfy his own mind that it was
> not supposed by the makers of it at the time but that some subjects were
> left a little ambiguous and uncertain. It was a great thing to get so many
> difficult subjects definitely settled at once. If they could all be agreed in, it
> would compact the Government. The few that were left a little unsettled
> might, without any great risk, be settled by practice or by amendments in
> the progress of the Government. He believed this subject of the rival
> powers of legislation and treaty was one of them; the subject of the militia
> was another, and some question respecting the judiciary another. When he
> reflected on the immense difficulties and dangers of that trying occasion –
> the old Government prostrated, and a chance whether a new one could be
> agreed in – the recollection called to him nothing but the most joyful sensa-
> tions that so many things had been so well settled, and that experience had
> shown there was very little difficulty or danger in settling the rest.[60]

IV

It is urged by the opponents of judicial control that, whatever may have
been the purpose of the members of the Philadelphia Convention, the ratifying
conventions in the states gave the final legal sanction to the Constitution, and a
sound rule of interpretation would compel us to ascertain the opinion of these

bodies on the point at issue. This contention cannot be gainsaid; but a full examination of the materials on the state conventions, as any one can see, would require years of research into the lives and opinions of several hundred members. The author of this paper does not pretend to have made this research, and this essay is limited principally to a consideration of the purpose of the framers, not the enactors, of the Constitution. However, it is of interest to note what materials bearing on the purpose of the enactors with regard to this point are contained in Elliott's *Debates*.

If the members of the Virginia convention which ratified the federal Constitution were in the dark in this matter, or had any doubts as to the probable implications of the judicial article, they must have been enlightened by the clear and unmistakeable language of John Marshall. In replying to objections which had been raised regarding the danger of an extension of federal jurisdiction at the cost of the states, he pointed out that the proposed federal government was one of the enumerated and limited powers.

> Has the government of the United States power to make laws on every subject? . . . Can they make laws affecting the mode of transferring property, or contracts, or claims between citizens of the same state? Can they go beyond the delegated power? If they were to make a law not warranted by any of the powers enumerated it would be considered by the judges as an infringement of the Constitution which they are to guard. They would not consider such a law as coming under their jurisdiction. They would declare it void.[61]

In the course of the discussion Mr. Grayson said: "If the Congress cannot make a law against the Constitution I apprehend they cannot make a law to abridge it. The judges are to defend it."[62] Mr. Pendleton declared: "The fair inference is that oppressive laws will not be warranted by the Constitution, nor attempted by our representatives, who are selected for their ability and integrity, and that honest, independent judges will never admit an oppressive construction."[63]

The Maryland convention was by no means uninformed regarding the possible functions of the judiciary under the proposed Constitution. In his famous letter directed to the legislature of the state, Luther Martin said:

> Whether, therefore, any laws or regulations of the Congress or any act of its president or the officers are contrary to, or not warranted by, the Constitution, rests only with the judges who are appointed by Congress to determine; by whose determination every state must be bound.[64]

If the member of the Pennsylvania ratifying convention had any doubts regarding the probable exercise of judicial control over legislation under the new Constitution, these must have been removed by one of Mr. Wilson's

speeches in defence of the judiciary. Some members of the convention expressed the apprehension that, inasmuch as the federal courts were to have
jurisdiction in all cases in law and equity arising under the Constitution and the
laws of the United States, the power enjoyed by the judges might be indefi-
nitely extended if Congress saw fit to make laws not warranted by the Constitution. On this point Mr. Wilson said:

> I think the contrary inference true. If a law should be made inconsistent
> with those powers vested by this instrument in Congress, the judges, as a
> consequence of their independence, and the particular powers of govern-
> ment being defined, will declare such law to be null and void. For the
> power of the Constitution predominates. Anything therefore that shall be
> enacted by Congress contrary thereto will not have the force of law.[65]

In New York, the members of the Convention must have known the clear
and cogent argument for judicial control made by Hamilton in *The Federalist.*

If the members of the Connecticut convention were unaware of the fact
that under the provisions of the Constitution the judiciary would enjoy the
power to pass upon the Constitutionality of federal and state statutes, it was
their own fault; for, in his speech of January 7, 1788, on the power of Congress
to lay taxes, Oliver Ellsworth carefully explained the new system. He said:

> This constitution defines the extent of the powers of the general govern-
> ment. If the general legislature should at any time overleap their limits, the
> judicial department is a constitutional check. If the United States go be-
> yond their powers, If they make a law which the Constitution does not
> authorize, it is void; and the judicial power, the national judges, who, to
> secure their impartiality, are to be made independent, will declare it to be
> void.[66]

It would be entirely misleading to conclude, from this fragmentary evidence, that the question of judicial control over acts of Congress was ade-
quately considered in the state conventions. It was judicial control over state
statutes that aroused the most serious apprehensions of critics of the new
frame of government. That they thought much—or cared much—about what
might happen to acts of Congress is not apparent.[67] Still it cannot be said that
they were kept in the dark in this respect, or that they could not easily have
learned, if the matter had interested them, what the framers of the Constitution intended and expected. And it may pertinently be asked what our constitutional position would be today, if it were recognized that each branch of the
federal government, in addition to the clearly expressed powers conferred
upon it, possesses those additional powers only which were understood, by the
ratifying conventions of the states, to have been impliedly conferred!

V

Those who hold that it was not the intention of the framers of the Constitution to establish judicial control of legislation make much of the opposition

aroused by the sporadic attempts of a few state courts to exercise such a control prior to 1787. Dean Trickett cites the cases and exclaims: "These then are the precedents!" Mr. Boudin cites them and also exclaims: "Such were the state 'precedents,' and such was the temper of the people at the time the Philadelphia Convention met to frame the Constitution of the United States." The only trouble with this line of argument is that it leaves out of account the sharp political division existing in the United States in 1787 and the following years.

The men who framed the federal Constitution were not among the paper-money advocates and stay-law makers whose operations in state legislatures and attacks upon the courts were chiefly responsible, Madison informs us, for the calling of the Convention. The framers of the Constitution were not among those who favored the assaults on vested rights which legislative majorities were making throughout the Union. On the contrary, they were, almost without exception, bitter opponents of such enterprises; and they regarded it as their chief duty, in drafting the new Constitution, to find a way of preventing the renewal of what they deemed "legislative tyranny." Examine the rolls of the state conventions that ratified the Constitution after it came from the Philadelphia Convention, and compare them with the rolls of the legislatures that had been assailing the rights of property. It was largely because the framers of the Constitution knew the temper and class bias of the state legislatures that they arranged that the new Constitution should be ratified by conventions. The framers and enactors of the federal Constitution represented the solid, conservative, commercial and financial interest of the country—not the interest which denounced and proscribed judges in Rhode Island, New Jersey and North Carolina, and stoned their houses in New York. The conservative interests, made desperate by the imbecilities of the Confederation and harried by state legislatures, roused themselves from their lethargy, drew together in a mighty effort to establish a government that would be strong enough to pay the national debt, regulate interstate and foreign commerce, provide for national defence, prevent fluctuations in the currency created by paper emissions and control the propensities of legislative majorities to attack private rights.

It is in the light of the political situation that existed in 1787 that we must inquire whether the principle of judicial control is out of harmony with the general purpose of the federal Constitution. It is an ancient and honorable rule of construction, laid down by Blackstone, that any instrument should be interpreted, "by considering the reason and spirit of it; or the course which moved the legislator to enact it. . . . From this method of interpreting laws, by the reason of them, arises what we call equity." It may be, therefore, that the issue of judicial control is a case in equity. The direct intention of the framers and enactors not being clearly expressed on this point, we may have recourse to the "reason and spirit" of the Constitution.

Now the essence of the doctrine of judicial control is that the judiciary, rather than the legislative or executive department, is best fitted to pronounce the final word of interpretation on the Constitution in cases involving private rights. Assuredly it is best fitted to secure the purposes which the framers had in mind—the construction of a government strong enough to carry out certain great national functions and at the same time firm enough to secure the rights of persons and of property against popular majorities, no matter how great.[68]

No historical fact is more clearly established than the fact that the framers of the Constitution distrusted democracy and feared the rule of mere numbers. Almost every page of Madison's record bears witness to the fact that the Convention was anxiously seeking to solve the problem of establishing property rights on so firm a basis that they would be forever secure against the assaults of legislative majorities. If any reader needs a documented demonstration of this fact, he will do well to turn to the *Records of the Convention,* so admirably compiled by Professor Farrand. Let him go through the proceedings of the Convention and see how many of the members expressed concern at the dangers of democracy and were casting about for some method of restraining the popular branch of the government. The very system of checks and balances, which is undeniably the essential element of the Constitution, is built upon the doctrine that the popular branch of the government cannot be allowed full sway, and least of all in the enactment of laws touching the rights of property. The exclusion of the direct popular vote in the election of the president; the creation, again by indirect election, of a Senate which the framers hoped would represent the wealth and conservative interest of the country; and the establishment of an independent judiciary appointed by the president with the concurrence of the Senate—all these devices bear witness to the fact that the underlying purpose of the Constitution was not the establishment of popular government by means of parliamentary majorities.

Page after page of *The Federalist* is directed to that portion of the electorate which was disgusted with the "mutability of the public councils." Writing on the presidential veto Hamilton says:

> The propensity of the legislative department to intrude upon the rights, and absorb the powers, of the other departments has already been suggested and repeated. . . . It may perhaps be said that the power of preventing bad laws included the power of preventing good ones; and may be used to the one purpose as well as the other. But this objection will have little weight with those who can properly estimate the mischiefs of that inconstancy and mutability in the laws which form the greatest blemish in the character and genius of our governments. They will consider every institution calculated to restrain the excess of law-making and to keep things in the same state in which they happen to be at any given period, is more likely to do good than harm; because it is favorable to greater stability in the system of legislation. The injury which may be possibly done by defeating a few good laws will be amply compensated by the advantage of preventing a number of bad ones.[69]

In the face of the evidence above adduced, in the face of political doctrines enunciated time and again on diverse occasions by the leaders in the

Convention, it certainly is incumbent upon those who say that judicial control was not within the purpose of the men who framed and enacted the federal Constitution to bring forward positive evidence, not arguments resting upon silence. It is incumbent upon them to show that the American federal system was not designed primarily to commit the established rights of property to the guardianship of a judiciary removed from direct contact with popular electorates.[70] Whether this system is outworn, whether it had unduly exalted property rights, is a legitimate matter for debate; but those who hold the affirmative cannot rest their case on the intent of the eighteenth-century statesmen who framed the Constitution.

VI

The great justice who made the theory of judicial control operative had better opportunities than any student of history or law today to discover the intention of the framers of the federal Constitution. Marshall, to be sure, did not have before him Elliot's *Debates,* but he was of the generation that made the Constitution. He had been a soldier in the Revolutionary War. He had been a member of the Virginia convention that ratified the Constitution; and he must have remembered stating in that convention the doctrine of judicial control,[71] apparently without arousing any protest. He was on intimate, if not always friendly, relations with the great men of his state who were instrumental in framing the Constitution. Washington once offered him the attorney-generalship. He was an envoy to France with two members of the Convention, Charles Cotesworth Pinckney and Elbridge Gerry. He was a member of Congress for part of one term in Adams's administration; he was secretary of state under Adams; and he was everywhere regarded as a tower of strength to the Federalists. It was, therefore, no closet philosopher, ignorant of the conditions under which the Constitution was established and unlearned in the reason and spirit of that instrument, who first enunciated from the supreme bench in unmistakable language the doctrine that judicial control over legislation was implied in the provisions of the federal Constitution.[72]

Those who hold that the framers of the Constitution did not intend to establish judicial control over the federal legislation sometimes assert that Marshall made the doctrine out of whole cloth and had no precedent or authority to guide him. This is misleading. It is true that it was Marshall who first formally declared an act of Congress unconstitutional; but the fact should not be overlooked that in the case of Hylton *v.* The United States[73] the Supreme Court, with Ellsworth[74] as chief justice and Paterson as associate (both members of the Convention), exercised the right to pass upon the constitutionality of an act of Congress imposing a duty on carriages. On behalf of the appellant in this case it was argued that the law was unconstitutional and void in so far as it imposed a direct tax without apportionment among the states. The court sustained the statute. If it was not understood that the court had the power to hold acts of Congress void on constitutional grounds, why was the case carried before it? If the court believed that it did not have the power to declare the act void as well as the power to sustain it, why did it assume jurisdiction at all or take the trouble to consider and render an opinion on the constitutionality of the tax?

The doctrine of judicial control was a familiar one in legal circles throughout the period between the formation of the Constitution and the year 1803, when Marshall decided the Marbury case. In Hayburn's case, already cited, the federal judges had refused to execute a statute which they held to be unconstitutional. This was in 1792. In 1794, in the case of Glass *v.* The Sloop Betsey,[75] the Supreme Court heard the doctrine of judicial control laid down by the counsel of the appellants:

> The well-being of the whole depends upon keeping each department within its limits. In the state governments several instances have occurred where a legislative act has been rendered inoperative by a judicial decision that it was unconstitutional; and even under the federal government the judges, for the same reason, have refused to execute an act of Congress. . . . To the judicial and not to the executive department, the citizen or subject naturally looks for determinations upon his property; and that agreeably to known rules and settled forms, to which no other security is equal.

In the case of Calder *v.* Bull,[76] decided in 1798, the counsel for the plaintiffs in error argued "that any law of the federal government or of any of the state governments contrary to the Constitution of the United States is void; and that this court possesses the power to declare such law void." Justice Chase however refused to pass upon the general principle, because it was not necessary to the decision of the case before him. He said:

> Without giving an opinion at this time whether this court has jurisdiction to decide that any law made by Congress is void, I am fully satisfied that this court has no jurisdiction to determine that any law of any state legislature contrary to the constitution of such state is void.[77]

In the same case Justice Iredell said:

> If any act of Congress or of the legislature of a state violates those constitutional provisions, it is unquestionably void; though I admit, that as the authority to declare it void is of a delicate and awful nature, the court will never resort to that authority but in a clear and urgent case.

In view of the principles entertained by the leading members of the Convention with whom Marshall was acquainted, in view of the doctrine so clearly laid down in number 78 of *The Federalist,* in view of the argument made more than once by eminent counsel before the Supreme Court, in view of Hayburn's case and Hylton v. The United States, in view of the judicial opinions several times expressed, in view of the purpose and spirit of the federal Constitution, it is difficult to understand the temerity of those who speak of the power asserted by Marshall in Marbury v. Madison as "usurpation."[e]

NOTES

a. Walter F. Murphy and C. Herman Pritchett, eds., *Courts, Judges, & Politics: An Introduction to the Judicial Process,* 4th ed. (New York: Random House, 1986), 485–86.

b. *The Doctrine of Judicial Review* (Gloucester, Mass.: Peter Smith, 1963), 11.

c. Warren E. Burger, "The Doctrine of Judicial Review: Mr. Marshall, Mr. Jefferson, and Mr. Marbury," in *Views from the Bench: The Judiciary and Constitutional Politics,* ed. Mark W. Cannon and David M. O'Brien (Chatham, N. J.: Chatham House, 1985), 8.

d. *Political Science Quarterly* 27 (March 1912): 1–35.

e. Beard's "Note on the Views of Thomas Jefferson" is not reproduced here.

1. The author desires to acknowledge his indebtedness to Mr. Birl E. Schultz, a graduate student in the School of Political Science of Columbia University, for preparing a bibliographical note on the writings of members of the Convention and for special researches in the papers of Roger Sherman and of John Dickinson.

2. *Cf.* Chief Justice Walter Clark, of North Carolina, Address before the Law Department of the University of Pennsylvania, April 27, 1906; reprinted in *Congressional Record,* July 31, 1911. Dean William Trickett, of the Dickinson Law School, "Judicial Dispensation from Congressional Statutes," *American Law Review,* vol. xli, pp. 65 *et seq.* L. B. Boudin, of the New York Bar, "Government by Judiciary," POLITICAL SCIENCE QUARTERLY, vol xxvi (1911), pp. 238 *et seq.* Gilbert Roe, of the New York Bar, "Our Judicial Oligarchy" (second article), *La Follette's Weekly Magazine,* vol. iii, no. 25, pp. 7–9, June 24, 1911.

3. *Cf infra,* pp. 152, 153, 155–56.

4. Thayer's Cases in Constitutional Law, vol. i, p. 55.

5. That the decision could have been reached without invoking this power, as Mr. Boudin argues, *loc. cit.,* p. 245, note I, does not affect the value of the decision as evidence of Blair's belief in the existence of the power.

6. Wilson, as we shall see later, had taken a strong stand, both in the constituent Convention and in the ratifying Pennsylvania convention, in favor of judicial control of legislation. *Cf. infra,* pp. 157, 165–66.

7. Hayburn's Case, 2 Dallas, 409.

8. *Cf infra,* p. 158.

9. *Cf infra,* p. 161.

10. Farrand, vol. ii, p. 299.

11. Ford Pamphlets on the Constitution of the United States, p. 184.

12. *Cf. infra,* p. 166.

13. *Cf infra,* p. 158.

14. Farrand, vol. i, p. 97.

15. Annals of Congress, vol. i, p. 491. See also p. 596.

16. Elliot's Debates, vol. iv, p. 393.

17. The Federalist, no. 78.

18. Farrand, vol. i, p. 98.

19. *Ibid.,* p. 109.

20. *Ibid.,* vol. ii, p. 74.

21. *Ibid.*

22. Writings of James Madison, vol. viii, p. 406.

23. Farrand, vol. ii, p. 430.

24. Writings, vol. v, pp. 293, 294.

25 Elliot's Debates, vol. iv, pp. 382, 383.

26. Cf Madison's letter of August, 1830, to Everett; Writings, vol. ix, p. 383.

27. Farrand, vol. ii, p. 76. For further evidence of Martin's attitude, cf. infra, p. 165.

28. Farrand, vol. ii, p. 78.

29. Ibid., pp. 75 et seq.

30 Ibid., p. 299.

31. Benton, Abridgement of Debates in Congress, vol. ii, p. 550

32. 2 Dallas, 409.

33. Moncure Conway, Edmund Randolph, p. 145.

34. American State Papers, Class X, Miscellaneous, vol. i, p. 23.

35. Farrand, vol. ii, p. 376.

36. Farrand, vol. ii, p. 73.

37. Ibid, p 391.

38. Cf. infra, p. 165–66.

39. Annals of Congress, vol. i, p. 51.

40. For further evidence in the case of Paterson cf. infra, p. 33.

41. Farrand, vol. i, p. 469.

42. Annals of Congress, vol. i., p. 582.

43. Farrand, vol. iii, p. 383.

44. Ibid, p. 370. Cf. infra, pp. 163, 164.

45. Annals of Congress, vol. i, pp. 18, 51.

46. American State Papers, Class X, Miscellaneous, vol. i, p. 340.

47. A proposition to make provision for submitting the case to judicial determination was defeated in the House on January 27, 1803. Annals of Congress, Second Session, 7th Congress, p. 439.

48. Thayer's Cases, vol. i, p. 55. Cf supra, p. 151.

49. Annals of Congress, vol. i, p. 51. Cf. supra, p. 158.

50. Cf. supra, pp. 151, 152.

51. Farrand, vol. i, p. 100.

52. Ibid., vol ii, p. 298.

53. Coxe, An Essay on Judicial Power, pp 248 et seq and 385.

54. Annals of Congress, vol. i, p. 51.

55. Loc cit., pp 248, 249.

56. Farrand, vol. i, p. 109.

57. Ibid., pp. 96 et seq

58. Farrand, vol. ii, p. 186.

59. Sparks, Life of Morris, vol. iii, p. 323.

60. Farrand, vol. iii, p. 369.

61 Elliot's Debates, vol. iii, p. 553.

62. Ibid., p. 567.

63. Elliot's Debates, vol. iii, p. 548.

64. Ibid, vol. i, p. 380.

65. McMaster and Stone, Pennsylvania and the Federal Constitution, p 354.

66. Elliot's Debates, vol. ii, p. 196. Cf. Farrand, vol. iii, p 240.

67. It is interesting to note that when, ten years later, the Kentucky and Virginia Resolutions raised the question of judicial control, and the other states had occasion to express a direct opinion on this point, none of them seems to have approved the doctrine expressed in the Resolutions. Cf. Ames, State Documents on Federal Relations, p. 16.

The Massachusetts legislature replied to Virginia, on February 9, 1709: "This legislature are persuaded that the decision of all cases in law and equity arising under the Constitution of the United States and the construction of all laws made in pursuance thereof are exclusively vested by the people in the judicial courts of the United States." *Ibid.,* pp. 18 *et seq.* The Rhode Island assembly declared that "the words, to wit, 'The judicial power shall extend to all cases arising under the laws of the United States,' vest in the federal courts exclusively, and in the Supreme Court of the United States ultimately, the authority of deciding on the constitutionality of any act or law of the Congress of the United States." *Ibid.,* p. 17. The New Hampshire legislature resolved: "That the state legislatures are not the proper tribunals to determine the constitutionality of the laws of the general government; that the duty of such decision is properly and exclusively confided to the judicial department." Elliot's Debates, vol. iv, p. 539 (ed. 1861). The Vermont legislature asserted: "It belongs not to state legislatures to decide on the constitutionality of laws made by the general government, this power being exclusively vested in the judiciary courts of the Union." *Ibid* The House of Representatives of Pennsylvania replied to Kentucky that the people of the United States "have committed to the supreme judiciary of the nation the high authority of ultimately and conclusively deciding upon the constitutionality of all legislative acts." Ames, *op cit*, p 20. The Senate of New York replied to Virginia and Kentucky that the decision of all cases in law and equity was confided to the federal judiciary and that the states were excluded from interference. *Ibid.,* p. 23.

68. The Federalist, no. 10.

69. The Federalist, no. 73.

70 See the article on this point by President Arthur T. Hadley, of Yale University. *The Independent,* April 16, 1908.

71. *Cf supra,* p. 25. In Marshall's argument in the case of Ware *v.* Hylton before the Supreme Court in 1796, Marshall said: "The legislative authority of any country can only be restrained by its own municipal constitution. This is a principle that springs from the very nature of society, and the judicial authority can have no right to question the validity of a law unless such a jurisdiction is expressly given by the Constitution." 3 Dallas, 211 Here, however, Marshall was arguing as counsel, not stating his own personal views.

72. It has not escaped close observers that the law which Marshall declared unconstitutional in Marbury *v.* Madison was a part of the Judiciary Act of 1789, which had been drafted and carried through by men who had served in the Convention. An analysis of the decision shows, however, that the section set aside was at most badly drawn and was not in direct conflict with the Constitution. Had Marshall been so inclined he might have construed the language of the act in such a manner as to have escaped the necessity of declaring it unconstitutional. *The Nation,* vol. lxxii, p. 104. The opportunity for asserting the doctrine, however, was too good to be lost, and Marshall was astute enough to take advantage of it. In view of the recent Jeffersonian triumph, he might very well have felt the need of having the great precedent firmly set

73. 3 Dallas, 171 (1796).

74. Ellsworth did not take part in the decision, for he had just been sworn into office.

75. 3 Dallas, 13.

76. 3 Dallas, 396.

77. Of course, as everybody knows, Chase adhered stoutly to the doctrine of federal judicial control.

III

The Compatibility Question

They [the courts] are to be rendered
totally independent, both of the people
and the legislature, both with respect to
their offices and salaries. No errors they
may commit can be corrected by any
power above them, if any such power
there be, nor can they be removed from
office for making ever so many erroneous
adjudications.

—ROBERT YATES in "Brutus XI"

11

An Antifederalist View of the Undemocratic Nature of the Judiciary

---

BEHIND THE QUESTION of the usurpation of power lurks a related issue. It is the equally difficult problem of the compatibility of judicial review with democratic values. Democratic sensibilities are offended by the spectacle of nine persons invalidating acts of popularly selected representatives of the people. Moreover, the judiciary is independent of the people and their elected representatives. The result is a third branch free from popular control. Is judicial review a menace to popular democracy? Alternatively, is review a way to perfect democractic government? In essence, is there any way to reconcile the practice of judicial review with democratic theory? This part of the book is devoted to exploring these recurring questions.

We turn first to the arguments of Robert Yates, a leading opponent of the ratification of the proposed constitution crafted at Philadelphia. Yates, Alexander Hamilton, and John Lansing had comprised the New York delegation to the Constitutional Convention. Yates and Lansing walked out on the Convention some two and one-half months before its work was completed. The two joined other Americans in making speeches and writing pamphlets, essays, and letters opposing ratification of the Constitution. Collectively, they came to be called Antifederalists. The other side of the debate was represented successfully by the Federalists.

As is often the case for winners and losers, much is widely known about Federalist thought, but little is understood about Antifederalist thinking. Fundamentally, this loosely knit group believed that the great choice facing humankind was between despotism or republicanism. The latter is based on consent of the governed or self-government, and the former is ensured by force. The Antifederalists believed that the proposed constitution granted too much power to the people's representatives without providing an effective countercheck. They reasoned that persons of privilege would benefit from the proposed constitution at the expense of ordinary people. They feared that unless restrictions could be placed on all three constitutional branches of the central government the potential for despotism would become a reality. Though the Antifederalists lost the ratification debate, their philosophy was in good part responsible for the addition of the Bill of Rights to our constitutional structure.[a]

Writing under the pseudonym *Brutus*, Robert Yates, then a judge of the New York Supreme Court, makes the case against the excesses of Article III. In the process of showing why the new government would prove destructive of political happiness, he argues that due to the nature of judicial review members of the Court possessed such overwhelming power that they could "mould the government into almost any shape they please."

This argument followed for the most part from two facts. First, there was no limit to the amount of power the Court could imply from the Constitution since interpretation would not be restricted to the "letter" of the Constitution, that is, to the "words in their common acception." Thus, the Court could build through implication from nebulous "spirit" and "intent" of the document. Second, and even more to be feared, the Court was not held accountable to either the people or their representatives. As such, the Court constituted a will independent of society, a will that could be "controlled" only by an appeal to the sword.

Yates was one delegate to the Philadelphia Convention who had no doubt that the proposed constitution contained within its meaning the power of judicial review. He finds it particularly alarming because the judges are "rendered totally independent, both of the people and the legislature, both with respect to their offices and salaries. No errors they may commit can be corrected by any person above them, if any such power there be."

The probable impact of the federal judiciary upon states' rights was central to Antifederalist republican principles and concerns. Every enlargement of federal power will restrict state power. This will happen, according to Yates, because the Necessary and Proper Clause of Article I, section 8, may be interpreted by the federal judiciary to permit the Congress to do "which in their best judgement is best." To be sure, the employment of the "elastic clause" has been a source of continuing controversy over the two-hundred-year history of the Constitution.

Readers interested in the concept of judicial independence will find *Brutus* XV provocative. Though Yates approves of judicial independence, he argues that the type of independence contained in the proposed constitution was unknown anywhere in the world, including England. Judges in both England and under the proposed constitution hold office during good behavior and possess fixed salaries. In England Parliament may override judicial decisions, but no such analogous power was contemplated for the would-be Congress of the United States.

Yates's interpretation of history is important. English judges were given life tenure and salary guarantees so that the king would no longer influence them to support royal claims to the detriment of the liberties of the people. The great difference is that in the United States there is no hereditary monarch with a vested interest in maintaining power at the expense of liberty. Government officials are elected in this country by the people and are consequently controlled by them. There is no need, according to Yates, to create uncontrolled power unless the goal is autonomy not from a despotic king, but from the democratic tendencies of a free people. Alexander Hamilton addresses this very point in the readings presented in the next chapter.

Letters of Brutus

Robert Yates
New York Journal and Weekly Register, 1788
January 31, February 7 and 14, March 20

BRUTUS XI
January 31, 1788

THE NATURE AND EXTENT of the judicial power of the United States, proposed to be granted by this constitution, claims our particular attention.

Much has been said and written upon the subject of this new system on both sides, but I have not met with any writer, who has discussed the judicial powers with any degree of accuracy. And yet it is obvious, that we can form but very imperfect ideas of the manner in which this government will work, or the effect it will have in changing the internal police and mode of distributing justice at present subsisting in the respective states, without a thorough investigation of the powers of the judiciary and of the manner in which they will operate. This government is a complete system, not only for making, but for executing laws. And the courts of law, which will be constituted by it, are not only to decide upon the constitution and the laws made in pursuance of it, but by officers subordinate to them to execute all their decisions. The real effect of this system of government, will therefore be brought home to the feelings of the people, through the medium of the judicial power. It is, moreover, of great importance, to examine with care the nature and extent of the judicial power, because those who are to be vested with it, are to be placed in a situation altogether unprecedented in a free country. They are to be rendered totally independent, both of the people and the legislature, both with respect to their offices and salaries. No errors they may commit can be corrected by any power above them, if any such power there be, nor can they be removed from office for making ever so many erroneous adjudications.

The only causes for which they can be displaced, is, conviction of treason, bribery, and high crimes and misdemeanors.

This part of the plan is so modelled, as to authorise the courts, not only to carry into execution the powers expressly given, but where these are wanting or ambiguously expressed, to supply what is wanting by their own decisions.

That we may be enabled to form a just opinion on this subject, I shall, in considering it,

1st. Examine the nature and extent of the judicial powers – and

2d. Enquire, whether the courts who are to exercise them, are so constituted as to afford reasonable ground of confidence, that they will exercise them for the general good.

With a regard to the nature and extent of the judicial powers, I have to regret my want of capacity to give that full and minute explanation of them that the subject merits. To be able to do this, a man should be possessed of a degree of law knowledge far beyond what I pretend to. A number of hard words and technical phrases are used in this part of the system, about the meaning of which gentlemen learned in the law differ.

Its advocates know how to avail themselves of these phrases. In a number of instances, where objections are made to the powers given to the judicial, they give such an explanation to the technical terms as to avoid them.

Though I am not competent to give a perfect explanation of the powers granted to this department of the government, I shall yet attempt to trace some of the leading features of it, from which I presume it will appear, that they will operate to a total subversion of the state judiciaries, if not, to the legislative authority of the states.

In article 3d, sect. 2d, it is said, "The judicial power shall extend to all cases in law and equity arising under this constitution, the laws of the United States, and treaties made, or which shall be made, under their authority, &c."

The first article to which this power extends, is, all cases in law and equity arising under this constitution.

What latitude of construction this clause should receive, it is not easy to say. At first view, one would suppose, that it meant no more than this, that the courts under the general government should exercise, not only the powers of courts of law, but also that of courts of equity, in the manner in which those powers are usually exercised in the different states. But this cannot be the meaning, because the next clause authorises the courts to take cognizance of all cases in law and equity arising under the laws of the United States; this last article, I conceive, conveys as much power to the general judicial as any of the state courts possess.

The cases arising under the constitution must be different from those arising under the laws, or else the two clauses mean exactly the same thing.

The cases arising under the constitution must include such, as bring into question its meaning, and will require an explanation of the nature and extent of the powers of the different departments under it.

This article, therefore, vests the judicial with a power to resolve all questions that may arise on any case on the construction of the constitution, either in law or in equity.

1st. They are authorised to determine all questions that may arise upon the meaning of the constitution in law. This article vests the courts with authority to give the constitution a legal construction, or to explain it according to the rules laid down for construing a law. These rules give a certain degree of latitude of explanation. According to this mode of construction, the courts are to give such meaning to the constitution as comports best with the common, and generally received acceptation of the words in which it is expressed, regarding their ordinary and popular use, rather than their grammatical propriety. Where words are dubious, they will be explained by the context. The end of the clause will be attended to, and the words will be understood, as having a view to it; and the words will not be so understood as to bear no meaning or a very absurd one.

2d. The judicial are not only to decide questions arising upon the meaning of the constitution in law, but also in equity.

By this they are empowered, to explain the constitution according to the reasoning spirit of it, without being confined to the words or letter.

"From this method of interpreting laws (says Blackstone) by the reason of them, arises what we call equity;" which is thus defined by Grotius, "the correction of that, wherein the law, by reason of its universality, is deficient["]; for since in laws all cases cannot be foreseen, or expressed, it is necessary, that when the decrees of the law cannot be applied to particular cases, there should some where be a power vested of defining those circumstances, which had they been foreseen the legislator would have expressed; and these are the cases, which according to Grotius, ["]lex non exacte definit, sed arbitrio boni viri permittet."

The same learned author observes, "That equity, thus depending essentially upon each individual case, there can be no established rules and fixed principles of equity laid down, without destroying its very essence, and reducing it to a positive law."

From these remarks, the authority and business of the courts of law, under this clause, may be understood.

They will give the sense of every article of the constitution, that may from time to time come before them. And in their decisions they will not confine themselves to any fixed or established rules, but will determine, according to what appears to them, the reason and spirit of the constitution. The opinions of the supreme court, whatever they may be, will have the force of law; because there is no power provided in the constitution, that can correct their errors, or controul their adjudications. From this court there is no appeal. And I conceive the legislature themselves, cannot set aside a judgment of this court, because they are authorised by the constitution to decide in the last resort. The legislature must be controuled by the constitution, and not the constitution by them. They have therefore no more right to set aside any judgment pronounced upon the construction of the constitution, than they have to take from the president, the chief command of the army and navy, and commit it to some other person. The reason is plain; the judicial and executive derive their authority from the same source, that the legislature do theirs; and therefore in all cases, where the constitution does not make the one responsible to, or controulable by the other, they are altogether independent of each other.

The judicial power will operate to effect, in the most certain, but yet silent and imperceptible manner, what is evidently the tendency of the constitution:—I mean, an entire subversion of the legislative, executive and judicial powers of the individual states. Every adjudication of the supreme court, on any question that may arise upon the nature and extent of the general government, will affect the limits of the state jurisdiction. In proportion as the former enlarge the exercise of their powers, will that of the latter be restricted.

That the judicial power of the United States, will lean strongly in favour of the general government, and will give such an explanation to the constitution, as will favour an extension of its jurisdiction, is very evident from a variety of considerations.

1st. The constitution itself strongly countenances such a mode of construction. Most of the articles in this system, which convey powers of any considerable importance, are conceived in general and indefinite terms, which are either equivocal, ambiguous, or which require long definitions to unfold the extent of their meaning. The two most important powers committed to any government, those of raising money, and of raising and keeping up troops, have already been considered, and shewn to be unlimitted by anything but the discretion of the legislature. The clause which vests the power to pass all laws which are proper and necessary, to carry the powers given into execution, it has been shewn, leaves the legislature at liberty, to do everything, which in their judgment is best. It is said, I know, that this clause confers no power on the legislature, which they would not have had without it – though I believe this is not the fact, yet, admitting it to be, it implies that the constitution is not to receive an explanation strictly, according to its letter; but more power is implied than is expressed. And this clause, if it is to be considered, as explanatory of the extent of the powers given, rather than giving a new power, is to be understood as declaring, that in construing any of the articles conveying power, the spirit, intent and design of the clause, should be attended to, as well as the words in their common acceptation.

This constitution gives sufficient colour for adopting an equitable construction, if we consider the great end and design it professedly has in view – these appear from its preamble to be, "to form a more perfect union, establish justice, insure domestic tranquility, provide for the common defence, promote the general welfare, and secure the blessings of liberty to ourselves and posterity." The design of this system is here expressed, and it is proper to give such a meaning to the various parts, as will best promote the accomplishment of the end; this idea suggests itself naturally upon reading the preamble, and will countenance the court in giving the several articles such a sense, as will the most effectually promote the ends the constitution had in view – how this manner of explaining the constitution will operate in practice, shall be the subject of future enquiry.

2d. Not only will the constitution justify the courts in inclining to this mode of explaining it, but they will be interested in using this latitude of interpretation. Every body of men invested with office are tenacious of power; they feel interested, and hence it has become a kind of maxim, to hand down their offices, with all its rights and privileges, unimpared to their successors; the same principle will influence them to extend their power, and increase their rights; this of itself will operate strongly upon the courts to give such a meaning to the constitution in all cases where it can possibly be done, as will enlarge the sphere of their own authority. Every extension of the power of the general legislature, as well as of the judicial powers, will increase the powers of the courts; and the dignity and importance of the judges, will be in proportion to the extent and magnitude of the powers they exercise. I add, it is highly probable the emolument of the judges will be increased, with the increase of the business they will have to transact and its importance. From these considerations the judges will be interested to extend the powers of the courts, and to construe the constitution as much as possible, in such a way as to favour it; and that they will do it, appears probable.

3d. Because they will have precedent to plead, to justify them in it. It is well known, that the courts in England, have by their own authority, extended their jurisdiction far beyond the limits set them in their original institution, and by the laws of the land.

The court of exchequer is a remarkable instance of this. It was originally intended principally to recover the king's debts, and to order the revenues of the crown. It had a common law jurisdiction, which was established merely for the benefit of the king's accomptants. We learn from Blackstone, that the proceedings in this court are grounded on a writ called quo minus, in which the plaintiff suggests, that he is the king's farmer or debtor, and that the defendant hath done him the damage complained of, by which he is less able to pay the king. These suits, by the statute of Rutland, are expressly directed to be confined to such matters as specially concern the king, or his ministers in the exchequer. And by the articuli super cartas, it is enacted, that no common pleas be thenceforth held in the exchequer contrary to the form of the great charter: but now any person may sue in the exchequer. The surmise of being debtor to the king being matter of form, and mere words of course; and the court is open to all the nation.

When the courts will have a precedent before them of a court which extended its jurisdiction in opposition to an act of the legislature, is it not to be expected that they will extend theirs, especially when there is nothing in the constitution expressly against it? and they are authorised to construe its meaning, and are not under any controul?

This power in the judicial, will enable them to mould the government, into almost any shape they please. – The manner in which this may be effected we will hereafter examine.

BRUTUS

BRUTUS XII
February 7 and 14, 1788

IN MY LAST, I shewed, that the judicial power of the United States under the first clause of the second section of article eight, would be authorized to explain the constitution, not only according to its letter, but according to its spirit and intention; and having this power, they would strongly incline to give it such a construction as to extend the powers of the general government, as much as possible, to the diminution, and finally to the destruction, of that of the respective states.

I shall now proceed to shew how this power will operate in its exercise to effect these purposes. In order to perceive the extent of its influence, I shall consider,

First. How it will tend to extend the legislative authority.

Second. In what manner it will increase the jurisdiction of the courts, and

Third. The way in which it will diminish, and destroy, both the legislative and judicial authority of the United States.

First. Let us enquire how the judicial power will effect an extension of the legislative authority.

Perhaps the judicial power will not be able, by direct and positive decrees, ever to direct the legislature, because it is not easy to conceive how a question can be brought before them in a course of legal discussion, in which they can give a decision, declaring, that the legislature have certain powers which they have not exercised, and which, in consequence of the determination of the judges, they will be bound to exercise. But it is easy to see, that in their adjudications they may establish certain principles, which being received by the legislature, will enlarge the sphere of their power beyond all bounds.

It is to be observed, that the supreme court has the power, in the last resort, to determine all questions that may arise in the course of legal discussion, on the meaning and construction of the constitution. This power they will hold under the constitution, and independent of the legislature. The latter can no more deprive the former of this right, than either of them, or both of them together, can take from the president, with the advice of the senate, the power of making treaties, or appointing ambassadors.

In determining these questions, the court must and will assume certain principles, from which they will reason, in forming their decisions. These principles, whatever they may be, when they become fixed, by a course of decisions, will be adopted by the legislature, and will be the rule by which they will explain their own powers. This appears evident from this consideration, that if the legislature pass laws, which, in the judgment of the court, they are not authorised to do by the constitution, the court will not take notice of them; for it will not be denied, that the constitution is the highest or supreme law. And the courts are vested with the supreme and uncontroulable power, to determine, in all cases that come before them, what the constitution means; they cannot, therefore, execute a law, which, in their judgment, opposes the constitution, unless we can suppose they can make a superior law give way to an inferior. The legislature, therefore, will not go over the limits by which the courts may adjudge they are confined. And there is little room to doubt but that they will come up to those bounds, as often as occasion and opportunity may offer, and they may judge it proper to do it. For as on the one hand, they will not readily pass laws which they know the courts will not execute, so on the other, we may be sure they will not scruple to pass such as they know they will give effect, as often as they may judge it proper.

From these observations it appears, that the judgment of the judicial, on the constitution, will become the rule to guide the legislature in their construction of their powers.

What the principles are, which the courts will adopt, it is impossible for us to say; but taking up the powers as I have explained them in my last number, which they will possess under this clause, it is not difficult to see, that they may, and probably will, be very liberal ones.

We have seen, that they will be authorized to give the constitution a construction according to its spirit and reason, and not to confine themselves to its letter.

To discover the spirit of the constitution, it is of the first importance to attend to the principal ends and designs it has in view. These are expressed in the preamble, in the following words, viz. "We, the people of the United States, in order to form a more perfect union, establish justice, insure domestic tranquility, provide for the common defence, promote the general welfare, and secure the blessings of liberty to ourselves and our posterity, do ordain and establish this constitution," &c. If the end of the government is to be learned from these words, which are clearly designed to declare it, it is obvious it has in view every object which is embraced by any government. The preservation of internal peace—the due administration of justice—and to provide for the defence of the community, seems to include all the objects of government; but if they do not, they are certainly comprehended in the words, "to provide for the general welfare." If it be further considered, that this constitution, if it is ratified, will not be a compact entered into by states, in their corporate capacities, but an agreement of the people of the United States, as one great body politic, no doubt can remain, but that the great end of the constitution, if it is to be collected from the preamble, in which its end is declared, is to constitute a government which is to extend to every case for which any government is instituted, whether external or internal. The courts, therefore, will establish this as a principle in expounding the constitution, and will give every part of it such an explanation, as will give latitude to every department under it, to take cognizance of every matter, not only that affects the general and national concerns of the union, but also of such as relate to the administration of private justice, and to regulating the internal and local affairs of the different parts.

Such a rule of exposition is not only consistent with the general spirit of the preamble, but it will stand confirmed by considering more minutely the different clauses of it.

The first object declared to be in view is, "To form a perfect union." It is to be observed, it is not an union of states or bodies corporate; had this been the case the existence of the state governments, might have been secured. But it is a union of the people of the United States considered as one body, who are to ratify this constitution, if it is adopted. Now to make a union of this kind perfect, it is necessary to abolish all inferior governments, and to give the general one compleat legislative, executive and judicial powers to every purpose. The courts therefore will establish it as a rule in explaining the constitution to give it such a construction as will best tend to perfect the union or take from the state governments every power of either making or executing laws. The second object is "to establish justice." This must include not only the idea of instituting the rule of justice, or of making laws which shall be the measure or rule of right, but also of providing for the application of this rule or of administering justice under it. And under this the courts will in their decisions extend the power of the government to all cases they possibly can, or otherwise they will be restricted in doing what appears to be the intent of the constitution they should do, to wit, pass laws and provide for the execution of them, for the general distribution of justice between man and man. Another end declared is "to insure domestic tranquility." This comprehends a provision against all private breaches of the peace, as well as against all public commotions or general insurrections; and to attain the object of this clause fully, the government must exercise the power of passing laws on these subjects, as well as of appointing magistrates with authority to execute them. And the courts will adopt these ideas in their expositions. I might proceed to the other clause, in the preamble, and it would appear by a consideration of all of them separately, as it does by taking them together, that if the spirit of this system is to be known from its declared end and design in the preamble, its spirit is to subvert and abolish all the powers of the state government, and to embrace every object to which any government extends.

As it sets out in the preamble with this declared intention, so it proceeds in the different parts with the same idea. Any person, who will peruse the 8th section with attention, in which most of the powers are enumerated, will perceive that they either expressly or by implication extend to almost every thing about which any legislative power can be employed. But if this equitable mode of construction is applied to this part of the constitution; nothing can stand before it.

This will certainly give the first clause in that article a construction which I confess I think the most natural and grammatical one, to authorise the Congress to do any thing which in their judgment will tend to provide for the general welfare, and this amounts to the same thing as general and unlimited powers of legislation in all cases.

BRUTUS

BRUTUS XII
Continued from February 7, 1788 paper
February 14, 1788

THIS SAME MANNER of explaining the constitution, will fix a meaning, and a very important one too, to the 12th [18th] clause of the same section, which authorises the Congress to make all laws which shall be proper and necessary for carrying into effect the foregoing powers, &c. A voluminous writer in favor of this system, has taken great pains to convince the public, that this clause means nothing: for that the same powers expressed in this, are implied in other parts of the constitution. Perhaps it is so, but still this will undoubtedly be an excellent auxilliary to assist the courts to discover the spirit and reason of the constitution, and when applied to any and every of the other clauses granting power, will operate powerfully in extracting the spirit from them.

I might instance a number of clauses in the constitution, which, if explained in an *equitable* manner, would extend the powers of the government to every case, and reduce the state legislatures to nothing; but, I should draw out my remarks to an undue length, and I presume enough has been said to shew, that the courts have sufficient ground in the exercise of this power, to determine, that the legislature have no bounds set to them by this constitution, by any supposed right the legislatures of the respective states may have, to regulate any of their local concerns.

I proceed, 2d, To inquire, in what manner this power will increase the jurisdiction of the courts.

I would here observe, that the judicial power extends, expressly, to all civil cases that may arise save such as arise between citizens of the same state, with this exception to those of that description, that the judicial of the United States have cognizance of cases between citizens of the same state, claiming lands under grants of different states. Nothing more, therefore, is necessary to give the courts of law, under this constitution, complete jurisdiction of all civil causes, but to comprehend cases between citizens of the same state not included in the foregoing exception.

I presume there will be no difficulty in accomplishing this. Nothing more is necessary than to set forth, in the process, that the party who brings the suit is a citizen of a different state from the one against whom the suit is brought, and there can be little doubt but that the court will take cognizance of the matter, and if they do, who is to restrain them? Indeed, I will freely confess, that it is my decided opinion, that the courts ought to take cognizance of such causes, under the powers of the constitution. For one of the great ends of the constitution is, "to establish justice." This supposes that this cannot be done under the existing governments of the states; and there is certainly as good reason why individuals, living in the same state, should have justice, as those who live in different states. Moreover, the constitution expressly declares, that "the citizens of each state shall be entitled to all the privileges and immunities of citizens in the several states." It will therefore be no fiction, for a citizen of one state to set forth, in a suit, that he is a citizen of another; for he that is entitled to all the privileges and immunities of a country, is a citizen of that country. And in truth, the citizen of one state will, under this constitution, be a citizen of every state.

But supposing that the party, who alleges that he is a citizen of another state, has recourse to fiction in bringing in his suit, it is well known, that the courts have high authority to plead, to justify them in suffering actions to be brought before them by such fictions. In my last number I stated, that the court of exchequer tried all causes in virtue of such a fiction. The court of king's bench, in England, extended their jurisdiction in the same way. Originally, this court held pleas, in civil cases, only of trespasses and other injuries alledged to be committed *vi et armis*. They might likewise, says Blackstone, upon the division of the *aula regia*, have originally held pleas of any other civil action whatsoever (except in real actions which are now very seldom in use) provided the defendant was an officer of the court, or in the custody of the marshall or prison-keeper of this court, for breach of the peace, &c. In process of time, by a fiction, this court began to hold pleas of any personal action whatsoever; it being surmised, that the defendant has been arrested for a supposed trespass that "he has never committed, and being thus in the custody of the marshall of the court, the plaintiff is at liberty to proceed against him, for any other personal injury: which surmise of being in the Marshall's custody, the defendant is not at liberty to dispute." By a much less fiction, may the pleas of the courts of the United States extend to cases between citizens of the same state. I shall add no more on this head, but proceed briefly to remark, in what way this power will diminish and destroy both the legislative and judicial authority of the states.

It is obvious that these courts will have authority to decide upon the validity of the laws of any of the states, in all cases where they come in question before them. Where the constitution gives the general government exclusive jurisdiction, they will adjudge all laws made by the states, in such cases, void *ab initio*. Where the constitution gives them concurrent jurisdiction, the laws of the United States must prevail, because they are the supreme law. In such cases, therefore, the laws of the state legislatures must be repealed, restricted, or so construed, as to give full effect to the laws of the union on the same subject. From these remarks it is easy to see, that in proportion as the general government acquires power and jurisdiction, by the liberal construction which the judges may give the constitution, will those of the states lose its rights, until they become so trifling and unimportant, as not to be worth having. I am much mistaken, if this system will not operate to effect this with as much celerity, as those who have the administration of it will think prudent to suffer it. The remaining objections to the judicial power shall be considered in a future paper.

BRUTUS

BRUTUS XV
March 20, 1788

I SAID IN MY LAST NUMBER, that the supreme court under this constitution would be exalted above all other power in the government, and subject to no controul. The business of this paper will be to illustrate this, and to shew the danger that will result from it. I question whether the world ever saw, in any period of it, a court of justice invested with such immense powers, and yet placed in a situation so little responsible. Certain it is, that in England, and in the several states, where we have been taught to believe, the courts of law are put upon the most prudent establishment, they are on a very different footing.

The judges in England, it is true, hold their offices during their good behaviour, but then their determinations are subject to correction by the house of lords; and their power is by no means so extensive as that of the proposed supreme court of the union—I believe they in no instance assume the authority to set aside an act of parliament under the idea that it is inconsistent with their constitution. They consider themselves bound to decide according to the existing laws of the land, and never undertake to controul them by adjudging that they are inconsistent with the constitution—much less are they vested with the power of giving an *equitable* construction to the constitution.

The judges in England are under the controul of the legislature, for they are bound to determine according to the laws passed by them. But the judges under this constitution will controul the legislature, for the supreme court are authorised in the last resort, to determine what is the extent of the powers of the Congress; they are to give the constitution an explanation, and there is no power above them to set aside their judgment. The framers of this constitution appear to have followed that of the British, in rendering the judges independent, by granting them their offices during good behaviour, without following the constitution of England, in instituting a tribunal in which their errors may be corrected; and without adverting to this, that the judicial under this system have a power which is above the legislative, and which indeed transcends any power before given to a judicial by any free government under heaven.

I do not object to the judges holding their commissions during good behaviour. I suppose it a proper provision provided they were made properly responsible. But I say, this system has followed the English government in this, while it has departed from almost every other principle of their jurisprudence, under the idea, of rendering the judges independent; which, in the British constitution, means no more than that they hold their places during good behaviour, and have fixed salaries, they have made the judges *independent,* in the fullest sense of the word. There is no power above them, to controul any of their decisions. There is no authority that can remove them, and they cannot be controuled by the laws of the legislature. In short, they are independent of the people, of the legislature, and of every power under heaven. Men placed in this situation will generally soon feel themselves independent of heaven itself. Before I proceed to illustrate the truth of these assertions, I beg liberty to make one remark—Though in my opinion the judges ought to hold their offices during good behaviour, yet I think it is clear, that the reasons in favour of this establishment of the judges in England, do by no means apply to this country.

The great reason assigned, why the judges in Britain ought to be commissioned during good behaviour, is this, that they may be placed in a situation, not to be influenced by the crown, to give such decisions, as would tend to increase its powers and prerogatives. While the judges held their places at the will and pleasure of the king, on whom they depended not only for their offices, but also for their salaries, they were subject to every undue influence. If the crown wished to carry a favorite point, to accomplish which the aid of the courts of law was necessary, the pleasure of the king would be signified to the judges. And it required the spirit of a martyr, for the judges to determine contrary to the king's will.—They were absolutely dependent upon him both for their offices and livings. The king, holding his office during life, and transmitting it to his posterity as an inheritance, has much stronger inducements to increase the prerogatives of his office than those who hold their offices for stated periods, or even for life. Hence the English nation gained a great point, in favour of liberty. When they obtained the appointment of the judges, during good behaviour, they got from the crown a concession, which deprived it of one of the most powerful engines with which it might enlarge the boundaries of the royal prerogative and encroach on the liberties of the people. But these reasons do not apply to this country, we have no hereditary monarch; those who appoint the judges do not hold their offices for life, nor do they descend to their children. The same arguments, therefore, which will conclude in favor of the tenor of the judge's offices for good behaviour, lose a considerable part of their weight when applied to the state and condition of America. But much less can it be shewn, that the nature of our government requires that the courts should be placed beyond all account more independent, so much so as to be above controul.

I have said that the judges under this system will be *independent* in the strict sense of the word: To prove this I will shew—That there is no power above them that can controul their decisions, or correct their errors. There is no authority that can remove them from office for any errors or want of capacity, or lower their salaries, and in many cases their power is superior to that of the legislature.

1st. There is no power above them that can correct their errors or controul their decisions—The adjudications of this court are final and irreversible, for there is no court above them to which appeals can lie, either in error or on the merits.—In this respect it differs from the courts in England, for there the house of lords is the highest court, to whom appeals, in error, are carried from the highest of the courts of law.

2d. They cannot be removed from office or suffer a diminution of their salaries, for any error in judgement or want of capacity.

It is expressly declared by the constitution,—"That they shall at stated times receive a compensation for their services which shall not be diminished during their continuance in office."

The only clause in the constitution which provides for the removal of the judges from office, is that which declares, that "the president, vice-president, and all civil officers of the United States, shall be removed from office, on impeachment for, and conviction of treason, bribery, or other high crimes and misdemeanors." By this paragraph, civil officers, in which the judges are included, are removable only for crimes. Treason and bribery are named, and the rest are included under the general terms of high crimes and misdemeanors.— Errors in judgement, or want of capacity to discharge the duties of the office, can never be supposed to be included in these words, *high crimes and misde-*

meanors. A man may mistake a case in giving judgment, or manifest that he is incompetent to the discharge of the duties of a judge, and yet give no evidence of corruption or want of integrity. To support the charge, it will be necessary to give in evidence some facts that will shew, that the judges committed the error from wicked and corrupt motives.

3d. The power of this court is in many cases superior to that of the legislature. I have shewed, in a former paper, that this court will be authorised to decide upon the meaning of the constitution, and that, not only according to the natural and obvious meaning of the words, but also according to the spirit and intention of it. In the exercise of this power they will not be subordinate to, but above the legislature. For all the departments of this government will receive their powers, so far as they are expressed in the constitution, from the people immediately, who are the source of power. The legislature can only exercise such powers as are given them by the constitution, they cannot assume any of the rights annexed to the judicial, for this plain reason, that the same authority which vested the legislature with their powers, vested the judicial with theirs—both are derived from the same source, both therefore are equally valid, and the judicial hold their powers independently of the legislature, as the legislature do of the judicial.—The supreme court then have a right, independent of the legislature, to give a construction to the constitution and every part of it, and there is no power provided in this system to correct their construction or do it away. If, therefore, the legislature pass any laws, inconsistent with the sense the judges put upon the constitution, they will declare it void; and therefore in this respect their power is superior to that of the legislature. In England the judges are not only subject to have their decisions set aside by the house of lords, for error, but in cases where they give an explanation to the laws or constitution of the country, contrary to the sense of the parliament, though the parliament will not set aside the judgement of the court, yet, they have authority, by a new law, to explain a former one, and by this means to prevent a reception of such decisions. But no such power is in the legislature. The judges are supreme—and no law, explanatory of the constitution, will be binding on them.

From the preceding remarks, which have been made on the judicial powers proposed in this system, the policy of it may be fully developed.

I have, in the course of my observation on this constitution, affirmed and endeavored to shew, that it was calculated to abolish entirely the state governments, and to melt down the states into one entire government, for every purpose as well internal and local, as external and national. In this opinion the opposers of the system have generally agreed—and this has been uniformly denied by its advocates in public. Some individuals, indeed, among them, will confess, that it has this tendency, and scruple not to say, it is what they wish; and I will venture to predict, without the spirit of prophecy, that if it is adopted without amendments, or some such precautions as will ensure amendments immediately after its adoption, that the same gentlemen who have employed their talents and abilities with such success to influence the public mind to adopt this plan, will employ the same to persuade the people, that it will be for their good to abolish the state governments as useless and burdensome.

Perhaps nothing could have been better conceived to facilitate the abolition of the state governments than the constitution of the judicial. They will be able to extend the limits of the general government gradually, and by insensible degrees, and to accommodate themselves to the temper of the people. Their decisions on the meaning of the constitution will commonly take place in cases which arise between individuals, with which the public will not be generally acquainted; one adjudication will form a precedent to the next, and this to a following one. These cases will immediately affect individuals only; so that a series of determinations will probably take place before even the people will be informed of them. In the mean time all the art and address of those who wish for the change will be employed to make converts to their opinion. The people will be told, that their state officers, and state legislatures are a burden and expence without affording any solid advantage, for that all the laws passed by them, might be equally well made by the general legislature. If to those who will be interested in the change, be added, those who will be under their influence, and such who will submit to almost any change of government, which they can be persuaded to believe will ease them of taxes, it is easy to see, the party who will favor the abolition of the state governments would be far from being inconsiderable. – In this situation, the general legislature, might pass one law after another, extending the general and abridging the state jurisdictions, and to sanction their proceedings would have a course of decisions of the judicial to whom the constitution has committed the power of explaining the constitution. – If the states remonstrated, the constitutional mode of deciding upon the validity of the law, is with the supreme court, and neither people, nor state legislatures, nor the general legislature can remove them or reverse their decrees.

Had the construction of the constitution been left with the legislature, they would have explained it at their peril; if they exceed their powers, or sought to find, in the spirit of the constitution, more than was expressed in the letter, the people from whom they derived their power could remove them, and do themselves right; and indeed I can see no other remedy that the people can have against their rulers for encroachments of this nature. A constitution is a compact of a people with their rulers; if the rulers break the compact, the people have a right and ought to remove them and do themselves justice; but in order to enable them to do this with the greater facility, those whom the people chuse at stated periods, should have the power in the last resort to determine the sense of the compact; if they determine contrary to the understanding of the people, an appeal will lie to the people at the period when the rulers are to be elected, and they will have it in their power to remedy the evil;

but when this power is lodged in the hands of men independent of the people, and of their representatives, and who are not, constitutionally, accountable for their opinions, no way is left to controul them but *with a high hand and an outstretched arm.*

Brutus

NOTES

a. W. B. Allen and Gordon Lloyd, eds., *The Essential Antifederalist* (Washington, D.C.: Univ. Press of America, 1985), viii–xiv.

12

The Judiciary as a Barrier
to Encroachments of Representative Bodies

LIKE THE ANTIFEDERALISTS, proponents of the ratification of the proposed constitution published their arguments. These appeared in New York newspapers from October 27, 1787, to August 16, 1788. Alexander Hamilton, James Madison, and John Jay, writing under the name *Publius,* prepared eighty-five short essays referred to as *The Federalist.*

It is fair to characterize the *Federalist Papers* as political propaganda, designed to persuade delegates to the New York Ratifying Convention to vote in favor of the proposed constitution. However, it is also true that the arguments found in these papers represent an important contribution to political theory and rank behind only the Constitution and the Declaration of Independence as the most cherished of American political writings.[a]

Alexander Hamilton authored or participated in writing more than half of the *Federalist Papers.* It is believed that he wrote the articles dealing with the federal judiciary, numbers 78 through 83. Hamilton was regarded as a distinguished attorney before he reached his thirtieth birthday. During the Revolutionary War he was an aide to General George Washington and later was named by the first president as the nation's first secretary of the treasury.

Hamilton was a delegate to the Philadelphia Convention and was strongly distrusted by his New York colleagues, including Robert Yates, for his advocacy of a strong national government.[b] Later, as a member of Washington's cabinet, he became the leader of what came to be called the Federalist Party; Hamilton was Thomas Jefferson's chief antagonist in and out of government. In 1804 he died in a duel with former Vice-President Aaron Burr. Though it is debatable whether this strong-willed person made contributions to the new nation for the good of all, Hamilton's statement on the judicial function is regarded as a classic defense of the apparently undemocratic nature of the judiciary.

The influential constitutional scholar Edward S. Corwin noted: "Hamilton's later argument in Federalist 78 and 81 seems to have been inspired by the effort of Yates, an opponent of the Constitution, to inflate judicial review to the dimensions of a bugaboo, and thereby convert the case for it into an argument against the constitution."[c] This seems all the more apparent when we examine *Federalist* 29, published in the *Daily Advertiser* on January 19, 1778, coincident with the *Brutus* letters. Hamilton observed:

> In reading many of the publications against the Constitution, a man is apt to imagine that he is perusing some ill-written tale or romance, which, instead of natural and agreeable images, exhibits to the mind nothing but frightful and distorted shapes —
>
> "Gorgons, hydras, and chimeras dire"; discoloring and disfiguring whatever it represents, and transforming everything it touches into a monster.[d]

Returning to this theme in *Federalist* 78, Hamilton wrote of his constitutional adversaries' "rage for objection, which disorders their imaginations and judgments." He proposed, nevertheless, to discuss those unreasoned objections in light of the constitutional provisions for the appointment and tenure of judges, the partition of authority to various courts, and the relation of those courts to one another. Out of all of these provisions, the major objection was to "the tenure by which the judges are to hold their places: this chiefly concerns their duration in office; the provisions for their support; and the precautions for their responsibility."

The crux of the matter lay in the constitutional provision for responsibility. Hamilton's argument is precisely what we would expect it not to be. Rather than showing how the judiciary is accountable to the people, how their will is not insulated from or independent of society, Hamilton emphasized the lack of direct responsibility, and why this ought to be celebrated and not feared. Tyranny, as Madison had observed in *Federalist* 48, was to be feared from the legislative branch more than any other owing to the nature of our form of government.

The sort of despotism most likely in a democratic republic would follow from "the encroachments and oppressions of the representative body."

If tyranny were most likely to stem from the branch of government most responsible to the very source of that tyranny, the people, it would hardly seem wise to make the judiciary responsible to that tyrannical majority when the purpose of judicial review is to check it. Thus, the criticism found in *Brutus* is well-founded; judicial power may be used to check the will of the people's elected representatives. It should be understood that Hamilton was reflecting in some part the views of the commercial class. During the preceding decade (1777–87) they experienced to their horror and detriment the practice of state legislatures of giving in to the demands of the debtor classes. The excesses of the majority were at least one reason for the scrapping of the Articles of Confederation in favor of the Philadelphia proposal. Though clearly admitting that the judiciary may not be accountable to the elected representatives of the people, Hamilton argued that there is no cause for alarm since the judiciary has "neither FORCE nor WILL, but merely judgment; and must ultimately depend upon the executive arm even for the efficacy of its judgments."

It can easily be discerned why the judiciary lacks force. Obviously, the judicial branch must depend upon the executive for enforcement of its will. However, it is not so easy to understand why judicial will is only "judgment" and therefore not will. After all, if the judiciary is to check the legislative branch it must have a will of its own, regardless of whether the success of that check depends upon executive cooperation. What Hamilton means is that insofar as the judiciary must depend upon the executive, the federal courts have no *meaningful will.*

The Court's will is not enforced unless it is also the will of the executive. Thus while the Court and its determination of will remain independent of society in terms of responsibility, the application of that will is never independent since it occurs through the chief executive, who is accountable. Though the judiciary can at times possess a will independent of society and which differs from the will of the executive, it may not be applied and thus is not to be feared. This is the case because an independent will that cannot be acted upon is hardly a meaningful will. This argument should be evaluated in light of the occasional president, such as Franklin Roosevelt and Richard Nixon, who were in conflict with the judiciary of their time but were still bound by them.

Federalist 81 reinforces the view expressed in *Federalist* 78.

Hamilton answers the charge that "the errors and usurpations of the Supreme Court . . . will be uncontrollable and remediless."

First, it is argued that the powers of the federal judiciary are no different in principle from those enjoyed by the state judiciaries. The power of courts to limit legislative acts stems from the general theory of limited government, and does not follow directly from a novel authority granted to the federal bench in the proposed constitution. Second, it is not true, as some have claimed, that state legislatures or the English Parliament may correct an undesirable court decision. In this sense, the federal judiciary under the proposed constitution would be no more uncontrollable than those in Britain and in the states. The final point is a reiteration of the least-dangerous-branch argument made in *Federalist* 78, with an additional consideration. Hamilton doubts whether judicial encroachment upon legislative prerogatives will ever become extensive. If per chance it does, the impeachment power can be employed: "this alone is a complete security." Whatever might be the merits of Hamilton's first two arguments, historical experience points to the dubious quality of the last.

The Federalist

FEDERALIST NO. 78

Alexander Hamilton

To the People of the State of New York:
We PROCEED now to an examination of the judiciary department of the proposed government.

In unfolding the defects of the existing confederation, the utility and necessity of a federal judicature have been clearly pointed out. It is the less necessary to recapitulate the considerations there urged, as the propriety of the institution in the abstract is not disputed; the only questions which have been raised being relative to the manner of constituting it, and to its extent. To these points, therefore, our observations shall be confined.

The manner of constituting it seems to embrace these several objects: 1st. The mode of appointing the judges. 2d. The tenure by which they are to hold their places. 3d. The partition of the judiciary authority between different courts, and their relations to each other.

First. As to the mode of appointing the judges; this is the same with that of appointing the officers of the Union in general, and has been so fully discussed in the two last numbers, that nothing can be said here which would not be useless repetition.

Second. As to the tenure by which the judges are to hold their places: this chiefly concerns their duration in office; the provisions for their support; the precautions for their responsibility.

According to the plan of the convention, all judges who may be appointed by the United States are to hold their offices *during good behavior;* which is conformable to the most approved of the State constitutions, and among the rest, to that of this State. Its propriety having been drawn into question by the adversaries of that plan, is no light symptom of the rage for objection, which disorders their imaginations and judgments. The standard of good behavior for the continuance in office of the judicial magistracy, is certainly one of the most valuable of the modern improvements in the practice of government. In a monarchy it is an excellent barrier to the despotism of the prince; in a republic it is a no less excellent barrier to the encroachments and oppressions of the representative body. And it is the best expedient which can be devised in any government, to secure a steady, upright, and impartial administration of the laws.

Whoever attentively considers the different departments of power must perceive, that, in a government in which they are separated from each other, the judiciary, from the nature of its functions, will always be the least dangerous to the political rights of the Constitution; because it will be least in a capacity to annoy or injure them. The Executive not only dispenses the honors, but holds the sword of the community. The legislature not only commands the purse, but prescribes the rules by which the duties and rights of every citizen are to be regulated. The judiciary, on the contrary, has no influence over either the sword or the purse; no direction either of the strength or of the wealth of the society; and can take no active resolution whatever. It may truly be said to have neither FORCE nor WILL, but merely judgment; and must ultimately depend upon the aid of the executive arm even for the efficacy of its judgments.

This simple view of the matter suggests several important consequences. It proves incontestably, that the judiciary is beyond comparison the weakest of the three departments of power;[1] that it can never attack with success either of the two; and that all possible care is requisite to enable it to defend itself against their attacks. It equally proves, that though individual oppression may now and then proceed from the courts of justice, the general liberty of the people can never be endangered from that quarter; I mean so long as the judiciary remains truly distinct from both the legislature and the Executive. For I agree, that "there is no liberty, if the power of judging be not separated from the legislative and executive powers."[2] And it proves, in the last place, that as liberty can have nothing to fear from the judiciary alone, but would have every thing to fear from its union with either of the other departments;

that as all the effects such a union must ensure from a dependence of the former on the latter, notwithstanding a nominal and apparent separation; that as, from the natural feebleness of the judiciary, it is in continual jeopardy of being overpowered, awed, or influenced by its coordinate branches; and that as nothing can contribute so much to its firmness and independence as permanency in office, this quality may therefore be just regarded as an indispensable ingredient in its constitution, and, in a great measure, as the citadel of public justice and the public security.

The complete independence of the courts of justice is peculiarly essential in a limited Constitution. By a limited Constitution, I understand one which contains certain specified exceptions to the legislative authority; such, for instance, as that it shall pass no bills of attainder, no *ex-post-facto* laws, and the like. Limitations of this kind can be preserved in practice no other way than through the medium of courts of justice, whose duty it must be to declare all acts contrary to the manifest tenor of the Constitution void. Without this, all the reservations of particular rights or privileges would amount to nothing.

Some perplexity respecting the rights of the courts to pronounce legislative acts void, because contrary to the constitution, has arisen from an imagination that the doctrine would imply a superiority of the judiciary to the legislative power. It is urged that the authority which can declare the acts of another void, must necessarily be superior to the one whose acts may be declared void. As this doctrine is of great importance in all the American constitutions, a brief discussion of the ground on which it rests cannot be unacceptable.

There is no position which depends on clearer principles, than that every act of a delegated authority, contrary to the tenor of the commission under which it is exercised, is void. No legislative act, therefore, contrary to the Constitution, can be valid. To deny this, would be to affirm, that the deputy is greater than his principal; that the servant is above his master; that the representatives of the people are superior to the people themselves; that men acting by virtue of powers, may do not only what their powers do not authorize, but what they forbid.

If it be said that the legislative body are themselves the constitutional judges of their own powers, and that the construction they put upon them is conclusive upon the other departments, it may be answered, that this cannot be the natural presumption, where it is not to be collected from any particular provisions in the Constitution. It is not otherwise to be supposed, that the Constitution could intend to enable the representatives of the people to substitute their *will* to that of their constituents. It is far more rational to suppose, that the courts were designed to be an intermediate body between the people and the legislature, in order, among other things, to keep the latter within the limits assigned to their authority. The interpretation of the laws is the proper and peculiar province of the courts. A constitution is, in fact, and must be regarded by the judges, as a fundamental law. It therefore belongs to them to ascertain its meaning, as well as the meaning of any particular act proceeding from the legislative body. If there should happen to be an irreconcilable variance between the two, that which has the superior obligation and validity ought, of course, to be preferred; or, in other words, the Constitution ought to be preferred to the statute, the intention of the people to the intention of their agents.

Nor does this conclusion by any means suppose a superiority of the judicial to the legislative power. It only supposes that the power of the people is superior to both; and that where the will of the legislature, declared in its statutes, stands in opposition to that of the people, declared in the Constitution, the judges ought to be governed by the latter rather than the former. They ought to regulate their decisions by the fundamental laws, rather than by those which are not fundamental.

This exercise of judicial discretion, in determining between two contradictory laws, is exemplified in a familiar instance. It not uncommonly happens, that there are two statutes existing at one time, clashing in whole or in part with each other, and neither of them containing any repealing clause or expression. In such case, it is the province of the courts to liquidate and fix their meaning and operation. So far as they can, by any fair construction, be reconciled to each other, reason and law conspire to dictate that this should be done; where this is impracticable, it becomes a matter of necessity to give effect to one, in exclusion of the other. The rule which has obtained in the courts for determining their relative validity is, that the last in order of time shall be preferred to the first. But this is a mere rule of construction, not derived from any positive law, but from the nature and reason of the thing. It is a rule not enjoined upon the courts by legislative provision, but adopted by themselves, as consonant to truth and propriety, for the direction of their conduct as interpreters of the law. They thought it reasonable, that between the interfering acts of an *equal* authority, that which was the last indication of its will should have the preference.

But in regard to the interfering acts of a superior and subordinate authority, of an original and derivative power, the nature and reason of the thing indicate the converse of that rule as proper to be followed. They teach us that the prior act of a superior ought to be preferred to the subsequent act of an inferior and subordinate authority; and that accordingly, whenever a particular statute contravenes the Constitution, it will be the duty of the judicial tribunals to adhere to the latter and disregard the former.

It can be of no weight to say that the courts, on the presence of a repugnancy, may substitute their own pleasure to the constitutional intentions of the legislature. This might as well happen in the case of two contradictory statutes, or it might as well happen in every adjudication upon any single statute. The courts must declare the sense of the law; and if they should be disposed to exercise WILL instead of JUDGMENT, the consequence would equally be the substitution of their pleasure to that of the legislative body. The observation, if it prove anything, would prove that there ought to be no judges distinct from that body.

If, then, the courts of justice are to be considered as the bulwarks of a limited Constitution against legislative encroachments, this consideration will afford a strong argument for the permanent tenure of judicial offices, since nothing will contribute so much as this to that independent spirit in the judges which must be essential to the faithful performance of so arduous a duty.

This independence of the judges is equally requisite to guard the Constitution and the rights of individuals from the effects of those ill humors, which the arts of designing men, or the influence of particular conjunctures, sometimes disseminate among the people themselves, and which, though they speedily give place to better information, and more deliberate reflection, have a tendency, in the meantime, to occasion dangerous innovations in the government, and serious oppressions of the minor party in the community. Though I trust the friends of the proposed Constitution will never concur with its enemies,[3] in questioning that fundamental principle of republican government, which admits the right of people to alter or abolish the established Constitution, whenever they find it inconsistent with their happiness, yet it is not to be inferred from this principle, that the representatives of the people, whenever a momentary inclination happens to lay hold of a majority of their constituents, incompatible with the provisions in the existing Constitution, would, on that account, be justifiable in a violation of those provisions; or that the courts would be under a greater obligation to connive at infractions in this shape, than when they had proceeded wholly from the cabals of the representative body. Until the people have, by some solemn and authoritative act, annulled or changed the established form, it is binding upon themselves collectively, as well as individually; and no presumption, or even knowledge, of their sentiments, can warrant their representatives in a departure from it, prior to such an act. But is easy to see, that it would require an uncommon portion of fortitude in the judges to do their duty as faithful guardians of the Constitution, where legislative invasions of it had been instigated by the major voice of the community.

But it is not with a view to infractions of the Constitution only, that the independence of the judges may be an essential safeguard against the effects of occasional ill humors in the society. These sometimes extend no farther than to injury of the private rights of particular classes of citizens, by unjust and partial laws. Here also the firmness of the judicial magistracy is of vast importance in mitigating the severity and confining the operation of such laws. It not only serves to moderate the immediate mischiefs of those which may have been passed, but it operates as a check upon the legislative body in passing them; who, perceiving that obstacles to the success of iniquitous intention are to be expected from the scruples of the courts, are in a manner compelled, by the very motives of the injustice they mediate, to qualify their attempts. This is a circumstance calculated to have more influence upon the character of our governments, than but few may be aware of. The benefits of the integrity and moderation of the judiciary have already been felt in more States than one; and though they may have displeased those whose sinister expectations they may have disappointed, they must have commanded the esteem and applause of all the virtuous and disinterested. Considerate men, of every description, ought to prize whatever will tend to beget or fortify that temper in the courts; as no man can be sure that he may not be tomorrow the victim of a spirit of injustice, by which he may be a gainer today. And every man must now feel, that the inevitable tendency of such spirit is to sap the foundations of public and private confidence and to introduce in its stead universal distrust and distress.

That inflexible and uniform adherence to the rights of the Constitution, and of individuals, which we perceive to be indispensable in the courts of justice, can certainly not be expected from judges who hold their offices by a temporary commission. Periodical appointments, however regulated, or by whomsoever made, would, in some way or other, be fatal to their necessary independence. If the power of making them was committed either to the Executive or legislature, there would be danger of an improper compliance to the branch which possessed it; if to both, there would be an unwillingness to hazard the displeasure of either; if to the people, or to persons chosen by them for the special purpose, there would be too great a disposition to consult popularity, to justify a reliance that nothing would be consulted but the Constitution and the laws.

There is yet a further and a weightier reason for the permanency of the judicial offices, which is deducible from the nature of the qualifications they require. It has been frequently remarked, with great propriety, that a voluminous code of laws is one of the inconveniences necessarily connected with the advantages of a free government. To avoid an arbitrary discretion in the courts, it is indispensable that they should be bound down by strict rules and precedents, which serve to define and point out their duty in every particular case that comes before them; and it will readily be conceived from the variety of controversies which grow out of the folly and wickedness of mankind, that the records of those precedents must unavoidably swell to a very considerable bulk, and must demand long and laborious study to acquire a competent knowledge of them. Hence it is, that there can be but few men in the society who will have sufficient skill in the laws to qualify them for the stations of judges. And making the proper deductions for the ordinary depravity of human nature, the number must be still smaller of those who unite the requisite integrity with the requisite knowledge. These considerations apprise us, that the government can have no great option between fit character; and that a temporary duration in office, which would naturally discourage such characters from quitting a lucrative line of practice to accept a seat on the bench, would have a tendency to throw the administration of justice into hands less able, and less well qualified, to conduct it with utility and dignity. In the present circumstances of this country, and in those in which it is likely to be for a long time to come, the disadvantages on this score would be greater than they may at first sight appear; but it must be confessed, that they are far inferior to those which present themselves under the other aspects of the subject.

Upon the whole, there can be no room to doubt that the convention acted wisely in copying from the models of those constitutions which have established *good behavior* as the tenure of their judicial offices, in point of duration; and that so far from being blamable on this account, their plan would have been inexcusably defective, if it had wanted this important feature of good government. The experience of Great Britain affords an illustrious comment on the excellence of the institution.

PUBLIUS

FEDERALIST NO. 81

Alexander Hamilton

To the People of the State of New York:
Let us now return to the partition of the judiciary authority between different courts, and their relations to each other.

"The judicial power of the United States is" (by the plan of the convention) "to be vested in one Supreme Court, and in such inferior courts as the Congress may, from time to time, ordain and establish."[4]

That there ought to be one court of supreme and final jurisdiction, is a proposition which is not likely to be contested. The reasons for it have been assigned in another place, and are too obvious to need repetition. The only question that seems to have been raised concerning it, is, whether it ought to be a distinct body or a branch of the legislature. The same contradiction is observable in regard to this matter which has been remarked in several other cases. The very men who object to the Senate as a court of impeachments, on the ground of an improper intermixture of powers, advocate, by implication at least, the propriety of vesting the ultimate decision of all causes, in the whole or in a part of the legislative body.

The arguments, or rather suggestions, upon which this charge is founded, are to this effect: "The authority of the proposed Supreme Court of the United States, which is to be a separate and independent body, will be superior to that of the legislature. The power of construing the laws according to the *spirit* of the Constitution, will enable that court to mould them into whatever shape it may think proper; especially as its decisions will not be in any manner subject to the revision or correction of the legislative body. This is as unprecedented as it is dangerous. In Britain, the judicial power, in the last resort, resides in the House of Lords, which is a branch of the legislature; and this part of the British government has been imitated in the State constitutions in general. The Parliament of Great Britain, and the legislatures of the several States, can at any time rectify, by law, the exceptionable decisions of their respective courts. But the errors and usurpations of the Supreme Court of the United States will be uncontrollable and remediless." This upon examination, will be found to be made up altogether of false reasoning upon misconceived fact.

In the first place, there is not a syllable in the plan under consideration which *directly* empowers the national courts to construe the laws according to the spirit of the Constitution, or which gives them any greater latitude in this respect than may be claimed by the courts of every State. I admit, however, that the Constitution ought to be the standard of construction for the laws, and that wherever there is an evident opposition, the laws ought to give place to the Constitution. But this doctrine is not deducible from any circumstances peculiar to the plan of the convention, but from the general theory of a limited Constitution; and as far as it is true, is equally applicable to most, if not to all the State governments. There can be no objection, therefore, on this account, to the federal judicature which will not lie against the local judicatures in general, and which will not serve to condemn every constitution that attempts to set bounds to legislative discretion.

But perhaps the force of the objection may be thought to consist in the particular organization of the Supreme Court; in its being composed of a distinct body of magistrates, instead of being one of the branches of the legislature, as in the government of Great Britain and that of the State. To insist upon this point, the authors of the objection must renounce the meaning they have labored to annex to the celebrated maxim, requiring a separation of the departments of power. It shall, nevertheless, be conceded to them, agreeably to the interpretation given to that maxim in the course of these papers, that it is not violated by vesting the ultimate power of judging in a *part* of the legislative body. But though this be not an absolute violation of that excellent rule, yet it verges so nearly upon it, as on this account alone to be less eligible than the mode preferred by the convention. From a body which had even a partial agency in passing bad laws, we could rarely expect a disposition to temper and moderate them in the application. The same spirit which had operated in making them, would be too apt in interpreting them; still less could it be expected that men who had infringed the Constitution in the character of legislatures, would be disposed to repair the breach in the character of judges. Nor is this all. Every reason which recommends the tenure of good behavior for judicial offices, militates against placing the judiciary power, in the last resort, in a body composed of men chosen for a limited period. There is an absurdity in referring the determination of causes, in the first instance, to judges of permanent standing; in the last, to those of a temporary and mutable constitution. And there is still greater absurdity in subjecting the decisions of men, selected for their knowledges of the laws, acquired by long and laborious study, to the revision and control of men who, for want of the same advantage, cannot but be deficient in that knowledge. The members of the legislature will rarely be chosen with a view to those qualifications which fit men for the stations of judges; and as, on this account, there will be great reason to apprehend all the ill consequences of defective information, so, on account of the natural propensity of such bodies to party divisions, there will be no less reason to fear that the pestilential breath of faction may poison the fountains of justice. The habit of being continually marshalled on opposite sides will be too apt to stifle the voice both of law and of equity.

These considerations teach us to applaud the wisdom of those States who have committed the judicial power, in the last resort, not to a part of the legislature, but to distinct and independent bodies of men. Contrary to the supposition of those who have represented the plan of the convention, in this respect, as novel and unprecedented, it is but a copy of the constitutions of New Hampshire, Massachusetts, Pennsylvania, Delaware, Maryland, Virginia, North Carolina, South Carolina, and Georgia; and the preference which has been given to those models is highly to be commended.

It is not true, in the second place, that the parliament of Great Britain, or the legislatures of the particular States, can rectify the exceptionable decisions of the respective courts, in any other sense than might be done by a future legislature of the United States. The theory, neither of the British, nor the State constitutions, authorizes the revisal of a judicial sentence by a legislative act. Nor is there anything in the proposed Constitution, more than in either of them, by which it is forbidden. In the former, as well as in the latter, the impropriety of the thing, on the general principles of law and reason, is the sole obstacle. A legislature, without exceeding its province, cannot reverse a determination once made in a particular case; though it may prescribe a new rule for future cases. This is the principle, and it applies in all its consequences, exactly in the same manner and extent, to the State governments, as to the national government now under consideration. Not the least difference can be pointed out in any view of the subject.

It may in the last place be observed that the supposed danger of judiciary encroachments on the legislative authority, which has been upon many occasions reiterated, is in reality a phantom. Particular misconstructions and contraventions of the will of the legislature may now and then happen; but they can never be so extensive as to amount to an inconvenience, or in any sensible degree to affect the order of the political system. This may be inferred with certainty, from the general nature of the judicial power, from the objects to which it relates, from the manner in which it is exercised, from its comparative weakness, and from its total incapacity to support its usurpations by force. And the inference is greatly fortified by the consideration of the important constitutional check which the power of instituting impeachments in one part of the legislative body, and of determining upon them in the other, would give to that body upon the members of the judicial department. This is alone a complete security. There never can be danger that the judges by a series of deliberate usurpations on the authority of the legislature, would hazard the united resentment of the body intrusted with it, while this body was possessed of the means of punishing their presumption, by degrading them from their stations. While this ought to remove all apprehensions on the subject, it affords, at the same time, a cogent argument for constituting the Senate a court for the trial of impeachments. . . .

PUBLIUS

NOTES

a. *The Guide to American Law*, s.v. "Federalist Papers and the Role of the Judiciary," by Stephen B. Presser.

b. *The Federalist* (New York: Modern Library, 1941), xxiii.

c. *Court Over Constitution* (Gloucester: Peter Smith, 1957), 45–46.

d. *The Federalist*, 180.

1. The celebrated Montesquieu, speaking of them, says: "Of the three powers above mentioned, the judiciary is next to nothing." "Spirit of Laws," vol. i, page 186. – PUBLIUS.

2. *Idem.* Page 181. – PUBLIUS.

3. *Vide* "Protest of the Minority of the Convention of Pennsylvania," Martin's Speech, etc. – PUBLIUS.

4. Article 3, sec. 1, – PUBLIUS.

Judicial Review
as a Democratic Institution

NEITHER ROBERT YATES nor Alexander Hamilton believed judicial review to be democratic. Yates condemned it for that reason, whereas Hamilton applauded it as a necessary check on the majority. In this chapter we discover a third view: Eugene Rostow argues that judicial review is in fact democratic.

Eugene Victor Rostow has had a distinguished career as a lawyer, economist, government official, and educator. He has been a law professor at a number of important institutions and was dean at the prestigious Yale Law School. The article reproduced here first appeared in a 1952 issue of the *Harvard Law Review* and is widely regarded as one of the best defenses of judicial review.

It is not surprising that Rostow prefaces his article by acknowledging widespread "uneasiness, and even guilt" about judicial review. Certainly by the end of World War II, the activist posture of the Supreme Court which resulted in striking down state and federal government economic regulation during the first third of the twentieth century was thoroughly discredited. Judicial self-restraint had become part of the liberal credo. However, by the late 1940s and early 1950s the difficult issues reaching the Supreme Court were no longer government regulation of the economy. Rather they involved subversive control, religious freedom, minority rights, and the application of the Bill of Rights to the states through the Due Process Clause of the Fourteenth Amendment. The liberal impulse is to come to the aid of political minorities and the underrepresented in society. But how could the Supreme Court justify its intervention without renouncing the lessons of the past? Rostow's essay may be interpreted as an attempt to show the way.

Rostow maintains that it is erroneous to define democracy solely in terms of a direct vote by the people on every issue. The real task is to ensure that both elected and appointed officials are ultimately responsible to the people for their acts. Moreover, Supreme Court justices are not the only governmental officers who are unaccountable through the electoral process. Other unelected officials such as admirals, generals, and members of the independent regulatory agencies are not perceived to be acting undemocratically. Why then should Court justices be so considered?

Besides, Rostow continues: "the final responsibility of the people is appropriately guaranteed by the provisions for amending the Constitution itself, and by the benign influence of time, which changes the personnel of courts. Given the possibility of constitutional amendment, there is nothing undemocratic in having responsible and independent judges act as important constitutional mediators." Article V of the Constitution, the amendment provision, requires votes of two-thirds and three-fourths depending upon the procedures employed; and thus Rostow has not so subtly substituted simple majority rule with extraordinary majority rule. Also note that most recent U.S. presidents have usually appointed no more than two justices to the nine-member high court, thereby requiring special patience and faith in the "benign influence of time."

For the sake of argument, one may concede the point that the Supreme Court is ultimately responsible to the people. But this proves only that our governmental system is based on popular sovereignty. It does not prove that the Supreme Court's use of judicial review to strike down acts of representative bodies is democratic.

Among the most important ideas contributed by Rostow to the judicial review debate is the notion that the Supreme Court may contribute to democracy by helping to maintain "a pluralistic equilibrium in society." It can mediate conflict between political institutions so as to ensure the maintenance of rights for all citizens. Thus we find the seed of a most important idea. One way to judge how democratic institutions may be is to study what they do. That is, the substance of decisions may be at least as important as the procedures employed to make those decisions. Rostow attacks what he regards as the overreliance upon judicial self-restraint as a failure to ensure the democratic character of U.S. society. His criticism of the Court's opinion in the most famous subversive control case of post–World War II America, *Dennis v. United States,* illustrates the point.

The Democratic Character of Judicial Review

Eugene V. Rostow

> It would require an uncommon portion of fortitude in the judges to do their duty as faithful guardians of the Constitution, where legislative invasions of it had been instigated by the major voice of the community.
> —ALEXANDER HAMILTON[1]

A THEME OF UNEASINESS, and even of guilt, colors the literature about judicial review. Many of those who have talked, lectured, and written about the Constitution have been troubled by a sense that judicial review is undemocratic. Why should a majority of nine Justices appointed for life be permitted to outlaw as unconstitutional the acts of elected officials or of officers controlled by elected officials? Judicial review, they have urged, is an undemocratic shoot on an otherwise respectable tree. It should be cut off, or at least be kept pruned and inconspicuous. The attack has gone further. Reliance on bad political doctrine, they say, has produced bad political results. The strength of the courts has weakened other parts of the government. The judicial censors are accused of causing laxness and irresponsibility in the state and national legislatures, and political apathy in the electorate. At the same time, we are warned, the participation of the courts in this essentially political function will inevitably lead to the destruction of their independence and thus compromise all other aspects of their work.

I

The idea that judicial review is undemocratic is not an academic issue of political philosophy. Like most abstractions, it has far-reaching practical consequences. I suspect that for some judges it is the mainspring of decision, inducing them in many cases to uphold legislative and executive action which would otherwise have been condemned. Particularly in the multiple opinions of recent years, the Supreme Court's self-searching often boils down to a debate within the bosoms of the Justices over the appropriateness of judicial review itself.

The attack on judicial review as undemocratic rests on the premise that the Constitution should be allowed to grow without a judicial check. The proponents of this view would have the Constitution mean what the President, the Congress, and the state legislatures say it means.[2] In this way, they contend, the electoral process would determine the course of constitutional development, as it does in countries with plenipotentiary parliaments.

But the Constitution of the United States does not establish a parliamentary government, and attempts to interpret American government in a parliamentary perspective break down in confusion or absurdity. One may recall, in another setting, the anxious voice of the *Washington Post* urging President Truman to resign because the Republican Party had won control of the Congress in the 1946 elections.

It is a grave oversimplification to contend that no society can be democratic unless its legislature has sovereign powers. The social quality of democracy cannot be defined by so rigid a formula. Government and politics are after all the arms, not the end, of social life. The purpose of the Constitution is to assure the people a free and democratic society. The final aim of that society is as much freedom as possible for the individual human being. The Constitution provides society with a mechanism of government fully competent to this task, but by no means universal in its powers. The power to govern is parcelled out between the states and the nation and is further divided among the three main branches of all governmental units. By custom as well as constitutional practice, many vital aspects of community life are beyond the direct reach of government—for example, religion, the press, and, until recently at any rate, many phases of educational and cultural activity. The separation of powers under the Constitution serves the end of democracy in society by limiting the roles of the several branches of government and protecting the citizen, and the various parts of the state itself, against encroachments from any source. The root idea of the Constitution is that man can be free because the state is not.

The power of constitutional review, to be exercised by some part of the government, is implicit in the conception of a written constitution delegating limited powers. A written constitution would promote discord rather than order in society if there were no accepted authority to construe it, at the least in cases of conflicting action by different branches of government or of constitutionally unauthorized governmental action against individuals. The limitation and separation of powers, if they are to survive, require a procedure for independent mediation and construction to reconcile the inevitable disputes over the boundaries of constitutional power which arise in the process of government. British Dominions operating under written constitutions have had to face the task pretty much as we have, and they have solved it in similar ways. Like institutions have developed in other federal systems.

So far as the American Constitution is concerned, there can be little real doubt that the courts were intended from the beginning to have the power they have exercised. The Federalist Papers are unequivocal; the Debates as clear as debates normally are. The power of judicial review was commonly exercised by the courts of the states, and the people were accustomed to judicial construction of the authority derived from colonial charters.[3] Constitutional interpretation by the courts, Hamilton said, does not

> by any means suppose a superiority of the judicial to the legislative power. It only supposes that the power of the people is superior to both; and that where the will of the legislature, declared in its statutes, stands in opposition to that of the people, declared in the Constitution, the judges ought to be governed by the latter rather than the former. They ought to regulate their decisions by the fundamental laws, rather than by those which are not fundamental.[4]

Hamilton's statement is sometimes criticized as a verbal legalism.[5] But it has an advantage too. For much of the discussion has complicated the problem without clarifying it. Both judges and their critics have wrapped themselves so successfully in the difficulties of particular cases that they have been able to evade the ultimate issue posed in the Federalist Papers.

Whether another method of enforcing the Constitution could have been devised, the short answer is that no such method has developed. The argument over the constitutionality of judicial review has long since been settled by history. The power and duty of the Supreme Court to declare statutes or executive action unconstitutional in appropriate cases is part of the living Constitution. "The course of constitutional history," Mr. Justice Frankfurter recently remarked, has cast responsibilities upon the Supreme Court which it would be "stultification" for it to evade.[6] The Court's power has been exercised differently at different times: sometimes with reckless and doctrinaire enthusiasm; sometimes with great deference to the status and responsibilities of other branches of the government; sometimes with a degree of weakness and timidity that comes close to the betrayal of trust. But the power exists, as an integral part of the process of American government. The Court has the duty of interpreting the Constitution in many of its most important aspects, and especially in those which concern the relations of the individual and the state. The political proposition underlying the survival of the power is that there are some phases of American life which should be beyond the reach of any majority, save by constitutional amendment. In Mr. Justice Jackson's phrase, "One's right to life, liberty, and property, to free speech, a free press, freedom of worship and assembly, and other fundamental rights may not be submitted to vote; they depend on the outcome of no elections."[7] Whether or not this was the intention of the Founding Fathers, the unwritten Constitution is unmistakable.

If one may use a personal definition of the crucial word, this way of policing the Constitution is not undemocratic. True, it employs appointed officials, to whom large powers are irrevocably delegated. But democracies need not elect all the officers who exercise crucial authority in the name of the voters. Admirals and generals can win or lose wars in the exercise of their discretion. The independence of judges in the administration of justice has been the pride of communities which aspire to be free. Members of the Federal Reserve Board have the lawful power to plunge the country into depression or inflation. The list could readily be extended. Government by referendum or town meeting is not the only possible form of democracy. The task of democracy is not to have the people vote directly on every issue, but to assure their ultimate responsibility for the acts of their representatives, elected or appointed. For judges deciding ordinary litigation, the ultimate responsibility of the electorate has a special meaning. It is a responsibility for the quality of the judges and for the substance of their instructions, never a responsibility for their decisions in particular cases. It is hardly characteristic of law in democratic society to encourage bills of attainder, or to allow appeals from the courts in particular cases to legislatures or to mobs. Where the judges are carrying out the function of constitutional review, the final responsibility of the people is appropriately guaranteed by the provisions for amending the Constitution itself, and by the benign influence of time, which changes the personnel of courts. Given the possibility of constitutional amendment, there is nothing undemocratic in having responsible and independent judges act as important constitutional mediators. Within the narrow limits of their capacity to act, their great task is to help maintain a pluralist equilibrium in society. They can do much to keep it from being dominated by the states or the Federal Government, by Congress or the President, by the purse or the sword.

In the execution of this crucial but delicate function, constitutional review by the judiciary has an advantage thoroughly recognized in both theory and practice. The power of the courts, however final, can only be asserted in the course of litigation. Advisory opinions are forbidden, and reefs of self-limitation have grown up around the doctrine that the courts will determine constitutional questions only in cases of actual controversy, when no lesser ground of decision is available, and when the complaining party would be directly and personally injured by the assertion of the power deemed unconstitutional. Thus the check of judicial review upon the elected branches of government must be a mild one, limited not only by the detachment, integrity, and good sense of the Justices but by the structural boundaries implicit in the fact that the power is entrusted to the courts. Judicial review is inherently adapted to preserving broad and flexible lines of constitutional growth, not to operating as a continuously active factor in legislative or executive decisions.

The division and separation of governmental powers within the American federal system provides the community with ample power to act, without compromising its pluralist structure. The Constitution formalizes the principle that a wide dispersal of authority among the institutions of society is the safest foundation for social freedom. It was accepted from the beginning that the judiciary would be one of the chief agencies for enforcing the restraint of the Constitution. In a letter to Madison, Jefferson remarked of the Bill of Rights:

> In the argument in favor of a declaration of rights you omit one which has great weight with me; the legal check which it puts into the hands of the

judiciary. This is a body, which, if rendered independent and kept strictly
to their own department, merits great confidence for their learning and
integrity. In fact, what degree of confidence would be too much, for a body
composed of such men as Wythe, Blair and Pendleton? On characters like
these, the *'civium ardor prava pubentium'* would make no impression.[8]

Jefferson, indeed, went further. He regretted the absence in the Constitution of
a direct veto power over legislation entrusted to the judiciary, and wished that
no legislation could take effect for a year after its final enactment.[9] Within
such constitutional limits, Jefferson believed, American society could best
achieve its goal of responsible self-government. "I have no fear," he wrote, "but
that the result of our experiment will be, that men may be trusted to govern
themselves without a master."[10]

Democracy is a slippery term. I shall make no effort at a formal definition
here. Certainly as a matter of historical fact some societies with parliamentary
governments have been and are "democratic" by standards which Americans
would accept, although it is worth noting that almost all of them employ second chambers, with powers at least of delay, and indirect devices for assuring
continuity in the event of parliamentary collapse, either through the crown or
some equivalent institution, like the president in France. But it would be scho-
lastic pedantry to define democracy in such a way as to deny the title of
"democrat" to Jefferson, Madison, Lincoln, Brandeis, and others who have
found the American constitutional system, including its tradition of judicial
review, well adapted to the needs of a free society.[11] As Mr. Justice Brandeis
said,

the doctrine of the separation of powers was adopted by the Convention of
1787, not to promote efficiency but to preclude the exercise of arbitrary
power. The purpose was, not to avoid friction, but, by means of the inevitable friction incident to the distribution of governmental powers among
three departments, to save the people from autocracy.[12]

It is error to insist that no society is democratic unless it has a government of unlimited powers, and that no government is democratic unless its
legislature has unlimited powers. Constitutional review by an independent
judiciary is a tool of proven use in the American quest for an open society of
widely dispersed powers. In a vast country, of mixed population, with widely
different regional problems, such an organization of society is the surest base
for the hopes of democracy.[13]

II

There is another fundamental aspect of the sustained attack on the legitimacy of judicial review. Men like James Bradley Thayer have urged that if the
propertied classes come to regard the courts as their protectors against popular government they will neglect government. Local and national government, shorn of power, will be indifferently conducted. The people will fail to

meet their political responsibilities.[14] This position is translated by some judges into the doctrine that they serve the cause of democracy by refusing to decide important questions of a political cast, thus forcing the elected agencies of government to settle or postpone them.

This contention has been belied by the course of history: legislatures today, despite almost sixty more years of considerable pressure from their judicial censors, are a good deal less "belittled" and "demoralized" than they were when Thayer wrote.[15] Nor does it stand up as a persuasive argument even in the terms Thayer and his followers used. The existence of the power of judicial review is hardly an adequate explanation for the lapses of legislatures, then or now. The election of petty and irresponsible men to state and national legislatures reflects cultural and sociological forces of far greater significance and generality. Political apathy and ignorance can hardly be explained by the hypothesis that the mass of non-voting citizens, or the larger mass who accept and support government by bosses, are comfortably relying on the courts to protect them. The reasons for the occasional low estate of legislators and congressmen must be sought in the history and development of American society—the ways in which the population has grown, the deplorable level of popular education, the nature of political tradition, the acceptance of graft, the concentration of American energies in business and other non-political activities. It is certainly not true today, and was not true in 1893, that dependence on the courts leads people to "become careless as to whom they send to the legislature; too often they cheerfully vote for men whom they would not trust with an important private affair, and when these unfit persons are found to pass foolish and bad laws, and the courts step in and disregard them, the people are glad that these few wiser gentlemen on the bench are so ready to protect them against their more immediate representatives."[16]

Actually Thayer's papers on constitutional law were written in the setting of different problems from those which face American public life today. It is doubtful whether if applied to the constitutional issues of the 1950's his views would have had the same emphasis that he gave them in discussing those of the last years of the nineteenth century. Thayer was preoccupied with the cycle of cases after the Civil War through which, in Mr. Justice Holmes' phrase, the Court wrote Herbert Spencer's *Social Statics* into the Constitution. He was resisting the practice of declaring all sorts of regulatory legislation illegal as unreasonable in the light of the Due Process Clause of the Fourteenth Amendment or as outside the scope of the commerce power. There is little if any reference in his writings to the function of the courts in enforcing the civil rights listed in the Constitution and the Bill of Rights. He quoted with approval Chief Justice Marshall's statement that the Court on which he served "never sought to enlarge the judicial power beyond its proper bounds, nor feared to carry it to the fullest extent that duty required." "That," Professor Thayer remarked, "is the safe twofold rule; nor is the first part of it any whit less important than the second; nay, more; today it is the part which most requires to be emphasized."[17]

In our time, however, the problem has changed. The constitutional revolution which began in 1937 has had its unmistakable impact. There is little or no risk that the present Supreme Court will become again a Third Chamber annulling a wide variety of regulatory legislation. The breadth of the commerce power, the freedom of the states to legislate in the realm of business, the wide discretionary powers of administrative bodies, state and national— these features of the constitutional scene are not the subject of significant disagreement among the Justices. And public opinion has become acutely conscious of the fact that state and national legislatures have enormous powers which are frequently exercised. While the problems of the future may provoke a new constitutional crisis over the powers of government, today the people are well aware that their own political exertions, and not the long arm of the Supreme Court, must be their chief reliance in molding the body of regulatory legislation to their heart's desire.

The risk today, and it is a real one, is that the Supreme Court is not giving sufficient emphasis to the second part of Marshall's "twofold rule." The freedom of the legislatures to act within wide limits of constitutional construction is the wise rule of judicial policy only if the processes through which they act are reasonably democratic. Chief Justice Stone put emphasis on the fact that in many instances legislative acts are directed against interests which are not or cannot be represented in the legislature: out-of-state interests, where the purpose of legislation is local economic protection, or politically impotent minorities, where the thrust of the act is discrimination or repression. This line of thought led him to the arresting conclusion that statutes which affected interests beyond political protection, or which limited the full democratic potentialities of political action, were not to be approached by the Court with the deference it usually accorded legislative decisions, by way of "presumption" or otherwise.[18]

Chief Justice Stone's distinction brings out an element which cannot easily be dismissed or disregarded in determining the weight to be given the constitutional judgment of the legislature in a judicial decision as to the constitutionality of its action. After all, the form and character of our present legal attack on communism and "disloyalty" is largely determined by the impotence of communism as a domestic political force. France or Italy, confronting communist parties to which one-third of the electorate is loyal, could not consider the kind of direct legal proceedings against communism which we have undertaken. Dealing with an infinitely more serious threat, the French and Italian governments must rely only on police action, in the narrower sense, and on political struggle in the market place of ideas.

III

The argument that action by the courts in protecting the liberties of the citizens is futile in bad times, and unnecessary in good ones, is fundamentally wrong. Judge Learned Hand has given the contrary view its strongest and most eloquent form. In a speech called "The Contribution of an Independent

Judiciary to Civilization,"[19] he reviews the main tasks of judges. In applying "enacted law" – commands of an organ of government "purposely made responsive to the pressure of the interests affected" – he believes that the judiciary should pursue a course of "unflinching" independence in seeking loyally to enforce the spirit of the enactment as it was made.[20] In a society which makes law by the procedures of democratic and representative government, "enacted laws" are always compromises of competing forces, and "to disturb them by surreptitious, irresponsible and anonymous intervention imperils the possibility of any future settlements and protanto upsets the whole system." The power of the judges to legislate in the field of customary law he regards as an anomaly which could not exist in "a pitilessly consistent democracy." Moreover, he points out, modern legislatures can pass laws more readily than ancient parliaments. But so long as the judges live by "a self-denying ordinance which forbids change in what has not already become unacceptable," the old system works out very well as it is, "for the advantages of leaving step by step amendments of the customary law in the hands of those trained in it, outweigh the dangers." As to the constitutional functions of the American judiciary, he makes a distinction. Insofar as the constitution is "an instrument to distribute political power," he would defend entrusting its construction to an independent judiciary, as in the case of interpreting "enacted law." Conflicts over authority are inevitable in a system of divided power. It was "a daring expedient" to have them settled by

> judges deliberately put beyond the reach of popular pressure. And yet, granted the necessity of some such authority, probably independent judges were the most likely to do the job well. Besides, the strains that decisions on these questions set up are not ordinarily dangerous to the social structure. For the most part the interests involved are only the sensibilities of the officials whose provinces they mark out, and usually their resentments have no grave seismic consequences.

Judge Hand's use of "ordinarily," "for the most part," and "usually" in the two preceding sentences may be appropriate as a matter of statistics, but it conceals some dramatic exceptions, of which the explosions of 1937 are only the most recent instance.

The next part of his lecture, however, distinguishes another class of constitutional questions and advances to the attack:

> American constitutions always go further. Not only do they distribute the powers of government, but they assume to lay down general principles to insure the just exercise of those powers. This is the contribution to political science of which we are proud, and especially of a judiciary of Vestal unapproachability which shall always tend the Sacred Flame of Justice. Yet here we are on less firm ground.

In a passage of Browningesque passion and obscurity, he advances the thesis that the judiciary will lose the independence it needs for its other functions unless it resolutely refuses to decide on constitutional questions of this order.

The general constitutional commands of fairness and equality, which he nowhere indentifies in detail, are "moral adjurations, the more imperious because inscrutable, but with only that content which each generation must pour into them anew in the light of its own experience. If an independent judiciary seeks to fill them from its own bosom, in the end it will cease to be independent." If the judges are "intransigent but honest, they will be curbed; but a worse fate will befall them if they learn to trim their sails to the prevailing winds." The price of judicial independence, he concludes, is that the judges

> should not have the last word in those basic conflicts of "right and wrong—between whose endless jar justice resides." You may ask what then will become of the fundamental principles of equity and fair play which our constitutions enshrine; and whether I seriously believe that unsupported they will serve merely as counsels of moderation. I do not think that anyone can say what will be left of those principles; I do not know whether they will serve only as counsels; but this much I think I do know—that a society so riven that the spirit of moderation is gone, no court *can* save; that a society where that spirit flourishes, no court *need* save; that in a society which evades its responsibility by thrusting upon the courts the nurture of that spirit, that spirit in the end will perish.

This gloomy and apocalyptic view is a triumph of logic over life. It reflects the dark shadows thrown upon the judiciary by the Court-packing fight of 1937. Judge Hand is preoccupied with a syllogism. The people and the Congress have the naked power to destroy the independence of the courts. Therefore the courts must avoid arousing the sleeping lion by venturing to construe the broad and sweeping clauses of the Constitution which would "demand the appraisal and balancing of human values which there are no scales to weigh." Presumably he would include in this catalogue of forbidden issues problems of freedom of speech, the separation of church and state, and the limits, if any, to which "the capable, the shrewd or the strong" should "be allowed to exploit their powers." Are we to read the last phrase as encompassing the right of habeas corpus, the central civil liberty and the most basic of all protections against the authority of the state? Would it deny the possibility of constitutional review by the courts for laws denying the vote to Negroes, for searches and seizures without warrant, for bills of attainder or test oaths?

In the first place, the judicial decisions which brought on the storm in 1937 were not in this area at all. They concerned the division of power between the states and the nation,[21] and between Congress and the President[22]— issues which Judge Hand regards as inescapably within the province of the courts and "not likely in any event to have seismic consequences." Further, it is important to reiterate the obvious but sometimes forgotten fact that the historic conception of the Supreme Court's duties, however challenged in 1937, prevailed in that struggle. In the end that idea of the Court's function was sustained, against the reluctant and half-hearted opposition of a Congress which did not really believe in President Roosevelt's proposal and took its first opportunity to abandon it.

The possibility of judicial emasculation by way of popular reaction against constitutional review by the courts has not in fact materialized in more than a century and a half of American experience. When the Court has differed from the Congress and the President in its notions of constitutional law— whether in the realm of the eternal verities or in interpreting the scope of the commerce power—time has unfailingly cured the conflicts, such as they were. Against that history, should we weigh the chance that Congress would suppress or intimidate the Supreme Court as ominously as Judge Hand does? Is it a reason for denying the Court competence in the broader reaches of constitutional law, or a bogey-man?

If the courts persist, Judge Hand warns, in seeking to impose their ideas as to the Higher Law of the Constitution upon the litigants before them, the end will be the destruction of society. The independence of the courts will be compromised, and social life will "relapse into the reign of the tooth and claw."[23] Is this dire vision justified? If the courts, for example, refused to defend the rights of Negroes in the name of the Fourteenth Amendment, or the right of political groups to assemble and make speeches, would the result be more order or more disorder in society? While no statistical answer to such questions is possible, I for one believe that the defense of civil rights by the courts is a force not only for democratic values but for social order. If repressed by those who control the local police, the social and political aspirations of the people would often spill over into rioting or sullen disaffection, which would be worse. Nothing has destroyed the essential solidarity of a people more effectively than policies of repression imposed by the strong on the weak. Such policies, not those of open discussion and political equality, have led modern societies to the rule of the tooth, the claw, and the tommy gun.

It may of course be true that no court can save a society bent on ruin. But American society is not bent on ruin. It is a body deeply committed in its majorities to the principles of the Constitution and both willing and anxious to form its policy and programs in a constitutional way. Americans are, however, profoundly troubled by fears—intense and real fears, raised by unprecedented dangers and by the conduct of perilous tasks unprecedented in the history of the Government. It is difficult for legislators confronting the menace of the world communist movement to reject any proposals which purport to attack communism or to protect the community from it. This does not mean, however, that the President and the Congress would refuse to obey the Supreme Court's rulings on the constitutionality of some of the means with which they have chosen to attack—and often, alas, merely to exorcise—the evil. Ruin can come to a society not only from the furious resentments of a crisis. It can be brought about in imperceptible stages by gradually accepting, one after another, immoral solutions for particular problems. The "relocation camps" conducted during the last war for Japanese residents and for Americans of Japanese descent is the precedent for the proposal that concentration camps be established for citizens suspected of believing in revolutionary ideas.[24] Thus can the protection of the writ of habeas corpus be eroded, and the principle lost that criminal punishment can be inflicted only for criminal behavior and then only after a trial by jury conducted according to the rules of the Bill of Rights. Thus can we be led to accept the ideas and techniques of the police state.

Nor, more broadly, is it true as a matter of experience that a vigorous lead from the Supreme Court inhibits or weakens popular responsibility in the same area. The process of forming public opinion in the United States is a continuous one with many participants—Congress, the President, the press, political parties, scholars, pressure groups and so on. The discussion of problems and the declaration of broad principles by the Courts is a vital element in the community experience through which American policy is made. The Supreme Court is, among other things, an educational body, and the Justices are inevitably teachers in a vital national seminar. The prestige of the Supreme Court as an institution is high, despite the conflicts of the last fifteen years, and the members of the Court speak with a powerful voice.

Can one doubt, for example, the immensely constructive influence of the series of decisions in which the Court is slowly asserting the right of Negroes to vote and to travel, live, and have a professional education without segregation? These decisions have not paralyzed or supplanted legislative and community action. They have precipitated it. They have not created bigotry. They have helped to fight it. The cycle of decisions in these cases—influential because they are numerous, cumulative, and on the whole, consistent—have played a crucial role in leading public opinion and encouraging public action towards meeting the challenge and burden of the Negro problem as a constitutional—that is, as a moral[25]—obligation. The Court's stand has stimulated men everywhere to take action, by state statutes, by new corporate or union policies, in local communities, on university faculties, in student fraternities, on courts, and in hospitals. The Negro does not yet have equality in American society, or anything approaching it. But his position is being improved, year by year. And the decisions and opinions of the Supreme Court are helping immeasurably in that process.

The Court's lead has also been constructive, on the whole, in reforming state criminal procedures—here again in a long series of decisions which year by year are having their effect on the conduct of police officers and on the course of trials.[26] This slow and evolutionary process requires a good deal of litigation: a single bolt from the blue could not overcome the inertia of long years of bad practice, nor the natural desire of policemen and prosecutors to win their cases. The pressure of the Court's opinions in this area requires thought and action in every state legislature and, indeed, in every court and police station of the land. The Court has not stilled or prevented responsible democratic action on these problems. It has required it. Lawless police action has not yet been banished from American life, but the most primitive police sergeant is learning that third degree methods may backfire.

Other examples, both of action and of inaction, could readily be listed. Even the tortuous and often maddening cases in which the Court considers whether state action unduly burdens or discriminates against the national commerce or conflicts with national legislation in the same field impose some limits on the degree of economic autarchy states can practice, and provide ammunition to those who urge the preservation of the national economy as a single continental market.[27]

In the field of civil rights itself, the libertarian cases of the early Thirties helped prevent during the Second World War many of the repressive and unnecessary acts which distinguished the course of public policy during and after the First World War. Where the Court failed to follow its own traditions, as in the Japanese-American cases, the results were painful. I have elsewhere contended that earlier decisions[28] required new trials, at the least, in the *Korematsu* and *Hirabayashi cases.*[29] Even there, Congress has in part atoned for the weakness of the Supreme Court.[30] And in *Duncan v. Kahanamoku*[31] the Court itself has come some distance towards repairing the rent in its doctrines.

The reciprocal relation between the Court and the community in the formation of policy may be a paradox to those who believe that there is something undemocratic in the power of judicial review. But the work of the Court can have, and when wisely exercised does have, the effect not of inhibiting but of releasing and encouraging the dominantly democratic forces of American life. The historic reason for this paradox is that American life in all its aspects is an attempt to express and to fulfill a far-reaching moral code. Some observers find this a handicap to coldly realistic policy making.[32] Others see in it the essential greatness and appealing power of America as an idea and a world force.[33] The prestige and authority of the Supreme Court derive from the fact that it is accepted as the ultimate interpreter of the American code in many of its most important applications.

IV

The distrust of judicial review has been reflected in several aspects of the Supreme Court's work, but nowhere more clearly than in its consideration of politically sensitive issues. One of the central responsibilities of the judiciary in exercising its constitutional power is to help keep the other arms of government democratic in their procedures. The Constitution should guarantee the democratic legitimacy of political decisions by establishing essential rules for the political process. It provides that each state should have a republican form of government. And it gives each citizen the political as well as the personal protection of the Bill of Rights and other fundamental constitutional guarantees. The enforcement of these rights would assure Americans that legislative and executive policy would be formed out of free debate, democratic suffrage, untrammeled political effort, and full inquiry.

A series of recent cases in the Supreme Court throws doubt on the zeal with which the present-day Court will insist on preserving the personal and political liberties essential to making political decisions democratic. The language and reasoning of the Justices' opinions are full of unresolved doubts about the extent—and indeed the propriety—of their powers. Contradictory and obscure, they represent not the final word, but a hesitant step towards the formulation of constitutional doctrine adequate to the needs of American society in its present state of siege.

The contradictions and inconsistencies of the constitutional ideas which occupy the minds of several of the Justices are clearly presented by Elliot Richardson in a recent article in this *Review* called "Freedom of Expression and the Function of Courts."[34] I find it difficult to be sure of the ultimate position Mr. Richardson takes on the courts' function in protecting freedom of expression. He says he is not against judicial review as such, although he quotes with enthusiasm those who strongly disapprove it. He is against "the interventionist view" but concedes to history that the courts are under a constitutional obligation to strike down "clearly bad laws." "Clearly bad," he repeatedly points out, means "unconstitutional," and not merely "unwise." For it is "plainly untenable," he says, that the Constitution be considered a "source of specific directions for the solution of every issue of political wisdom," even where freedom of expression is involved. Not "every issue," but some issues. For in interpreting the limitations of the First and Fourteenth Amendments the courts must be free to disagree with the legislature and the executive sometimes, since

> once having conceded the power of the judiciary to enforce the Constitution, the very meaning of the First Amendment is that freedom of expression embodies values that must not be supplanted by short-sighted surges of bigotry and intolerance, however faithfully reflected by the legislature. The court must, therefore, having so far as possible determined what interests the legislature had in view, accept the responsibility of measuring their long-run importance against the values protected by the First Amendment. The courts have not yet articulated—and it is hardly to be expected that language apt for the purpose can be found—any standards of measurement. The triviality of the interests in unlittered streets, at one extreme, and the major importance of the interest in the national security, at the other, are easily recognized. Judgments in the area between must largely rest on "an intuition of experience which outruns analysis." The question is—whose intuition?[35]

The answer he gives is that in the end, the "intuition" of the judges must and does govern. The judges cannot escape the obligation of deciding matters of this kind, even when they give every degree of deference short of blind submission to the views of the legislature and the executive. Their judgment, after meticulously weighing the conflicting interests involved, will contain a final and decisive element of "wisdom" and even of "intuition" – "constitutional" wisdom and intuition, to be sure, as distinguished from the components of "legislative" judgment, but human choice nonetheless.

What standards are to guide the courts in exercising this extraordinary power, rather grudgingly conceded to exist? While I find much in Mr. Richardson's careful analysis of the elements of decision in this class of cases which helps to clarify the role and the responsibility of the judiciary, I can trace little or no connection between the conclusions of his analysis and his general philosophy of judicial review. Indeed, they seem to be in irreconcilable conflict. For his belief in the democratic character of judicial abstinence is so strong as apparently to overcome even his distaste for decisions which fail to measure up to his standards of procedure in the exercise of the courts' constitutional function.

Whatever the exact nuance of meaning other readers will find in his article, to me the broad argument of Mr. Richardson's paper stands with the view deprecating and seeking to limit the Supreme Court's constitutional function as "undemocratic" and dangerous. The Court is not an elected body, but a bench of judges appointed for life. Therefore, he seems to be saying, it is an undemocratic institution.[36] It would be preferable in a democracy if the courts lacked the power to declare statutes or executive action unconstitutional, even in the area of civil rights. Although the power exists historically, reasons of democratic principle require that its exercise be kept to an irreducible minimum.

Although I believe that unresolved doubts on this score have led Mr. Richardson, and others, to tortured and untenable judgments about the work of the Court, this is not a conclusion he can admit. An inner conflict about the democratic propriety of judicial review is translated into an advocacy of extreme self-restraint in the exercise of the Court's acknowledged powers.

Few people would disagree with Mr. Richardson that in exercising their powers of judicial review, the courts should be as wise and statesmanlike as their capacities and temperaments permit – wise as judges, wise in their concern for the effectiveness of their occasional interventions into public affairs, and wise too in adapting the Constitution to changing conditions over centuries of development. The policy against judicial excess does not derive from an unhappy sense that the Supreme Court is "undemocratic," but from an awareness of the limited but vital historical place it occupies in American public life. These limitations stem in considerable part from the fact that, as a court, it can pass only on issues presented at random in the course of litigation, often long after the action being reviewed has taken place. "The only check upon our own exercise of power," Justice Stone said, "is our own sense of self-restraint."[37] But "self-restraint," he made clear both there and elsewhere, is not an excuse for inaction. It is rooted in a respect for the dignity and high purpose of the other branches of government, and a sympathetic understanding of the problems they must try to resolve.

That the Supreme Court's power is limited is perhaps the key to its extraordinary influence. Of course the Justices should give the utmost consideration to the views of other branches of the Government, in civil rights as in other constitutional cases. Of course the Court should keep its powder dry and avoid wasting its ammunition in petty quarrels. Of course in the end the Court must balance even the policy in favor of freedom of speech against the right of the state to protect itself from mobs, riots in the streets, pornography, espionage, and revolution. It must consider whether means are reasonably adapted to ends; whether the Government could have chosen alternative means which would raise fewer constitutional doubts; whether in fact circumstances justify the means adopted.

But when all the facts and arguments are before a court, in a suitable case and on a suitable record, it must decide, and invariably does decide, since a refusal to do so is a decision in favor of the constitutionality of the action being reviewed. The judges cannot refuse to decide cases because they personally believe the United States would be a more democratic country without judicial review. A preoccupation with the prudent and statesmanlike exercise of their duties can hardly be allowed to deny the existence of those duties. Anxious as they may be not to compromise the Court as an institution, and to avoid when possible the intense political pressures of hard cases, they should recall too that their great power exists to be used at the right times, not lost in atrophy. The Court can be destroyed by the weakness as well as the recklessness of its members. The maxim *justitia fiat* has a place in the history of law at least as honorable as the Fabian counsel of prudence. There are times when the hard, great, politically sensitive cases do come before the bar. In times of crisis they are likely to come frequently, and in acute form; indeed, if the cases were not hard, there would be little point in bringing them to the Supreme Court. It is not because people expect the Supreme Court to avoid difficult and vital cases that it has gained its peculiar prestige and authority in popular opinion. Visitors to Washington piously bring their children to the Supreme Court because they believe it is a place where vitally important rights are vindicated against all comers—where The Law in some primitive but meaningful sense is supreme even against the mighty forces of society.

Mr. Richardson cannot bring himself to accept Judge Learned Hand's monkish rule of complete abstinence,[38] though he quotes it with approval.[19] The courts cannot avoid some responsibility for enforcing the political and civil rights declared by the Constitution, although he warns that dependence on the courts as protectors of liberty would sap self-discipline, and lead to "suspicion, intolerance, bigotry and discrimination which the sporadic forays of the judiciary are helpless to check." While Judge Hand's statement should not be taken literally, it should serve as a "counsel of moderation" for judges. The transition is difficult to follow. If it destroys the spirit of self-reliance to submit large political issues to litigation, surely a little more or less of the hemlock cup will not make much difference. This is a strong poison, fatal in small doses. But Mr. Richardson urges a distinction. "Ten opinions striking down ten doubtfully bad laws," he contends, "surely are not twice as effective in their educational impact as five opinions striking down five clearly bad laws. There is much to be said, in any event, for the educational value of opinions *refusing* to invalidate as unconstitutional what is merely unwise."

Since no one in recent years has revived Jefferson's proposal to make the Supreme Court a third house of the national legislature or advocated the invalidation of "doubtful" laws, this part of the argument strikes at men of straw. The question, and the only question, is what criteria the Court should employ in deciding that a statute or executive action is "clearly" contrary to one or another of the provisions of the Constitution. Unless we are to say that the Supreme Court, like a jury, should not declare statutes unconstitutional save by unanimous vote, the criterion of limiting judicial review to "clear" cases is one for the minds and souls of the justices. Dissenters normally believe the law is just as clear as their brethren in the majority. In cases dealing with freedom of expression the Court sits as the ultimate guardian of the liberties on which the democratic effectiveness of political action depends. Their decisions in this area help to determine whether the citizen, whatever his color or his opinions, can live in dignity and security. Mr. Richardson contends, however, that even on such questions the normal presumptions in favor of the constitutionality of legislation should apply with full force. The Court must decide, he repeats over and over again, not that a statute is unwise, but that its provisions fall outside the area of reasonable judgment: in other words, to paraphrase his text, that the competing considerations resolved by its enactment have been arbitrarily resolved, and that the inferences from the data upon which they rest have been irrationally drawn.[40]

There are alternative ways to define the Court's task in passing on the constitutionality of legislation or official action. The language of "presumptions" is often used. And it is commonly said that the Supreme Court should not invalidate action by other branches of the Government if "any" rational basis for upholding it could be found. Formulae of this kind obscure more than they illuminate. The real problem for the Court must balance competing considerations: rights of privacy against the right to speak; order against freedom; safety against the privileges of political action. In reaching a judgment that must accommodate society to such conflicts, the Court is hardly aided by the proposition that it must uphold the act of government if "any" rational basis for it exists. As Justice Frankfurter has said, "those liberties of the individual which history has attested as the indispensable conditions of an open as against a closed society" must be given an altogether different weight by the Court than other privileges altered by legislative or executive order.[41] Society is more deeply affected by a statute limiting political action than by a zoning ordinance, however restrictive.

However, even Mr. Richardson's formula for stating the Court's function in judicial review doesn't settle the cases. The difficulty under his rule comes in deciding whether competing considerations have been "arbitrarily" resolved or inferences from data "irrationally" drawn.

When Mr. Richardson applies his general view of the Court's function to the cases, I find a sharp difference between the two halves of his thesis. In the *Dennis* case,[42] the jury had found the defendants guilty under the Smith Act of "teaching and advocating" the doctrine of overthrowing the state by force and of conspiring to teach and advocate such doctrines. There were strong competing interests: the right of the state to protect itself against subversion or revolution and the interest of the state and of the defendants in protecting freedom of speech, of thought, and of political organization and action. Presumably Mr. Richardson would defend the decision upholding the conviction, either as a "doubtful" case which the Court should have refused to decide, or as one where legislative and executive judgment, however unwise, clearly fell within the zone of rationality. Yet the Court had no record before it which could permit a judicial judgment on the final constitutional issue as Mr. Richardson defines it.

There was no legislative judgment that the organized promulgation of these doctrines by the Communist Party threatened the security of the state at the time of the trial. The statute underlying the prosecution was passed in 1940, with a meager and obscure legislative history, in language which has been invoked since 1798, with few variations, whenever American legislatures have become alarmed over seditious doctrines and their effect on public order.[43] The Act was hardly aimed in terms or otherwise at the Communist Party, and in fact its first application was directed against bitter enemies of that Party. While Congress has passed many statutes against the communist threat, it has not declared that membership in the Communist Party is a crime. The decision to try the leaders of the Communist Party under the Smith Act was not a legislative judgment but an executive one. For the period from June 22, 1941, when Germany invaded Russia, until some time after the end of the war, presumably neither the legislative nor the executive branches of the Government would have invoked the statute against the Communist Party. The development of world political pressures and the change in the policies of the Communist Party within the United States, however, led to the executive branch of the Government to proceed against it under the Act, although other statutes could have been chosen as more direct and appropriate bases for the prosecution.

In terms of Mr. Richardson's analysis, the Court's constitutional task should have led it to consider evidence on the probability and gravity of the evil sought to be suppressed and on the "necessity" of restricting speech in order to prevent it. In this case, the Court's examination could hardly have been aided by a presumption in favor of a legislative determination of the danger, and of the necessity for the application of the legislation to the defendants, for no such legislative determinations had been made.

Judge Learned Hand, for the court of appeals, fell back on judicial notice for evidence that restriction of speech was necessary to protect the state against the communist conspiracy. Reviewing the state of world politics in 1948, when the indictment was presented, he found sufficient evidence in the reality of Soviet strength and of Soviet plans for direct and indirect aggression to support the conclusion that the activities of the defendants in organizing and directing the American Communist Party were a "present danger" to the security of the United States. The conspirators did not plan to strike until war broke out or until other circumstances presented them with a favorable opportunity. But in 1948 Soviet-American relations were such that war could break out at any moment. "We shall be silly dupes," Judge Hand wrote,

> if we forget that again and again in the past thirty years, just such preparations in other countries have aided to supplant existing governments, when the time was ripe. Nothing short of a revived doctrine of *laissez-faire,* which would have amazed even the Manchester School at its apogee, can fail to realize that such a conspiracy creates a danger of the utmost gravity and of enough probability to justify its suppression. We hold that it is a danger "clear and present."[44]

The Chief Justice's opinion, formally accepting the "clear and present danger" test as the starting point of analysis, similarly treated the case as if it were a prosecution for conspiracy to overthrow the Government by force. Since the indictment charged only the organized teaching and advocacy of revolutionary doctrine, however, the court was able to avoid the historic distinctions between criminal "preparations" and criminal "attempts" which might have complicated a direct prosecution for revolutionary action. By assuming, on the basis of judicial notice, that the defendants were guilty of a crime for which they had been neither indicted nor convicted, the Court could find that the crime charged was within the limits of what could be done constitutionally. Both the opinion of Judge Hand and that of the Chief Justice are at pains to indicate that the defendant's advocacy of revolution could be made criminal only because the defendants were part and parcel "of an apparatus designed and dedicated to the overthrow of the Government, in the context of world crisis after crisis. . . . It is the existence of the conspiracy which creates the danger. . . . If the ingredients of the reaction are present, we cannot bind the Government to wait until the catalyst is added."[45] Yet this crucial element, which seemed to make the "teaching and advocacy" of revolution a crime, was established by the uncontrolled process of judicial notice.

Mr. Justice Jackson, in a typical statement of the fainéant judicial philosophy he sometimes espouses, refused to put judgement on so slender a foundation. A serious application of a "clear and present danger" test, he wrote, would require the courts to assess imponderables "which baffle the best informed foreign offices and our most experienced politicians . . . . The judicial process simply is not adequate to a trial of such far-flung issues."[46] He therefore rested his vote for affirmance on the broader ground that the organized teaching and advocacy of revolutionary doctrine, without particular qualification as to surrounding circumstance, could be made criminal in the name of defending the state.

Mr. Justice Frankfurter, who also concurred in the result, did not go far into the central doctrinal and procedural problems of the case. His opinion passes off the issue with a quip. "Mr. Justice Douglas," he wrote, "quite properly points out that the conspiracy before us is not a conspiracy to overthrow the Government. But it would be equally wrong to treat it as a seminar in political theory."[47] It would be absurd, he said—despite his formal acceptance of the "clear and present danger" test—"To make the validity of legislation depend on judicial reading of events still in the womb of time . . . ."[48] He would not say that a legislature was beyond the limits of its constitutional powers in concluding that under present political circumstances the "recruitment of additional members for the Party would create a substantial danger to national security."[49] While there was no reliable evidence in the record tracing acts of sabotage or espionage directly to the defendants, a report of the Canadian Royal Commission on the role of the communist movement in Canadian espionage, and the experience of Klaus Fuchs—who, the Justice thought, had been led into the service of the Soviet Union through communist indoctrination—were invoked to help support and justify what the Justice treated throughout his opinion as the judgment of Congress that the statute should apply to the Communist Party:

> Congress was not barred by the Constitution from believing that indifference to such experience would be an exercise not of freedom but of irresponsibility. . . . Congress has determined that the danger created by advocacy of overthrow justifies the ensuing restriction on freedom of speech. . . . Can we establish a constitutional doctrine which forbids the elected representatives of the people to make this choice? Can we hold that the First Amendment deprives Congress of what it deemed necessary for the Government's protection?[50]

For a variety of reasons drawn from his philosophy of judicial review, he shrinks from such a conclusion.

The transmutation of the "clear and present danger test" in these opinions is quite remarkable. It begins as the principle that since the First Amendment cannot be considered to mean what it says, the Court will decide for itself whether attempted restrictions on freedom of speech are justified by evidence of an imminent and serious danger arising from the speech. Judge Learned Hand finds a present danger of a future coup d'etat in the activities of defendants, viewed against the background of world and domestic politics in 1948. The Chief Justice's opinion says that the danger need not be one that the Government will be overthrown; it is enough that an attempt may some day be made. Nor must the danger be "present" in any immediate sense. The injury to the state sought to be prevented by the Act, he indicates, is both the physical and the political damage which may be occasioned by extremist parties and their more extreme activities. Since the "clear and present danger" test in this form permits the Court to consider not only present but also possible future injuries, the problem of anticipating the future becomes inscrutable, if not insoluble, and the Court says it can find no ground for overruling the supposed judgment of Congress that the teaching and advocacy of revolution is illegal, at least in the case of the twelve leaders of the Communist Party.

To all this Justice Douglas' answer was a powerful one. The record, he urges, contains no evidence on the key factual issue of the case: whether the defendants' conspiracy to teach and advocate the communist theory of revolution constituted a clear and present danger to the nation. While the purposes and capabilities of the Soviet Union in world politics would be relevant evidence on the clear and present danger of the defendants' advocacy of revolution within the United States, they hardly exhaust the issue. The Court could not say that the defendants' conspiracy to teach revolution in the United States "is outlawed because Soviet Russia and her Red Army are a threat to world peace."[51] If it were proper to approach the question on the basis of judicial notice, Mr. Justice Douglas observed, he would conclude that the Communist Party was impotent and discredited as a political force within the United States, that it had been exposed and destroyed as an effective political faction by free speech and vigorous counteraction. "Some nations less resilient than the United States, where illiteracy is high and where democratic traditions are only budding, might have to take drastic steps and jail these men for merely speaking their creed. But in America they are miserable merchants of unwanted ideas; their wares remain unsold. The fact that their ideas are abhorrent does not make them powerful."[52] The weakness of the Communist Party as a political entity is not the end of the matter, however. In determining whether their advocacy of revolution would endanger the Republic, he continued, it would be necessary to examine the extent to which they had infiltrated key areas of Government and of economic life.

> But the record is silent on these facts. If we are to proceed on the basis of judicial notice, it is impossible for me to say that the Communists in this country are so potent or so strategically deployed that they must be suppressed for their speech. I could not so hold unless I were willing to conclude that the activities in recent years of committees of Congress, of the Attorney General, of labor unions, of state legislatures, and of Loyalty Boards were so futile as to leave the country on the edge of grave peril. To believe that petitioners and their following are placed in such critical positions as to endanger the Nation is to believe the incredible. It is safe to say that the followers of the creed of Soviet Communism are known to the F.B.I.; that in case of war with Russia they will be picked up overnight as were all prospective saboteurs at the commencement of World War II; that the invisible army of petitioners is the best known, the most beset, and the least thriving of any fifth column in history. Only those held by fear and panic could think otherwise.
>
> This is my view if we are to act on the basis of judicial notice. But the mere statement of the opposing views indicates how important it is that we know the facts before we act. Neither prejudice nor hate nor senseless fear should be the basis of this solemn act. Free speech—the glory of our system of government—should not be sacrificed on anything less than plain and objective proof of danger that the evil advocated is imminent. On this

record no one can say that petitioners and their converts are in such a
strategic position as to have even the slightest chance of achieving their
aims.[53]

Mr. Richardson is concerned with this phase of the *Dennis* case. He dis-
agrees with Justice Frankfurter, who, he says, supports the supposed legislative judgment by taking judicial notice of facts which the legislature could not
have considered when the statute was passed. He argues that

> To assure that the facts of which it proposes to take notice are properly
> subject to notice, the court should give the defendant an opportunity to
> controvert these facts, although reserving to itself the final determination
> as to whether they are genuinely disputable. Disregard of the disputed
> facts may still leave an undisputed residue adequate to fill in the back-
> ground of inherent probability. If not, there would remain no alternative
> but to take testimony on the issue.[54]

And he is equally troubled by the failure of the Court explicitly to exercise its
own judgment as to the rationality of the Government's view that the defendants' organized advocacy of revolution constituted a danger to the state:

> The legislative judgment expressed in the Smith Act could not, any more
> than that expressed in the New York statute involved in the *Gitlow* case,
> foreclose the question whether the circumstances justified the suppression
> of any sort of "discourse" teaching or advocating violent overthrow of or-
> ganized government, no matter how "redundant" and no matter how lim-
> ited its circulation. Supplementing the legislative judgment in the *Dennis*
> case, however, in contrast with the *Gitlow* case, were the jury's findings
> that the conspiracy to teach and advocate embraced a systematic course of
> indoctrination, not a single discourse, and was to be carried by a rigidly
> disciplined organization "as speedily as circumstances would permit." Both
> the legislative judgment and the jury's findings, moreover, were strength-
> ened in the *Dennis* case by facts subject to judicial notice which bore on the
> already existing probability of the apprehended evils, while in the *Gitlow*
> case such facts were insignificant. But the inexplicitness of the *Dennis*
> affirming opinions, their differences in emphasis, and the very fact that
> none was able to secure a majority leaves uncertain the weight to be given
> in future cases to legislative judgments that a certain type of utterance
> contributes to the probability of an apprehended evil.[55]

The *Dennis* case is by all odds the most important and far-reaching of the
recent civil rights cases. In disposing of it, the Supreme Court had several
alternatives. It could have reversed for a further trial on the factual justification for a conclusion that the defendants' organized advocacy of revolution
gave rise to a present danger of anticipated future action to achieve that end.
Such a decision would have put the Court's performance of its own function, in
reviewing the constitutionality of a statute outlawing "the teaching and advo-

cacy" of revolutionary ideas, on a more orderly and rational basis. Or it could have held that the statute, as applied to the defendants, violated the First Amendment. A result on this ground would have forced the executive to prosecute the communists on the direct charge that the Communist Party is not a political party, but a conspiracy to subvert the state. No one doubts the constitutionality of statutes making it a crime to attempt to overthrow the Government, or to conspire to that end.[56] In such a prosecution, the propaganda arms of the Communist Party would be considered as an integral part of a central conspiratorial plan before the Court in its entirety.

As the case was disposed of, however, we are left with a series of paradoxes. Insofar as the Justices' opinions can be brought into a single focus, they declare that the systematic teaching and advocacy of revolution can be made a crime, at least (and perhaps only) if the organization for spreading such ideas is an aspect of a serious and potentially important attempt to attack the Government by other means. The case is confusing, however, because the qualifications of factual circumstance considered decisive of constitutionality were established entirely on the basis of judicial notice. The Court purports to accept the "clear and present danger" test of the Holmes-Brandeis dissents as prevailing law. That approach to the constitutional problem in civil rights cases is designed to give the courts considerable discretion in passing on the constitutionality of legislative or executive action. Yet the Court applies the Holmes-Brandeis formula in a way which makes it extremely difficult to conceive of a successful case against the reasonableness of the government's decision to prosecute.

In the end, the *Dennis* case is strongly colored – perhaps determined – by the view that cloistered and appointed Justices should not pit their judgment of the Constitution against that of the elected representatives of the people, who have to deal with these difficult problems at first hand. Some of the Justices, indeed, come perilously close to denying that they have any duty to review the constitutional judgment of the legislature and the executive at all. Much of the reasoning in the various opinions, like that in other recent cases, draws strength from the premise that the power of judicial review is somehow tainted, and of undemocratic character, and that the courts should not interfere with the attempts of Congress and the President to deal with wars and emergencies.

V

When the Supreme Court falters, as I believe it has in this and some other recent civil rights cases, we need not conclude that the Constitution is dead. Mr. Justice Brandeis used to say that no case is ever finally decided until it is rightly decided. The example of the Holmes and Brandeis dissents, and their ultimate acceptance, should encourage the present dissenters on the Court to persevere. Even though all their arguments are not of equal weight, their effort and example are a force which can in time help to restore sounder views. For civil liberties in the United States are in a state of grave crisis, and I venture to hope that the recent decisions of the Supreme Court will not prove to be its lasting position. The problem of security is concededly most serious, and the state has every right to protect itself against attack. But the Court has the correlative duty to inquire whether repressive acts are reasonably adapted to the end of security. Do we really protect the state against spies and saboteurs by making professors of music take oaths, and by combing through the lives of all Government employees for scattered espisodes of sin, enthusiasm, and folly? It is proper to attack the Communist Party for "teaching and advocating" subversion of the state–a doctrine which could have jailed Calhoun and the participants in the Hartford Convention, and perhaps Thoreau as well–when the Party could have been prosecuted for what it was and undoubtedly is, a conspiracy to overthrow the Government by force? Can the real and pressing danger of the Communist Fifth Column be met by police measures, as some qualified students of the problem urge,[57] or by a general movement to silence heterodoxy, create doubts in the relation of man to man, make universities hesitate to appoint young firebrands, and lead honest men to wonder whether they should continue to visit their friends?

NOTES

a. *Harvard Law Review* 66 (December 1952): 193-224. Copyright © 1952 by the Harvard Law Review Association. Used by permission.

1. THE FEDERALIST, No. 78 at 509 (Modern Library ed. 1937).
2. Many writers have distinguished the authority of the Supreme Court to deny effect to an unconstitutional act of Congress or the President from its duty under Article VI to declare unconstitutional provisions of state constitutions or statutes, although Article VI declares even federal statutes to be "the supreme Law of the Land" only when made in pursuance of the Constitution. HOLMES, *Law and the Court* in COLLECTED LEGAL PAPERS 291, 295-6 (1920); JACKSON, THE STRUGGLE FOR JUDICIAL SUPREMACY 15 *et seq.* 1941); THAYER, *The Origin and Scope of the American Doctrine of Constitutional Law* in LEGAL ESSAYS I, 35-41 (1908); THAYER, JOHN MARSHALL 61-65 (1901); HAINES, THE AMERICAN DOCTRINE OF JUDICIAL SUPREMACY 131-35, 511-12 (2d ed. 1932).
3. The evidence is reviewed in THAYER, *The Origin and Scope of the American Doctrine of Constitutional Law* in LEGAL ESSAYS I, 3-7 (1908); BEARD, THE SUPREME COURT AND THE CONSTITUTION (1912); and HAINES, *op. cit. supra* note 3, 44-49, 88-121. A useful bibliography appears in DODD, CASES ON CONSTITUTIONAL LAW 8-18 (3d ed. 1941).
4. THE FEDERALIST, No. 78 at 506 (Modern Library ed. 1937).
5. See THAYER, JOHN MARSHALL 96 (1901); THAYER, *The Origin and Scope of the American Doctrine of Constitutional Law* in LEGAL ESSAYS I, 12-15 (1908); HAINES *op. cit. supra* note 2, at 518-27.
6. Rochin v. California, 342 U.S. 165, 173 (1952).
7. West Virginia State Board of Educ. v. Barnette, 319 U.S. 642, 638 (1943).

8. JEFFERSON, LIFE AND SELECTED WRITINGS 462 (Modern Library ed. 1944). This passage, Griswold comments, "suggests that while [Jefferson] relied on the Court to safeguard the Bill of Rights, he was also counting on the bill to ensure a long-run democratic tendency on the part of the Court. History has borne out the acumen of this thought. . . . The Court's vested responsibility for our civil liberties has kept it anchored to democratic fundamentals through all kinds of political weather." A. W. Griswold, *Jefferson's Republic—The Rediscovery of Democratic Philosophy,* Fortune, April, 1950, p. 111, at 130. Later in life, of course, Jefferson strongly differed with many of the decisions and opinions of the Supreme Court and expressed his disagreement in terms which sometimes seemed to repudiate the constitutionality of the judicial review itself.

9. JEFFERSON, LIFE AND SELECTED WRITINGS 437, 441, 460 (Modern Library ed. 1944).

10. 6 THE WRITINGS OF THOMAS JEFFERSON 151 (Lipscomb and Bergh ed. 1940).

11. See, *e.g.,* Lincoln, *First Inaugural Address* in 6 MESSAGES AND PAPERS OF THE PRESIDENTS 5-12 (Richardson ed. 1897); WILSON, CONSTITUTIONAL GOVERNMENT IN THE UNITED STATES c. 6 (1911).

12. Myers v. United States, 272 U.S. 52, 293 (1926) (dissenting opinion).

13. See CARDOZO, THE NATURE OF THE JUDICIAL PROCESS 92-94 (1921): The great ideals of liberty and equality are preserved against assaults of opportunism, the expediency of the passing hour, the erosion of small encroachments, the scorn and derision of those who have no patience with general principles, by enshrining them in constitutions, and consecrating to the task of their protection a body of defenders. By conscious or subconscious influence, the presence of the restraining power, aloof in the background, but none the less always in reserve, tends to stabilize and rationalize the legislative judgment, to infuse it with the glow of principle, to hold the standard aloft and visible for those who must run the race and keep the faith. I do not mean to deny that there have been times when the possibility of judicial review has worked the other way. Legislatures have sometimes disregarded their own responsibility, and passed it on to the courts. Such dangers must be balanced against those of independence from all restraint, independence on the part of public officers elected for brief terms, without the guiding force of a continuous traditions. On the whole, I believe the latter dangers to be the more formidable of the two. Great maxims, if they may be violated with impunity, are honored often with lip-service, which passes easily into irreverence. The restraining power of the judiciary does not manifest its chief worth in the few cases in which the legislature has gone beyond the lines that mark the limits of discretion. Rather shall we find its chief worth in making vocal and audible the ideals that might be otherwise silenced, in giving them continuity of life and expression, in guiding and directing choice within the limits where choice ranges. This function should preserve to the courts the power that now belongs to them, if only the power is exercised with insight into social values, and with suppleness of adaptation to changing social needs.

14. See THAYER, *The Origin and Scope of the American Doctrine of Constitutional Law* in LEGAL ESSAYS I, 39-41 (1908); HAINES, THE AMERICAN DOCTRINE OF "JUDICIAL SUPREMACY 500-40 (2d ed. 1932); L. HAND, *The Contribution of an Independent Judiciary to Civilization* in THE SPIRIT OF LIBERTY 172 (Dilliard ed. 1952); COMMAGER, MAJORITY RULE AND MINORITY RIGHTS 57-83 (1943), Wyzasnski, Book Review, 57 HARV. L. REV. 389 (1944); Clark, *The Dilemma of Ameri-*

can Judges, 35 A.B.A.J. 8 (1949). For other views of the proper extent of judicial review, see M. COHEN, *Constitutional and Natural Rights* in THE FAITH OF A LIBERAL 175 (1946); PEKELIS, LAW AND SOCIAL ACTION 194-203 (1950); CURTIS, LIONS UNDER THE THRONE 24-34 (1947); FREUND, ON UNDERSTANDING THE SUPREME COURT 37-41 (1949); Braden, *The Search for Objectivity in Constitutional Law,* 57 YALE L. J. 571 (1948).

15. THAYER, *The Origin and Scope of the American Doctrine of Constitutional Law* in LEGAL ESSAYS I, 39 (1908), originally published in 1893 in 7 HARV. L. REV. 129.

16. THAYER, JOHN MARSHALL 104 (1901).

17. Id. at 106.

18. Building on a suggestion in McCulloch v. Maryland, 4 Wheat. 316, 428 (U.S. 1819), and other early cases, Chief Justice Stone contended that the court should give less than the normal weight to the legislative judgment where normal electoral safeguards against legislative abuse are not present or where the legislative act would itself tend to restrict the effectiveness of "those political processes which can ordinarily be expected to bring about the repeal of undesirable legislation. . . ." United States v. Carolene Products Co., 304 U.S. 144, 152 n. 4 (1938). See also McGoldrick v. Berwind-White Coal Mining Co., 309 U.S. 33, 46 (1940); South Carolina State Highway Dep't v. Barnwell Bros., Inc., 303 U.S. 177, 185 (1938); Southern Pacific Co. v. Arizona, 325 U.S. 761, 767-68 (1945); Minersville School District v. Gobitis, 310 U.S. 586, 603-07 (1940) (dissenting opinion); Dowling, *The Methods of Mr. Justice Stone in Constitutional Cases,* 41 COL. L. REV. 764, 785-800 (1946).

19. Address on 250th anniversary of Supreme Judicial Court of Massachusetts, Nov. 21, 1942, reprinted in THE SPIRIT OF LIBERTY 172 (Dilliard ed. 1952). See also Freund, *The Supreme Court and Civil Liberties,* 4 VAND. L. REV. 533, 551-54 (1951).

20. This and the following quotations, until otherwise indicated are from L. HAND, *The Contribution of an Independent Judiciary to Civilization* in THE SPIRIT OF LIBERTY 172-81 (Dilliard ed. 1952). This is not the occasion to comment on these remarks as the starting point for a theory of statutory construction.

21. See, *e.g.,* United States v. Butler, 297 U.S. 495 (1936).

22. See, *e.g.,* Schechter Poultry Corp. v. United States, 295 U.S. 495 (1935). See also Youngstown Sheet & Tube Co. v. Sawyer, 343 U.S. 579 (1952).

23. L. HAND, *Chief Justice Stone's Concept of the Judicial Function* in THE SPIRIT OF LIBERTY 201, 208 (Dilliard ed. 1952).

24. See Subchapter II of the Internal Security Act of 1950, 64 STAT. 1019, 50 U.S.C. sec. 811-26 (Supp. 1952); see O'Brian, *Changing Attitudes toward Freedom,* 9 WASH. & LEE L. REV. 157 (1952).

25. See MYRDAL, AN AMERICAN DILEMMA (1944).

26. See, *e g,* Boskey and Pickering, *Federal Restrictions on State Criminal Procedure,* 13 U. OF CHI. L. REV. 266 (1946); Frank, *The United States Supreme Court,* 1950-51, 19 U. OF CHI. L. REV. 165, 201-09 (1952), and earlier surveys cited at 165; Comment, 58 YALE L. J. 268 (1949).

27. See Rostow, *The Price of Federalism,* Fortune, Dec., 1948, p. 162.

28. Reaffirmed in Sterling v. Constantin, 287 U.S. 378 (1932).

29. Korematsu v. United States, 323 U.S. 214 (1944), and Hirabayshi v. United States, 320 U.S. 81 (1943), discussed in Rostow, *The Japanese American Cases—A Disaster,* 54 YALE L. J. 489 (1945).

30. " . . . to redress these loyal Americans in some measure for the wrongs in-

flicted upon them . . . would be simple justice." H.R. REP. No. 732, 80th Cong., 1st Sess. 5 (1947). See 62 STAT. 1231 (1948), 50, U.S.C. App. sec. 1981 *et seq.* (Supp. 1952).

31. 327 U.S. 304 (1946).

32. See KENNAN, AMERICAN DIPLOMACY, *1900-1950*, 95–103 (1951), Mc-Dougal, Book Review, 46 A.B.A.J. 102 (1952).

33. See MYRDAL, AN AMERICAN DILEMMA 3–6 (1944).

34. 65 HARV. L. REV. I (1951). Until otherwise indicated the following quotations are from *id.* at 50–53.

35. *Id.* at 39–40.

36. See *id.* at I, 54.

37. United States v. Butler, 297 U.S. I, 79 (1936) (dissenting opinion).

38. See pp. 203–05 *supra.*

39. Richardson, *supra* note 34, at 52–53. Quotations in this paragraph are from *id.* at 52–53.

40. *Id* at 50.

41. Kovacs v. Cooper, 336 U.S. 77, 95 (1949) (concurring opinion).

42. Dennis v. United States, 341 U.S. 494 (1951).

43. See CHAFEE, FREE SPEECH IN THE UNITED STATES 439–46, 462–84 (1941).

44. United States v. Dennis, 183 F. 2d 201, 213 (2d Cir. 1950).

45. Dennis v. United States, 341 U.S. 494, 510–11 (1951).

46. *Id.* at 570.

47. *Id.* at 546.

48. *Id* at 551.

49. *Id.* at 547.

50. *Id.* at 548–51.

51. *Id.* at 588.

52. *Id.* at 588–89.

53. *Id.* at 589–90.

54. Richardson, *Freedom of Expression and the Function of Courts,* 65 HARV. L. REV. I, 30–31 (1951).

55. *Id.* at 35.

56. See Nathanson, *The Communist Trial and the Clear-and-Present Danger Test,* 63 HARV. L. REV. 1167 (1950).

57. PHILBRICK, I LED THREE LIVES 299–300 (1952).

14

The Antidemocratic Nature of Judicial Review and a Good Democracy

D EAN ROSTOW'S ARGUMENT in the preceding chapter
suggests that democracy entails more than procedural majority rule. Democracy also entails the protection of minority rights. Indeed, for Rostow, judicial review is not only
compatible with democracy, it is, in fact, democratic.

The bulk of the first essay presented below was written by George
Mace and was published in the *California Law Review* in 1972. It was
originally intended as a rebuttal to Rostow's piece. In its present
enlarged form, it contains a more complete discussion of other views
on judicial review, including those found in Antifederalist and Federalist writings. Mace argues that Rostow would have been closer to the
truth had he written in terms of the compatibility of the Supreme
Court's exercise of judicial review with democracy rather than the
"democratic character" of judicial review. The exercise of judicial review is neither democratic nor undemocratic; rather it is antidemocratic.

Ironically, it is precisely the antidemocratic character of judicial
review that imparts a major and beneficial contribution to the democratic system of which it is a part. In Aristotelian terms, judicial review
contributes to our "good democracy."

The classical distinction between bad and good democracies is
crucial to a justification of judicial review. To be sure, processes and
procedures play a central role in any democracy. However, it is not the
whole of the matter. A good democracy is directed to the interests of
the whole people, including both majorities and minorities. The Supreme Court must resist the other branches or divisions of government

236

when they act tyrannically, whether against majorities or minorities. When the Court exercises a check against an abusive majority it acts in an antidemocratic fashion. But it is precisely this antidemocratic feature known as judicial review that makes our governmental system a good democracy.

After considering what we regard as the most defensible justification for judicial review, readers should consider at least briefly a related practical question faced by the Court in carrying out its responsibility. How may the antidemocratic Supreme Court protect itself from institutional attack? It is the branch of government least able to defend itself because it is so dependent on the other branches for support in carrying out its functions. Yet the other branches are most subject to majority sentiments and, therefore, least disposed to come to the Court's aid.

The second reading in this chapter is a review of a book by Jesse H. Choper, dean of the University of California Law School. Dean Choper is reacting to contemporary attacks upon the Court for its judicial activism. He recommends that the Court reserve its institutional capital for what he regards as its most important function, namely, the protection of individual rights against the transgressions of majorities. All other matters, including, for example, federal-state relations, should not be handled by the Court; the political process should be allowed to work its will in such matters.

For the reasons outlined in the book review, we do not agree with Dean Choper's recommendations for limiting the exercise of judicial review. Nonetheless, Choper has noted an important practical problem the Supreme Court faces when it functions to make this a "good democracy." The fact that his book and others with similar themes have been published during the 1980s emphasizes the continued importance of the issue of judicial review for our democratic society.

The Democratic Compatibility of Judicial Review [a]

George Mace

JUDICIAL REVIEW THRUSTS the American judiciary into the heart of areas that in most other countries remain purely political. Accordingly, the Supreme Court has been vulnerable to criticism for political behavior that is seemingly inconsistent with the appointive status of its members. And although Justice Roberts once claimed that judicial review is merely a process of comparing legislation to the Constitution and deciding whether the two are compatible, as noted in Chapter 1, such is obviously not the case. Since judicial review unquestionably has played an extraordinary role in shaping our political-legal system, not to mention the manner in which judicial review itself was established, it is difficult to regard Roberts's view as anything other than apocryphal. Judicial review clearly involves something other than a simple comparison of words possessing readily discernible and unchanging meanings. It is a process of judicial interpretation, a kind of interpretation not far removed from legislation.

Given Court rulings that in the final analysis appear to be legislative rulings, despite the fact that judicial "legislators" are not held accountable directly through the electoral process, many have claimed that to permit the judiciary such power is inconsistent with the principles and operation of a democratic government.

In his essay, appearing in the previous chapter, Eugene Rostow strove to answer such attacks on judicial review by ascertaining which things may rightly be regarded as democratic. Several points that are crucial to his subsequent argument appear questionable and merit close examination. In the process the proposition that judicial review is democratic will be shown to be equally questionable.

The first point is found in Rostow's assertion that "the attack on judicial review as undemocratic rests on the premise that the Constitution should be allowed to grow without a judicial check."[1] Although the attack by some may be rooted in such a premise, it simply is untrue that significant charges have not rested on other foundations. One of the earliest and most telling is found in Robert Yates's *Letters of Brutus*.[2]

Essentially, Yates attacked judicial review not because it would function to check constitutional growth, but because it would be the very vehicle of that growth. However, his basic thrust against judicial review did not stem simply from the nature and extent of the power; it lay primarily in the fact that "those to be vested with it, are to be placed in a situation altogether unprecedented in a free country. They are to be rendered totally independent, both of the people and the legislature, both with respect to their offices and salaries."[3] Because the Court would not be held accountable to either the people or their representatives, the Constitution "made the judges *independent* in the fullest sense of the word. There is no power above them to controul any of their decisions. There is no authority that can remove them, and they cannot be controuled by the laws of the legislature. In short, they are independent of the people, of the legislature, and of every power under heaven. Men placed in this situation will generally soon feel themselves independent of heaven itself."[4]

Thus in light of both the nature of the power of judicial review and the independence of the body that wielded it, Yates portrayed the Court as a "will independent of society," which he feared could be controlled only by "a high hand and an outstretched arm."[5]

In *Federalist* 78 Alexander Hamilton addressed himself to the objections raised by Yates.[6] Rather than refute Yates's charges that the Court was responsible to no one and therefore constituted a will independent of society, Hamilton attempted to demonstrate an absolute necessity for such a lack of responsibility. Hamilton returned to a theme introduced earlier by James Madison, the notion that judicial independence is the best means of preventing tyranny.

Rostow rightly saw that separation of powers plays a major role in the realization of limited government in our polity. Moreover, he was further correct in attributing a primary role in the maintenance of separation of powers to judicial review.[7] However, some question may be raised as to whether Rostow realized the full implications of that role. Madison, like Hamilton, held that separation of powers was intended to prevent the "accumulation of all powers, legislative, executive and judicial, in the same hands, whether of one, a few, or many, and whether hereditary, self-appointed, or elective, may justly be pronounced the very definition of tyranny."[8] Moreover, separation of powers in general and judicial review in particular, it may be said, were intended primarily as a check or barrier to the encroachments and oppressions of Congress.

Why should the most democratic branch of our government be the primary target? This seems all the more curious since the *Federalist Papers* insist that the government they explain is wholly popular.[9] The answer lies in Madison's admonishments in *Federalist* 48. It is precisely due to the fact that the majority rule we must fear is tyranny from below more than from above. Madison first distinguished between a representative republic and a direct democracy, noting that the only difference was representation in the former. He continued that, in a representative government

> where the executive magistracy is carefully limited, both in the extent and duration of its power; and where the legislative power is exercised by an assembly, which is inspired, by a supposed influence over the people, with an intrepid confidence in its own strength; . . . it is against the enterprising ambition of this department that the people ought to indulge all their jealousy and exhaust all their precautions.[10]

In *Federalist* 51 Madison further indicated that the legislature was the primary target of separation of powers in his discussion of the necessity of the executive veto power. However, not even the devices of separation of powers, judicial review, and executive veto were considered sufficient barriers to the legislature. Further protection was necessary since

> it is not possible to give to each department an equal power of self-defence. In republican government, the legislative authority necessarily predominates. The remedy for this inconveniency is to divide the legislature into different branches; and to render them, by different modes of election and

> different principles of action, as little connected with each other as the nature of their common functions and their common dependence on the society will admit.[11]

Thus it was hoped the division of the legislature itself, the principle of legislative balances and checks, would serve as a further barrier.[12]

The greatest threat of tyranny in our system stems from a majority faction working through the legislature, what most modern commentators refer to as a *tyrannical majority*. To the constitutional fathers, a faction was "a number of citizens, whether amounting to a majority or minority of the whole, who are united and actuated by some common impulse of passion, or of interest, adverse to the rights of other citizens, or to the permanent and aggregate interests of the community."[13] A minority faction could be checked by

> the republican principle, which enables the majority to defeat its sinister views by regular vote. It may clog the administration, it may convulse the society; but it will be unable to execute and mask its violence under the forms of the Constitution. When a majority is included in a faction, the form of popular government, on the other hand, enables it to sacrifice to its ruling passion or interest both the public good and the rights of other citizens.[14]

However, the principle of majority rule that enables the majority to overcome a minority faction is the very principle that allows a tyrannical majority to run roughshod over any minority. If separation of powers and judicial review are to be directed against a majority, they must obviously be relatively independent of that majority. Any other arrangement would be futile, for a body can hardly be expected to control its controllers.

Thus Hamilton could and did argue for the necessity of just such judicial independence. Though judicial review was relatively independent of a majority and, as we shall see, completely independent of a simple majority, Hamilton argued that this held little threat to the people. The fact that judicial responsibility is missing constitutes no danger since the judiciary can exercise "neither FORCE nor WILL but merely judgment; and must ultimately depend upon the executive arm even for the efficacy of its judgments."[15]

It is true that the judiciary is dependent upon the executive branch to enforce its judgments. Moreover, Hamilton's statement that the judiciary lacks a will seems to indicate that he felt the judiciary lacked a meaningful will because of this dependence. The appointed Court, with no direct responsibility, could render judgments, but the elected executive, responsible to the people, could decide whether or not to enforce these judgments. What emerges then is an indirect control over the judiciary.

Although Hamilton's argument may have assuaged the doubts of eighteenth-century America, it no longer rings true. Today the chief executive is bound by decisions of the Supreme Court because the general public acknowledges that the Constitution empowers the Court to express its will and have that will enforced. The question is not whether the public agrees with the Court's decisions—and often, of course, it does not—but whether the Court's decisions are constitutional and therefore legitimate and binding. In general, public opinion decrees that they are.

Thus the major considerations in the question of the democratic character of judicial review do not concern the constitutionality of that power. They concern the identification of democracy and, accordingly, what things are democratic. Rostow knew the perplexities involved in these questions and consequently wrote:

> Democracy is a slippery term. I shall make no effort at a formal definition here. Certainly as a matter of historical fact some societies with parliamentary governments have been and are "democratic" by standards which Americans would accept, although it is worth noting that almost all of them employ second chambers, with powers at least of delay, and indirect devices for insuring continuity in the event of parliamentary collapse, either through the crown or some equivalent institution like the presidency in France. But it would be scholastic pendantry to define democracy in such a way as to deny the title of "democrat" to Jefferson, Madison, Lincoln, Brandeis, and others who have found the American constitutional system, including its tradition of judicial review, well adapted to the needs of a free society. As Mr. Justice Brandeis said, "the doctrine of the separation of powers was adopted by the Convention of 1787, not to promote efficiency but to preclude the exercise of arbitrary power. The purpose was, not to avoid friction, but, by means of the inevitable friction incident to the distribution of governmental powers among three departments, to save the people from autocracy."[16]

Certainly democracy is a slippery term, and Rostow's informal inferential definition seems equally subtle. However, it is fair to suggest that his definition derives from certain arguments by association which may not be legitimate. In the first case Rostow seems to imply a similarity between American "democracy" and British "democracy" and between the Supreme Court and the British House of Lords. We rather suspect that he would be hard put indeed to find Americans, including Jefferson, Madison, Lincoln, and Brandeis, who considered titles of nobility and an aristocratic branch of government in any way democratic. Of course, this is not really what Rostow says. He refers instead to the political system of which they are a part, reasoning that seems to be a major flaw throughout his essay. As we shall see, rather than proving the democratic character of judicial review, or even of the Supreme Court, his endeavors primarily are directed to proving the democratic character of American government. Indeed, even this may be claiming too much since he concludes, at this point, not that the American political-legal system and judicial review are democratic, but that they are "well adapted to the needs of a free society." We shall return to these points below.

At present, however, let us look more closely at the government that allegedly Americans would consider "democratic." First, the parliamentary form of government hardly appears "adapted to the needs of a free society." After all, any system in which the legislative and executive powers are lodged in the same hands, in this case parliament, hardly squares with a doctrine of separation of powers intent upon saving the people from autocracy through a distribution of governmental powers among *three* departments. Another, equally substantial, obstacle to American acceptance is the matter of the House of Lords. The British system was, and remains, a mixed form of government. It is a combination of monarchic, aristocratic, and democratic elements. Admittedly the monarchic element has been reduced to ceremonial functions, although it retains the responsibility for calling elections. Further, today the House of Lords can do little more than delay. However, few Americans would consider such a body, made up of members selected because of birth (or knighthood for various claims to excellence) and having any power to thwart a popularly elected chamber, to be democratic. This is, indeed, a body with a will independent of society. Not even the U.S. Supreme Court is so independent. If Rostow has in mind other parliamentary governments, in which the "second chamber" comprises elected members, obviously this reservation would not apply. However, it must be noted that for Rostow they are nevertheless undemocratic due to their violation of a separation of powers.

Rostow's second assertion concerned four "democrats," namely, Jefferson, Madison, Brandeis, and Lincoln. Essentially, we are asked to accept the implication that because these men were "democrats" and they considered our political-legal system "well adapted to the needs of a free society," the system (including judicial review) must therefore be democratic. In addition to the more obvious deficiencies of this *ad hominem* argument, there are certain other apparent errors that merit discussion. The first of these is the implication that Jefferson favored judicial review, the second, that democracy can be equated with liberty; and the third, that any of these four men considered judicial review democratic.

As we shall see, one of the major reasons our political-legal system is, in fact, "well adapted to the needs of a free society" is that it contains certain antidemocratic features. As a rule we tend to identify all things democratic as good. Conversely, those things that are antidemocratic seem, *a priori*, bad. Thus, since it is difficult to reconcile things democratic with legislators not directly responsible through an electoral process, or even indirectly responsible through a supraordinate who is responsible, it is not surprising to find that themes of uneasiness and guilt color the literature about judicial review.

A major thesis of this essay is that all things democratic are not good and that the primary reason judicial review is good is because it is antidemocratic. This is not a new idea. Jefferson, for example, was aware that antidemocratic agencies were both necessary and good. The proof of this lies in the very material Rostow cites as evidence of Jefferson's acceptance of judicial review. A survey of this material is worthwhile, as it will serve to demonstrate two things: (1) Jefferson had substantial reservations about majority rule and favored counterbalances to it, and (2) Jefferson did not favor judicial review as we know it.

In presenting his themes that a viable separation of powers is a prerequisite to a free society and that judicial review maintains such a separation of powers through checking the elected branches, Rostow wrote:

> The division and separation of governmental powers within the American federal system provides the community with ample power to act, without compromising its pluralist structure. The Constitution formalizes the principle that a wide dispersal of authority among the institutions of society is the safest foundation for social freedom. It was accepted from the beginning that the judiciary would be one of the chief agencies for enforcing the restraints of the Constitution. In a letter to Madison, Jefferson remarked of the Bill of Rights:
>
>> In the arguments in favor of a declaration of rights, you omit one which has great weight with me; the legal check which it puts into the hands of the judiciary. This is a body, which, if rendered independent and kept strictly to their own department, merits great confidence for their learning and integrity. In fact, what degrees of confidence would be too much, for a body composed of such men as Wythe, Blair and Pendleton? On characters like these, the 'civium ardor prava pubentium' would make no impression.[17]

Rostow continued:

> Jefferson, indeed, went further. He regretted the absence in the Constitution of a direct veto power over legislation entrusted to the judiciary, and wished that no legislation could take effect for a year after its final enactment. Within such constitutional limits, Jefferson believed, American society could best achieve its goal of responsible self-government. "I have no fear," he wrote, "but that the result of our experiment will be, that men may be trusted to govern themselves without a master."[18]

For Rostow these remarks proved that Jefferson favored judicial review and even wished "to make the Supreme Court a third house of the national legislature"[19] In fact, it was only later in life that "Jefferson strongly differed with many of the decisions and opinions of the Supreme Court and expressed his disagreement in terms which sometimes seemed to repudiate the constitutionality of judicial review itself."[20]

Turning first to an examination of Jefferson's remarks concerning the Bill of Rights, we find two key clauses. First, to merit confidence, the judiciary must be rendered independent and "kept strictly to their own department." Second, the check that the judiciary is to exercise is a legal one and is to be directed against the "civium ardor prava pubentium." The second clause tells us what Jefferson fears most—not tyranny from above, from a nonresponsive, closed government corporation, but tyranny resulting from the excessive ardor and passion of the people, in other words, from a faction. This is also why

Jefferson favored a judicial veto and a year's delay in the passage of legislation. In a letter to Madison, Jefferson wrote: "The instability of our laws is really an immense evil. I think it would be well to provide in our constitutions, that there shall always be a twelve month between the engrossing a bill and passing it; that it should then be offered to its passage without changing a word; and that if circumstances should be thought to require a speedier passage, it should take two-thirds of both Houses, instead of a bare majority."[21]

In the same letter he endorsed the executive's veto power and suggested that perhaps such authority should instead have been vested in the judiciary. The form of judicial check that Jefferson favored is far from the present conception of judicial review as the final and absolute determination of the constitutionality of acts of Congress, much less that of other branches of federal and state governments. For Jefferson the ultimate say rested with two-thirds of the membership of Congress. Moreover, the scope concerned only congressional acts, whereas judicial review as now practiced goes far beyond review of federal legislative acts. In light of the fact that Jefferson preferred an either/or proposition – either give the veto to the judiciary or give it to both the executive and the judiciary – anyone following Rostow's reasoning that the veto power is the same as judicial review is forced to conclude that Jefferson also favored an "executive review." This line of reasoning is as specious as that resulting in the conclusion that Jefferson wished to make the Supreme Court a third house of the legislature, for on this basis we must conclude that Jefferson also wished to make the executive a third house.

Let us consider the form of judicial check that Jefferson actually favored. Jefferson's earlier statements seem to indicate two things. First, as we have seen, the principle for which he contended was not judicial review as we understand that power, but judicial review as an extension of separation of powers. Second, the fact that he held the judiciary to be "the most harmless and helpless of all organs" of government indicates that he did not foresee the development of the present form of judicial review.

Jefferson was in France during the Philadelphia Constitutional Convention and missed the Virginia Ratifying Convention as well.[22] At the Virginia Convention, Marshall argued eloquently in favor of the Constitution because of its provisions for judicial review as he interpreted it. That Jefferson felt he could best remove Marshall from the political arena by offering him a judgeship clearly illustrates how ineffectual he regarded the judiciary to be.

It was not at all inconsistent, therefore, for Jefferson to later regard judicial review as practiced and advocated by Marshall as a true threat to both states' rights and the separation of powers. It is only when one reads into his notion of a judicial veto the additional element of a final and binding determination as now exists in judicial review that his later remarks "seem" at odds with earlier ones as Rostow believes.

However, if anything can put to rest the question of whether Jefferson favored judicial review, it must be his remarks in the 1804 letter to Abigail

Adams cited in Chapter 4: "the opinion which gives to judges the right to decide what laws are constitutional and what not, not only for themselves in their own sphere of action, but for the legislature and executive also, in their spheres, would make the judiciary a despotic branch."[23] Jefferson believed that each branch would have to decide independently whether acts are constitutional. It seems clear, then, that Jefferson's concept of a judicial check was one not binding upon the other branches, and that he regarded judicial review not only as inconsistent with the principle of separation of powers but despotic as well, and therefore scarcely "well adapted to the needs of a free society."

It is necessary at this point to raise the question of whether Jefferson's belief that judicial review is despotic proves that it is. One of the obvious deficiencies of Rostow's argument is that of moving away from the identification of what things are democratic on the basis of the constituent elements of democracy to the identification of what things are democratic on the basis of citing men who are democrats and insisting that what they approve is democratic and what they disapprove is undemocratic.

As with Jefferson, examination of the statements of Madison and Lincoln indicate that judicial review is directed primarily against the majority. We have seen above that Madison was so convinced; *Federalist* 48 and 51 make the point. In the case of Lincoln, we need only look to the material Rostow cites. Lincoln argued,

> the candid citizen must confess that if the policy of the Government upon vital questions affecting the whole people is to be irrevocably fixed by decisions of the Supreme Court, the instant they are made in ordinary litigation between parties in personal actions the people will have ceased to be their own rulers, having to that extent practically resigned their government into the hands of that eminent tribunal. Nor is there in this view any assault upon the court or the judges. It is a duty from which they may not shrink.[24]

In the case of Brandeis, two points need amplification. First, the material Rostow cites does not seem to prove his point. Brandeis wrote of the doctrine of separation of powers, not the principle of judicial review. Second, it is a curious thing indeed to cite a case concerning the presidential power of removal, related to the separation of powers but not judicial review, as a vehicle for proving something about judicial review. Moreover, Rostow cites Brandeis's dissenting opinion, that is, he looks to a dissent to the rule of law established by judicial review.

Rostow's scholarship offers firm evidence that judicial review has functioned to nurture and to protect our liberty. However, it appears that his unjustified equation of *good, libertarian* or *utilitarian* with *democratic* leads to other distortions. His use of admirals, generals, and the Federal Reserve Board is a case in point. Obviously, few would deny the goodness or utility of such officials. But Rostow's argument respecting these functionaries is precisely the same kind as his argument respecting the democrats, Jefferson *et al.,* that is, since the whole is democratic the parts must be. In similar fashion, he focuses attention not upon the democratic character of the offices and powers of admirals, generals, and members of the Federal Reserve Board, but upon the system of which they are a part.

For Rostow, democracy's real task "is not to have the people vote directly on every issue, but to assure their ultimate responsibility for the acts of their representatives, elected or appointed."[25] Admirals, generals, and members of the Federal Reserve Board, like Supreme Court justices, are not held accountable through the electoral process. Since the former do not make our constitutional system undemocratic, why should Supreme Court justices armed with the power of judicial review make it so? It is quite true that the existence of such officials does not make the system of which they are a part undemocratic. However, when we consider that the subject of Rostow's essay is the character of judicial review rather than the character of our political-legal system, we find that Rostow has demonstrated little more than a similarity between admirals and generals, for example, and Supreme Court justices. Thus with respect to the character of judicial review, Rostow has demonstrated that the Court's exercise of judicial review is just about as democratic as a general's exercise of his power of command. It is unlikely that members of the armed forces would consider their power democratic. Moreover, there is excellent reason for arguing that the armed forces are more democratic than the Court. In the first place, the armed forces do not exercise political power, whereas the Court does. Second, they are directly under the control of an elected official, the president, but the Court is not. At least military personnel are held indirectly responsible through simple majority vote. Nor is the Federal Reserve Board any less independent, being the creation of Congress and therefore subject to destruction by statute.

Although Rostow is correct in seeing the difficulties inherent in defining the term *democracy,* there is nevertheless an essential aspect of democracy without which no form of government is democratic. There has been agreement at least from Jefferson's time to ours that the fundamental prerequisite is majority rule. For Jefferson the *"lex majoris partis . . .* is a fundamental law of nature," by which alone self-government can be exercised by a society."[26] In another place he insisted:

> The first principle of republicanism is that the *lex majoris partis* is the fundamental law of every society of individuals of equal rights; to consider the will of the society enounced by the majority of a single vote as sacred as if unanimous, is the first of all lessons in importance, yet the last which is thoroughly learnt. This law once disregarded, no other remains but that of force, which ends necessarily in military despotism.[27]

Making specific reference to our constitutional system, Jefferson noted that "the fundamental principle of the government is that the will of the majority is to prevail." For him all "governments are more or less republican, as they have more or less the element of popular election and control in their composition."[28] Applying his criteria to the government of his own state, he found that "the purest republican feature . . . is the House of Representatives. . . . The executive still less, because not chosen by the people directly. The Judiciary seriously anti-republican, because [appointed] for life."[29] In unequivocal fashion Jefferson summed up all of his statements by noting that "action by the citizens in person, in affairs within their reach and competence, and in all others by representatives, chosen immediately and removable by themselves, constitutes the essence of a republic."[30] Given the evolution of language, what modern Americans mean by *democratic* is precisely what the Founding Fathers meant by *republican*. Regardless of where we look, we find there is an essential ingredient in the democratic or republican stew — majority rule.

The most thought-provoking material Rostow presented in this regard was his suggestion that the task of democracy was to assure the ultimate responsibility of the people for the acts of their appointed and elected representatives. Rostow suggested that the judges' responsibility is guaranteed by changes in the personnel of courts and by the possibility of constitutional amendment. Since he lists the latter factor, not the former, as the real element making the Court's exercise of judicial review democratic, we can see that even he had some misgivings about whether the "benign influence of time" really makes the Court responsible and/or democratic.

At first glance the factor of changes in personnel seems hardly to the point, and little more than a makeweight argument. History seems reluctant to verify that time and change of personnel are necessarily beneficial. Besides the fact that things do not necessarily get better by replacing one person with another, we must keep sight of the fact that the second appointee will be no more responsible than the first unless provisions are introduced to secure his or her responsibility.

Perhaps what Rostow had in mind was a kind of indirect responsibility stemming from the process of appointment. A page from history, perhaps, would serve to introduce this point. Recalling the example of the "nine old men" and their "battle" with President Roosevelt in the early days of the New Deal, we can see that a firmly established constitutional doctrine was at stake, substantive due process. Although the beginning of this doctrine may be found earlier, it was well established in the decision in *Dred Scott* v. *Sanford* (19 Howard 393) in 1857. Previously, due process had generally concerned only the rights of persons accused of crimes in criminal cases, and proper notice, hearing, and compensation in civil cases. Chief Justice Taney firmly established that due process involved the substance of the matter at hand as well as these appropriate measures.

In succeeding cases the Court restricted the area encompassed by the Commerce Clause through the application of substantive due process and the Tenth Amendment, thus narrowing the regulatory power of the federal government. This limitation was expanded to include the states through *Lochner*

v. *New York* (198 U.S. 45), and certain areas of commerce were thus freed from *any* federal or state regulation. Not until the "switch in time that saved nine" in *West Coast Hotel Co.* v. *Parrish* (300 U.S. 379) did the Court reverse itself, allowing that Congress could indeed regulate in the areas so long forbidden.

Although the position that the Court reversed itself because of fear of court packing has been a subject of debate, it is a fact that Congress and the president have the power to appoint an unlimited number of new justices whenever they please. Thus the extent to which the Court's awareness of this authority actually influences their behavior is beside the point. New justices holding views similar to the president, Congress – and by extension a popular majority – *can* be placed upon the Court to override the old justices. Of course, once the new justices are sworn in, they become just as independent as the old and as little likely to reflect the wishes of a future majority. Thus the process in no way makes the Court more responsible.

It is more likely that what Rostow had in mind was not the possibility of court packing, but the matter of appointment in the ordinary course of replacement. This seems true since, in the final analysis, we find that Rostow does not mean that providing for "the final responsibility of the people" at the same time provides for responsible judges. Indeed, in the case of ordinary litigation we find that the people must assume a twofold duty of ensuring the *quality* of the judges and "the substance of their instructions." Thus their responsibility is to ensure that their elected officials appoint good judges. This in no way touches the matter of responsibility of judges to the people. As Rostow had noted, "It is hardly characteristic of law in democratic society . . . to allow appeals from the courts in particular cases to legislatures or mobs."[31] On the other hand, in the case of the extraordinary litigation of the Supreme Court, the people are afforded an opportunity for direct participation through the possibility of amendment, which does appear to touch the matter of responsibility.

However, in this regard it is important to note that for Rostow what ultimately makes judicial review democratic is the *possibility* of amendment. In this way Rostow indicated his awareness of the difficulties involved in that process and of the unlikelihood of using it to check the Court. But even when the difficulties of constitutional amendment are put aside, it is difficult to see how that process makes the Court accountable unless, of course, the amendment is directed to the very nature of the Court. Since overturning an action of the Court in no way makes it hold any other will on the matter, any future interpretation of the amendment by the Court would likely reflect the Court's original will. Thus the reason the Court can be said to be responsible at all in this respect is because of the more important possibilities of either making the Court directly accountable through suffrage or even amending the Court out of existence. However, the fact that a method exists to make a nondemocratic Court democratic does not mean that the Court in its present form is democratic.

Given these possibilities, Rostow is correct in seeing that the Court is ultimately responsible to the people. By showing that the Court does not constitute a "will independent of society," taken together with the fact that amendments can change almost any aspect of our form of government, Rostow demonstrated beyond doubt that our political-legal system is rooted in popular sovereignty. Nevertheless, this does not prove that the Court is not a will independent of a majority of society. In order to propose an amendment to the Constitution, two-thirds of both houses of Congress must vote to do so or a minimum of two-thirds of the states must request a convention to propose amendments. To ratify an amendment proposed by either method, the legislatures or conventions of three-fourths of the states must give approval. This is not now, nor was it intended to be, an extension of the principle of majority rule. It was an extension of the principle of popular sovereignty requiring a majority that is extraordinary in terms of size and geographic extent. No simple majority could initiate or realize a constitutional amendment. Basing calculations on the census figures of 1790, we find that of the original thirteen states four with less than 10 percent of the population (352,354) could have prevented the remaining nine states with more than 90 percent of the population (3,285,527) from amending the Constitution. On the other hand, the ten states with the smallest populations still comprise almost 57 percent of the total population. To pass an amendment in 1790 it would have been necessary to carry states possessing between a minimal 57 percent to a maximal 94 percent of the population.

Thus even in this final aspect of indirect control the Court, and even the political-legal system, can be seen as antidemocratic. That is, they are antidemocratic if it is correct to assume that majority rule is "the inescapable necessity of the democratic state." However, as we have seen, this is not to say that checks against the the majority are bad. Not only are they both good and essential, they also give evidence of who ultimately rules in our system—the majority. To see that this is so we must accept the fact it is possible to have bad democracies. Aristotle was one of the first to note this distinction. The crucial difference between good and bad forms of democracy (or between good and bad forms of monarchy and aristocracy) did not turn upon the kinds of offices held by citizens, nor upon the accidental basis of number, but rather upon the idea of social class. Accordingly, bad democracy (what he termed *democracy*) was rule by the whole people. On the other hand, good democracy (*polity*) was rule by the many in the interests of the whole people, rather than just the poor. And it is this sort of government that contemporary Americans regard as our form of government.

Although Aristotle took exception to the etymological meaning of democracy, at the same time he pointed to a crucial distinction. A government is known by the interest to which it is directed *as well as* the sort of participation involved. It is not determined simply on the basis of whether rule is by the one, the few, or the many. Perhaps, in the *Politics* Aristotle is actually saying that there are two kinds of government—good and bad. The three good forms are kinship, aristocracy, and polity. The three bad forms—tyranny, oligarchy, and democracy—are perversions of the good forms.

There can be little doubt that Jefferson was aware of this distinction, since he rested the authority of the Declaration of Independence upon the statements of the day as "expressed in conversation, in letters, printed essays, or in the elementary books of public right, as Aristotle, Cicero, Locke, Sidney, or etc."[32] And listed first among those acts that marked George as a tyrant rather than a good king is that "he has refused his Assent to Laws, the most wholesome and necessary for the public good." Furthermore, he refused "to pass other laws for the accommodation of large districts of people." Not only did he impose his will upon legislation, but he made "Judges dependent on his will alone" as well. The definition is so Aristotelian we can see readily the influence of Aristotle's "book of public right."

To Aristotle, process or participation distinguished kinds of government. It did not distinguish a good form from its bad or perverted form; thus there are good and bad democracies. Otherwise, what we refer to today as *the tyrannical majority,* or what Talmon refers to as *totalitarian democracies,*[33] would really be as good as we consider the government of the United States to be. Totalitarian democracies are morally comparable to what Aristotle would have called *perverted constitutions;* that is, they are directed to the interest of a particular social class. A good democratic government is directed to the interest of the whole people—the many *and* the few, the poor *and* the rich.

In this sense Lincoln's trilogy takes on meaning other than simply an ideological statement on the nature of the *federal* union, or just rhetorical flair. "Government of the people, by the people, and for the people" could be understood as government responsible to *all* the people, exercised by a representative *portion* of the people, and directed to the interest of *all* the people.

This is not to suggest the personification of that interest in an artificial whole such as the state. For a good democratic government ultimately must be responsible to the people. What is intended here is the recognition by the government of the importance of the individual as such in a situation of relations with and among other individuals. Government must not merely concern itself with the interest of majorities, nor simply with the interest of minorities. It must concern itself with the interest of both. Since most fact or value situations involving majorities and minorities find each with interests that tend to be in conflict, good democracy assumes compromise; as Madison suggested in *The Federalist,* justice consists in half a loaf for everyone.[34]

Since a minimum requisite of good democracy is that the government be responsive to the interest of the whole people, there are at least two reasons why a suffrage is so necessary in such a political-legal system. First, history has demonstrated that governments not held accountable to an electorate have been less responsive to the people. The second reason is perhaps even more cogent. A good democratic government must be directed to the interest of the whole people; this interest we refer to as the *common interest, public good, justice,* and *general will.* There is great enough difficulty in resolving majority-minority conflicts even with such "guides" as distilled wisdom, public opinion, and pressure-group activity. It is even more difficult to bring conflict resolution in line with the interest of the whole people in its other aspect as common interest, public good, justice, or general will. There is no guarantee that any government can at any time, or even most of the time, determine what the interest of the whole people is in either of its aspects. Therefore, some kind of protection is needed from a government that though honestly directed to the interest of the whole people cannot say what that interest is.

This has led some to believe that good democracy is merely process. Abraham Kaplan is perhaps typical. "We are characters in search of an author, while the greatness of the drama lies just in this: that the characters themselves take over the plot. Democracy means that you carry no banner but your own."[35] Kaplan believes that a democratic statesman concerns himself not with the vision of ends "but with the greatness of the journey."[36] However, *good democracy* is not just some way of arriving at social policy, it is a very special kind of way. It is not just a suffrage providing for responsiveness to every demand of any majority at every point in time. It is also compromise and consensus in the interest of the whole people, and it is that very interest that Kaplan assumes is present in process alone. If this were true, how can the experiences of many Latin American countries be explained? For that matter, what of the "people's democracies"? It may be argued that these countries actually do not have a suffrage. This may be true. However, they certainly have the structure for suffrage. They have to Kaplan's way of thinking the most important criterion for a "way" to "*the* way." That is, unless process in itself is not really good democracy.

Kaplan's argument could be summarized in the following manner. Good democracy is incompatible with enforced homogeneity in pursuit of monolithic, government-stated goals. By "the greatness of the journey" he could mean simply that the greatness of democracy is in its insistence on preserving individual spontaneity with respect to goals. He would say that the only interest of the whole, as far as it can be stated concretely, is to preserve the process.

However, it is not solely the process that in fact is responsible for that preservation. If it were, we would not have to concern ourselves with the notion of bad democracies. Heterogeneity is also a positive value that Kaplan envisions as part of the process, and which Talmon and the historical experience of many nations deny. The governments of such nations have in fact enforced homogeneity on the part of some of the people to monolithic, government-stated goals. This may be stated in other terms: pluralism is now a political fact, and the reflection of that pluralism is a positive value. But the value lies not in government that resolves conflict only on the basis of either majority or minority interests. That resolution must reflect the interests of both, which cannot be accomplished without a notion of the public good—

which encompasses something more than just the preservation of a system that reflects majority wishes.

Process plays an essential role, but that role is not the whole of the matter. A good democratic government is directed to the interest of the whole people, and in our good democratic system the agency ultimately charged with the protection of that interest is the Supreme Court. Resistance to the other branches of government when they act tyrannically, whether because they refuse to reflect the will of the majority or because they do reflect the will of a tyrannical majority, is the constitutionally imposed duty of the judiciary. Unquestionably, therefore, since to resist a majority the judiciary must be independent of that majority, the character of judicial review is antidemocratic. And this is good. Moreover, we have seen that although the Court is independent of a simple majority, it is not independent of society. Thus there can be no equation of its antidemocratic character with a monarchic, tyrannic, aristocratic, or oligarchic character. It is simply one of the primary means whereby the constitutional fathers expected "to secure the public good and private rights against the danger of such a faction, and at the same time to preserve the spirit and form of popular government."[37]

To the extent that the Court, possessed of the power of judicial review, is antidemocratic, the political-legal system of which it is a part is less democratic. But this is true of all governments in historical fact. Even Athenian "democracy" does not qualify as wholly democratic. Although the whole body of male citizens formed the assembly, this body had a minor role in the formation and discussion of policy. Neither have there been any pure monarchies, actual states in which total rule was in the hands of a single individual. Thus governments are democratic, monarchic, and so on to some degree depending upon how close they fall to the pure end of the continuum. However, in the case of our democracy the strand of impurity results not from an admixture of monarchic or aristocratic elements. It is due primarily to rule by extraordinary majority rather than a simple one. Thus it might be correct to say that our government is less democratic than, for example, the Swiss cantons, but it would not be correct to say our government is not democratic.

It appears that the feelings of guilt concerning judicial review are not justified simply because that power is antidemocratic. This fact does not make the system of which it is a part undemocratic. What it does is to help make it a *good democracy*.

Limiting Supreme Court Jurisdiction[b]

Judicial Review and the National Political Process: A Functional Reconsideration of the Role of the Supreme Court, by Jesse H. Choper (Chicago: University of Chicago Press, 1980)

Albert P. Melone

JESSE H. CHOPER, a noted professor of law at the University of California, Berkeley, has made an interesting and provocative contribution to the continuing debate over the proper role of the United States Supreme Court. Readers will react either in praise or damnation to the startling and apparently radical proposals for limiting the Court's exercise of judicial review.

The author's major theme is that, when the exercise of judicial review is not necessary to preserve individual rights, the Court should not intervene. In other words, the Court should rule that federalism issues and disputes between the executive and congressional branches are matters beyond the reach of constitutional adjudication, unless such disputes involve claims that individual rights were violated. It must be noted that the prescribed limitations upon the exercise of judicial review in no way interfere with the Court's traditional task of statutory interpretation, and the Court could still settle disputes involving restrictions upon judicial authority.

The author's proposals are founded upon at least two interrelated premises. First, the exercise of judicial review is not consistent with the principle of majority rule. When the Court exercises review, it may flout the majority and expend precious institutional capital. Second, because the state and central governments possess political power and because the executive and congressional branches do, too, they can resolve conflicts within the political arena without the intervention of the Court and the possible diminution of its good will.

But because individuals are weak in relation to government and since individual rights are perilously at the mercy of the majority, the Court must act as the guardian of minority rights. And although other branches of government can protect their own interests, the judiciary lacks political clout so the Court may properly employ the judicial process to protect the Court's own interests. In search of a basis for principled decisionmaking, Choper looks not to mere expediency (for example, the familiar selective employment of judicial self-restraint for the purpose of momentary institutional self-protection) but to a political theory of relative power.

Despite the author's fine review of existing impact and historical accounts, I remain skeptical that the Court will make a significant contribution toward the preservation of its institutional capital by holding federalism and executive-congressional disputes nonjusticiable. Because the Court refuses to rule on these matters does not mean that the public will fail to react strongly to particular individual rights cases, as Choper himself acknowledges (page 169).

In fact, public and elite reaction may depend upon the emotional saliency of the issue before the Court and not upon the division or branch of government whose constitutional boundaries are being litigated. In other words, the preservation of institutional capital may not be a zero-sum game at all. The fact is that in recent decades it has been Court decisions involving individual rights and not federalism or executive-congressional judicial rulings which have produced the greatest negative reactions.

Consider a related point, and one which puts the author's concern in greater doubt. Empirical studies tend to demonstrate that while the public and even elites may disapprove of specific Court decisions, a deep reservoir of support for the Court as an institution remains relatively high.[38] The myths surrounding the Court may be so powerful that disapproval of specific Court decisions does not significantly erode its deeply acculturated diffuse support. Moreover, if the Court should abdicate its boundary-defining role with respect to federalism and executive-congressional relations, the unfulfilled expectations of both the mass public and elites may well result in less and not more support for the Court.

From a systemic viewpoint, the author's proposals are disturbing. While purporting to displace institutional heat away from the Court, Choper argues that the rest of the political system can dissipate it without serious problems. But judicial review functions both as a boundary-defining mechanism and as a legitimating tool of government.

Much of U.S. history has been charged with Court decisions settling and adjusting difficult conflicts between the state and federal governments and, to a lesser extent, between the executive and legislative branches. The fact is that the Constitution is imprecise and ambiguous in many areas likely to produce conflict, such as "Commerce . . . among the . . . states," "executive Power," "Republican Form of Government," and the Tenth Amendment.

It is true, as Choper maintains, that through the give and take of politics the meanings of the vague and ambiguous constitutional provisions can be defined. But ultimately, under Choper's proposals, the answers depend more upon the exercise of power than the perception of legitimacy. As practiced for nearly 200 years, a strength of the constitutional system is that the loser in a political conflict can retreat to a court for a "definitive" decision. If he loses again (often the case), he may find it easier to accept defeat in the knowledge that he has had his day in court.

This book, which represents years of careful study, calls into question the conventional wisdom and strongly challenges the existing paradigm. Professor Choper should be congratulated for his courage. But rebuttal is often the price of boldness. Judging from his own style, he will no doubt relish the many encounters which will surely follow the widespread reading of this book.

NOTES

a. This essay is an enlarged version of an earlier article: "The Anti-Democratic Character of Judicial Review," *California Law Review* 60 (1972) 1140–49. George Mace is grateful to Albert P. Melone for his editorial assistance in writing this latest version.

1. Eugene V. Rostow, "The Democratic Character of Judicial Review," *Harvard Law Review*, 66:194. Hereafter cited as Rostow. Reprinted in Chapter 13 of this volume. See 211 for quotation.
2. These articles appeared in the *New York Journal and Weekly Register* during the latter part of 1787 and early 1788. See Chapter 11 of this volume for Numbers XI, XII, and XV, comprising the major attack upon the Court.
3. See Chapter 11, this volume, 180.
4. Ibid , 190.
5. Ibid., 194.
6. See Chapter 12 of this volume for complete text.
7. Rostow, especially 195-9. See also Chapter 13, 211-14.
8. *Federalist* 47, in Alexander Hamilton, John Jay, and James Madison, *The Federalist* (New York: Modern Library, 1941), p. 313. Hereafter cited as *Federalist.*
9. See *Federalist* 10, p. 53; *Federalist* 14, p. 81; see also Martin Diamond, "The Federalist," in *History of Political Philosophy,* ed. Leo Strauss and Joseph Cropsey (Chicago: Rand McNally, 1963), 581.
10. *Federalist* 48, 322-23.
11. *Federalist* 51, p. 338.
12. Ibid. Also see *Federalist* 9, p. 48.
13. *Federalist* 10, p. 54.
14. Ibid., p. 57.
15. *Federalist* 78, p. 504. Also see Chapter 12, this volume, 199.
16. Rostow, 199. See also Chapter 13, this volume, 214.
17. Ibid., 198. Also see: Chapter 13, this volume, 213-14.
18. Ibid., 199. Also see: Chapter 13, this volume, 214.
19. Ibid., 214. Also see: Chapter 13, this volume, 225.
20. Ibid., 199. Also see: Chapter 13, this volume, 233, n.8.
21. *The Writings of Thomas Jefferson,* ed. Albert Ellery Bergh (Washington, D.C.: Thomas Jefferson Memorial Association, 1927), VI:393. Hereafter cited as Bergh.
22. See Chapter 2, this volume, for greater elaboration.
23. H. A. Washington, ed., *The Writings of Thomas Jefferson* (Washington, D.C.: Taylor and Maury, 1854), IV:561, hereafter cited as Washington; Paul L. Ford, ed., *The Writings of Thomas Jefferson* (New York: G. P. Putnam's Sons, 1896), VIII:311, hereafter cited as Ford.
24. Abraham Lincoln, *First Inaugural Address,* in *Messages and Papers of the Presidents,* ed. James D. Richardson (n.p.: Bureau of National Literature, n.d.), VIII: 3210-11; and Rostow, 199, especially n. 11. Also see Chapter 13, this volume, 214, 233, n.11.
25. Rostow, 197. Also see: Chapter 13, this volume, 213.
26. Ford, VII:417.
27. Washington, VII:75.
28. Ibid., VI:608.
29. Ford, X:29; Washington, VI:606.

30. Washington, VI:591.

31. Rostow, 197. Also see: Chapter 13, this volume, 213.

32. Bergh, 118-19.

33. See J. L. Talmon, *Origins of Totalitarian Democracy* (New York: Praeger, 1960).

34. *Federalist* 10, pp. 56-57.

35. Abraham Kaplan, "The Great Journey," *Saturday Review* (December 23, 1961): 26.

36. Ibid.

37. *Federalist* 10, pp. 57-58.

b. This book review first appeared in *Judicature* 64 (February 1981): 335-36. Used by permission.

38. Murphy and Tanenhaus, *Public Opinion and the United States Supreme Court: Mapping of Some Prerequisites for Court Legitimation of Regime Changes,* 2 LAW & SOC'Y REV. 357 (1968); Daniels, *The Supreme Court and Its Publics,* 37 ALBANY L. REV. 632 (1973); Murphy and Tanenhaus, PUBLIC EVALUATIONS OF CONSTITU-TIONAL COURTS, ALTERNATIVE EXPLANATIONS. Sage Professional Papers in Comparative Politics, vol. 4 series no. 01-045 (Beverly Hills: Sage Publications, 1973); Casey, *The Supreme Court and Myth: An Empirical Investigation,* 8 LAW & SOC'Y REV. 385 (1974); Melone, *System Support Politics and the Congressional Court of Appeals,* 51 N. DAKOTA L. REV. 597 (1975); Jaros and Roper, *The U S. Supreme Court; Myth, Diffuse Support, Specific Support, and Legitimacy,* 8 AM. POL. Q. 85 (1980). [Also see: Chapter 15, this volume, 259-60.]

15

Judicial Review and Public Awareness

W E HAVE ATTEMPTED in this volume to acquaint readers with a number of difficult questions regarding the role of the United States Supreme Court in the American political system. In particular, the exercise of judicial review has often placed the Court at the heart of political controversies, and this circumstance has raised serious questions concerning that role.

The first concerns the origins of judicial review. Many have insisted that the Court usurped law-making power when claiming this function. The writings of Judge Gibson and Louis Boudin are illustrative of this viewpoint. Others, including Mr. Justice Lurton and Charles Beard, argue that there is sufficient historical evidence to support the conclusion that the constitutional Framers intended judicial review and that it is a desirable feature of our governmental system. Still others, such as James B. Thayer, accept judicial review as an authority properly possessed but counsel restraint in its employment.

We believe it is difficult to make a case one way or the other with absolute certitude. Indeed, we have a modest disagreement that starts with the observation that the proof is not overwhelming. One of us believes the weight of the evidence supports the usurpation charge; the other has concluded that it tends to refute the charge. Our disagreement lends credence to the old saying that reasonable persons may disagree. In the end, neither of us is willing to stake his professional reputation on an unequivocal answer. Any conclusion must be qualified.

However, we agree on the certainty that judicial review is a fact of political life, usurpation or not. The Supreme Court has exercised and will continue to exercise the authority, although the use of the judicial veto has from time to time generated serious opposition for the Court. Yet through it all the high bench has been able to maintain its extraordinary authority, a power masterfully seized by John Marshall in *Marbury* v. *Madison.*

In Part III of this volume we have focused upon the second great and difficult query surrounding the exercise of judicial review: is judicial review compatible with democracy? In this case the two of us agree on the answer.

It is significant that both Robert Yates and Alexander Hamilton held that judicial review is inconsistent with the democratic principle that government ought to be accountable to the people. But, of course, each came to different conclusions about its desirability. Yates, the Antifederalist, argued against the proposed constitution and judicial review because the Court would constitute a will independent of society. Hamilton applauded review because the Court's independence of society would serve as a safeguard against the tyranny of the elected representatives of the people.

A third view is expressed in Eugene Rostow's article. It is an argument positively proclaiming the democratic character of judicial review. According to this view, the judiciary is accountable to the people for its decisions. Further, judicial review must not be assessed solely in procedural terms; it must also be judged in terms of the ends it serves. Therefore, to the extent that judicial review protects precious rights and liberties it is consistent with democratic theory, and the justices of the Supreme Court should feel no guilt about its use.

There is at least one additional view, a perspective shared by both of us. It is the view articulated in the previous chapter by George Mace. Judicial review is neither democratic nor undemocratic. Rather it is antidemocratic. Because it is antidemocratic, it is consistent with the Aristotelian notion of a "good democracy." Therefore, we support judicial review as a functional tool in the service of important democratic values. Although review is antidemocratic it is nonetheless compatible with democracy. It operates to guard against threats to liberty and human happiness.

It is clear to us that whatever the legitimacy of its origins, judicial review may be justified in terms of democratic theory. It is also plain that many proponents of judicial supremacy find it difficult to defend. This is especially true when Court decisions seem removed from prevailing public opinion. Obviously, not all exercises of judicial review have placed the Court under severe attack. The justices themselves have attempted to protect the Court from attack through the exercise of judicial self-restraint. However, rational political calculation is not the only explanation for this behavior. No doubt, as Eugene Rostow explained, there is a sense of guilt surrounding the use of the judicial veto. It is an uneasiness that does not seem to disappear, despite repeated usage and the passing of time.

Supreme Court justices, judges of other courts, constitutional scholars, bar association representatives, members of Congress and of the executive branch, and others have felt compelled to justify the Court's power. Though no responsible public figure has in recent years called for an end to judicial review, there have been forcefully presented criticisms of its uses and alleged misuses.

Contemporary conservatives such as Chief Justice William Rehnquist and Judge Robert Bork have written and spoken about the importance of exercising judicial self-restraint. Justice William Brennan and Judge Frank Johnson, whom many would characterize as liberals, are representative of those arguing for the importance of an activist posture: courts must function so as to articulate and protect valuable constitutional rights. President Ronald Reagan's Justice Department asserts the importance of following the Framers' "original intent" when the Court interprets constitutional provisions.[a] At the same time, there have been recurrent calls for curbing the Court, including the introduction of legislation that would remove appellate jurisdiction from the Supreme Court to hear cases involving certain controversial issues.[b]

We believe the recurring debate about the Court's role is traceable to the fundamental question of legitimacy, which centers on the issues of usurpation and compatibility. However, what is rarely acknowledged, and will be denied by many, is an underlying uncertainty about whether ordinary Americans can understand the intellectual justification for judicial review without coming to a conclusion that may contribute to the instability of the political system. An empirical study reported in 1986 found that public confidence in the incumbents of the Court is related to judicial activism. The conventional wisdom that the Court skates on thin ice when it invalidates federal statutes is substantiated by the data.[c] However, confidence in particular justices of the

Supreme Court is probably different from support for the Court as an institution. Empirical studies demonstrate that, whereas specific support for Court decisions may wane from time to time, diffuse support for the Supreme Court remains relatively high and favorable.[d] It is also true that political elites have a tendency to come to the aid of the Court when direct institutional attacks are made upon its authority.[e]

Empirical evidence has not linked a diminution of public confidence in Supreme Court justices or in the exercise of judicial review with a drastic decline in diffuse support. Nonetheless, it is conceivable that at some point public acquiescence may turn to intolerance, resulting in the removal of the deep reservoir of public support so necessary for the Court to continue its historic role in U.S. politics.

The fear of popular misunderstanding or rejection of judicial supremacy is well-illustrated by the rash of criticisms that greeted the 1979 publication of Bob Woodward and Scott Armstrong's runaway bestseller, *The Brethren.* Though some critics concede the point that the Court is a political institution, they fear a little knowledge (or information not entirely accurate or reliable) could be dangerous, engendering widespread feelings of alienation or, worse, rebellion.

The last essay in this volume addresses the questions raised by the reactions to the publication of *The Brethren.* The judicial myth is rejected as an inaccurate description of judicial processes and behavior. The myth can be summed up in the saying that judges only find the law, they do not make it. It has been expressed in a number of different ways, including Mr. Justice Roberts's famous decision in *United States* v. *Butler*—an opinion best characterized as an exercise in mechanical jurisprudence. It is true that myths may be functional for system stability. However, democratic theory properly assumes that the political system functions best with a well-informed citizenry.

We are mindful of the impact of political socialization and cultural norms upon the maintenance of institutions. We are also cognizant of the importance played by irrationality and self-interest in human affairs. But in the end, we possess a Jeffersonian belief in the educability and good sense of the American people. Whether or not our assumptions are mistaken, we are certain that the pursuit of truth is ill served by the propagation of myths. It is hoped that this volume has contributed to the goals of a life of reason and a political system based upon an informed consent of the governed.

Paradoxically, because the judicial review debate refuses to go away, the use of that power is made more secure. Proponents and opponents of the judicial veto are compelled to carefully assess and reassess its costs against its benefits. The debate serves as a reminder that in a democratic society all power must be limited.

A Political Scientist Writes in Defense of *The Brethren*[1]

Albert P. Melone

The Brethren has been both widely read and generally criticized.[1] The former is commendable; the latter should not go unchallenged. As is usually the case with ambitious and worthwhile projects, the authors, Bob Woodward and Scott Armstrong, have made some errors. Yet the mistakes of fact and even of judgment are far outweighed by the book's potential for creating a more realistic appraisal of the Court's role in the American political system.

The Brethren is indeed gossipy and reveals little-known and sometimes embarrassing information about the personal habits and tastes of the Supreme Court justices. Woodward and Armstrong have extended the current journalistic analysis of executive and legislative officials to the judiciary. But however distasteful the analysis might be, one must certainly admit that judges, like other political leaders, are mere mortals. Their quest for power, their egocentricity, and their petty behavior can hardly be considered unusual in contemporary society.

The authors have made technical errors in the book, even to the point of misstating the facts and the Court's holdings in a few opinions. These errors are undoubtedly disconcerting to serious students of constitutional law. However, the book is clearly intended as a journalistic account of judicial politics and not a legal treatise. The authors highlight not the law as such but rather the judicial decision-making process, and they thus focus on how justices negotiate for a given result and how and why they may trade a vote today for one tomorrow.

If the naive view prevailed that a justice always votes his conscience, then institutional paralysis would surely result. Indeed, no political system could long endure without compromise, logrolling, and the formation of alliances. What Woodward and Armstrong do is to show that the Supreme Court must also use these methods.

The use of information supplied by the law clerks is a common criticism of this book, and perhaps the authors do place too much reliance on the clerks' self-inflating words. In one instance, some 30 clerks have specifically repudiated a report attributed to them by the authors.[2] The accuracy of the information thus is attacked not only because the critics allege that the sources are unreliable but also because the sources themselves – the clerks – claim that the authors have misrepresented the facts. Woodward and Armstrong have anticipated this criticism by stressing that they always verified the story with other sources, such as different clerks, unpublished written materials, other Court employees, and some of the justices themselves.[3]

The Rules of the Game

While the issue of the validity of the authors' information is often raised, what especially irritates critics is that the clerks violated the rules of the game. Clerks are not only well-situated institutionally to learn how the decision-making process works but also to participate in it to a limited extent. The clerks are bearers of gossip and informal messages between and among the chambers of the justices. Given the volume of their work, the justices cannot perform their duties without the aid of competent assistants.

In light of their privileged position, critics think the clerks who washed the Court's dirty linen in public violated the norms of polite society concerning discretion and silence. Apparently many clerks, and probably some of the justices, broke this gentlemen's code.

But the consequences of unbecoming conduct are not as ruinous as one might suppose. Although justices may suppress any open display of hostility, they can hardly suppress hostility, especially in a group as small as the Supreme Court. But so what? In the unlikely event that some justices are shocked and embarrassed by the revelations of the book, one need not conclude that the justices will now become even less cooperative than they were before. Surely mature and experienced public figures understand that sometimes lofty argument degenerates into personal animosity and ill-will. Moreover, they recognize the importance of putting such unprofessional feelings aside and getting on with the public's business. It is doubtful that the Court will now experience less internal cohesion.

The possible diminution of public respect for the Marble Palace is a greater source of concern. In light of the book's revelations about the Court's internal workings and personalities, might we surmise that public support for the judicial system will wane and that the rule of law will be questioned? It is true that myths are often functional for the maintenance of social and political systems. But democratic theory assumes that the political system functions best with a well-informed citizenry.[4]

The Myth Behind the Judiciary

The Brethren attacks the myth that judges only discover the law, they do not make it. Like most other myths, the judicial myth is useful for gaining the kind of unreasoning, blind obedience and respect that parents might expect from children. The book's popular appeal is its irreverent and clear message that the Supreme Court is a political institution. Defenders of mystery and magic may flinch at the suggestion, but the American public is fully capable of acquiring a realistic knowledge of the judicial system without growing alienated or, worse, rebellious in the process.

As lawyers know very well, the rules contained in constitutions, statutes, or case law are often vague, ambiguous, or otherwise not self-evident. Justices are compelled to give meaning to so-called principles such as "due process of law," "unreasonable restraint of trade," or "obscenity." Only by drawing upon those values and attitudes grounded in their life experiences and world views can they arrive at a decision in a given case or controversy.

This is not to say that the justices are without restraint, and that they can come to any decision they wish. They must provide justification in the form of written opinions. But the mere existence of written opinions does not make the reasoning any less teleological. *The Brethren* is replete with examples of how the justices first decided on the most desirable outcome for a case and then spent arduous hours justifying it and building the coalition necessary to win a majority vote.

The Court's 1972 abortion decision provides a graphic example of how justices sometimes agonize over the paucity of legal principles or rules to guide their decision-making behavior. Justice Harry Blackmun, working for many months on the abortion question during the Court's 1971 term, could not produce an acceptable draft opinion. When the Court's summer interlude began, Justice Blackmun began studying the question intensely at the world-famous Mayo Clinic in Rochester, Minnesota. Because he had served the clinic as counsel for many years, he was remarkably familiar with the field of medicine. Hence, it should come as no surprise that the medical distinction of the trimester pregnancy is now as much a part of Blackmun's opinion as the tenuous legal concept of the right to privacy.

Thus, the state's constitutional ability to interfere with a woman's right to an abortion today turns on a medically based formula to protect the woman's health in the second trimester of pregnancy and to protect the potential life of the fetus after the beginning of the last trimester. Because the phrase "right to privacy" does not appear in the Constitution and because it is such a new judicial concept, one might say that in this case – as in many others before it – the Court could no longer sustain the idea of mechanical jurisprudence as a description of the judicial process: it simply lacks intellectual viability.

The Appearance of Impartiality

Though they must choose among competing sets of ideas, it does not necessarily follow that justices are guilty of personal favoritism, prejudice, or bias toward the particular litigants coming before the Court. The authors make this point by noting the many instances in which justices disqualified themselves from participation in cases where even the slightest hint of personal bias might be suspected.

For example, because his old law firm had once been the bond counsel for the Denver School Board, and even though he had been away from there for 13 years, Justice White felt compelled to disqualify himself from the Denver school desegregation case (*Keyes v. School District No. 1*).

Likewise, because he had been chairman of the Richmond, Virginia, School Board from 1952 to 1961, Justice Powell felt it necessary to disqualify himself in a 1972 case involving a federal district court-ordered city-suburb merger of the Richmond School district.

As an official of the Justice Department, William Rehnquist had drafted President Nixon's original position on executive privilege; he had also worked closely with both Halderman and Ehrlichman and was a close personal friend of Kleindienst. Without offering any reason (and none was necessary under the circumstances), Justice Rehnquist disqualified himself from the Watergate tapes case involving the President. However, as Justice Rehnquist has suggested, in the attempt to appear more virtuous than Caesar's wife, a preoccupation with the appearance of impartiality may result in the justices failing to perform their fundamental responsibility to decide cases.[5]

The authors provide a concrete example of how impartial members of the Court can be. Justices Black and Brennan responded quickly to overt lobbying on behalf of a client by Thomas B. Corcoran, a former official of the Roosevelt Administration and a well-known Washington lawyer. When Corcoran strolled into the justices' office to argue for a rehearing petition that was pending before the Court, both Black and Brennan asked Corcoran to leave, and Brennan later disqualified himself from the case. Thus, Woodward and Armstrong demonstrate that the justices are impartial toward the litigants, though they are hardly neutral toward the great issues of the day. Impartiality to litigants reinforces the Court's reputation for fairness, but neutrality on issues denies the necessity of choice in the cases the Court encounters each term.

Interpersonal Relationships

The Brethren directs public attention to the interpersonal influences and small group dynamics of the Supreme Court. It alerts the general public to what students of the Court have long understood, namely, judicial policy-making is significantly affected by the quality of the personal and professional interactions among Court members. Identifying the quality of interactions is important for understanding the Court as a social and political organization.

Most commentators point to the unusual social and task leadership traits of John Marshall as a significant basis for the development of the Supreme Court as a powerful political institution.[6] As a talented social leader, Marshall minimized interpersonal conflicts; as a task leader he improved the Court's internal procedures and offered forceful intellectual guidance.[7]

Chief Justice Taft is best understood as a mediator of social conflict within the Court but not as a particularly gifted intellectual or task leader; he depended upon Associate Justice Van Devanter to guide the Court as a group through the intellectual nooks and crannies of the day's great constitutional labyrinth.[8] Compared to Hughes, Chief Justice Stone is remembered as both an ineffective social and task leader.[9]

In this book, critics interpret the authors' focus upon Warren Burger's leadership traits as an attempt to victimize him, suggesting that these liberal journalists are guilty of malicious intent or that they are using *ad hominen* arguments. But the authors present an engrossing and vivid account of Burger's personal, social, political and organizational style, and, though it seems unflattering, it furnishes the discerning reader with a sufficient number of cues to create sympathy for Burger because of the difficulty of the tasks confronting him.

As Woodward and Armstrong point out, Burger succeeded a very popular leader of the Court, Earl Warren, who was certainly the first among equals, personally charming to all and intellectually compatible with the liberal bloc. In contrast, Burger was appointed by a President who was almost universally despised by liberals on and off the Court. Since Burger interpreted his appointment as a conservative mandate to change the Court's liberal course, he could expect little else but trouble from the confirmed liberals such as Black, Douglas, Brennan, and Marshall.

Through his prerogatives as Chief Justice, Burger has manipulated his institutional power—especially assigning opinions—to achieve conservative goals. But ever since John Marshall did away with seriatim opinions and assigned most cases to himself, chief justices have recognized and employed, with varying degrees of acumen and success, their institutional authority to achieve desired political ends.[10] Burger is no exception.

In addition to dealing with the disputatious liberals, Burger has had to cope with independent-oriented moderates, such as Stewart and White, and with his intellectually arrogant fellow conservative, Rehnquist. It is little wonder that Burger welcomed as a relief the nomination to the Court of Harry Blackmun, his childhood friend. All in all, Woodward and Armstrong present sufficient information for the objective reader to come to the fair conclusion that given the times and cast of characters, it would be most difficult for any human being to perform both task and social duties with great distinction.

Is The Brethren *Useful?*

Some critics condemn *The Brethren* as unscholarly because it lacks the kind of documentation that directs scholars to law libraries or computer centers. But the authors do not pretend to be constitutional lawyers, historians, or even political scientists. Their *modus operandi* is that of investigative journalists, and their writing is designed to gain the attention of the reading public, not to cultivate specialist audiences. In light of its obvious scholarly limitations, is *The Brethren* useful to serious students of the judiciary? The answer is a qualified yes.

Scholars should regard *The Brethren* as a searching mission (not search and destroy) to uncover and construct testable propositions. From a theoretical perspective, it is not particularly significant that Justice X holds Justice Y in high or low esteem. What is significant is that personal interactions have public consequences; in this respect, *The Brethren* offers nothing new.

In at least one research area, however, the authors compel us to consider seriously the organizational roles of the law clerks. Heretofore, scholars have tended to minimize the roles of the clerks; textbook writers might mention how clerks are chosen and the roles they play in certiorari decisions, and an occasional author would recite the long-standing debate whether clerks are influential in policy-making. But generally, conventional wisdom maintains that the evidence is inconclusive.

Woodward and Armstrong remind us, however, that the clerks are at the center of a communication network. They facilitate the work of the individual justices by carrying informal messages from chamber to chamber, saving justices from intellectual embarrassments and helping to create necessary coalitions for deciding cases. The clerks may both facilitate and impair the decision-making process, however; they lubricate the system and yet contribute to its friction. Because Woodward and Armstrong rely so heavily on information provided by the clerks, the clerks' influence may be overstated. Exaggeration or not, *The Brethren* should encourage renewed scholarly interest in the roles the clerks play.

Overall, *The Brethren* is a worthwhile venture. A mature and realistic understanding of our political institutions is what we need today. Over time, reason and not myth is the best support for the rule of law. Genuine respect and support for our most honorable political institution should be based upon knowledge, not mystery. With this relatively short book, two journalists have made a valuable contribution to public awareness.

NOTES

a. Stuart Taylor, Jr., "*Meese v. Brennan*: Who's Right About the Constitution," *New Republic* (January 6 and 13, 1986): 17–21. For a convenient look at the various viewpoints of justices and judges see Mark W. Cannon and David M. O'Brien, eds., *Views from the Bench: The Judiciary and Constitutional Politics* (Chatham, N. J.: Chatham House, 1985); and The Federalist Society, *The Great Debate: Interpreting Our Written Constitution* (Washington, D.C.: The Federalist Society, 1986).

b. Albert P. Melone, "System Support Politics and the Congressional Court of Appeals," *North Dakota Law Review* 51 (1975): 597–613. For a contemporary discussion

of limiting federal court jurisdiction and whether Congress may do so, see the entire
issue of *Judicature* 65 (October 1981).

    c. Gregory A. Caldeira, "Neither the Purse nor the Sword: Dynamics of Public
Confidence in the Supreme Court," *American Political Science Review* 80 (December
1986): 1222.

    d. Walter F. Murphy and Joseph Tanenhaus, "Public Opinion and The United
States Supreme Court: A Preliminary Mapping of Some Prerequisites for Court Legitimation of Regime Changes," *Law and Society Review* 2 (1968): 357–82; Walter F. Murphy,
Joseph Tanenhaus, and Daniel Kastner, *Public Evaluations of Constitutional Courts: Alternative Explanations* (Beverly Hills, Calif.: Sage Publications, 1973); Joseph Tanenhaus
and Walter F. Murphy, "Patterns of Public Support for the Supreme Court: A Panel
Study," *Journal of Politics* 43 (1981): 24–39.

    e. Melone, "System Support Politics."

    f. *Judicature* 64 (September 1980): 140–44. Used by permission.

    1. For a convenient summary of the criticisms, *see: What other critics are saying,*
63 JUDICATURE 347 (February, 1980). See also: Ashman, *The Court's latest portrait:
over-exposed, underdeveloped,* 63 JUDICATURE 346 (February, 1980); Lewis, *Supreme
Court Confidential,* 27 N.Y. REV. OF BOOKS (February 7, 1980); Daniels, *The Clerks
Talk: Commentary and Analysis of the Brethren,* 44 ALBANY L. REV. 732–737 (1980).

    2. Lewis, *supra* n. 1, at 3.

    3. For Woodward and Armstrongs' rebuttal to Lewis and Lewis's reply, *see* Arm-
strong, Woodward and Lewis, *The Evidence of the Brethren: An Exchange,* 27 N.Y. REV.
OF BOOKS 47–53 (June 12, 1980).

    4. For a fine discussion of myth and reason, *see* Miller, THE SUPREME COURT:
MYTH AND REALITY (Westport, Conn.: Greenwood Press, 1978).

    5. *See* Woodward and Armstrong, *The Brethren,* 261 (1969); Rehnquist, *Sense and
Nonsense about Judicial Ethics,* 28 RECORD 694–713 (1973).

    6. *See, e.g.,* Beveridge, THE LIFE OF JOHN MARSHALL Vol. 4, 82–96; Vol. 2,
563–564 (Boston: Houghton Mifflin, 1916–1919). Severn, JOHN MARSHALL: THE
MAN WHO MADE THE SUPREME COURT 170–173 (1969).

    7. Schmidhauser, THE SUPREME COURT: ITS POLITICS, PERSONALI-
TIES, AND PROCEDURES 109, 111–114 (New York, Holt Rinehart and Winston,
1960).

    8. Danelski, *The Influence of the Chief Justice in the Decisional Process,* in Murphy
and Pritchett, COURTS, JUDGES, AND POLITICS: AN INTRODUCTION TO THE
JUDICIAL PROCESS 696–697 (New York: Random House, 1979).

    9. *Id.,* at 698–699.

    10. Murphy, ELEMENTS OF JUDICIAL STRATEGY 39, 82–89, 100–101, 184–
185 (Chicago: University of Chicago Press, 1964); and Schmidhauser, *supra* n. 7, at 103–
127.

Bibliography

Abraham, Henry J. *Freedom and the Court: Civil Rights and Liberties in the United States,* 4th ed. New York: Oxford Univ. Press, 1980.

———. *The Judicial Process: An Introductory Analysis of the Courts of the United States, England and France,* 5th ed. New York: Oxford Univ. Press, 1986.

Advisory Commission on Intergovernmental Relations. *A Framework for Studying the Controversy Concerning the Federal Courts and Federalism.* Washington, D.C.: 1986.

Agresto, John. *The Supreme Court and Constitutional Democracy.* Ithaca, N.Y.: Cornell Univ. Press, 1984.

Allen, W. B., and Lloyd, Gordon, eds. *The Essential Antifederalist.* Washington, D.C.: University Press of America, 1985.

Association of American Law Schools. *Selected Essays on Constitutional Law.* 5 vols. Chicago: Foundation, 1938.

Attansio, John B. "Everyman's Constitutional Law: A Theory of the Power of Judicial Review." *Georgetown Law Journal* 72 (Aug. 1984): 1665–1723.

Ball, Howard. *Judicial Craftsmanship or Fiat?* Westport, Conn: Greenwood, 1978.

Barrett, Edward L. *The Structure of Government.* New York: Foundation, 1981.

Beard, Charles A. *The Supreme Court and the Constitution.* New York: Macmillan, 1912.

———. "The Supreme Court – Usurper or Grantee?" *Political Science Quarterly* 27 (March 1912): 1–35.

———. *An Economic Interpretation of the Constitution of the United States.* New York: Macmillan, 1935.

———. *The Supreme Court and the Constitution.* Englewood Cliffs, N.J.: Prentice-Hall, 1962.

Benton, Thomas H. *Examination of the Dred Scott Case.* New York: Appleton, 1857.

Berger, Raoul. *Congress v. the Supreme Court.* Cambridge: Harvard Univ. Press, 1969.

_____. "A Political Scientist as Constitutional Lawyer: A Reply to Louis Fischer." *Ohio State Law Journal* 41, no.1 (1980): 147–75.

_____. *Government by Judiciary: The Transformation of the Fourteenth Amendment.* Cambridge: Harvard Univ. Press, 1981.

_____. "Paul Brest's Brief for an Imperial Judiciary." *Maryland Law Review* 40 (1981): 1–38.

_____. "The Role of the Supreme Court in a Democratic Society." *Villanova Law Review* 26 (Jan. 1981) 414–32.

Beveridge, Albert J. *The Life of John Marshall.* Vol. 4. Boston: Houghton Mifflin, 1916.

Bickel, Alexander M. *The Least Dangerous Branch: The Supreme Court at the Bar of Politics.* Indianapolis: Bobbs-Merrill, 1962.

Billikopf, David M. *The Exercise of Judicial Power.* New York: Vantage, 1973.

Birkby, Robert H. *The Court and Public Policy.* Washington D.C.: C. Q. Press, 1983.

Bizzell, William B. *Judicial Interpretation of Political Theory.* New York: B. Franklin, 1974.

Black, Charles L., Jr. *Old and New Ways in Judicial Review.* Brunswick, Maine: Bowdoin College, 1958.

_____. *The People and the Court: Judicial Review in a Democracy.* New York: Macmillan, 1960.

_____. *Decision According to Law.* New York: W. W. Norton, 1981.

Bobbit, Philip. *Constitutional Fate.* New York: Oxford Univ. Press, 1984.

Boudin, Louis B. "Government by Judiciary." *Political Science Quarterly* 26 (June 1911): 238–70.

_____. *Government by Judiciary.* 2 vols. New York: William Godwin, 1932.

Brest, Paul. *Brest's Processes of Constitutional Decisionmaking.* Boston: Little, Brown, 1977.

_____. *The Misconceived Quest for the Original Understanding.* Boston University *Law Review* 60 (March 1980): 204–38.

_____. *Processes of Constitutional Decisionmaking.* Boston: Little, Brown, 1983.

Bridwell, Randall. *The Constitution and the Common Law.* Lexington, Mass: Lexington Books, 1977.

Brown, Robert E. *Charles A. Beard and the Constitution: A Critical Analysis of "An Economic Interpretation of The Constitution."* Princeton: Princeton Univ. Press, 1956.

Bruce, William R. *The Bruce Resolution Debate.* Glen Rock, N. J.: Microfilming Corp. of America, 1976.

Burton, Harold. "The Cornerstone of Constitutional Law: The Extraordinary Case of Marbury v. Madison." *American Bar Association Journal* 36 (October 1950) 805–8.

Cahn, Edward. *Supreme Court and Supreme Law.* Bloomington: Indiana Univ. Press, 1954.

Caldeira, Gregory A. "Neither the Purse Nor the Sword: Dynamics of Public

Confidence in the U.S. Supreme Court." *American Political Science Review* 80 (Dec. 1986): 1209–26.

Calhoun, John C. *A Disquisition on Government.* Columbia, S.C.: A. S. Johnson, 1851.

_____. *A Discourse in the Constitution and Government of the United States.* 1851. Post Edition. Indianapolis: Bobbs-Merrill, 1953.

Cannon, Mark W., and O'Brien, David M., eds. *Views from the Bench: The Judiciary and Constitutional Politics.* Chatham, N.J.: Chatham House, 1985.

Cardozo, Benjamin N. *The Nature of the Judicial Process.* New Haven: Yale Univ. Press, 1921.

Carr, Robert K. *The Supreme Court and Judicial Review.* Westpoint, Conn.: Greenwood, 1942.

Chief Justice Earl Warren Conference on Advocacy in the United States. *The Courts: The Pendulum of Federalism.* Washington, D.C.: Foundation, 1979.

_____. *The Courts: Separation of Powers.* Washington, D.C.: Roscoe-Pound American Trial Lawyers Foundation, 1983.

Childes, Steven A. *Federal Standards of Review.* New York: Wiley, 1986.

Choper, Jesse H. *Judicial Review and the National Political Process: A Functional Reconsideration of the Role of the Supreme Court.* Chicago: Univ. of Chicago Press, 1980.

Clark, Walter. "The Next Constitutional Convention of the United States." *Yale Law Journal* 16 (Dec. 1906): 65–93.

_____. "Is the Supreme Court Constitutional?" *Independent* 63 (1907):723.

_____. *Judicial Supremacy.* 1911. Wickliffe, Ohio: Monetary Science, 1980.

Clinton, Robert Lowry. "The Populist-Progressive Reinterpretation of American Constitutional History: The Scapegoating of John Marshall, His Court, and the Founding Fathers." Ph.D. diss. University of Texas, Austin, 1984.

Clinton, Robert N. "Judges Must Make Law a Realistic Appraisal of the Judicial Function in a Democratic Society." *Iowa Law Review* 67 (May 1982): 711–41.

Coke, Brinton. *An Essay on Judicial Power and Unconstitutional Legislation.* New York: Da Capo, 1970.

Conkle, Daniel O. "The Legitimacy of Judicial Review in Individual Rights Cases: Michael Perry's Constitutional Theory and Beyond." *Minnesota Law Review* 69 (Feb. 1985): 587–665.

Cooley, Thomas M. *A Treatise on the Constitutional Limitations Which Rest Upon the Legislative Power of the Status of the American Union.* Boston: Little, Brown, 1868.

_____. *General Principles of Constitutional Law.* Boston: Little, Brown, 1880.

_____. *Constitutional History of the United States.* New York: G. P. Putnam's Sons, 1889.

Cope, Alfred. *Franklin D. Roosevelt and the Supreme Court.* Lexington, Mass: D. C. Heath, 1969.

Corwin, Edward S. "The Supreme Court and Unconstitutional Acts of Congress." *Michigan Law Review* 4 (1906).

_____. "The Establishment of Judicial Review." *Michigan Law Review* 9 (1910).

_____. *The Doctrine of Judicial Review and Other Essays.* Princeton: Princeton Univ. Press, 1914.

_____. *John Marshall and the Constitution.* New Haven: Yale Univ. Press, 1919.

_____. "The Progress of Constitutional Theory Between the Declaration of Independence and the Meeting Of the Philadelphia Convention." *American History Review* 30 (1925): 511.

_____. *The Twilight of the Supreme Court.* New Haven: Yale Univ. Press, 1934.

_____. *Court Over Constitution.* Princeton: Princeton Univ. Press, 1938.

Cox, Archibald. "The Role of the Supreme Court in American Society." *Marquette Law Review* 50 (June 1967): 575–93.

Coxe, Brinton. *An Essay on Judicial Power and Unconstitutional Legislation.* Philadelphia: Kay & Brother, 1983.

Crosskey, William W. *Politics and the Constitution in the History of the United States.* Chicago: Univ. of Chicago Press, 1953.

Cushman, Robert E. *Leading Constitutional Decisions,* 7th ed. New York: F. S. Crofts, 1940.

Davis, Horace A. *The Judicial Veto.* New York: Da Capo, 1971.

Dean, Howard E. *Judicial Review and Democracy.* New York: Random House, 1966.

Dewey, Donald O. *Marshall Versus Jefferson: The Political Background of Marbury v. Madison.* New York: Alfred A. Knopf, 1970.

Dicey, A. V. *Law and Public Opinion in England.* New York: Macmillan, 1905.

Dimond, Paul R. "Strict Construction and Judicial Review of Racial Discrimination Under the Equal Protection Clause: Meeting Raoul Berger on Interpretivist Grounds." *Michigan Law Review* 80, (Jan. 1982): 462–511.

Doolittle, James R. *The Veto Power of the Supreme Court." Chicago Law Times* (1887): 177.

Ducat, Craig R. *Modes of Constitutional Interpretation.* St. Paul: West Publishing, 1978.

Dver, William Alexander. *The Constitutional Jurisprudence of the United States.* New York: Burt Franklin, 1856.

Elliott, Charles B. "The Legislatures and the Courts: The Power to Declare Statutes Unconstitutional." *Political Science Quarterly* 5(1891): 224.

Ellis, Richard E. *The Jeffersonian Crisis: Courts and Politics in the Young Republic.* New York: Norton, 1974.

Ely, John H. *Democracy and Distrust.* Cambridge: Harvard Univ. Press, 1980.

Ewing, Cortez A. *The Judges of the Supreme Court, 1789–1937.* Minneapolis: Univ. of Minnesota Press, 1938.

Fairman, Charles. *Mr. Justice Miller and the Supreme Court.* Cambridge: Harvard Univ. Press, 1939.

Farrand, Max. "The Judiciary Act of 1801." *American History Review* 5(1899–1900): 682–86.

──────. *Records of the Federal Convention.* Vol. 2. New Haven: Yale Univ. Press, 1911.

Federalist Society. *The Great Debate: Interpreting Our Written Constitution.* Washington, D.C.: Federalist Society, 1986.

Forte, David F. *The Supreme Court in American Politics: Judicial Activism vs. Judicial Restraint.* Lexington, Mass.: D. C. Heath, 1972.

Frank, Jerome. *Law and the Modern Mind.* New York: Coward-McCann, 1930.

Frankfurter, Felix. *Law and Politics.* Edited by Archibald MacLeish and E. F. Prichard, Jr. New York: Harcourt, Brace, 1939.

Frankfurter, Felix, and Landis, James M. *The Business of the Supreme Court.* New York: Macmillan, 1927.

Free Congress Research and Education Foundation. *A Blueprint for Reform.* Washington, D.C.: Free Congress Research and Education Foundation, 1981.

Freyer, Tony A. *Harmony and Dissonance.* New York: New York Univ. Press, 1981.

Gabin, Sanford Byron. *Judicial Review and the Reasonable Doubt Test.* Port Washington, N.Y.: Kennikat, 1980.

Galie, Peter J. "The Other Supreme Courts: Judicial Activism Among State Supreme Courts." *Syracuse Law Review* 33 (Summer 1982): 731–93.

Garvey, Gerald. *Constitutional Bricolage.* Princeton: Princeton Univ. Press, 1971.

Gilbert, Wilfred C. *Provisions of Federal Law Held Unconstitutional by the Supreme Court of the United States.* Westport, Conn.: Greenwood, 1976.

Grey, T. C. "Do We Have an Unwritten Constitution?" *Stanford Law Review* 27 (1975):703-18.

Haines, Charles Grove. *The Conflict Over Judicial Powers in the United States to 1870.* New York: Columbia Univ. Press, 1909.

──────. *The Supreme Court of the United States.* New York: Columbia Univ. Press, 1928.

──────. *The Revival of Natural Law Concepts.* Cambridge: Harvard Univ. Press, 1930.

──────. *American Doctrine of Judicial Supremacy.* Berkeley: Univ. of California Press, 1932.

──────. *The Conflict Over Judicial Powers.* 1909. New York: AMS, 1970.

Hall, Kermit. *The Supreme Court and Judicial Review in American History.* Washington, D.C.: American Historical Association, 1985.

Hamilton, Alexander; Jay, John; and Madison, James. *The Federalist.* New York: Modern Library, 1941.

Hampton, Carson L. *The Supreme Court of the United States.* Philadelphia: John Y. Yuber, 1891.

Harris, Robert. *The Judicial Power of the United States.* Port Washington, N. Y.: Kennikat, 1972.

Haskins, George L. "Law Versus Politics in the Early Years of the Marshall Court." *Pennsylvania Law Review* 130 (Nov. 1981): 1–27.

Henschen, Beth M. "Judicial Use of Legislative History and Intent in Statutory Interpretation." *Legislative Studies Quarterly* 10 (Aug. 1985): 353–71.

Higgins, Thomas J. *Judicial Review Unmasked.* West Hanover, Mass.: Christopher, 1981.

Hirschfield, Robert S. *The Constitution and the Court.* New York: Random House, 1962.

Horowitz, David. *The Courts and Social Policy.* Washington, D.C.: Brookings Institution, 1977.

Hughes, Charles E. *The Supreme Court of the United States.* New York: Columbia Univ. Press, 1928.

Hyneman, Charles S. *The Supreme Court on Trial.* New York: Atherton, 1963.

Jackson, Robert. *The Struggle for Judicial Supremacy.* New York: Alfred A. Knopf, 1941.

Jacobsohn, Gary J. "Abraham Lincoln 'on this Question of Judicial Authority': The Theory of Constitutional Aspiration." *Western Political Quarterly* 36 (March 1983): 52-70.

Johnson, Julia E. *Limitation of Power of Supreme Court to Declare Acts of Congress Unconstitutional.* New York: H. W. Wilson, 1935.

Johnston, Richard E. "The Burger Court and Federalism: A Revolution in 1976?" *Western Political Quarterly* 33 (June 1980): 197–216.

Kaczorowski, Robert J. *The Politics of Judicial Interpretation.* Dobbs Ferry, N.Y.: Oceana, 1985.

Kaden, Lewis B. "Judges and Arbitrators: Observations on the Scope of Judicial Review." *Columbia Law Review* 80 (March 1980): 267–98.

Kaufman, Irving R. "Maintaining Judicial Independence: A Mandate to Judges." *American Bar Association Journal* 66 (April 1980): 470–72.

Kelly, Alfred H.; Harbison, Winfrend A.; and Belz, Herman. *The American Constitution: Its Origins and Development,* 6th ed. New York: W. W. Norton, 1983.

Kenyon, Cecelia, ed. *The Antifederalists.* Indianapolis: Bobbs-Merrill, 1966.

Kurland, Philip B. "Curia Regis: Some Comments on the Divine Right of Kings and Courts 'To say what Law is.'" *Arizona Law Review* 23 (1981): 581–97.

Levy, Beryl H. *Our Constitution: Tool or Testament?* New York: Alfred A. Knopf, 1941.

Levy, Lenard. *Judicial Review and the Supreme Court.* New York: Harper and Row, 1967.

Library of Congress, Legislative Reference Service. *Provisions of Federal Law Held Unconstitutional by the Supreme Court of the United States.* Westport, Conn: Greenwood, 1976.

Lowenstein, Karl. *Political Power and the Governmental Process.* Chicago: Univ. of Chicago Press, 1957.

Lurton, Horace H. "A Government of Law or a Government of Men?" *North American Review* (Jan. 1911): 9–25.

Lusky, Louis. *By What Right?* Charlottesville, Va.: Michie, 1975.

Mace, George. "The Anti-Democratic Character of Judicial Review." *California Law Review* 60 (1972): 1140–49.

Main, Jackson Turner. *The Anti-Federalists: Critics of the Constitution.* New York: W. W. Norton, 1974.

Mason, Alpheus Thomas. "The Federalist—A Split Personality." *American Historical Review* 57 (April 1952): 625–43.

Mathias, Charles McC., Jr. "The Federal Courts Under Seige in the American Judiciary." *Annals of the American Academy of Political and Social Science* 462 (July 1982): 26–33.

Mayers, Lewis. *The Machinery of Justice.* Totowa, N.J.: Littlefield, Adams, 1973.

McDonald, Forrest. *We the People: The Economic Origins of the Constitution.* Chicago: Univ. of Chicago Press, 1958.

McLaughlin, Andrew C. *The Confederation and the Constitution.* Vol. 10, *The American Nation.* New York: Harper and Brothers, 1905.

———. *A Constitutional History of the United States.* New York: D. Appleton-Century, 1935.

Meese, Edwin III. *Address of the Honourable Edwin Meese III, Attorney General of the United States, Before the American Bar Association, Grosvernor House, London, England.* Washington, D.C.: Department of Justice, 1985.

Melone, Albert P. "A Political Scientist Writes in Defense of *The Brethren.*" *Judicature* 61 (Sept. 1980): 140–46.

———. "Limiting Supreme Court Jurisdiction." Review of *Judicial Review and the National Political Process: A Functional Reconsideration of the Role of the Supreme Court,* by Jesse H. Choper. *Judicature* 64 (Feb. 1981): 335–36.

Melone, Albert P., and Mace, George. "Judicial Review: The Usurpation and Democracy Questions." *Judicature* 71 (Dec.-Jan. 1988): 202–10.

Mendelson, Wallace. "Jefferson on Judicial Review: Consistency Through Change." *University of Chicago Law Review* 29 (Winter 1962): 327–37.

———. *Supreme Court Statecraft: The Rule of Law and Men.* Ames, Iowa: Iowa State Univ. Press, 1985.

Miller, Arthur S. *Politics, Democracy, and the Supreme Court.* Westport, Conn: Greenwood, 1985.

Moore, Blaine F. *The Supreme Court and Unconstitutional Legislation.* New York: AMS, 1968.

Moschzisker, Robert von. *Judicial Review of Legislation.* New York: Da Capo, 1971.

Murphy, Walter F., and Pritchett, C. Herman. *Court, Judges, and Politics: An Introduction to the Judicial Process,* 4th ed. New York: Random House, 1986.

Nagel, Robert F. "How Useful Is Judicial Review in Free Speech Cases?" *Cornell Law Review* (Jan. 1984): 302–40.

Neuborne, Burt. "Judicial Review and the Separation of Powers in France and the United States." *New York University Law Review* 57 (June 1982):363–442.

Parsons, Theophilus. *The Constitution: Its Origin, Function, and Authority.* Boston: Little, Brown, 1861.

Paul, Arnold M. *Conservative Crisis and the Rule of Law.* New York: Harper and Row, 1969.

Pennock, J. Roland. *Administration and the Rule of Law.* New York: Farrar & Rinehart, 1941.

Perry, Michael J. *The Constitution, the Courts, and Human Rights.* New Haven: Yale Univ. Press, 1982.

Posner, Richard A. "The Meaning of Judicial Self-Restraint." *Indiana Law Journal* 59 (1983): 1–24.

Powell, Thomas R. *Vagaries and Varieties in Constitutional Interpretation.* New York: AMS, 1967.

Pritchett, C. Herman. *The Political Offender and the Warren Court.* New York: Russell and Russell, 1967.

_____. *Constitutional Law of the Federal System.* Englewood Cliffs, N.J.: Prentice-Hall, 1984.

Provine, Doris M. *Case Selection in the United States Supreme Court.* Chicago: Univ. of Chicago Press, 1980.

Read, Conyers, ed. *The Constitution Reconsidered.* New York: Columbia Univ. Press, 1938.

Redish, Martin H. "Judicial Review and the 'Political Question.' " *Northwestern University Law Review* 79 (Dec. 1984–Feb. 1985): 1031–61.

Rodell, Fred. *Nine Men: A Political History of the Supreme Court of the United States from 1790 to 1955.* New York: Vintage Books, 1955.

Rodgers, William H., Jr. "Judicial Review of Risk Assessments: The Role of Decision Theory in Unscrambling the Benzene Decision." *Environmental Law* 11 (Winter 1981): 301–20.

Rostow, Eugene V. "The Democratic Character of Judicial Review." *Harvard Law Review* 66 (Dec. 1952): 193–224.

_____. *The Sovereign Prerogative.* Westport, Conn: Greenwood, 1974.

Schlueter, David A. "Federalism and Supreme Court Review of Expansive State Court Decisions: A Response to Unfortunate Impressions." *Hastings Constitutional Law Quarterly* 11 (Summer 1984): 523–50.

_____. "Judicial Federalism and Supreme Court Review of State Court Decisions: A Sensible Balance Emerges." *Notre Dame Law Review* 59 (1984): 1079–17.

Schmidhauser, John R. *Judges and Justices: The Federal Appellate Judiciary.* Boston: Little, Brown, 1979.

Schubert, Glendon A. *The Presidency in the Courts.* New York: Da Capo, 1973.

Sedgwick, Theodore. *A Treatise on the Rules which Govern the Interpretation and Construction of Statutory and Constitutional Law*. Littleton, Colo.: F. B. Rothman, 1980.

Sedler, Robert A. "The Legitimacy Debate in Constitutional Adjudication: An Assessment and a Different Perspective." *Ohio State Law Journal* 44 (1983): 93–97.

Siegan, Bernard H. *The Supreme Court's Constitution*. New Brunswick, N.J.: Transaction, 1986.

Smith, William French. "Urging Judicial Restraint." *American Bar Association Journal* 68 (Jan. 1982): 59–61.

Solberg, Winton U., ed. *The Federal Convention and the Formation of the Union of the American States*. Indianapolis: Bobbs-Merrill, 1958.

Spaeth, Harold J. "Burger Court Review of State Court Civil Liberties Decisions." *Judicature* 68 (Feb.–Mar. 1985): 285–91.

Storing, Herbert J. *The Complete Anti-Federalist*. Vol. 7. Chicago: Univ. of Chicago Press, 1981.

Story, Joseph. *Commentaries on the Constitution of the United States*. Vol. 3. Boston: Little, Brown, 1858.

Street, Robert. "How Far Questions of Policy May Enter Into Judicial Decisions." *Report of the American Bar Association* 6 (1983): 179.

Surrency, Erwin C. "The Judiciary Act of 1801." *American Journal of Legal History* 2 (1958): 53–65.

Swindler, William F. *Sources and Documents of the United States Constitutions*. Dobbs Ferry, N.Y.: Oceana, 1979.

"Symposium: Judicial Review Versus Democracy." *Ohio State Law Journal* 42 (1981).

Taylor, Stuart, Jr. "Meese v. Brennan: Who's Right About the Constitution?" *New Republic* 94 (January 6 and 13, 1986): 17–21.

Thayer, James Bradley. "The Origin and Scope of the American Doctrine of Constitutional Law." *Harvard Law Review* 7 (Oct. 1983): 129–56.

Tiedeman, Christopher. *The Unwritten Constitution of the United States*. New York: Putnam, 1890.

Tugwell, Rexford G. *The Compromising of the Constitution*. Notre Dame: Univ. of Notre Dame Press, 1976.

Twiss, Benjamin R. *Lawyers and the Constitution: How Laissez-Faire Came to the Supreme Court*. Princeton: Princeton Univ. Press, 1942.

U.S. Congress. Senate. Committee on the Judiciary. *Hearings before the Subcommittee on Separation of Powers, Federalism and the Federal Judiciary*. 98th, 1st sess. 1984.

———. *Hearings before the Subcommittee on Administrative Practice and Procedure, Legislative Veto and the "Chadha" Decision*, 98th, 2d sess. 1983.

Van Alstyne, William W.. "A Critical Guide to *Marbury* v. *Madison*." *Duke Law Journal* (Feb. 1969): 1–47.

Waggoner, Michael J. "Log-rolling and Judicial Review." *University of Colorado*

Law Review (Fall 1980): 33–47.

Warren, Charles. *The Supreme Court in United States History.* 3 vols. Boston: Little, Brown, 1922.

_____. *Congress, the Constitution, and the Supreme Court.* Boston: Little, Brown, 1925.

Wasby, Stephen L. *The Supreme Court in the Federal Judicial System.* New York: Holt, Rinehart and Winston, 1978.

Wechsler, Herbert. *Principles, Politics and Fundamental Law.* Cambridge: Harvard Univ. Press, 1961.

Wellington, Harry H. "The Nature of Judicial Review." *Yale Law Journal* (Jan. 1982): 486–520.

Witt, Elder, ed. *Congressional Quarterly's Guide to the U.S. Supreme Court.* Washington, D.C.: Congressional Quarterly, 1979.

Wolfe, Christopher. "A Theory of U.S. Constitutional History." *Journal of Politics* 43 (May 1981): 292–325.

_____. *The Rise of Modern Judicial Review.* New York: Basic Books, 1986.

Wood, Gordon S. *The Creation of the American Republic, 1776–1787.* New York: W. W. Norton, 1972.

Woodward, Bob, and Armstrong, Scott. *The Brethren: Inside the Supreme Court.* New York: Simon & Schuster, 1979.

Wright, Benjamin F. "Natural Law in American Political Theory." *Southwestern Political and Social Science Quarterly* 4 (1923): 202–20.

_____. "American Interpretations of Natural Law." *American Political Science Review* 20 (1926): 219–25.

_____. *The Growth of American Constitutional Law.* Boston: Houghton Mifflin, 1942.

INDEX

Executive power (*continued*)
  Commander-in-chief; President;
    Presidential power
Executive privilege, 18
"Executive review," 244
Executive veto power, 239. *See also*
    Presidential power
  Jefferson's view, 244

Fabius, 151
Faction, 240
Fair Labor Standards Act, 18
Farm Mortgage Act of 1935, 13
Farrand, Max, 168
Federal Convention of 1787. *See*
    Philadelphia Convention
Federal Election Campaign Act of 1971,
    18
Federal government
  defined, 22
  examples of, 22
  judicial review
    role of, 23–26
    Thayer's view of, 94–95
  state relationship, 21
Federalism, 21–22, 23
  tensions between central and state
    government, 213, 237
Federalist, The, 152–53, 166, 168, 170,
    195, 198
Federalist 10, 250
Federalist 48, 196, 239, 245
Federalist 51, 239, 245
Federalist 78, 170, 196–97, 198, 210, 212,
    239
Federalist 81, 196–97, 204
Federalist Papers, xiii, 195, 211, 212, 239.
    See also *Federalist, The*
Federalists
  1796 election, 38
  1800 election, 38, 42
  judicial power, 10
  party coalesces with Antifederalists,
    195–96
  party differences with Antifederalists,
    9, 37
  proponents of ratification, 177, 236
Federal Reserve Board, 213, 245, 246

Fereira *v.* United States, 131
Few, William, 160
Fifteenth Amendment, 15
Fifth Amendment, 16
First Amendment, 14, 218, 227
  clear and present danger test, 227, 228
Fletcher *v* Peck, 33
Ford, Gerald R., 17
Forms of government, Aristotle's
    classification, 249–50, 252
Fourteenth Amendment. *See also* Due
    Process; Equal Protection
  application of, 3, 12, 13, 14, 15, 16,
    208
  Bill of Rights, 208
Framers' intent, 247
  and judicial review, 119, 122, 123,
    126–29, 145–48, 212, 257
    Beard's evidence, 148–61 (*see also*
      Boudin; Lurton; Thayer)
France, 79, 109, 169, 214, 216, 241, 244
Frankfurter, Felix, 14, 15, 77, 212, 225,
    227–28
Fuchs, Klaus, 228

Generals, undemocratic nature of, 212,
    245–46
Georgia
  constitution, 206
  1808 court decision on judicial review,
    86
Germany, 79, 226
Gerry, Elbridge
  judicial control, 152, 153
  and Marshall, 169
Gibson, John, xii, 67–69, 76, 78, 88, 90,
    119, 129–30, 132
  civil power of judiciary, 70
  De Chastellue *v.* Fairchild, 69
  Eakin *v* Raub, 67, 69–75, 76, 132–33,
    257
  judicial function, 67, 68, 69–70, 132–33
  Norris *v.* Clymer, 95n
  political power of judiciary, 70
Gideon *v* Wainwright, 16
Gitlow *v.* New York, 14, 230
Glass *v.* The Sloop Betsey, 170
Good behavior